NEW ESSAYS BY DE QUINCEY

NEW ESSAYS BY

De Quincey

HIS CONTRIBUTIONS
TO THE
Edinburgh Saturday Post
AND THE
Edinburgh Evening Post
1827-1828

STUART M. TAVE

PRINCETON, NEW JERSEY

PRINCETON UNIVERSITY PRESS

1966

PR
4532
T3

Publication of this book has been aided
by the Whitney Darrow Publication Reserve
Fund of Princeton University Press

Printed in the United States of America
by Princeton University Press
Princeton, New Jersey

TO EDEL

Acknowledgments

There are debts of gratitude to many institutions and individuals which I am happy to acknowledge in this easy and inexpensive way, since they are not otherwise payable. First, to the owners of the manuscripts printed at length, quoted or cited in the text and editorial matter: the Bodleian Library, the Pierpont Morgan Library, the Henry W. and Albert A. Berg Collection of the New York Public Library, the Houghton Library of Harvard and Carlyle's House, Chelsea; all have granted permission with grace and speed, and specific acknowledgments are made in the appropriate places. Then to the libraries that provided the films, pictures, books and facilities: the British Museum, the Edinburgh Public Library, the National Library of Scotland, the Kendal Public Library, the Huntington, the Newberry and the University of Chicago. To Mr. Gordon Ray and the Guggenheim Foundation, who gave me the opportunity of free time during which I began this book—though this book was not what I intended to do when I asked for and accepted their money. To the many people who so kindly answered my queries, drawing upon their sources of special knowledge and sometimes special material in their possession: Mrs. Esther Rhoads Houghton, Messrs. Richard Bruère, John Clive, Kenneth Curry, Albert Goldman, John E. Jordan, Sir John Murray, Messrs. Charles Richard Sanders, Alan Lang Strout and William S. Ward. To my friends at the University of Chicago for their help, patience and encouragement. To Miss Maureen Byers, who typed a difficult manuscript with an accuracy and handsomeness that delighted but did not surprise me. To Mrs. James Holly Hanford of Princeton University Press, who edited the manuscript with an understanding of its peculiar problems that was always helpful and always pleasant.

ACKNOWLEDGMENTS

To my wife, who reads Danish like a native, a virtue that here provided a scholarly bonus I did not anticipate when I married her for other reasons, and who is never upset by the difficulties of understanding minor authors, from Jens Baggesen to the present.

Contents

List of Articles

This list gives the date and page number of the newspaper issue in which each article was published. Titles in square brackets have been supplied by me.

LIST OF ARTICLES

NEW ESSAYS BY DE QUINCEY

Introduction

The late 1820's are years "lightly documented" in De Quincey's biography: this on the word of his most thorough biographer.[1] But we can do a little better than has been done and, in fact, there are more documents than have been used.

To begin with, there is a puzzling letter he wrote to Charles Knight, from Westmorland, on July 23, 1829, in which he says:

> merely to stave off the extreme pressure of my pecuniary embarrassments, in the summer of 1827 . . . I quitted my home at this place for Edinburgh, and there I continued until the 12th of last month, writing, but of necessity consuming a great part of my emoluments on a separate establishment in that city. This was managed with great economy, but still was a heavy burden upon me, as you may suppose, when I go on to add that in the autumn of that year, 1827, feeling myself depressed by this entire separation from my family, and recollecting besides that the education of my two eldest children was now urgently calling for my attention, I resolved to bring them up to my own lodgings in Edinburgh. Accordingly, on the 3rd of October, 1827, I went down to Carlisle, where they met me, and the next day I brought them (my eldest son and daughter) on to Edinburgh; and there they stayed, one of them, however, for more than a year of the time, at the houses of old friends until the said June 12, 1829.

> In 1828, for many important arrangements which my Philistines (*Duns videlicet*) made necessary, Mrs. De Quincey joined me in Edinburgh, so that

[1] Horace Eaton, *Thomas De Quincey* (New York, 1936), p. 312.

for three-quarters of a year we had a larger establishment in Edinburgh than in Westmoreland.[2]

What was De Quincey writing from the summer of 1827 to June 12, 1829? His only known works are the "Toilette of the Hebrew Lady," a translation from a chapter of German, in the March 1828 issue of *Blackwood's*; the "Elements of Rhetoric," in the December *Blackwood's*; "The Duke of Wellington and Mr. Peel," in the March 1829 *Blackwood's*; and an article on John Wilson, published in the *Edinburgh Literary Gazette* in three parts, June 6 and 20 and July 4, 1829. Not much to show for two years, especially at a time when he was writing under extreme pressure for money and his emoluments were sufficient for him to maintain, precariously, a separate establishment in Edinburgh.[3] He seems to have had steady work,[4] since he remained in Edinburgh and sent for his two eldest children and then his wife. What kind of writing was it that paid, but paid poorly, and required

[2] Alice A. Clowes, *Charles Knight* (1892), pp. 168-69. De Quincey had done a couple of translations for *Knight's Quarterly Magazine* and Knight had been kind to him. A portion of the letter was in Knight's *Passages of a Working Life* (1864), I, 340-42.

[3] He also says in the letter to Knight that by good management and better luck he contrived to silence his duns by Candlemas [February 2], 1829. This would seem to be before he received the £500 that came with the complicated transaction that made him the owner of The Nab; see M. L. Armitt, *Rydal* (Kendal, 1916), pp. 690-97. At least so the chronology that he gives in the letter to Knight seems to indicate; and if it is accurate, he may have been able to clear himself by Candlemas with money he was making by writing. February was evidently a crucial month in his economic history; see his mother's letter in *De Quincey Memorials*, ed. Alexander H. Japp (1891), II, 166. But then there were many such months in his life.

[4] And he seems to have been in fairly steady working order. On September 23, 1828, he told Matthew Davenport Hill, who called on him in Edinburgh, that he hadn't tasted opium in one hundred and eighty days. Rosamund and Florence Davenport Hill, *The Recorder of Birmingham* (1878), p. 85.

his continued residence in Edinburgh? It sounds like newspaper work.[5]

It was in these years that he met Carlyle and Carlyle knew what De Quincey was doing. In a letter to his brother John, written from Edinburgh (Comley Bank) on November 29, 1827, Carlyle says:

> The 'Edinburgh Review' is out some time ago, and the 'State of German Literature' has been received with considerable surprise and approbation by the Universe. Thus, for instance, De Quincey praises it in his 'Saturday Post'. . . . De Quincey was here last Wednesday and sate till midnight. He is one of the smallest men you ever in your life beheld; but with a most gentle and sensible face, only that the teeth are destroyed by opium, and the little bit of an under lip projects like a shelf. He speaks with a slow, sad, and soft voice in the politest manner I have almost ever witnessed, and with great gracefulness and sense, were it not that he seems decidedly given to prosing. Poor little fellow! It might soften a very

[5] Dorothy Wordsworth, in a letter to De Quincey, written November 16, 1826, reports to him a conversation she has had with De Quincey's wife: "She then said that you had at present some literary employments at Edinburgh; and had, besides, had an offer (or something to this effect) of a permanent engagement, the nature of which she did not know; but that you hesitated about accepting it, as it might necessitate you to settle in Edinburgh. To this I replied, 'Why not settle there for the time at least that this engagement lasts. . . .' I then added that it was my firm opinion that you could never regularly keep up your engagements at a distance from the press. . . . I would venture to request you well to consider the many impediments to literary employments to be regularly carried on in limited time, at a distance from the press, in a small house, and in perfect solitude" (*Letters of William and Dorothy Wordsworth: The Later Years*, ed. Ernest De Selincourt [Oxford, 1939], I, 257-58). Dorothy writes out of a general knowledge of De Quincey's character and history, but one particular instance she and De Quincey may well have had in mind was his attempt and failure to write for and edit successfully the *Westmorland Gazette*, in 1818-19, while living at a distance from the press.

5

hard heart to see him so courteous, yet so weak and
poor; retiring *home* with his two children to a miserable lodging-house, and writing all day for the king
of donkeys, the proprietor of the 'Saturday Post.' I
lent him Jean Paul's autobiography, which I got
lately from Hamburgh, and advised him to translate
it for Blackwood, that so he might raise a few
pounds, and fence off the Genius of Hunger yet a
little while. Poor little De Quincey! He is an innocent man, and, as you said, extremely *washable*
away.[6]

The entire passage has been given to show that Carlyle
is a good witness: observant, detailed, patronizing, no
doubt, but also sympathetic. He is getting his information on De Quincey's activities from De Quincey himself,
who visits his home and sits with him till midnight: the
detail about the two children in the lodgings is both first-
hand and recent.[7] And he is professionally interested in
what De Quincey is doing: De Quincey, who had damned

[6] James Anthony Froude, *Thomas Carlyle* (New York, 1882), I,
339. I do not know why Carlyle called the proprietor the king of
donkeys, unless this is an impersonal comment on the old-clothes
Toryism of his newspaper. In an undated letter (by internal evidence approximately July 1828) he lists the *Post* with two other
"equally vapid and stupid" Scotch newspapers which he reads;
[Henry Inglis], "Some Early Letters of Mr. Carlyle," *Glasgow
Herald*, February 16, 1882, p. 3, col. 3. De Quincey himself, Carlyle said, was "one of the most irreclaimable Tories now extant";
letter to Mill, April 18, 1833, *Letters of Thomas Carlyle to John
Stuart Mill*, etc., ed. Alexander Carlyle (1923), p. 48.

[7] It is in another letter of the same day, which also deplores the
writing De Quincey is doing for a newspaper; after talking of
Jeffrey as a new acquaintance, Carlyle says: "—What do you
think too? I am an acquaintance almost a friend of—The Opium-
Eater's! Poor Dequincey! He is essentially a gentle and genial
little soul; only that the Liver is diseased, and the '*I-ety*' is strong;
and both together sometimes overset his balance. Poor soul! One
of the most perfect *gentlemen* I have ever seen; and yet here he
is living in *lodgings*, with two of his little children (writing for
bread in the paltriest of all newspapers) while his wife with other

6

his translation of *Wilhelm Meister,* in "a very vulgar and brutish Review,"[8] only three years earlier, now knows and respects him and is giving him a good review. We know that he saw De Quincey again on January 17, 1828, and went to his lodgings on March 11.[9] In May Carlyle moved to Craigenputtock; on December 11 he sent De Quincey a kindly letter from himself and Jane ("often thinking of you with the old friendly feelings"), extending a most pleasant invitation to visit.[10] That letter was

two resides in Westmoreland,—as a kind of 'hostage' to his creditors!" Letter dated November 29, 1827, to Mrs. Montagu; MS. in Carlyle House, Chelsea.

[8] Letter to John Carlyle, January 22, 1825, in *Early Letters of Thomas Carlyle,* ed. Charles Eliot Norton (1886), II, 302-03. De Quincey's review had been in the August 1824 *London Magazine.* The change in relationship was dramatic and Carlyle enjoyed it. He wrote to John Taylor on December 30, 1827, from Edinburgh, "Mr. De Quincey is here also; and what may seem still stranger, he and I, the Reviewer and the Reviewed, are very good friends! Do not such instances of magnanimity ennoble the history of Letters? Your Opium-eater is in truth a most interesting man and must awaken a respectful sympathy go where he may" (MS. in the Berg Collection, New York Public Library [kindly transcribed by Professor Charles Richard Sanders]). Carlyle's later memories of their first meeting after the review were that De Quincey was in great fear; Carlyle's *Reminiscences,* ed. Norton (1887), II, 151-52 and *Letters of Charles Eliot Norton* (Boston and New York, 1913), I, 483. But they are not borne out by his letters written at the time.

In fact, De Quincey had given Carlyle the German student a bad review even more recently, in the *Post* of July 28, 1827 (pp. 37-39 below). It is clear from the contrast of that review and the review of November 24 (pp. 203-204 below) that they must have met between those dates, probably closer to the latter. On November 29 Carlyle was "an acquaintance almost a friend" of the Opium-Eater; by December 30 they were "very good friends."

[9] Letter to B. W. Procter, from Comley Bank, January 17, 1828, in Moncure Conway, *Thomas Carlyle* (New York, 1881), p. 244; letter to John Carlyle, March 12, 1828, in Froude, I, 349; see also *Letters of Thomas Carlyle, 1826-36,* ed. Norton (1888), I, 132.

[10] *Memoirs of the Life and Writings of Thomas Carlyle,* ed. Richard Herne Shepherd (1881), I, 60-66.

According to James Hogg, "Nights and Days with De Quincey,"

delivered by Henry Inglis, for whom it was also a letter of introduction to De Quincey; and in his covering letter to Inglis, also dated December 11, 1828, Carlyle gave directions for locating De Quincey: "here is a letter for the *Opium-eater*, whose address, if you cannot find it elsewhere, you will learn at the office of the *Saturday Post* in Register Street."[11] De Quincey's name reappears in Carlyle's correspondence in succeeding years, but these are the only notices relevant to our purposes. De Quincey in 1827 and 1828 was writing for the *Edinburgh Saturday Post*, later called the *Edinburgh Evening Post*, a weekly newspaper, whose office address, as Carlyle knew, or as any reader would know, because it was given in the colophon of each issue, was Register Street. The "State of German Literature," whose success Carlyle celebrates in his letter of November 29, 1827, was his article in the *Edinburgh Review* for October; there is a review of that issue of the *Edinburgh* in the *Saturday Post* of November 24, in which Carlyle's article is praised, and Carlyle's immediate information that De Quincey was the author is also well supported by the internal evidence (pp. 204-11, below). Carlyle also knew that De Quincey was doing a great deal of writing for the *Saturday Post*.

Furthermore, Carlyle was not the only one who knew of De Quincey's connection with the *Post*. The *West-*

Harper's, LXXX (1890), 451-52, De Quincey remembered with profound gratitude how Mrs. Carlyle had nursed him during a severe illness—at the Carlyles' own home, if Hogg remembered rightly. This must have been in late 1827 or early 1828, since Carlyle says that after leaving Edinburgh he never again saw De Quincey (*Reminiscences*, II, 152-53), and it is further evidence of Carlyle's intimate knowledge of De Quincey's life at this time.

11 *Letters*, ed. Norton, I, 181-82. Inglis evidently did not see De Quincey; on March 31, 1829, Carlyle asked, "Have you ever seen De Quincey? He had been at his opium when you called, and indeed is rarely visible in these cases." *Ibid.*, I, 200.

minster Review, in an article on the provincial newspaper press, in January 1830, has this paragraph:

> The Saturday Evening Post is a sort of successor of the Beacon, of disgraceful notoriety. It stickles for church and state, the ascendancy of the aristocracy, and every one of the exploded or fading abuses in politics and political economy. Few take it for its opinions; but it is published on Saturday evening, after the arrival of the London mail, and so gives the very latest news of the week, and is an agreeable companion on Sunday morning. De Quincy has been engaged regularly by the Post. Two of its pages are filled by what they call Scottish Literary Gazette. The critical notices there are almost entirely written by Mr. Andrew Crichton, the author of several volumes, and are able, learned, and impartial. There is a much greater proportion of original writing in the Post than in any of the other Edinburgh papers.[12]

The *Post* replied to this article, defending itself and correcting some errors of fact. But one thing was true: "It is true that 'De Quincy is engaged regularly by the Post;' and we hope long to receive many able contributions from his pen" (January 16, p. 22, col. 1).

[12] XII, 85. The *Beacon* was a violent and ill-fated Edinburgh Tory newspaper in 1821.

I believe there is also a reference to De Quincey's connection with the *Post* in the December 1828 *Blackwood's* (XXIV, 699-700). In the "Noctes Ambrosianae," No. 40, the Shepherd says, "Faith there's the Embro' Saturday Evening Post turnin' out a maist capital paper. There's smeddum yonner, Mr. North." And North replies, "There *is* smeddum yonder, James. The pen of one first-rate writer may be traced in its leading articles, and occasionally elsewhere—and some of his coadjutors are apparently men of power and principle. It has—though young—a good circulation, and is sure to succeed. A true Tory." John Wilson ("Christopher North") knew De Quincey well, housed him in Edinburgh around the time in question, and probably knew of his connection with the newspaper.

Andrew Crichton, to whom the *Westminster* directs our attention, was a man then at the beginning of a long career as an editor of newspapers in Edinburgh; he was active enough, as editor, as contributor to periodicals, as author and compiler of books, to make his way into the *DNB*. And one of his obituaries, a source for the *DNB*, says this: "He commenced his connection with the newspaper press in 1828, by editing (at first in conjunction with De Quincy), the *Edinburgh Evening Post*."[13]

There is no other evidence that De Quincey may have been an editor of the *Post*, but he did write extensively for it and he helped establish its editorial policy. We have his manuscript of what must have been one of the political leaders he wrote for the paper, the Bodleian MS. Eng. Misc. d. 271 (pp. 349-56 below). De Quincey does not date this manuscript article, but the occasion of its composition, the resignation of Huskisson from Wellington's cabinet, gives us the date; the article was probably the leader in the *Post* of May 31, 1828.[14] Unfortunately, no

[13] Edward Walford, *Hardwicke's Annual Biography for 1856* (1856), p. 198. Some of Crichton's articles in the *Post* are reprinted in his *Reviews in the Case of the Rev. Dr. A. Thomson, and the Rev. Henry Grey, and of the Proceedings in the Presbytery of Edinburgh* (Edinburgh, n.d. but Preface dated October 3, 1828); they are articles of August and September 1828.

The names of some other men connected with the *Post*, proprietors and writers, are given in one of several articles on "The Newspaper Press of Scotland," in *Fraser's Magazine*, XVII (1838), 564, 566, 567-68. But not all the information there is accurate. Some other material on the history of the paper is R. M. W. Cowan's *The Newspaper in Scotland . . . 1815-1860* (Glasgow, 1946). Cowan says De Quincey contributed to the *Post*; his source is evidently the *Westminster Review*.

[14] See below, p. 349n.

An approximate date also seems to be established by a note on the back of the second page of the manuscript:

About half as much more remains: this will be ready by 11 o'clock to-night; and Mr. Abernethy can either send then, or as early to-morrow morng. as he chooses.

19 Pitt Street, 3rd. flat—right hand door.

A letter of De Quincey's printed by Miss Armitt (pp. 692-93) is

copy of the issue of May 31 has been located; but, by way of compensating luck, in the second paragraph of the manuscript article De Quincey proves his political foresight by referring the reader to what he had said on the 26th of January and by quoting for him a key sentence. That sentence is in the political leader of the *Post* of January 26. There are also other signs that the manuscript was written for the *Post* (pp. 356-57 below).

Finally, much of the internal evidence of material in the *Post* is so strong that it would be possible to attribute articles to De Quincey on that alone. The argument is given in the body of this book, after each article. But it is worth pointing out here that some of that evidence is more than similarity or identity of ideas or words with De Quincey's known writings. It is also, occasionally, as in the article of September 29, 1827 (pp. 145-46 below), biographical, where dates, names, and events establish the authorship of De Quincey and no one but De Quincey.

There are, then, several independent and different kinds of convincing evidence that De Quincey was writing for the *Post*. But the problem of finding his contributions remains, since all are anonymous or, a few of them, pseudonymous. Nor is it possible to establish exactly the chronological limits of his work because of the state of the files. The *Edinburgh Saturday Post* began publication on May 12, 1827, and continued under that name for one year, fifty-two issues, the last of them on May 3, 1828; there is a complete file at the British Museum

dated December 6, 1828, from 18 Pitt Street, Edinburgh. And by February 23, 1829, he had moved to Duncan Street (*De Quincey Memorials*, II, 166-68). The difference between 18 Pitt Street and 19 Pitt Street I cannot explain; perhaps Miss Armitt was in error—the *19* is quite plain in the Bodleian manuscript. Eaton also says he was at 18 Pitt Street in the fall of 1828 but gives no source (p. 313).

(Colindale). It then changed its name to the *Edinburgh Evening Post, and Scottish Literary Gazette*.[15] But the only known extant issues of the *Evening Post* for 1828 are May 24, June 14 and 28, July 12 and 26, in the Edinburgh Public Library. The only known issues of 1829 are March 28, May 30, and July 4, in the Edinburgh Public Library, and May 2, in the Huntington.

De Quincey's first contribution was, I believe, in the issue of July 28, 1827.[16] And though the *Westminster Review* and the *Post* itself say that he was writing for the paper in January 1830, he had certainly stopped before then.[17] The file for 1830, in the Edinburgh Public

[15] The standard bibliographies list the two names as independent publications but there is no question of the continuity. On April 12, 1828 (p. 388, col. 4), and in all three succeeding issues, the *Saturday Post* announced that its first year had been so successful that "On the 10th of May, this Journal will be published in a new and more extended shape, under the title of THE EDINBURGH EVENING POST, AND SCOTTISH LITERARY GAZETTE." The numbering of the issues is continuous. And the *Evening Post*, on October 2, 1830 (front page, first sentence), says, "this Journal was begun in the month of May 1827." Even after the change of title there are contemporary references to the *Evening Post* as the *Saturday Post*, or the *Saturday Evening Post*, as the *Westminster Review* called it.

[16] This judgment, based on internal evidence, may be confirmed by a writer in William Hone's *Table Book* (1827-28), II, 277-78, who reports that he saw De Quincey in the Lake country on July 20 and 21, 1827. The dates of De Quincey's departure and arrival would then fit rather neatly, though we also know, of course, that he did some travelling back and forth.

[17] The *Westminster Review's* information was not quite up to date. Evidently Crichton was no longer writing for the *Post* either; at least the *Post* said on November 20, 1830 (p. 372, col. 1), that Crichton had ceased to have any connection with that paper "upwards of twelve months ago, as was then announced."

Why the *Post* itself should say that De Quincey was still regularly employed is more puzzling, but it was probably because his name had value and the proprietor was pleased to use it. The proprietor at this time was also the proprietor of the *Edinburgh Literary Gazette*: in the same paragraph of January 16, 1830, in which he still claims De Quincey for the *Post*, he says that De Quincey is among the chief contributors to the *Gazette*; in the

Library, is not complete and copies are imperfect, but there is more than enough available to reveal his presence if he was still contributing. There is no sign of it. This is hardly surprising, since we know from his own letter to Knight, and also from a letter he wrote to Wordsworth,[18] that he left Edinburgh on June 12, 1829. He was now the owner of The Nab and there he remained for perhaps a year. In the letter to Knight he also says that on April 6, 1829, he came down from Edinburgh to Westmorland to arrange for the purchase of The Nab, found himself involved in an infinity of legal complications, some of which required a further journey, to Manchester, and so it was not until May 12 or May 11 that he could return to Edinburgh. The month following was occupied in winding up his Scottish affairs, the main part of which was arranging and burning papers, returning books and other "fash" which, as he said, "infests and dogs the movements of literary men."[19] It doesn't sound

---

Post of January 9 (p. 9, col. 3) he says that De Quincey appears regularly in the *Gazette*; and the *Gazette* is advertised in the *Post* to the same effect. But in fact De Quincey seems to have written for the *Gazette* only the one three-part article on Wilson, six and seven months earlier.

The *Post* continued to be interested in De Quincey's career, referring to him and his articles in *Blackwood's* several times in 1830. But the memory he left behind him tasted, too, of the sour disappointment that other of his employers knew. On November 13 (p. 364, col. 4) the *Post*, among its "Laconicisms," discharged this one at DE QUINCEY:

"Idleness is the root of all evil"—and a certain Oriental root is the cause of all idleness. With broken nerves, it is impossible that a person can be so industrious as the world, in the case of a man of splendid powers, would lead itself to wish. If such a one writes for the bettering of public morals, we may not inaptly say with Plutarch—

Αλλων ιατρος, αυτος ελπισι [for ἑλκεσι] βρυων

(Actually a fragment of Euripides: a physician of others, himself teeming with sores.)

18 Letter of July 19, 1829, in John E. Jordan, *De Quincey to Wordsworth* (Berkeley and Los Angeles, 1962), p. 332.

19 Clowes, *Charles Knight*, pp. 170-71.

as though he could have been doing much writing for the *Post* after early April 1829. I have not been able to ascribe to him anything after July 12, 1828, but of course there are almost no copies extant between then and the date of his departure.

Many of the articles are, as I have said, clearly his, the evidence such that I think no one can question it. With the security of these articles, and of the external evidence, I think we are justified in a rather larger boldness than would otherwise be prudent in attributing to him additional articles where the evidence is good but less conclusive. Actually the number of articles from which we must choose is, though large enough, limited by the nature of the newspaper. The *Post* was an eight-page weekly, each page closely printed in four long columns, and, as the *Westminster Review* said, it had more original material than comparable papers. But when one has deducted the advertisements, the Parliamentary reports, the law reports, the reprints from the London press, the accounts of "Dreadful Accident," and so forth, the number of original articles in each issue is not great. They are normally the front page commentaries, then the leaders, usually several, and then the literary reviews, also usually several. Deduct further the controversies on local Scottish affairs, especially ecclesiastical polemics, in which we know that Crichton was active (he was a divine as well as a Scot),[20] and the problem becomes manageable. Once one picks up the rhythm of the thing, and the sort of original contributions De Quincey was making, the task is not ungrateful.

We are told that Rufus Choate's "universal reading and his appreciation of De Quincey's eloquence made him infallible in discovering any work of his hand."[21]

[20] Some evidence of Crichton's work is given in n.13, above. The article in *Fraser's*, cited in the same note, gives the names of two other Scottish divines as early contributors to the *Post*.

[21] Mrs. James T. Fields, *A Shelf of Old Books* (New York, 1894), p. 111n.

Lacking these qualifications, I think I have been reasonably cautious. And though I may have assigned to De Quincey some things that are not his, it is probable that in sum I have not gone far enough. In particular, it is likely that he wrote more of the commentaries and leaders on events of the week, where in immediate subject matter there are no parallels to be found in De Quincey's known works and where other evidences, though nagging, do not seem persuasive enough. In any case, it seems certain that De Quincey did more work for the *Post* than we can or need recover: the evidence of the Bodleian manuscript is that he was also writing digests of the news; and so perhaps he was doing other journal tasks too, as he had for the *Westmorland Gazette*.

Those for whom there is already quite enough De Quincey available will not be much moved by having more of him. Those who are more receptive—as Baudelaire was, or D. H. Lawrence ("I can go on reading and reading him") or Jorge Luis Borges—will be interested in finding a substantial addition to the canon. They have here what is, I believe, the largest number of new essays since the *Posthumous Works* of 1891-93. The more general problems of canonical scholarship, in so extended an example of new attributions, may be of interest to those for whom De Quincey will be of only adventitious importance. Similarly, here is a contribution to the history of the newspaper, a form of publication that attracted some of the best talent of the nineteenth century, as De Quincey himself pointed out, and which offers more opportunities for study than have been accepted. One of these, illustrated by the essays reprinted here, is the running commentary by De Quincey on contemporary issues of the quarterlies and magazines as they appear. They elicit a varied response, from the most general characterization of their qualities to specific new attributions of authorship of particular articles and new essays in criticism. There is a striking attack on Macaulay; De Quincey is known to have had some slight connections with him,[22] but this is the only written comment we have and it is, especially in its characterization of Macaulay's style, a viciously Tory and acute early diagnosis. There are other biographical and critical materials to be found as we learn what De Quincey was doing in this portion of his life. They increase our knowledge of his relations with Carlyle and his opinions of Carlyle's early writing; he saw quickly that Carlyle was not an *Edinburgh Reviewer*. The extent to which thoughts of Wordsworth dominated De Quincey's mind is made convincingly clear here, to the degree that quotations from Wordsworth become an aid to the identification of De Quincey's authorship of articles. The exploitation of his personal knowledge of Wordsworth and Coleridge, which began on a large scale after Coleridge's death and was so disgusting to both families, begins here on a small scale and in a friendlier manner. In various other ways, too, De Quincey the journalist is working here a miscellaneous collection of subjects that entered his writing before and after this time, from the financing of empires to the digestion of rabbits to the quite brilliant analysis of Burke's mind

[22] De Quincey's mother was a friend and, for a time, a neighbor of Hannah More's and De Quincey's first knowledge of Macaulay came to him in a letter from his mother (June 8, 1811, in *De Quincey Memorials*, II, 92-95). The "Baby genius" (age 11) had just been sent from Hannah More's house, then overflowing with company, to spend a couple of days with Mrs. De Quincey. The powerful impression made by somebody else's "extraordinary" boy upon a woman who, to De Quincey's pain, did not like to hear praise of her own children could not have made for a happy introduction. Nor could the connection with Hannah More and the Saints. There were other, unimportant, contacts between the two men which can be traced in the biographies of De Quincey, especially Eaton's. In addition, strong dislike of Macaulay is expressed by the "English Opium-Eater" in one of the "Noctes Ambrosianae," *Blackwood's*, XXVII (1830), 680-84.

and style; the material in the *Post* establishes a continuity in his career.

Most notably, he is doing week-to-week Tory political commentaries at a critical point in the history of the second Tory party, when it is dying in convulsion, at a critical point in English history, when the issues are cash, corn and Catholicism, reform, slavery, revolutions abroad. De Quincey did more political writing than is generally recognized because most of it—the work he did on Wordsworth's *Convention of Cintra* (1809), the *Close Comments* (1818), the editorship of the *Westmorland Gazette* in 1818-19, and the articles in *Blackwood's* from 1829 to 1845—is not reprinted in his collected works. The present collection from the *Post*, incomplete as it necessarily is, is a sizable addition, is a connecting link between the *Gazette* and *Blackwood's*, and, when added to the material that is reprinted in the collected works, makes clear that from the beginning to the end of his literary career politics was a major concern.

De Quincey's politics are interesting. They are the politics of the English Opium-Eater, to whom the central experience is the lost paradise: a great unity and balance that once existed is now lost forever in dark chance and unresting, endless change. This makes them the politics of a certain type of mind and they have therefore a universal significance. They are interesting, but not, I think, edifying.

The key event is Waterloo. For twenty-two years, from the beginning of the war with France in 1793 until 1815, all political questions were merged and absorbed into a "sublime unity." There was only one question in this great agony of the world and the answer was clear for patriot or traitor.[23] It was a time of splendor and marvellous character of events, in which the greatest activities were reconciled in a single action. It was a drama. This

[23] P. 77 below.

drama was wound up fortunately and appropriately by "the solemn and unparallelled catastrophe of Waterloo." After a quarter-century, afflicted Europe had been brought to a "great Sabbath of repose." But there was no repose; the aspect of the political heavens became more portentous.[24] Still, the problems of sedition, of Peterloo, the Queen, or people like Brougham, which followed 1815, though seriously disturbing were not devastating, because the enemy was known by familiar marks and could be fought simply and successfully. The second key event—the one we see in progress in the *Post*—is the apostacy of Canning, when he left the "faithful armies" and formed his coalition with the Whigs.[25] That was a Lucifer-plunge and the Miltonic echoes accompany it. That was a "shattering blow" to the cohesion of parties, a destruction of equilibrium; followed quickly by the brief false hope of Wellington's ministry, which only magnified the final shock of his treachery in 1829;[26] and then, naturally, darkness, anarchy, reform. Looking back upon the wreck of Napoleon's system—the royal phantoms that rose from the earth at his bidding and then were dislimned, that rose and set within our personal ken—De Quincey is impressed with "a sense of shadowyness and unreality," "a feeling of non-reality" left behind by that gorgeous and perishable vision. Yet changes not less mighty nor less rapid have been unfolded in the post-Waterloo period of time and he is impressed with the same feelings.[27]

Canning was the great dissolver of known boundaries and predictable forces by whom politics were plunged

[24] "On the Approaching Revolution in Great Britain," *Blackwood's*, XXX (1831), 317-18; an important article for De Quincey's political ideas.
[25] Pp. 78, 283 below.
[26] "French Revolution," *Blackwood's*, XXVIII (1830), 555-56.
[27] "Approaching Revolution," pp. 317-18.

into "the utter chaos of chance combinations."[28] Words lost their meaning, as the old denominations of Whig and Tory, which can never become obsolete as long as the constitution stands, were discarded and attempts were made to substitute new names: "liberal" is the new word of the 1820's and, invidiously, "illiberal."[29]

Once the true ancient equilibrium is destroyed safety is committed to a "blind agency of chance." An "infinite succession of change" becomes certain, but the point of rest towards which it tends, the kind of catastrophe that will limit these changes is (unlike Waterloo) "wrapped up in unfathomable darkness." The state is "doomed to transmigrate through many shapes of revolution."[30] The language is the language of the English Opium-Eater. But the experience is not as convincing as his; the more one looks into it the less substance it has: it starts well but it is not true to itself.

The constitution destroyed by Canning, and the train of events he set in motion, is a work of nature; it was not struck out like the French Constitution of 1792 at one heat by human hands, but "grew up silently from age to age as a passive deposition from the joint and reciprocal action of every thing in law, manners, religion, institutions, and local necessities which can possibly combine to frame a durable product for a people living in the same soil and climate, and inheriting in every generation the same tastes, habits, and wants."[31] Actually, however, it would seem to have come into existence in the seventeenth century. The landed gentry which had arisen in Tudor times was a new order, a new power that could not incarnate itself in the old and imperfect organization of the political structure; the constitution was a growing thing whereas Charles I viewed it as a perfect whole long

[28] P. 352 below.
[29] Pp. 198, 353 below, and "Approaching Revolution," p. 318.
[30] "Approaching Revolution," p. 329.
[31] *Ibid.*, pp. 321-22.

19

since matured. Hence arose a necessary war. As a result
of that struggle it did mature and came to its final expansion and settlement and was ratified in 1688-89.[32] At
that point, evidently, the process stopped and Charles
would seem to have been wrong only in being a premature nineteenth-century Tory. Because if the constitution was once a growing thing that provided for the
incarnation of new powers it is now a machine. It is
balanced in an exquisite equilibrium, as by centrifugal
and centripetal action, by the reciprocal antagonism of
popular and aristocratic forces, each entrusted for its
preservation to a political party.[33] And if the language
of the machine is dynamic, achieving its stability by a
kinesis, the important point is that it cannot be disturbed; there is no longer place for new forces or new
combinations or shifts of direction; it cannot respond. It
seems likely that if a serious and persistent attempt had
been made to enforce De Quincey's policies of the 1820's
the bloody revolution of his fears would have been a
reality.

De Quincey is at work at the beginning of the "liberal"
age and there is a service to be performed. If it is the
weakness of the liberal mind to abstract or to mechanize,
to simplify and leave difficulties out of account, it is the
function of the conservative to see more complexities,
more history, a larger world, to be more imaginative. The
greatness of Burke and his legacy to the poets and essay-
ists, including those who most hated his conclusion, was
that he brought imagination to bear upon politics; he
showed that problems were not to be reduced, that there
were always more and always more varied powers to be
taken into account; that there was a play and interplay
of concrete objects and of spiritual forces, all with his-

[32] See esp. "A Tory's Account of Toryism, Whiggism, and Radicalism" (1835-36), M., IX, 320-26.
[33] See pp. 352-53, 356-57 below, and the further references there.

tories and continually in movement; that it required a comprehensive mind, intelligent and feeling, to be aware of these, to give them adequate weight, to see them as a whole; and that a various, knowledgeable, and impassioned rhetoric was necessary to enlarge the mind of the audience to the size of the problem. De Quincey, who was obviously indebted to Burke for some of his political ideas, saw the special quality of Burke's mind; he defended it against the commonplace attempts to reduce it to mere "fancy" as opposed to "judgment," knew that the imagination and the intellection, the emotion and the thought, were a unity. That unity was a mark of his own best work. But in his politics, though there is much feeling it is usually without thought, and though there is a good deal of thought it is too often without feeling. He performs no service in a liberal world because his is the narrower world, with its automatic responses and its fixed language that makes discussion impossible—in party politics a lifeless "equilibrium," in religion a "fine old patriotic chant of *No Popery*," in slavery a "panic of property," in political economy a "doctrine."

The last is worth brief special note. De Quincey's political economy is anomalous in a Tory—so much so that it is helpful in identifying the authorship of his articles.[34] It has gained him the praise of men whose politics are very different from his: Whig, Utilitarian, Fabian.[35] It might have been a recognition of a new power that prompted a rethinking of Tory principles. Or, a Tory interested in political economy might have humanized a dismal science. For De Quincey it is really without con-

[34] See pp. 119-20 below.
[35] See J. R. M'Culloch, *The Literature of Political Economy* (1845), p. 33, on the greatness of the "Dialogues of Three Templars," though M'Culloch was repelled by the manner of the *Logic of Political Economy* (p. 20); John Stuart Mill, *Principles of Political Economy* (1848), Book III, chaps. i-iii; Sidney Webb, in *Fabian Essays in Socialism*, ed. G. Bernard Shaw ("Dolphin Books" ed., a reprint of the 1889 ed.), p. 64.

sequence. Its attraction is that it is *a priori*, insulated, a fixed doctrine. Like his politics it tends to be a schematism that abstracts from reality; he came upon it as an escape from pain, a stimulant in a vacuum, and it remained that.[36] So far as it has value it is a weapon to sweep away someone like Robert Owen without the need to understand or to recognize a problem.[37] Southey did better than that.

De Quincey's politics are a failure of imagination. They are, recognizably, the politics of the English Opium-Eater, but the success of the Opium-Eater, the quality that drew men like Baudelaire and Lawrence to him, is the willing, exploratory imagination, with its vivid sense of the unusual in life, of incongruous, heterogeneous elements that fuse into a harmony of strange new shapes and transformations that require a comprehensive response. There are dangers and terrors in this vision, always dark passages, uncontrollable forces and endless vistas and loss of equilibrium, but the result is always a discovery and a probing of reality. The politics are a refusal of vision, understandable, but nonetheless a refusal, an unearned claim upon equilibrium and a fantasy of the past that converts the present to shadowiness and unreality. They make him terribly vulnerable because he is faced by a continual betrayal—by Liverpool, Canning, Wellington, Peel. The "new æra," the "lustration," the return to purity so longed for never comes; the unruly cattle are never permanently broken.[38] As each man comes to power he succumbs to inner weakness, outer pressure, cannot hold out against events, and De Quincey casts him off.

It is a drama worth watching. It has its points, its questions, its unspoken ironies. Who destroyed the Tory party? Who betrayed De Quincey?

[36] *Confessions* (both versions), M., III, 431-32.
[37] Pp. 106-22 below.
[38] Pp. 280, 349 below.

A Note on the Text

The text has been transcribed from microfilms of the originals. Obvious newspaper misprints—transposed letters, reduplicated syllables and such—have been corrected without comment. Otherwise the intention has been a faithful transcript and the *sic*'s have been used infrequently.

The general format is to give, first, the text of the article, including the original footnotes—often many and long, as is De Quincey's practice. These footnotes are keyed by asterisks, daggers, double daggers, letters, or whatever the (inconsistent) usage of the original. My annotations of the article are keyed by numerals. The text and notes are then followed by the reasons for attributing the article to De Quincey. Where an article appeared in two or more parts, in separate issues of the newspaper, the argument for attribution is given at the end of the last part. The sole exception is the very first article, which is preceded by some introductory material, for reasons that will be apparent there.

Since a case must be made for each article the arguments for attribution are sometimes repetitive; I have tried to eliminate this repetition as much as possible by the use of extensive cross-references, though these bring their own kind of lesser awkwardness. Other schemes, such as appendices and indices, might reduce this problem but only by introducing more complications than they remove. The general index is designed to include the advantages of an index of repetitive pieces of evidence.

In establishing attributions of this sort the best one can arrive at is a high degree of probability. I have, however, called those articles "certainly De Quincey's" where the evidence is so strong that I am confident the argument is proved beyond a reasonable doubt—where, as a question of probability, it would be extraordinary if De

Quincey were not the author. Because of the cross referencing some brief term was needed and this one at least makes clear my own presumption, in one sense or another.

In the notes the abbreviation "M." means *The Collected Writings of Thomas De Quincey*, 14 vols., ed. David Masson (Edinburgh, 1889-90). Masson's edition is not complete and has other serious defects for our purposes here, but it has many virtues, is the best we have, and is certainly necessary for convenience. Whenever M. contains the relevant passage or words the reference is to his text and title, though the original, especially the title, may have been somewhat different. References are given to the original, or to other editions, when M. doesn't reprint the relevant passage or words, or when he omits the entire essay. The largest group of omitted essays essential here are those found later by William E. A. Axon, "The Canon of De Quincey's Writings," *Transactions of the Royal Society of Literature*, 2nd ser., XXII (1914), 1-46; they are chiefly from *Blackwood's*.

In the notes and other editorial material the place of publication of a book is given only when it is other than London.

THE TEXT, NOTES,

ATTRIBUTION

July 28–August 4, 1827

This two-part review of the *Edinburgh Review* for June 1827, was, I believe, De Quincey's first contribution to the *Post*. The immediate occasion was Article XI of the *Edinburgh*, "The Present Administration." Liverpool, who had been Prime Minister since 1812, suffered a stroke in February 1827, and Canning succeeded him in April. The Catholic question, although it was not a "ministerial" question, was the chief problem in the reconstruction of the administration because Canning would not serve under an anti-Catholic, and several Tory ministers, including Wellington and Peel, refused to accept Canning's leadership. These Tories, individually or collectively, had other reasons to distrust Canning: his "liberal" position on foreign policy and on free trade; his lack of personal principle, as they saw him. When Canning was charged with the reconstruction they resigned from the cabinet and Canning was then joined by some of the Whigs in a coalition. The *Edinburgh* defended the Whigs and the coalition and attacked the Tories who had seceded; the *Post*, ultra-Tory, responded on July 21 (p. 81), identifying Macaulay[1] as the author of the offending article:

[1] Sydney Smith identified the author in a letter of July 1827, but his nineteenth-century editor deleted the name: "The article on the new Ministry is by ——; violent, but there is considerable power in it" (*Letters of Sydney Smith*, ed. Nowell C. Smith [Oxford, 1953], I, 467). Nowell Smith says the style strongly suggests Macaulay and he may be right: the material in the *Post* is at least further evidence that contemporary opinion assigned the article to Macaulay, and, since that evidence hasn't been gathered before, a long footnote is needed. The *Times* of July 21 (p. 2, col. 3) also seems to have Macaulay in mind: the article is "evidently the composition of a very young man, whose vehemence of tone and peremptoriness of judgment are in immense disproportion to his powers of reasoning, and to his knowledge: still he is not without talent"; and the *Times* quotes two passages "happily conceived, and expressed with sufficient point and energy." The *Times* obviously wanted the advantages of Macaulay's point and

It is with regret that we perceive the forthcoming
Edinburgh Review, has been made a vehicle for an
elaborate paper—not in favour of Mr. Canning—not
a recantation of the former descriptions of that gentleman, but a cento merely of the abuse which has
been so copiously poured on his quondam associates,—merely because they claimed their right as
British subjects to retire from office; for this is the
head of their offending. It is a sort of compound by
a Mr. Macauley [*sic*], we are told—(son of Mr. Zachary, of Sierra Leone celebrity) [2]—of all the garbage

energy while dissociating itself from his vehemence. The *Times*
is a good authority on the authorship because Brougham had close
connections with it. This, incidentally, weakens the possibility that
Brougham himself was the author; see Chester W. New, *The Life
of Henry Brougham to 1830* (Oxford, 1961), p. 442; see also
Brougham's article in the next issue of the *Edinburgh* (XLVI,
415), in which he seems to be disclaiming authorship of the June
article, and the comment of the *Post* on that occasion (p. 197
below). *Blackwood's*, in October 1827 (XXII, 403ff.), cites the
Times and attributes "The Present Administration" to Macaulay.
William Maginn, in a later attack on Macaulay's review of
Southey's *Colloquies*, also attributes this article to him and quotes
it at length; *Fraser's*, I (1830), 584-86. The unauthorized edition
of Macaulay's *Speeches* (New York, 1853) reprints it as his. Professor John Clive has supplied me with two additional pieces of
manuscript evidence that clinch the case. In a letter to his father,
August 3, 1827 (Trinity College Papers, Cambridge), Macaulay
refers to editorial revisions of an article of his in the *Edinburgh*;
the article is unidentified but evidently just published and the
date indicates the June issue, which was published in the last few
days of July. In the journal of his sister Selina (Huntington
Library) there is an entry for June 16, 1827, which says that Tom
is now very busy writing his article on the present ministry; she
adds that it was very complimentary of Jeffrey to have asked
Tom to write this piece.
It is also possible that Macaulay saw De Quincey's attack; he
wrote to his father on September 1, "I received the Edinburgh
paper which you sent me. Silly and spiteful as it is, there is a
little truth in it," etc. G. Otto Trevelyan, *Life and Letters of
Lord Macaulay* (New York, 1876), I, 141.
[2] Zachary Macaulay, a leader in the antislavery movement, had
been governor of the Sierra Leone colony of liberated slaves.

of the daily press, with the *matter* of Sir James Mac-
intosh's "single speech" in defence of coalitions,[3]
mixed up with rant about the French revolution,
and prophecies of what might have taken place, if
the late Ministry had not been dissolved. There is
in it some affected terseness of stile and some "fine
writing," as it is called; and this champion, like
Molineaux the black,[4] or some other African warrior,
curvettes on his hobby horse, and wields his point-
less javelin, and vows that he cannot find an adversary worthy to meet him, to break a spear withal!
And finding no higher game, he shoots a few en-
venomed arrows with great pride and pomp, at the
new Antijacobin Magazine,—a work, of which till
now, we never heard of.[5] It would have been well,
had Mr. Jeffrey himself dealt with this important
subject. From him we might have expected that
good taste, and right feeling, which, whatever may
be his leaning, would have kept him far aloof from
a participation in the vulgar system of political
pugilism, which seems to derive the hues of its character from the manners of "Gentlemen of the fist."
Mr. Macaulay may be quite assured, that he will
find in England,—and Scotland too—men who are
quite able, and not unwilling to measure swords with
him; and although he may be "a burning, and a shin-

[3] Sir James Mackintosh, who had been absent from the House
for a long time, took the occasion of a debate on Canning's policy
in Portugal to defend the coalition on June 8. Like the author of
the article in the *Edinburgh* he argued that there could be no objection to "coalitions in the abstract." The *Post* had reprinted his
speech on June 16: "his first and single appearance this season"
(p. 41). The phrase used in the present article is probably a
facetious allusion to "Single Speech" Hamilton.

[4] Tom Molineaux, an American-born former slave, had been
twice defeated by Tom Cribb for the boxing championship.

[5] The *New Anti-Jacobin Review*, a short-lived periodical of
1827, had been the ostensible subject of review by the *Edinburgh*
article.

ing light" among the saints,[6] he may yet be found a person of very slender dimensions, and limited dignity, when stripped of the gorgeous panoply which he has wrapped around him with so much self-complacency. We have seen the article to which we allude; but as the Review is not yet published, we do not feel ourselves at liberty to quote any part of it at present.

De Quincey seems to have been the challenger who then came forward to measure swords with the gorgeous young Whig. The editor of the *Post* was pleased to present him and his article to the public as fulfillment of the promise that Macaulay would find worthy adversaries in England—and in Scotland too:

Whatever may be the feelings of our readers, with respect to the topics which it discusses, men of all parties, we think, will admit that it is written with great acuteness, and in a gentlemanly spirit; and Mr. Macaulay will be compelled to acknowledge, that he has found one adversary, at last, with whom he may deign to break a lance. There are other men of the north who laugh to scorn his lofty airs,—who smile in compassion for a rash youth, rushing as he has done (to use his own fine figure) "into the mouth of an absurdity;" and who spare the rod, in this instance, only because they do not hate the child. His lucubrations would not have merited the notice which has been bestowed on them, had it not been for the channel through which they have been given to the public,—the only circumstance which could have saved them, even for a single day, from the oblivion to which they should have passed with the

---

[6] Zachary Macaulay was one of the "saints," the contemporary name given to the group later known as the Clapham Sect, and the *Post* assumes that his son too must be "a burning, and a shining light" (John 5:35).

30

numerous crudities of the London daily press. (August 4, p. 97.)

The editor had had in types, and ready for publication on July 28, another notice of the same issue of the *Edinburgh*. He printed that one too on August 4, saying that it had been superseded to give place to the communication from his new "very clever Correspondent" (p. 102). He goes on to say that he does not consider himself responsible for the strictures of his correspondent, but it is apparent that he had found a valuable contributor. The notices of the subsequent issues of the *Edinburgh*, the *Quarterly*, and *Blackwood's* (pp. 95, 129, 164, 189, 197, 212, 329 below) were by De Quincey, with a style and content similar to this notice and quite different from the dull effort that had been in types before De Quincey's appearance. From this time De Quincey is a regular contributor to the *Post*.

Edinburgh Review

No. 91. June, 1827

TO THE EDITOR OF THE
EDINBURGH SATURDAY POST

JULY 27, 1827.

SIR, I beg to trouble you with a few notices of the new number of the Edinburgh Review,—confining myself to those articles which, either from their subject or their execution, may be supposed to attract general attention.

ART. I.— (*Rise, Progress, Present State, and Prospects of the British Cotton Manufacture*) does not fall within this description; but I notice it, notwithstanding, for the sake of recording a little circumstance about it, which, however credible, previously to last winter, does certainly, at this date, confound all calculations built upon human prudence. The reputed author of the article, you are aware, is Mr. M'Culloch; and I suppose that nobody has yet forgotten the exposures made last winter by Mr. Mordecai Mullion, of the way in which that gentleman had up to that time conducted his British Manufacture of Political Economy.[1] The general impression was, that

[1] The author of the article was John Ramsay M'Culloch, a disciple of Ricardo and the *Edinburgh's* expert on political economy; see Frank Whitson Fetter, "The Authorship of Economic Articles in the *Edinburgh Review*, 1802-47," *Journal of Political Economy*, LXI (1953), 252. Mordecai Mullion was De Quincey's friend John Wilson of *Blackwood's Magazine*. A proposal had been made to establish a separate chair of political economy at the University of Edinburgh and to appoint M'Culloch. Wilson was Professor of Moral Philosophy and also Political Economy at the university, though he had never yet lectured on political economy; he considered the proposal an invasion of his territory and he succeeded in stopping it. He attacked M'Culloch in *Blackwood's* and in a pamphlet, *Some Illustrations of Mr. M'Culloch's Principles of Political Economy* (1826), signed Mordecai Mullion, in

Mr. Mullion had forever given the *coup de grace* to that
lucrative branch of industry. Judge, then, of my surprise,
when a friend, coming to the words "Mr. Malthus, whose
leanings, it ought to be observed, are all on the side of
agriculture," suddenly awoke as it were from slumber,—
and, in the very words of the Vicar of Wakefield to the
Cosmogony man, exclaimed—"I beg pardon for interrupting so much learning, but it seems to me that I have
read all this before." And sure enough it is so. The old
machinery, as my friend satisfied me, is again put in
motion, though I have not yet ascertained to what extent. I suppose Mr. M'Culloch says to himself—"Enough
has been given to party malice, or (if you will) to public
justice!—Let it suffice that Mullion has silenced me for
half a year. Vengeance is satisfied; and humanity now
requires that there should be a general *amnesty*—(especially of my past articles)." How far the Editor of the
Review will approve of this doctrine, is not for me to say.
But, undoubtedly, if *he* does, the public will not:—there
will soon get up a general outcry, whenever Mr. M'Culloch makes his appearance.—"By G—— here comes the
cosmogony man;" and Mr. Mullion, who has already
given us the *Rise and Progress*, will soon have to appear
with the *Present State and Prospects of the M'Culloch
article manufactory.* Of its *prospects* Mr. M'Culloch himself seems to think most favourably; for this is the manufactory he has evidently in his eye in the following passage, at p. 17:—"We have not, indeed, the slightest doubt
that weaving by machinery is destined, and at no distant
period, entirely to supersede weaving by the hand. There
are no limits to the power and resources of genius; the
various processes carried on in the weaving mills will be
constantly receiving new improvements; and the race of
weavers—a race that has always been proverbial for pov-

which he showed that M'Culloch was guilty of continual self-
plagiarism.

33

erty and want of forethought—will be changed to ma-
chine-makers."*

 * Not wishing to trouble your readers with any direct speculations of Political Economy during the summer heats and the
recess of Parliament, when people look for a vacation from that
kind of torment, I shall confine to a note the following charge
against Mr. M'C., of a worse species of plagiarism than that which
Mr. Mullion exposed. When Mr. M'C. pillages from himself, it is
doubtless unavoidable that the public should suffer in pocket by
paying twice—thrice—or 18 times, as it may happen, for the same
wares: but still the public is no particular object of compassion,—
having a very long purse. But, in appropriating to himself a doctrine brought to light by Mr. Ricardo, Mr. M'C. is guilty of an
encroachment on the claims of a private individual. Now, this is
done in the most audacious style throughout pp. 29, 30, and 31 of
this very article. There is no one discovery in Political Economy
more brilliant, or more incontestably the property of Mr. Ricardo
than this: That in a country where there is a large proportion of
machinery, increase of wages is so far from being any evil, that
it positively decreases the prices of many things; viz.—of all those
which are in any considerable degree the product of machinery.
One sentence will make this clear. Wages and profits vary in-
versely: whatever one gains, the other loses; and *vice versa*. Taken
jointly, therefore, they always compose the same sum. Now, upon
this previous doctrine, which also is Mr. Ricardo's, depends the
one in question. For, suppose wages in a given case of production,
to be 9d. and profits 3d. *i.e.* jointly a shilling, then let wages rise
to 10d.; what follows? Profits sink to 2d, still making jointly a
shilling. Thus far, then, the public are neither gainers nor losers;
because, whatever is saved to them upon the one fund, is lost
upon the other. And so it would always be in a country where all
production went on by unassisted human labour. But now, suppose machinery to be introduced, and then observe how this will
affect the case. Profits have sunk to 2d.: but this advantage is lost
and neutralized upon articles made by human labour; for, if
profits have sunk by a penny, wages have risen by a penny. On
the other hand, in articles made wholly by machinery, this advantage is *not* lost: profits have sunk; and this gain cannot be
neutralized by a corresponding rise on wages, because, by the supposition there *are* no wages, the article being wholly the product
of machinery. In this case, then, you have the *full* benefit of the
fallen profits; and in proportion to the degree in which machinery
enters into the production of the article, you have a *corresponding*
benefit from the fallen profits. Hence it appears, that every rise
in wages, by producing a fall in profits, must inevitably produce
a fall in price upon one very large class of commodities; viz.—all
those produced by machinery. And observe that this is an *increas-*

34

ART. II. *Memoirs of the Emperor Baber.*—This article, which general report ascribes to the Editor,[2] was doubtless intended to furnish something like a balance of amusement to the general dullness of the Number. But it is a failure. The writer acknowledges at the outset that "the strongest impression left on his mind" by the Memoirs, was the "uselessness" of the class to which they belong; and thinking it "in vain to recommend them as a portion of history," he proposes to do no more than "to extract a few of the traits which appear the most striking and characteristic." When history is read, or perhaps is of a nature to admit of being read, for no higher end—even this end is lost. Of the more eminent European princes we all read so much under some vague notion of reading for instruction, that afterwards memoirs and anecdotes relating to persons so familiarly known to us, gain a power to interest and amuse, which those identical narratives would not have had in any degree, if told of a stranger. The very same danger or escape happening to Henry IV. of France, or Charles I. of England, would have held us in breathless suspense, which is quite powerless when told of a shadow like Baber, who is no more to us than an algebraical quantity. And, over and above this want of previous acquaintance, we are not at home

---

ing class in every advancing country. And thus, in every thriving country, it tends more and more to become a general law—that increase of wages produces diminished prices.

Such is the splendid discovery of Mr. Ricardo, which is actually argued throughout the three pages already cited, with the air and tone of an original discoverer; and, to complete the climax of audacity (oh! for some fitter word!), a foot-note to p. 31 winds up the discussion in the following terms:—"See, for a farther illustration of this principle, Mr. Ricardo's Principles of Political Economy and Taxation, p. 34, 1st edit. and Mr. M'Culloch's Principles of Political Economy, p. 320." A farther illustration in the works of the whole and sole discoverer ! !

---

[2] The report was true; the article is reprinted in Jeffrey's *Contributions to the Edinburgh Review.*

in Oriental manners and Oriental feelings. And, finally, the want of resistance to the will, or conflict with the presiding passions, in which lie the elements of interest in any narrative, and which the condition of despotic power precludes, strip the history of an Eastern prince of all power to interest. Foreign enemies apart,—to him there can be nothing to fear; and to the reader, therefore, nothing to excite. So that, though Mr. Baber—or "the Tiger," as he is called—*for* a Tiger, is really not a bad Tiger; yet, when all is said and done, and Mr. Baber has taken himself off, we feel that there is no one thing on earth that we could more willingly have parted withal.

ART. VI.—*George III. and the Catholic Question.*— This is written by a low-bred fellow, as incapable of the feelings of a gentleman as of handling the question before him.[3] His chief care is to insult the late King, the Duke of York, and the Editor of the Correspondence, Dr. Phillpotts. His quarrel with the King is *risum teneatis*! on points of style and grammar. Now, as to the style, the King wrote like a gentleman, which is what the Reviewer will never do. Gentlemen are not apt, in their notes and confidential letters, to shew a finical and scholastic anxiety in the construction of their sentences: satisfied to be intelligible, they often express themselves with conversational freedom and negligence. And thus far the King may be amenable to criticism. Half a minute's care would have corrected every thing amiss in the

[3] The *Edinburgh* article was a review of *Letters from His Late Majesty to the Late Lord Kenyon* (1827). They are letters written 1795-1801, in which George expressed scruples about his coronation oath, in opposition to Pitt's forwarding of Catholic claims. Some letters from Pitt and from the Duke of York are in the same pamphlet. The editor was Henry Phillpotts, at this time a strong anti-Catholic; a few years later he became Bishop of Exeter, as a reward for supporting Wellington's Catholic Emancipation.

The author of the review may have been Brougham; New, *Brougham*, p. 442.

King's style, which is simply the undress style of a person not aware that he is going into public. The Reviewer, on the other hand, writes like a pedant, whom no discipline could polish into ease and elegance. Dr. Phillpotts is insulted as an "expectant beneficiary," who brings "posthumous adulation" to the late King, "at the risk of vilifying" the present. But surely of all courses for getting on in the church, it must be the most unpromising to address one's scurrility to a living King, and one's homage to a dead one. The reviewer himself, stupid fellow as he is, shews that he knows better where to plant his adulation and his brutality. As to the question itself (of the Coronation oath, in relation to the Catholic question,) it has been more learnedly treated in the newspapers. And the reviewer makes the small mistake of supposing Mr. Pitt, because a friend to the Catholic pretensions of 1801, coupled with adequate securities for Protestant ascendancy, of consequence a friend to those pretensions as they are shaped at this day.

ART. VII.—*Jean Paul Frederich* (read Friederich)[4] *Richter*. Here is the greatest oversight, on the part both of editor and reviewer that I remember throughout my whole acquaintance with periodical literature. The public is summoned to an elaborate critique of works, which are in no shape before them. A full summing up is delivered, and judgment given, on a case never brought into Court: the works of John Paul are not, as the French say, *en evidence*. What should we think of a minute critical examination, in England, of a picture-gallery at Pekin? In such a case it is not the justice

[4] Here and in two other places there are misprints, corrected by a notice of errata in the following week's paper. The corrections (incorporated in the present text) would be characteristic of De Quincey's meticulousness in these matters.

The *Edinburgh* article is by Carlyle. De Quincey's account of it is less than fair. The quotation about Taylor and Browne, for example, is taken out of context and distorts the meaning.

merely of the remarks, but their very meaning and purpose, that are made indeterminable from the absence of all the objects to which they are applied. It is true, that an entire class of works is sometimes brought under review in English journals, (as *English novels*, for example, *French Memoirs, Eloquence of the Senate*, &c.) although not then, more particularly than in any other month or year, at the public bar. But in such cases, the critic appeals to a general previous acquaintance, on the part of his readers, with the whole, or at least with a representative part of the whole body which he professes to examine. But, in the case of John Paul, not one considerable work of the vast number he has written, is before the English public: so that, to be verified, or even to be understood, the present critique must be laid up in lavender, probably for years to come. Any thing more injudicious, I have rarely known. In such a case, one would suppose that a moment's reflexion should have pointed out the propriety of very large specimens with very short criticisms; instead of which, we have, first of all, 17 pages of criticism; and, at the close of all, something less than one page of specimen, and *that* not translated in a way to recommend John Paul. The critique is much superior to the translation; being frequently able and original in its style of thinking. One defect, however, I must loudly tax the Reviewer with—and that is, an imperfect acquaintance with John Paul's writings. Some of the best he seems not even to have heard of. In one of these, by the way, *The Comet*, published about 1822, he would have found a list up to that time, of all Richter's works, drawn up by himself. The *Vorschule der Aesthetik*, which he speaks of at p. 183, I suspect that he has not accurately read; a great deal of it has nothing to do with "poetic art," and would be intelligible in any part of the world.—However, it will be time enough to

discuss John Paul when his works are before the English
public. Meantime, that opinion of the Reviewer, which
is most likely to attract notice and surprise, is one which
respects some of our own writers,—the Jeremy Taylors
and Sir Thomas Brownes, "whose way of thought," he
tells us, (p. 195) "has long ceased to be our way, and
the most valued of their merely intellectual opinions
have passed away." What he can possibly mean, is past
my skill to divine.

ART. X.—*Library of Useful Knowledge.* —*Tempestas
in matulâ!*[5] or, to speak in decorous English, a storm in
a gutter! So far as I can get at the honest man's meaning, he has an assortment of little books to sell; and is
very much enraged at some rival concern: which is exceedingly natural. But surely all this should have been
transferred to the cover of the Review.[6]

ART. XI.—*The Present Administration.*—But now
comes the salt which is to keep the Review in good odor
during this hot weather. Here lies the sting which is
properly put into the tail of the Review. Fit subject he
is, and ripe, this same Master Macaulay, for the *knout*
of Christopher North,[7] which I much doubt will be laid
into him in a memorable style next month. For my part,

[5] In less decorous English, a tempest in a piss-pot. It is not, in
any sense, a classical expression and no source has been located;
see below, p. 58.

[6] The cover would be where the advertisements were printed.
Blackwood's for October 1827 (XXII, 425ff.), attributes the account of the *Library of Useful Knowledge* to Brougham; De
Quincey's review of *Blackwood's* in the *Post* of September 29
(pp. 129-30 below) accepts the attribution and it is a reasonable
one. See New, *Brougham*, pp. 442-44. Brougham was the founder
of the Society for the Diffusion of Useful Knowledge (Peacock's
Steam Intellect Society), which had just begun to publish the
Library, and Brougham used the *Edinburgh* to publicize and defend the Society and its publications.

[7] Christopher North was John Wilson under his more famous
pseudonym, in *Blackwood's*, where he applied the knout to Whigs
and other criminals.

NEW DE QUINCEY ESSAYS

I am a bad hand at 'knouting' a man, though I could expose shallow logic *con amore*. Next week I shall trouble you with a paper at some length on this subject; for the present, I fear that I have already gone beyond the limits you prescribe to such communications.—Yours, very truly,

METACRITICUS.

August 4, 1827

Edinburgh Review

[*cont.*]

TO THE EDITOR OF THE
EDINBURGH EVENING POST

SIR,—According to my promise, I resume my letter on
the last No. of the Edinburgh Review, for the purpose
of commenting a little on its concluding article, (XI.)
entitled *The Present Administration.*

This article is to be understood, of course, as a manifesto from that division of the Whigs, (or *soi-disant*
Whigs,) who are parties to the late coalition, and as the
official vindication of that whole transaction: it has,
therefore, the character, in some degree, of a State-paper.
So much on the one hand. On the other hand, the reputed author is a young gentleman "upon town," of the
name of Macaulay. In the case of a King's Speech, constitutional reasons oblige us to consider it as the speech
of the ministers who compose it: but, in any other case
of a public *exposé* of principles and policy, we are entitled to consider it, indifferently, as the work of the
immediate author from whom it is known* to emanate,
or of the party by whom it is sanctioned and adopted.
I say that we are entitled to do so, if it will answer any
useful purpose. Now, it does certainly proclaim the indecorous precipitancy, and the recklessness of the party
whose appeal is here advocated; to contrast the solemnity of the task with the boyish immaturity of the hands
to which it has been confided. Too happy in their new-
born luxuries of place and power, these *parvenus* of office

* "*Known* to emanate," I say, because Mr. Macaulay, who cannot but have seen the newspaper statement, has not contradicted
it; and, because the internal evidence tallies with that statement.

41

(it would seem,) have no leisure for their own vindication; a great question of honour and public principle they are satisfied to see degraded into a contest of epigram and sneer; and, in a case where considerate men would feel themselves to be at the bar of public opinion, under a most heavy impeachment of integrity, they submit to have their defence so conducted,—

Ut pueris placeant, et declamatio fiant.[1]

Mr. Macaulay, the reputed author of this article, is the son of Mr. Zachary Macaulay, well known on other accounts, and also as the editor of the Christian Observer, a respectable religious journal, which may or may not exist at this moment. About two years ago, I remember that Mr. Macaulay, jun. first came into notice in London, on occasion of a speech which he delivered at some public meeting.[2] That speech, I and others, no friends to Mr. Macaulay's party, read and admired; understanding however, expressly, that the author was a very young man, and allowing to that consideration a most liberal weight in our judgments. Since, then, I hear that Mr. Macaulay's public appearances have disappointed the expectation he had raised; but *why*, I do not distinctly understand. Undoubtedly in some cases, not to have advanced, is to have retrograded: and, in particular, with regard to the weaknesses of youth, not to have out-grown them, is in some sense to have decayed. To be reminded of promises only by their non-fulfilment, and of hopes by their overthrow, is painful. And blossom, such as Mr. Macaulay's, which, after two years' expecta-

[1] Adapted from Juvenal, X, 167. In Dryden's translation: "To please the Boys, and be a Theme at School" (in Johnson's *Vanity of Human Wishes*, "To point a moral, or adorn a tale").

[2] Zachary Macaulay had edited the *Christian Observer*, the organ of the saints, from 1802 to 1806; it was still very much in existence. The speech of Mr. Macaulay, jun. had been made at a meeting of the Antislavery Society, June 25, 1824, and had been an enormous success.

tion, has borne no fruit, is more probably the harbinger
of a blight. Else, and upon any other principle, I do not
see why Mr. Macaulay should be said to have fallen off:
for the present article in the Edinburgh Review is the
very twin brother of his speech. The same rashness and
intemperance, the same petulance, are prominent in both;
and the same ambition of superfine rhetoric†: every sen-

† I am sorry to say, also,—the same inconsistency and careless-
ness to harmonize his assertions or his logic. I give a few instances:

1.—At p. 247, describing his own embarrassment as to the line
he will take in his defence, Mr. M. says, "A statement of facts,
may be contradicted; but the gentlemen of the Opposition do not
deal in statements. Reasonings may be refuted; but the gentlemen
of the Opposition do not reason." This is not amiss; being constructed on the model of the celebrated answers from the Tenth
Hussars when quartered in Dublin—"The Tenth do not dance,"—
"The Tenth never waltz,"—"The Tenth do not play l'ecarté," &c.[3]
Unfortunately, however, it happens, that for all the rest of the
article, Mr. M. does little else than "reason" after his fashion; and
against somebody, I presume, possibly against the Opposition.

He is also "unable to comprehend distinctly of what they" (the
Ministers) "are accused;" and yet, afterwards, is at great pains
to show that several weighty charges against them are groundless.

2.—The party in Opposition are described, p. 247, as one "which
for ignorance, intemperance, and inconsistency, has no parallel in
our annals" as a "scandal to the nation," &c.

On the other hand, at p. 257, the same party are described as
"men who had done their country noble service before—and of
many of whom, individually, it must be impossible to think otherwise than with respect."

3.—Of the Catholic question it is said, p. 253, that the opposition to it lies "with the people of England; and not with the
corrupt, not with the servile, not with the rude and uneducated,
&c., but with the great body of the middling orders; the lower
classes care nothing at all about the question."

Yet, at p. 254, having to upbraid his own party for their selfish
lukewarmness in this cause, Mr. M. says, "If, at the late election,
all our public men, who are favourable to emancipation, had
dared speak out, they might have lost a few votes; they might
have been compelled to face a few dead cats; but they would have
put down the prejudice effectually. Five or six friends of the

[3] In reference to incidents that had been much in the news in
1824, when the fashionable Tenth had been derided for its dandi-
fied and offensive conduct.

tence seems saturated with its separate charge of quicksilver; and paragraph after paragraph roll off in volleys
of minute explosions, flashes, raps, and bounces, like the
small artillery of a schoolboy, or a feu-de-joye of squibs
and crackers.

So furnished, and with graces of such a quality, Mr.
Macaulay is thought a fit organ of communication between the pseudo-Whigs and the public, and rates his
own pretensions in that character so highly, as to expect
the gratitude of the *New Anti-jacobin Review*, for having condescended to insult it. "We once," says he, "heard
a schoolboy relate, with evident satisfaction and pride,
that he had been horsewhipped by a Duke; we trust that
our present condescension will be as highly appreciated."

claims might have been unseated; but the claims would have been
carried."

Listen to this:—It is "the middling orders" that fling dead cats
(for "the lower classes care nothing at all about the question;)"
and people, who argue by dead cats, are to be reasoned out of
their "prejudices" by a course of speeches from the hustings of
one election.

And at p. 255, notwithstanding that "the lower classes care
nothing at all about the question," yet for all that "plain, spirited,
moderate treatises on the subject, should find their way into
every *cottage*."

4.—The "lowest" orders in "our manufacturing towns" are represented at p. 261, as insensible to any thing but gross physical
influences. "An abundant supply of the necessaries of life is with
them almost the only consideration. The difference between an
arbitrary and a limited monarchy vanishes, when compared with
the difference between one meal a-day and three meals a-day. It
is a poor consolation to the man who has had no breakfast, and
who expects no supper, that the King does not possess a dispensing power," &c.

Yet turn to p. 262, where Mr. M. has quite forgotten p. 261, (as
the practice is with epigrammatists), and you find it written, that
"people familiar with political inquiries attribute the grievances
under which they labour to defects in the original constitution of
the government. *Thus it is with a large proportion of our spinners,
our grinders, and our weavers.*"

At p. 261 "our grinders" care for nothing but breakfast and
supper; but at p. 262 they are "familiar with political inquiries."

Now, it is true, that Virgil's hero would occasionally suggest to any man whom he had knocked down—that, perhaps, it might console him to know that he was going to have his throat cut by the hands of the pious Æneas: and from Falstaff's account of Mr. Justice Shallow, we learn that he looked upon it as one of the trophies of his youth, that his head had been broken by John of Gaunt. But, John of Gaunt and Æneas were princes; and the latter in particular, *famâ super æthera notus;*[4] circumstances which, unfortunately for the tribute of gratitude here anticipated, are wanting in the Reviewer. But, leaving him to settle that matter with those whom it concerns, I must take leave to suppose that, however he may hold the relation of the Duke to the schoolboy, with regard to the anonymous persons whom he insults at the beginning of his article, he will suspect himself, on reflection, that he performs the part of schoolboy, in relation to the four Dukes, (Newcastle, Rutland, Buckingham, and Wellington,)[5] against whom he points his malice towards its conclusion. A more indecorous disproportion between the matter and the author, I have never seen: what might have worn the shape of political animosity in the hands of a known adequate representative of the faction in power, sinks into an impotent lampoon under the youth, youthful manner, and want of consideration in the state which attach to the person of the Reviewer. I shall say no more on this subject; and I have noticed it at all out of no ill-will to Mr. Macaulay, but as an evidence, in one view, of the ferocious *sansculloterie* of the Whig *parvenus.* Their accredited apologist, on this occasion, be his talents what they may, at all events, writes in a style stamped with the characters of youth, levity, inexperience and audacity. So much will be admitted; now, it is not possible, that any

[4] *Aeneid,* I, 379.
[5] All anti-Canningite Tories.

one thing should argue more an extinct sense of personal
dignity, in a political party, or a want of regard for it
in others, than lending their name and countenance to
persons, or to occasions, below the standard of a *public*
existence. If it is necessary to Whig purposes, that men
like the Duke of Wellington or the late Chancellor,[6] men
who have a *national* place and acceptance, should be
hauled out by name, (not in Parliament, but in a literary
journal,) as parties to a course of policy which is described as certain to have driven this country into a
"bloody revolution," (p. 260,) mere decent consideration
for the public, for the objects of the attack, and for
themselves as authorising the attack, demands that it
should be made in language, and with circumstances arguing a responsible *age* in the writer, with gravity and
thoughtfulness; and (if possible) supporting the illusion
of a writer clothed with something of a corresponding
weight of authority and character. Wilfully to neglect
these decencies, is to profess jacobinism. On that account, it is worthy of notice. Now for the *matter* of the
Whig apology.

I.—After a great deal of coyness and fighting shy,
much protesting that he does not know what thing it is
that his party are charged with;—never heard of it—has
not the least idea, and so forth—all at once, (p. 248,)
like a good fellow, the Reviewer takes to the charge
without more ado, and roundly admits that he knows
most perfectly what that thing is; and a thing it is which
has many names, amongst which he chooses to select
"deserted principles," and "unnatural coalition." On this
hint he speaks and undertakes to shew, that "coalitions
in the abstract," are no bad things. As I do not purpose
to speak of "things in the abstract," I shall decline going
over the whole of his ground, and content myself with
the sum of his argument, which is this—that, if Party

6 Eldon, one of the Tories who had seceded.

can be justified, Coalition can; both standing on the very
same footing. For what is party? It is a connexion in
which we consent to merge the minor points on which
we chance to differ, for the sake of giving fuller effect to
those great ones on which we agree. Now, this is just
what we do in coalitions. So that coalitions are a sort of
transcendant party: for "what coalitions are to parties,
parties are to individuals." Vastly pretty, I protest.
Quam bella persona! at cerebrum non habet.[7] As in
parties two individuals, so in coalitions two parties, sacrifice their less considerable differences to their paramount agreements. This, I take it, is the reviewer's meaning. Well: but, if two parties are already agreed about
the paramount points of policy and principle, in what
sense *are* they two parties? It must have been under
some prodigious blunder, that they have not coalesced
from the first, being in effect one and the same party,
and divided only by name. If it be replied, that they
were originally two parties, but have gradually approxi-
mated by mutual changes of opinion, here, undoubtedly,
there is opening made for an honourable coalition: but
then this amounts to no more than that, when people
have altered their way of thinking, it is their duty to
say so; a truth which nobody disputes, but availing little
in defence of coalitions as they are, which, (in our history at least) have been unions of parties, which would
not confess to any change of principle. *These* are the
coalitions for which the reviewer is to seek a defence.
For instance, at this moment, if Mr. Canning will say,
"I confess myself to have been in error for the greater
part of my life; Mr. Pitt was very well as an orator, but

[7] Cf. Phaedrus, I, 7:
    Personam tragicam forte vulpes viderat:
    O quanta species, inquit, cerebrum non habet!
In Christopher Smart's translation:
    A fox beheld a mask—"O rare
    "The head-piece, if but brains were there!"

no great politician: I now see the danger of anti-jacobin politics;" or, in case Mr. Canning refuses, if Mr. Brougham will read an abjuration of *his* political creed,—there can be no reason on earth why they should not coalesce; and no man would be entitled to call their coalition profligate: which, as things are, plain-spoken people take the liberty to do; because, under pretence of having recanted nothing, and professing therefore still to hold principles, which should, in all reason, divide them as far asunder as the poles, they have yet united for practical ends, and with the necessity, therefore, of sacrificing their principles on the one side or the other, as often as they stand in the way of those ends: which necessity would not exist, if either party had, in profession, as well as in practice, recanted his principles. The reviewer then, to speak coarsely, has "got the wrong sow by the ear,"—having addressed his defence to a case which nobody impeaches.

II.—More to the purpose, if only they were truly stated, are six cases of coalition, or pretended coalition, cited from the history of the last 140 years. Not one, however, is accurately stated in its circumstances and bearings. I give the first as an example. "The Revolution itself," says he, "was the fruit of a coalition between parties, which had attacked each other with a fury unknown in later times." This is not true: the Whigs and Tories of 1688-9 did *not* coalesce as to any one point on which they had ever differed. What they did was this: they suspended their standing differences, for the purpose of meeting one capital emergency, which would else have left them nothing to differ about: they agreed provisionally, and *quoad hoc*. Two parties, contending for the management of a ship, may, very consistently, unite to extinguish a fire, or to repel an external enemy. Their quarrel is for supremacy in the management of the ship, or perhaps about the principles on which the ship shall

be managed: it is surely an object paramount to *that*—
whether they shall have any ship at all to manage.

III.—The reader may think that it is not much to the
purpose to discuss the abstract idea of coalition, or even
the actual coalitions of past history; the question before
us being this particular coalition of 1827, which must
be justified, after all, on its own grounds. But here the
Reviewer gives an ingenious and colourable construction
to the line of argument he has taken: contending that,
if any possible or conceivable coalition can admit of justification, then *a fortiori* there will be a justification for
this particular coalition; because "never has the world
seen, and never is it likely to see, a junction between parties agreeing on so many points, and differing on so few."

At length, then, whether by a right road or a wrong
one, we are arrived at the true question. And, with respect to this, I am more anxious to say a word or two
on the erroneous shape in which it has been usually debated, than myself to debate it. For in no way is truth
more apt to suffer, or the just advantages of an argument to be forfeited, than by accepting unawares the
laws or the course and direction of a dispute from one's
antagonist. How often is the *onus probandi* inadvertently shifted upon the party to whom it does not belong;
and still oftener the question allowed to be thrown into
that shape which meets the purposes of our antagonist.
In the case before us, it is contended uniformly, that the
two coalescing parties have long been agreed as to all,
or nearly all, the great public questions. Now, first as to
the fact. Three such questions only have been assigned,
the Catholic Question, Free Trade, and our relations to
the South American Republics.[8] As to the first, every

[8] Though there were divisions of opinion, of varying seriousness,
on these questions, they were not obvious party issues. The Catholic Question, in both the Liverpool and the Canning ministries,
was carefully excluded from ministerial questions; both cabinets
contained "Catholics" and "Protestants." Free trade was an issue

man in Parliament being, in this instance, permitted to think as he pleased, agreement thus far was not necessarily more than an accident of taste or caprice, nor implying any other agreements; and not only an accident, but a most trivial accident, and leading to no practical result whatever, so long as it is a settled point, that nothing can be done in the business until the body of the English people are brought to look favourably upon the Catholic pretensions. Doubtless, the coalition conceit, that, by patronage, and so forth, they will have it in their power gradually to win over the spiritual guides of the English people, and thus to improve it into a practical question. But they are wrong there. For most of the coalition are elderly men; and, long before *that* scheme begins to tell, they will all (to use Hamlet's expression,) be "at supper"—*i.e.* "not where they will eat, but where they will be eaten."—So much I think that *I* may take upon me to prophecy. Next, as to Free Trade, that again was a point on which most men thought— not as their party prescribed, but as they had or had not an acquaintance with books of Political Economy, or according to the company they kept. Here, as before, the agreement was pure matter of accident, and pointed to no grounds or principles from which further agreements might be anticipated. Then, as to South America, what was it, I should be glad to know, upon which they ever *did* agree? The recognition of their independence?

---

that divided the manufacturing and the landed interests, though even there the division was not consistent; Huskisson, President of the Board of Trade in the later years of Liverpool's ministry and in Canning's ministry, worked successfully for the reduction of some tariffs and modification of the navigation laws; and the corn laws, of course, continued to be troublesome to both Whigs and Tories. Canning, as Liverpool's foreign minister, after Castlereagh's suicide, had extended recognition to several of the South American republics, but not as a party measure and not because he admired republics; he acted to protect British trade and to restrain possible French and American ambitions.

But *that* was a trifle compared with the question on which they had previously differed. "Aid, or no aid?" was rather a more vital question (I take it) to South America during the agony of her contest, than "recognition or no recognition?" after all was over. But, no matter how important, that step is now taken and irrevocable; and no second step depends upon it. So that, except for the pleasure of saying—How gloriously we agree! they might really, by this time, just as well have differed.

Thus, when the facts of the case are probed, how the fantastic imposture melts away! But, if not, of what consequence are such facts? Miserable delusion to think, that three, or even three score, agreements upon particular questions, or insulated measures, can be of any importance, in comparison with the great original *principles* in politics, from which, as from a fountain, all unanimity must flow that can be steadily relied on! What principles I allude to, can hardly be doubtful: they are those which the French revolution has put on record in every country—Jacobin and Anti-jacobin; principles as old as the human heart, but which the progress of social life has expanded into new activity and wider application; and, with regard to which, the differences between the two parties in coalition, are as notorious as they ought in reason to be irreconcilable. Every hour may bring up new events, or new aspects in political affairs, in which these principles are interested. Let a question arise about Alien intriguers, about a Manchester seditious meeting— about a suspension of the Habeas Corpus Act—about a reformer—a blasphemer—an Ogden—a Hone, &c. &c.[9] or

[9] De Quincey has in mind chiefly those measures by which the Tories took strong action against political agitation in the years after Waterloo: Peterloo in 1819; the suspension of habeas corpus in 1817; the imprisonment of William Ogden for sedition in 1817, and the subsequent parliamentary debate on his treatment in jail; the unsuccessful prosecution of William Hone for blasphemous and

thousands of other cases, such as the fermentation of society is eternally liable to breed, and a moment is sufficient to dissolve the hollow and skin-deep union,—a moment will betray the unfathomable gulf of separation, provided only the two parties were to abide by their former principles. I do not mean to insinuate that they *would* abide by them: for coalitions are not made with that view. But I mean to say, that here lies the real impossibility for any conscientious coalition, unless it be reasonable to suppose, that those who never yet agreed upon one such case, should, for the future, in honest sincerity, differ upon none. The principles concerned in these cases, are of somewhat deeper root, and larger range than those which govern a corn bill: yet precisely these it is that the writers on this question affectedly veil from view. In particular, the writer in the Edinburgh Review tells us, that the Whigs and Mr. Canning "were united in principle, and separated only by names, by badges, and by recollections." Argument, to a man that will say this, is idle. But answer him out of his own mouth. Jacobinism, it seems then, is simply "a name and a recollection." Now, turn to p. 261, where he describes the growth "in the bosom of the middling orders in England of a republican sect, as audacious, as unscrupulous in the choice of its means as the French Jacobins themselves, but far superior to the French Jacobins in acuteness and information—in caution, in patience, and in resolution." Next, turn to p. 262, where he says—"The history of our country, since the peace of 1815, is almost entirely made up of the struggles of the lower orders against the government, and of the efforts of the government to keep them down." Or, finally, read all which

seditious libel in 1817. The Alien Act, which gave the government special police powers over political refugees, had been the subject of periodic debates because it had to be renewed from time to time; in 1826 it was replaced by an alien Registration Act.

follows this passage to the end, where he enlarges on the portentous symptoms, as he interprets them, of imminent revolution in this country. Indirectly, and while occupied with another object, he betrays his panic apprehensions of those anti-social agencies and principles of convulsion—which, in connexion with Mr. Canning's name, he will not so much as mention but by allusion, and instantly dismisses as mere obsolete "recollections."

But "Leviathan is not so tamed:"[10] and Mr. Canning has no such flattery for himself. He of all men can least hide from his own eyes the vast abyss which separates him in principle from his new allies. Not in anger, but in sorrow, it is felt by those whom he has abandoned, that he can never regain his tranquillity, or his own perfect self-approbation. Too surely it is felt, that

> "—————————————Not Mandragora,
> Nor all the *drowsy syrups of the East,**
> Can ever med'cine him to that sweet sleep,"[11]

which by just right was his up to that hour, when he, the child and heir of Mr. Pitt's principles, and the express champion of the honours that had gathered round his memory, first dallied with the thoughts of an "accursed league"[12] with that man who had made it publicly his prayer, that upon his grave it might be found inscribed, as his most honourable distinction, *Here lies the enemy of William Pitt!*[13]

---

* I do not choose to invade the recesses of private life; but the particular allusion in this line will be intelligible to Mr. Canning's private friends.

---

[10] Cowper, *Task*, II, 322.

[11] *Othello*, III, iii, 330-32, misquoted. Canning used laudanum, a fact that would attract De Quincey's attention but not necessarily his sympathy.

[12] From Wordsworth's sonnet "A Prophecy" (1807), damning the Elector of Bavaria who allied himself with Napoleon.

[13] This was Brougham, who was not in the cabinet but had been the chief Whig in bringing about the coalition. In 1812, when he

Such, I think, are the leading points in the hollow pleadings I undertook to examine; but there remain several other gross mis-statements of facts, misconstructions, and sophisms, which somewhere or other ought to be exposed: and upon these, if you should have room for such a communication, I may perhaps trouble you again. Meantime, I remain, Sir, yours very truly,

METACRITICUS.

ATTRIBUTION

There is a fair amount of evidence connecting this two-part article with De Quincey's other work for the *Post* and with his acknowledged works. There is a reference back to a passage in this article (p. 44) in the article of November 24 (p. 197), which is certainly his. The essay by M'Culloch attacked here (p. 32) is attacked again in two later articles in the *Post*, November 10 (p. 177) and December 15 (p. 230); both of them are certainly De Quincey's.

Two subjects on which he wrote in later issues of the *Post*, as well as in his acknowledged works, appear in this article. One is political economy, a favorite topic of his in the years both before and after the *Post* and on which he became the *Post's* resident expert. Ricardo was his master here; the particular point made in this article (pp. 34-35n.) is repeated in De Quincey's "Ricardo and

---

had been one of the Whigs standing for election at Liverpool, and Canning had been one of the Tories there, Brougham made a speech in which he said, "I stand up in this contest against the friends and followers of Mr. Pitt, or, as they partially designate him, the immortal statesman now no more. *Immortal* in the miseries of his devoted country! Immortal in the wounds of her bleeding liberties!" etc. But as for himself, said Brougham, "may no such immortality ever fall to my lot . . . may I have an humble monument in some nameless stone, to tell that beneath it there rests from his labours in your service, *'an enemy of the immortal statesman—a friend of peace and of the people'.*" *Speeches of Henry Lord Brougham* (Edinburgh, 1838), I, 485-86.

Adam Smith. Part III," *Blackwood's*, LII (1842), 736ff.: "amongst his most brilliant discoveries," he said there of Ricardo, is the fact that a rise in wages actually lowers the price of articles produced by machinery.

The other subject is Jean Paul Richter (pp. 37-39). It was De Quincey and Carlyle, the author of the article in the *Edinburgh*, who introduced Richter to the general reading public in England. The method of offering short criticism but large specimens, which is recommended by the newspaper critic, was the method De Quincey had used in introducing Richter to the readers of the *London Magazine* in 1821-24 (M., XI, 259-93); in a note added in 1854 to "The Last Days of Kant" (M., IV, 343) he pointed out that he had been the first to give an English "specimen" of Richter. The anglicizing of Jean Paul as John Paul is a crotchet of De Quincey's, which has been twice noted: by V. R. in *Notes and Queries*, CLXXVII (1939), 190-91, and by Peter Michelsen, *Journal of English and Germanic Philology*, LXI (1962), 736n.; that form of the name appears again in a later article of the *Post*, which is certainly his (p. 133 below). The newspaper critic has some first-hand acquaintance with Richter, including the *Vorschule der Aesthetik*, which De Quincey too had looked into and mentioned in the *London Magazine* (M., XI, 267, 269-70); not many Englishmen, or Scotsmen, knew the *Vorschule*, of which no English translation has ever been published. Richter's *Comet*, noted in the same passage here, recently published (1820) and another little known work, was known to De Quincey: "Herder" (1823), M., IV, 390; "Gillies's German Stories," *Blackwood's*, XX (1826), 850. The "Dream Upon the Universe" he had translated in 1824 for the *London Magazine* (M., XI, 290-93) is from the *Comet*; see also M., VIII, 33-34 and p. 148 below. Also, the implied defense of Jeremy Taylor and Sir Thomas Browne, in the same passage, estab-

lishes a connection between the newspaper article and
De Quincey's article on "Rhetoric," which was published
in the following year (1828): he there brings Taylor,
Browne, and Richter together as the only three authors
of a species of composition he admires greatly (M., X,
104); Carlyle had included Hooker in his comparison,
but Hooker is omitted both here and in the article on
rhetoric.

The allusion to the cosmogony man of the *Vicar of
Wakefield* (p. 33) appears three times in De Quincey's
works: "Society of the Lakes," etc. (1840), M., II, 436;
Confessions (1856 ed.), M., III, 325-26; "System of the
Heavens" (1846), M., VIII, 32. The term "cosmogony
man," used here in the newspaper, is not in the *Vicar*,
but it is used by De Quincey two of the three times he
alludes to the story (and the other time he says "cosmogony friend").

The terrible consequences of the evil hour when Canning, the life-long disciple of Pitt, abandoned his principles, and formed an alliance with "that man" who had
prayed that his epitaph might be "Here lies the enemy
of William Pitt" (p. 53), are deplored by De Quincey
in two articles he wrote shortly after: first, in "The Duke
of Wellington and Mr. Peel," *Blackwood's*, XXV (1829),
295, where the identical epitaph is cited, though the
words are a condensed and altered version of what
Brougham actually said; and second, in "The Present
Cabinet in Relation to the Times," *Blackwood's*, XXIX
(1831), 155, where there are other verbal similarities.
In both *Blackwood* articles, as we shall see, there are
additional parallels to the articles in the *Post*. The presence in the same paragraph of an appropriate phrase
from a minor sonnet by Wordsworth (p. 53) is another bit of evidence; later articles in the *Post* will show
similar literary—and also personal—intimacy with Wordsworth.

The principle that many a good cause suffers in argument for failure to perceive when the "*onus probandi*" lies with one's opponent (p. 49) is also in De Quincey's "Philosophy of Roman History" (1839), M., VI, 447, where the same term is used. "Onus," in reference to the onus of an argument, appears in two other *Post* articles which show additional evidence of De Quincey's authorship: August 18, 1827 (p. 80) and February 16, 1828 (p. 313). "Onus," sometimes in reference to an argument and sometimes in other contexts, is common in De Quincey; there are at least twenty instances. The author's delight in his own felicity as a logician, both here on p. 49 and on p. 40, is the way of De Quincey, who in matters of logic held himself to be impeccable, *doctor seraphicus*: e.g., "Malthus on the Measure of Value" (1823), M., IX, 34; "Protestantism" (1847-48), M., VIII, 255n. The "*knout*" of Christopher North in the same passage on pp. 39-40, as an alternative mode of argument, is also in De Quincey's "Kant in His Miscellaneous Essays" (1830), VIII, 112; see too "Coleridge and Opium-Eating" (1845). M., V, 180-81, 197. Christopher's knout reappears in the article of September 8 (p. 95 below), which is certainly De Quincey's.

To come now to other phrases and words of various kinds. The phrase "the Whigs, or *soi-disant* Whigs" (p. 41) is used again in the article of January 26, 1828 (p. 280), which is certainly De Quincey's. His *Blackwood* article of 1831, "The Present Cabinet in Relation to the Times," refers to "the *soi-disant* Whigs" (p. 143), and an article he wrote in 1837, "On the Political Parties of Modern England," uses the phrase "*soi-disant* Whig party" (M., IX, 368). "Soi-disant" in other contexts, though less distinctive, is a frequent word in De Quincey. It is in the *Post* article of June 28, 1828 (p. 382n.), which is certainly his, and in more than a dozen of his known writings, both before and after this date, including letters and unpublished manuscripts.

The phrase "feu-de-joye of squibs and crackers" (p. 44) is De Quinceyan: "*feu-de-joie* of jests and playful fictions," is in "Recollections of Charles Lamb" (1838), M., III, 66; "*feu-de-joie* of fireworks," in "John Paul Frederick Richter" (1821), M., XI, 270, is a description of the *Vorschule der Aesthetik*; "feu-de-joie of laughter," is in "Mr. Schnackenberger" (1823), M., XII, 314; see also "Ireland," *Blackwood's*, LV (1844), 522n., and "System of the Heavens" (1846), M., VIII, 32, in the same passage as the allusion to the cosmogony man.

"Tempestas in matula" (p. 39), if not peculiarly De Quinceyan is at any rate unusual and favored by him; he uses it in "The Caesars" (1832), M., VI, 229, and in "Anti-Corn-Law Deputation," *Blackwood's*, LII (1842), 275; it is also in "Autobiography," *Tait's*, N. S. I (1834), 485, but when he revised that article in 1853 he substituted "storm in a slop-basin," which is what Masson prints (I, 324). "Leviathan is not so tamed" (p. 53) is in his article "The Late Cabinet," *Blackwood's*, XXVIII (1830), 976; see too "Coleridge and Opium-Eating" (1845), M., V, 205.

Among the more conventional, and therefore less helpful, quotations, "ut pueris," etc. (p. 42) and "fama super aethera notus" (p. 45) are both used by De Quincey, the first in the 1856 *Confessions* (M., III, 214), the second in "Society of the Lakes" (M., II, 375). And one can point to common phrases, which do not prove authorship but show consonance with De Quincey's known writings. "Risum teneatis" (p. 36), a tag from the *Ars Poetica*, is used also in the article of September 29, 1827 (p. 131), which is certainly his; it is also in "Ricardo and Adam Smith. Part III," *Blackwood's*, LII (1842), 737, the article in which he makes the same point about Ricardo which is made in this *Post* article;

the phrase is also in "Kant in His Miscellaneous Essays" (1830), M., VIII, 103, where Christopher's "*knout*" and "*soi-disant*" too are used; and it is in four other places. "*A fortiori*" (p. 49), used also in the articles of November 10, 1827 (p. 173) and February 9, 1828 (p. 301), is an uncommon favorite with De Quincey; it appears about forty times in his writings, including several of the articles cited already. "Coup de grace" (p. 33), "en evidence" (p. 37), "con amore" (p. 40), and "quoad hoc" (p. 48) are all in his repertory.

Klopstock, from the Danish

TO THE EDITOR OF THE
EDINBURGH SATURDAY POST

SIR,—The only sketch in our language (so far as I am aware,) of Klopstock's habits, conversation, and personal qualities, is contained in a private and anonymous memorandum of two visits paid to him towards the end of the last century, which memorandum was drawn up at the time, but not published until the year 1810, when Mr. Coleridge printed it, without alteration, in the original edition of "The Friend." In the second and *reformed* edition of that work, this memorandum was omitted; for what reason I do not exactly know.[1] Hence, however, and from the fact, that the first edition of "The Friend" was never in any proper sense *published*,[2] (having been printed amongst the mountains of Cumberland, and circulated only by the post,) we must explain how it has happened that the laborious, and all-comprehensive spirit of research, which distinguishes the German literati, should have missed so interesting and authentic a record of Klopstock's conversations and opinions. To many readers, that record will have an adventitious interest, as coming from the pen of Mr. Wordsworth the poet. I now send you another memorial of Klopstock, no less authentic than the one published by Mr. Coleridge,— and, like *that*, deriving a separate interest from the celebrity of the author, over and above the *primâ facie* interest from its subject. It is taken with a good deal of

[1] *Friend*, No. 18, December 21, 1809. It was omitted in the 1818 edition of the *Friend*, but it had been reprinted in *Biographia Literaria* (Satyrane's Letter III).

[2] Coleridge had made this point, in *Biographia Literaria* (ed. J. Shawcross [Oxford, 1907], I, 60n., 110), and in the Advertisement to the 1818 *Friend*.

compression, and some little change in the arrangement, from the first volume of the *'Labyrinten'* of Baggesen, a Danish writer of some note.[3] I would not be understood to compare Mr. Baggesen with Mr. Wordsworth. Mr. B. has no pretensions of that magnitude. But he holds a conspicuous place in the modern Danish literature; and, judging from my own limited acquaintance with his works, I am disposed to think not undeservedly. For he displays everywhere an unaffected sensibility, and an enthusiasm honourable to the early period of life at which this work was written, much good sense, and occasionally no inconsiderable originality of thought.

From the insufficient publication of "The Friend," in its first model, Mr. Coleridge thinks himself warranted to consider it "as good as MS.," and accordingly quotes it as such.[4]—Perhaps I have the same title, though on a different ground, for assuming my present communication to be "as good as MS." A Danish book, which has never been translated, although printed and well published at Copenhagen, Kiel, and Altona, may fairly be considered a sealed book to the world at large; there being probably not twenty people in Great Britain, merchants excepted, who cultivate any acquaintance with the Danish language or literature.

For the credit of my own judgment, I beg to be understood as in no respect coinciding with the preposterous estimate of Klopstock's merit, set up by most* Germans

---

* One weighty exception I remember in the person of Kant; and it does honour to his discernment, that he was so at a time when there were few dissenters in this point. The poetic sensibilities of this philosopher were not very profound, but they were true and healthy; and their direction lay chiefly towards the sublime. Hence he reverenced Milton; and, as a German, he desired to reverence Klopstock—but he felt the *falsetto* in his manner, and unwillingly considered him a pretender.

---

[3] Jens Baggesen (1764-1826). His *Labyrinth*, an account of his travels in Europe, was published 1792-93. As De Quincey indi-

and Danes. I am satisfied that his pretensions are vastly overrated; and I heartily assent to the spirit of Mr. Coleridge's repartee in answer to a person who assured him that Klopstock was the German Milton—"Yes, Sir, a very *German* Milton, most undoubtedly."[5]—I remain, Sir, your obedient servant,

X. Y. Z.

July 25, 1827

Professor Cramer and I had just arrived at Hamburgh from Poppenbütel, and had taken up our quarters at the *city of Copenhagen*,—an inn which now, as upon former occasions, I chose, like a good patriot, purely upon account of its name. Cramer had gone abroad, and I was engaged in writing, with, my head drooping over the paper, when a sound as gentle as the folding of a seraph's wings, awoke me from the dream which at this moment possessed me. I raised my head with a sudden start, looked round, and lo! it was Klopstock; it was the poet of the Messiah that stood behind me smiling with the radiance of—what shall I say? Not to repeat the word *seraph* too often,—of a cherub suppose, provided you can fancy to yourself a sexagenarian cherub. I had seen him two years before: but he now looked even more animated than at that time, and in more juvenile health.

Upon his proposal, we went down to his garden; and Cramer soon after joined us. The moment he appeared in sight, Klopstock stepped back with one foot,—threw himself into a fighting attitude, and playfully bade Cramer defend himself. Defend himself, for what? For his disloyal and treacherous treatment of Germany and her

---

cates, the translation is very free, and it is livelier than the original. It is also my impression that De Quincey tends to skip sentences which are more than ordinarily difficult to translate.

[4] *Biographia Literaria*, I, 60n.: "To the public at large indeed it is the same as a volume in manuscript."

[5] *Friend*, No. 18, p. 288: "a very *German* Milton indeed!!!"

language, in his attack on the German *ch.* "Saidst thou not," asked Klopstock, "that *ch* was a sound worthy of a crocodile? But now Cramer, be it known unto thee, that the three Graces in the language of all others most worthy of themselves, the language of Greece to wit, were known by a designation (*Charites*) beginning with that very opprobrious *ch* which thou, Cramer, wouldst proscribe as ultra German. This is my answer; and thus am I avenged. Thou art tried, dear Cramer, and found guilty: and now for judgment, and for punishment." And so saying, he advanced; and—cordially shook hands with him.

We were delighted to see him in such fine spirits; and we *expressed* our delight. Upon which he told us, with an air of exultation, that he had suffered greatly, especially during the past year, from rheumatic gout, but that it had never forced a shriek from him, or so much as a sigh: "once only," said he, "when it flew to my stomach, it forced me to grind my teeth."

From his own spasms, he made an adroit transition to the spasms which were convulsing the political world. (The French Revolution was now in its earliest stage.) Denmark, Sweden, Russia, he glanced at slightly: but FRANCE, FRANCE, was the subject at his heart. "Are you aware," said he, "that I have composed two new lyric poems on this occasion, one entitled, "*Louis the Greatest*," and the other "*The Convocation of the States General?*" We expressed our desire to hear them: and accordingly, in the summer-house of his garden, upon my hinting that I should translate the latter into Danish, he repeated it by heart: the other, he could not remember; and, to say the truth, considering the repulsiveness of the title, I was not sorry for it.

[Baggesen here gives the German original, and his own Danish translation, each consisting of five quatrains. The English reader will probably dispense with any attempt at giving further currency to a composition so radically unlyrical, when he hears the substance of it—which is this:—Every dog has his day; and at length, says Klopstock, "a morning, such as never had been dreamed of, has dawned upon France." Klopstock is thankful for having lived to see this morning; particularly, as it enables him to recant a Klopstockian prejudice of long standing: heretofore he had many times exhorted Germany to take warning by France; whereas, now he exhorts her loudly to take example by France. Another opinion there is also, which Klopstock desires to correct; viz.—that, whereas hitherto he had been in the habit of considering the proudest spectacle of the 18th century—Frederick of Prussia wielding his club, like another Hercules, against the potentates of Europe, and especially against the 'ladies' of Russia and Austria; now, on the contrary, he is far from holding that opinion. France is now the sight for *his* money—France arraying herself in a civic crown worth bushels of your blood stained laurels. Such is the Klopstockian—or, as Mr. Baggesen calls it, the Klopstockish conception of an ode. It is unfortunate, however, that when Mr. Wordsworth visited Klopstock about 10 years after, the premature exulter had found it necessary to recant all these recantations, and to indite a palinode upon his own palinode; making, altogether, a most dismal lesson on the necessity of *looking before you leap*.][6]

Klopstock told us that Rochefoucault* had taken a great deal of pains to translate this ode into French, but had not succeeded. And no blame to Rochefoucault

* Probably the Duc de la Rochefoucault Liancourt.[7]

[6] The brackets are De Quincey's.

[7] La Rochefoucauld-Liancourt. Burke mentions his name near the beginning of the *Reflections on the Revolution* because a letter by him had been printed, with Richard Price's sermon, by the Revolutionary Society.

All footnotes to the translation, incidentally, are De Quincey's, not Baggesen's.

either! The Klopstockian odes are not to be translated by *tours de phrase.* Of all languages the French is the poorest for purposes of poetry, and the richest for rhetoric. Now, with the German language, this is just reversed. France has orators, but no poets, (meaning, of course, poets in the most eminent sense, epic or lyric.) Germany, on the contrary, has poets, but—hitherto† at least—not a single orator. Our Danish language, without possessing all the strength of the German, or all the vivacity of the French, combines, however, so much of both, as to be a better representative (by translation) of the characteristic merits in either than it will ever be possible for those languages to be reciprocally to each other. Klopstock has acquired Danish enough to understand, in a case of necessity, any little that he ever reads in this language: that, however, is little indeed: since Ewald's time, none of our Danish poetry has reached him: with the merits of our modern authors—Pram, for example, Rahbek and Tode, I found him thoroughly un-

† *i.e.* Up to the time of the French Revolution, which is the time of which the Danish author speaks; and now, in 1827, we may add, nor up to this time. The reason of so remarkable a defect in the German pretensions, seems to be this: where the popular forms of government are wholly unknown,—where there are no national deliberative bodies, no senate, no hustings, &c. the main field is wanting for the cultivation of civil eloquence. One field only remains in this path, viz. the bar. But it is remarkable that, whenever the popular mind has had no influence on the *making* of the laws, it has, in no instance, taken any interest in the *administration* of the laws, and thus forensic eloquence also languishes in sympathy with the higher modes of civil eloquence. Sacred oratory still remains; and the low state of this in Germany it might be more difficult to account for, as it depends probably on complex causes. One cause, however, is undoubtedly the rude and uncultured state of German prose style. There is no good model of style in Germany; the most eminent writers, as to matter, being usually but just tolerable, and often *not* tolerable as to the manner. The Germans have yet to learn the art of composition in its first rudiments; and to break up their rude, shapeless, involved, and interminable periods into the grace and animation of a living and organic diction.

acquainted; and, altogether, his knowledge of our literature is shallow beyond what I could have supposed.

I will confess, that, in the case of any other less amiable and estimable person than Klopstock, situated as Klopstock is with regard to the Danish nation,‡ such a discovery would have put me into bad humour: so unaccountable, not to say so unreasonable, does it seem to me—that Klopstock, living *upon* Denmark, should, in no shape or pretence, live *in* Denmark or *for* Denmark. *In* Denmark he certainly does not live, although within sight of it: for no town upon earth is more essentially Anti-Danish than Hamburgh: and, in all cases of pensions to foreigners, no condition seems more reasonable than that they should be spent in the country whence they are derived. Undoubtedly, it is true, that Klopstock could not live in Copenhagen upon the same income which he finds sufficient in Hamburgh; and *that* is justification enough as respects *him*: but, as respects the Danish government, it would have been more politic— as better proclaiming its own munificence—to have raised his pension up to a Copenhagen standard. To live *in* a country, however, under the circumstances of Klopstock, is a far less weighty duty than to live *for* it as an influential person. One consumer more or less in a state, is, after all, not worth talking about. But Klopstock, in no respect, lives or labours for *us*, except in as far as he labours for the whole world: a kind of merit which he shares with others who have not burdened Denmark with a pension. Homer and Virgil, for example, and in modern literature Cervantes, Shakespeare, and Milton, have had a prodigious influence on the Danish literature; and yet, so far as I know, never drew a farthing from the Danish Exchequer. Not one page is there in all the immortal works of Klopstock, I grieve to say it, which points to any event in Danish history, as its principle

‡ Klopstock was pensioned by the Danish court.

of inspiration. With all this however, it is and will remain a monument of honour to the Danish nation, that the German Homer should have owed his subsistence to them: and woe to the un-Danish heart that is not grateful to the government for having directed the national patronage into so noble a channel.

The personal characteristics of Klopstock I shall not attempt to describe in detail, this having been done already to the satisfaction of myself, and every body else, by the author of the Notes upon Klopstock. In general, I shall say, that the expression of his exterior, is dignity, blended with confiding, and child-like simplicity. The Heaven of Heavens seems to preside in his poetry; and a spirit drawn from the very best of what is earthly, to govern his ordinary demeanour. As a man, he is of the earth—earthy; as a poet, he seems to make his dwelling beyond Uranus, and the limits of our planetary system. To express what I mean, and hoping that I shall not offend any religious reader,[8] I would say, that his soul seems already to have passed through the gates of death and of resurrection, whilst his body is still living upon earth; and that he is at once on this side and on the other side of the grave.

Hence arises a rare mixture of majesty, and almost infantine *naiveté*, and artlessness. No matter what the subject of conversation may be, from the highest to the lowest, from the convocation of the States-General in France, down to the beautiful pair of stirrups of which he has lately become possessed, he talks of all with an ardour more than juvenile. Indeed his stirrups, and the French convocation, are not so far apart as they might seem; both alike being to him representative symbols of the two subjects upon earth which most call out the fire of his nature, viz. horsemanship, and enlightened hatred of tyranny: for Klopstock manifests the same ardour of

[8] The parenthetical hope is De Quincey's, not Baggesen's.

sympathy with the new-born prospects of French liberty, and with the overthrow of despotic power, as he
does with the fiery motions of the noble animal which
he daily gallops over the plains about Hamburgh. The
saddle, and the tribune of the patriot, guiding the storm
of national justice, are, in his feeling, the two highest
stations of pleasurable power. No subject, in fact, can
ever come amiss to the sensibilities of Klopstock; since,
in the meanest woodcut of this earth, (to speak figura-
tively) he detects the latent marks of original painting,
rich in celestial inspiration. If there be any one subject
on which he does not speak with freedom and pleasure,
it is perhaps that of money.

Considering his advanced age, Klopstock's eye-sight is
tolerably good. In his younger days, he informed me, that
he had lived almost constantly amongst blind people. He
smiled upon my expressing a hope that he himself would
become blind before he died. "To some rules," said I,
"we cannot allow of exceptions; Homer was blind, Milton was blind, and Klopstock must doubtless prepare
himself for the same fate." "Why, as to *that*," he replied, in a lower tone, "I can thus far countenance your
hopes, that within this last year, I have actually been
aware of a considerable decline in my powers of sight;
and at some distance cannot, without effort, distinguish
a crow from a magpie."

His hearing is uncommonly acute, and catches every
syllable of what you utter. Unfortunately, he seems to presume upon the same degree of this faculty in all his hear-
ers; for his loudest *forte* does not exceed another man's
piano. I was once present at a party, where he read aloud
one of his odes; all the company having formed themselves into an ellipse about him. By good luck I was *in
perihelio*, by which means I came to hear about every
third line; but several of those who occupied the *aphelion*
assured me that they had not caught one single line.

The favourite topics of his conversation seemed to be the great acts and enterprizes of heroic nations, especially of those which moved under republican impulses,—and, above all, he delighted to expatiate upon the merits of that language which, with so peculiar a propriety, and in a double sense, he may call *his own.* Just now, however, the French Revolution has the foremost place in his interest, and, indeed, possesses his soul with the fervour of a second *Messiah.** At the mere sound of the word *France,* his face is suddenly illuminated, as if it were a mirror that reflected the "orient hues" of that great dawn of freedom. Newspapers are become more interesting to him than *Thucydides, Plutarch,* and *Tacitus*: his old age is more cheerful, and brighter with hope, than his youth: awakened liberty has awakened him also; and, in the evening of his life, himself a star of the first magnitude—just at the point of setting, he is called off from his own speedy disappearance, to contemplate, with undivided attention, the ascending glories in the east.

In the midst, however, of these cosmopolitical interests, Klopstock is alive to nothing so much as the personal interests of those with whom he is talking. Interrupt the most animated conversation by an account of some accident which has befallen yourself—drop a word of any suffering or inconvenience, and immediately Klopstock is all attention; counsel, remedies, sympathy, are all at your service; and, with so indescribable an air of earnestness and hearty sincerity, that your interest appears to be the weightiest concern of his life, and, in fact, for the time, it really *is* so. Never have I heard Klopstock, on such occasions, dealing out the chill common places of unmeaning consolation: he puts himself, in the fullest sense, into the condition of the complainer, no matter how insignificant he may be; and so little does his sympathy wear the aspect of an assumed feeling

* Meaning a Poem of that name.

or a mere practised courtesy, so entirely does it impress you as absolute nature, and the spontaneous growth of pure unaffected benignity, that he—more than any man I know, and in spite of the elevation and somewhat of a commanding air that is spread over his personal appearance—succeeds in winning confidence and love that dismisses all disguise.

Klopstock's exterior is simple, and in some respects almost ordinary and unimpressive. His eye expresses innocence and piety rather than poetic power, or any thing that could properly be called genius. On the other hand, he compensates these defects in his deportment; and his carriage, in particular, is in a high degree characteristic and original. There is an extraordinary grace diffused over his whole mien; which, however, it is not every eye that will detect under his common costume, of a little old-fashioned coat and a shabby wig: add to which, that his excessive use of snuff and tobacco a little disturbs the polish of his neatness. His smile is indescribably fascinating; but notwithstanding the spirit which is given to it by an expression of humour and good-natured irony, it is still the smile of a girl rather than a man.

As to his pecuniary circumstances,—greatly to the honour of our Danish government, and of the Margrave of Baden, he enjoys a moderate competence, which puts a few luxuries even within his reach,—such as a pretty little garden just out of the town, a horse for his own riding, and the means of now and then offering hospitalities to a small number of friends.

Many are the delightful hours which I have passed in the society of this great poet, and thoroughly good man; but none more so than when attending him in his riding excursions; on which occasions, mounted on his favourite Harold Harefoot, he surrendered himself without restraint to boyish exuberance of spirits. My pleasure, however, at these times, was a little disturbed by anxiety;

for he rides with great boldness—I may say, with rashness; and his horse is so headstrong, that he threatens at every moment to throw his poetic rider. In his study, where Klopstock passes the whole forenoon, he sits perpetually involved in a nebula of snuff, and in voluminous exhalations of tobacco-smoke: for, Klopstock has four principal accomplishments; and it is difficult to say which of these four is in greatest perfection—Epic Poetry, Riding, Skating and Smoking.

Such are my recollections of Klopstock, drawn chiefly from former visits to Hamburgh. Upon the present occasion, Cramer and I took an early leave of him, for a purpose, which was the only one that I know of, that could have reconciled us to the loss of Klopstock's company, viz. to see Schröder, the greatest of German actors, in *King Lear*—the mightiest beyond comparison of all human tragedies.[9]

ATTRIBUTION

This is certainly De Quincey's. The writer of the letter has a knowledge of Coleridge, particularly of the first edition of the *Friend*, which is more than casual. De Quincey says, in his article on Coleridge in 1834 (M., II, 190-93), that for the greater part of the time that Coleridge was publishing the *Friend* he saw him daily; Coleridge was borrowing his German books. De Quincey comments there too on the madness of printing the *Friend* in the mountains of Cumberland and depending on the post. We know also, from the correspondence of De Quincey, of Coleridge, and of the Wordsworths, that their associations were close at the time; that De Quincey solicited subscribers for the *Friend*; and that he and Coleridge had talked of setting up a private press at Grasmere: De

[9] The London *Standard* (see p. 92 below) reprinted this translation from the *Edinburgh Saturday Post* in its own issue of August 18, p. 2.

Quincey wanted to print the classics and Coleridge was, at the time, desirous of printing the *Friend* too at Grasmere.

De Quincey says earlier in the article of 1834 (M., II, 170-72) that Wordsworth's dialogue with Klopstock was "first printed (hardly *published*)" in the original or Lake edition of the *Friend*, but "in the recast of that work it was omitted." Not only is the same bibliographical information given here in the *Post*, but both the author in the *Post* and De Quincey know that it was Wordsworth who conversed with Klopstock. Coleridge, in his account, does not name the friend who carried on the conversation (in French) or whose notes he is transcribing. Furthermore, the one important point missed by the *Post*—that the conversation had been reprinted in *Biographia Literaria* —is missed also by De Quincey: he too thinks it appeared only in the first edition of the *Friend* (M., II, 172).

Coleridge's comment on Klopstock, "a very *German* Milton," is repeated by De Quincey in one of the passages on Klopstock and the *Friend* cited above (M., II, 171). He had used it earlier in "Herder" (1823), M., IV, 380. Both times the phrasing ("True, sir; a very *German* Milton," and "Yes,—a very *German* Milton") is closer to the form here in the *Post* than it is to Coleridge's own phrase, which had no prefatory "Yes, Sir."

Coleridge's phrase "as good as MS." had been used by De Quincey earlier in 1827, in the first of the papers "On Murder Considered as One of the Fine Arts" (M., XIII, 30); and he used it afterwards in "Russia as it was in the Summer and Winter of 1812," *Blackwood's*, XLIX (1841), 737, and in his General Preface of 1853 (M., I, 6). In each instance the reference is to little-known printed work, and in 1841 he used the phrase, as here in the *Post*, in the preface to a translation. In each instance the same phrase is used and each time, except

1841, it is attributed to Coleridge, though it is in fact a version of Coleridge's words.

The signature "X. Y. Z." is not unique, of course, but it had been used extensively by De Quincey in the *London Magazine* (1821-24), where he was known as both "the English Opium-Eater" and "X. Y. Z.," and in *Blackwoods*: see M., X, 425ff.; also III, 103; III, 397; III, 466; IV, 380 (the article on Herder, in which one of the references to Klopstock as "a very *German* Milton" also appears); V, 146; IX, 31; IX, 42 and 44ff.; X, 22, 32, 52, 63, 80; XIII, 11 (the 1827 paper on "Murder," in which the phrase "as good as manuscript" also appears); XIV, 46; and he used it again, after the *Post*, in his 1830 article, "Kant in His Miscellaneous Essays" (M., VIII, 126). It was also in an unpublished manuscript, "To the Editor of Blackwood's Magazine" (1828); see Richard H. Byrns, "Some Unpublished Works of De Quincey," *PMLA*, LXXI (1956), 996. Three subsequent articles in the *Post* carry the same signature: November 3, 1827, January 5 and January 12, 1828 (pp. 183, 262, 271); the last two are certainly by De Quincey.

The term *"prima facie,"* used in the prefatory letter, can't prove much, but it is worth pointing out that it is a favorite with De Quincey, appearing some forty times in his writings. It is used also in subsequent articles in the *Post*: November 24, 1827, and February 23, 1828 (pp. 197, 322), the first of which is certainly his.

As for the translation, the fact that it is a translation from Danish is evidence of De Quincey's authorship. A knowledge of Danish, as the prefatory letter says, was not common in Great Britain, but it was among De Quincey's accomplishments. He had used it in his earlier connection with a newspaper, to write "Danish Origin of the Lake Country Dialect" for the *Westmorland Gazette* in 1819-20 (M., XIII, 373-83, where only a part of the article is reprinted). See also M., X, 60-61n. (one of the

London Magazine articles signed "X. Y. Z."); M., IV, 118-19n.; M., I, 314; his *Uncollected Writings*, ed. James Hogg (1892), I, 265-74. Furthermore, he had already translated, and not long before this date, something from Baggesen. It was part of Baggesen's Danish version of Ludvig Holberg's *Niels Klim*; the manuscript has been edited by S. Musgrove (Auckland, 1953). It seems likely, therefore, that when De Quincey claims, in the passage on Wordsworth and Klopstock (M., II, 171), that he has authority for Klopstock's "accomplishment" in the art of skating, his authority is Baggesen and the present translation (p. 71).

The translator's footnote on the defects of German eloquence (p. 65) is very close to De Quincey on the same subject. In "Oxford" (1835), M., II, 39, he says that the lack of popular deliberative assemblies in Germany makes senatorial eloquence impossible; that forensic eloquence is unknown for similar reasons, that only the pulpit remains, but no good models have arisen; and later in the same series of articles (M., II, 65) he says that the Germans have no eloquence because of the immoderate length and complexity of their sentences. On the endless German prose sentences that make good style impossible, see also his "German Studies and Kant in Particular" (1836), M., II, 83. His essay on "Rhetoric," published in the year after this one in the *Post*, remarks on endless German sentences and the absence of forensic, senatorial, and pulpit eloquence in Germany (M., X, 122-23).

[Mr. Canning's Death]

We are of opinion, that a political journalist can do no better service to the cause which he supports, than by pointing a keen public attention to the falsehoods and delusions which the press is continually sowing in the public mind; especially at this moment, when a vast proportion of the political press is combined for purposes of mischief, with a harmony and activity of which there is no precedent. False and mischievous opinions, steadily repeated, are too often passively adopted by men who are nowise predisposed to them, and whom an impulse in a better direction from any quarter would immediately rouse to shake them off. — — — — — During the past week we have been more than usually disgusted with the quality of the sentiments put forth in connexion with the late melancholy event of Mr. Canning's death;[1] and to one or two of these we shall now address a few words of calm examination.

First, as to the amount of the loss which the nation has sustained on this occasion:—It is justly complained of by a London morning paper,[2] as one of the weaknesses besetting the English press in these times, that a disproportionate and hyperbolical importance is attached to whatsoever is *present*. This is one of the spasms of weakness which arises from the intense and morbid excitement of London life. We, who are accustomed to consult the past occasionally, for a just estimate of the present, remember very distinctly, that on the death of Mr. Pitt—of Mr. Fox—of Mr. Windham—of Mr. Sheridan—we were regularly assured that our last pillar of state was taken away;

---

[1] Canning died on August 8.

[2] The *Morning Herald*, a Tory in the same mold as the *Post*; the article referred to is reprinted in this issue of the *Post*, p. 114.

and, in particular, we remember, that to each of them in succession was applied the same reverential title of *ultimus Romanorum*. If, on any one of these occasions, Mr. Canning had been suggested as standing between us and the melancholy consummation implied in that title, the answer would have been a burst of contemptuous laughter. For our own parts, we never went that length; and are as little disposed at this time to go the fashionable length in the opposite direction. At the earliest of those dates, we were already admirers of Mr. Canning as a shewy—we may even say, brilliant debater; and at this moment, two and twenty years in advance of *that*, we sympathize fully with the public sorrow for the loss of a man of genius and of generous nature—of a very ornamental (if not a very useful) servant of the state—and of a splendid performer on the stage of political life. Thus far our feelings answer to the call made in the public journals. But when we are summoned to grieve as for a loss emphatically national—for the overthrow of a main prop and column of our public welfare,—we pause, and turn a more vigilant scrutiny to Mr. Canning's pretensions than we might else be disposed to do at this moment, when his recent death and sufferings, together with the unhappy errors which threw a shade upon his latter life,—all combine to give a character of tenderness and pity to the very sincere admiration with which we regard him.

Among orators, Mr. Canning is improperly described as belonging to the highest class: It is more true to say, that he occupied the very highest rank in the second. To occasions of moderate dignity, such as the ordinary course of public affairs brings forward, his powers were perfectly equal; and, within this field, it is no more than justice to say that he excelled all the men of his age. For he was the finest *artist* in his great displays that perhaps the world has ever seen; and he was also the most *ac-*

complished of orators; by which we mean to say, that he was furnished with the largest number of those accessories and subordinate adjuncts of his art,—such as wit, scholarship, manner, voice, personal appearance,—which, though not indispensable to the greatest effects of eloquence, yet aid so powerfully its general brilliancy of impression; which finish and *accomplish* an orator, though the very greatest of orators may happen to want them all. So much is true; but it is also true that, for impassioned oratory, in its highest form, he neither attained it nor attempted it; and under any occasion of a magnitude sufficient to transcend artificial aids, and majestic enough to reject ornament, his powers were not capable of supporting him.

As a statesman, it was the good fortune of Mr. Canning's youth to fall upon times too determinate in their character, and upon a patron too great and authentic in his example, to leave much room for error or indecision in the general outline of his politics. With the enlightened patriotism of Mr. Canning, and with his generous heart, it was not possible to go far astray on any great questions of foreign policy—such as were then likely to arise. There was, in fact, at that time, but one paramount question. For two and twenty years of Mr. Canning's political life, all other aspects and regards of political speculation merged and were absorbed in the sublime unity of that one tremendous question—our relation to revolutionary France, and the barbarizing system of Buonaparte. Through this long period, the requisites for a sound statesman—first and last—were little more than a just sense of national honour, and a reverence for the dignity of human nature. "Will you fight?" was almost the only demand which it was then worth while to make of an English senator: and to be a tolerably wise man, in this great agony of the world, it was sufficient to be altogether an honest one. This was the "palmy" period of

Mr. Canning's life; and upon this it is that the true friends of his reputation would do well to fix our regard. Through this period he fought under the banners of Mr. Pitt; and we do not scruple to add—of the first Lord Melville, whose exclusive merits with respect to the Egyptian expedition, (had he possessed no other merits,) should in all reason suffice to make the name of *Dundas* immortal amongst the statesmen of Christendom.[3] During this great anarchy of the social world, Mr. Canning took his station in the ranks of the "faithful armies;" and his name was not, in a single instance, inscribed on the roll of dastards or traitors in our national council, who were in those days summoned

"———————To judge of danger which they fear'd,
And honour which they did not understand."[4]

With the great day of Waterloo, this mighty drama was wound up: and from that same event the steadiness and consistency of Mr. Canning's politics might date their declension. The great determining principle, the grand distinction of Jacobin and Anti-jacobin, by the light of which he had hitherto guided himself, had now become obsolete, or less readily available: and, coming amongst events, of which the relation to human interests was less obvious and unmixed, he was perplexed by the novelty of the road, and his treading became insecure. From this stage of his life it is, however, that his present adulators draw the materials for their sycophancy; in particular, an elaborate eulogist of Mr. C., in the *New*

[3] Henry Dundas, first Lord Melville. As Pitt's Secretary for War he had planned the Egyptian campaign of 1801 and carried it out successfully, though Pitt and the King had opposed it. De Quincey does not "scruple" to add his name even though in 1805-06 Melville had been impeached for malversation.

[4] Adapted from the last two lines of Wordsworth's sonnet, "Another year!—another deadly blow," written in 1806 after the battle of Jena, published in 1807. The "faithful armies," just above, are from *Paradise Lost*, VI, 204.

Times,[5] describes as the "acts of policy which are to hand
down his name as a patriot and a minister," these three,*
—"the recognition of South America; the protection of
Portugal; the restoration of Greece;"[7]—a selection, by the
way, which unfortunately narrows the meritorious part
of his life to little more than the last year of it. Large
words are these,—*"protection"* and *"restoration;"* and for
the sake of distracted Portugal, and poor desolated
Greece, heartily should we rejoice to know that they were
other than airy bubbles, and the hollowest of mockeries.
As to the recognition of the South American republics,
that, from the mere necessity of the case, was at any rate
to be made sooner or later; and the whole merit of Mr.
Canning's policy must, in this instance, confine itself to

* The writer prudently declines adding to this list of Mr. Canning's distinctions, and his honours with posterity, the part he took
on the Catholic question; because, says he, that question "was not
his question;" meaning, not originally moved by him. Perhaps an
equally good reason for suppressing this claim, was the puerile
ignorance of Mr. Canning on many of the leading points connected
with that question, which, as exposed by Mr. Phillpotts, is now become notorious to the public.[6]

[5] A Tory journal now supporting the coalition and therefore
despised as an apostate. The quotations that follow are from the
last paragraph of a long obituary of Canning, August 9, p. 2,
col. 2.

[6] Phillpotts was the man attacked by the *Edinburgh* for his anti-
Catholicism (pp. 36-37 above). He had also published in 1827 two
letters to Canning on Catholic relief, which were used by Canning's
opponents to attack him.

[7] Canning had sent ships and troops to Portugal to support the
constitutionalists there against Spanish intervention; but the
Portuguese problem was not yet ended.

The Greek revolt against the Turks raised the dangers of Russian intervention and growth of power in the Near East; it had
also the sympathy of many Englishmen, from Byron to Eldon.
Canning tried to control independent Russian action by proposing
to Russia a joint demand for partial Greek independence; the
Treaty of London, to which England, Russia and also France
were parties, was signed on July 6, 1827. But there was trouble
to come.

On South America see p. 49 above.

the selection of the time. It is for our antagonists to shew, that in this selection there was any especial sagacity: the *onus* here is upon them; and there we leave it. But, for the two other cases, we should have supposed that the merest common sense would have restrained any writer from founding a claim of this extent upon measures so purely inchoate and immature, as to be less properly described as Mr. Canning's "*acts* of policy," than as Mr. Canning's schemes or intentions of policy. The *New Times* indeed assures us, that Mr. Canning would "have seen all completed, had he been spared a few months longer." Mr. Canning's policy is therefore countersigned by the *New Times*; and we have the guarantee of that worthy sycophant for its entire fulfilment. Much it would rejoice us to think that this were worth a rush; and that it might be so, for the sake of Greece in particular, we could desire that the *New Times* should have that degree of weight in Constantinople, which, unfortunately for so much merit, it has *not* in London, and should obtain that consideration in the Mahometan world which hitherto it has wanted in the Christian. Meantime, we suppose it to be evident, that whatever may have been Mr. Canning's good wishes for the "protection" of Portugal and the "restoration" of Greece, those desirable objects being as yet unadvanced by a single stage, must now owe their accomplishment (if accomplishment they are to have) to other acts than his, and to counsels which must submit to be guided, at every step, by events that are yet to arise.

So far with regard to the amount of our loss: Next, as to the immediate cause of it; for even this has been improved into an engine of faction and lying malignity. Temperate people are disposed to find ground enough for the rapid and fatal course of Mr. Canning's illness, in the known irritability of his constitution, combined with the exhausting fatigues of office, and the agitations of his

recent struggles. Eighteen months ago, a friend of our
own, who had an opportunity of observing Mr. Canning's
state of health pretty closely,[8] assured us, that his bodily
system betrayed at that time so marked a disposition to
inflammatory action as to make it very probable that, unless he quitted public life altogether, his death would be
sudden, and not very remote. Considering the maturity
which such a tendency must have gained in two sessions
of Parliament, no event could surely be less marvellous
than that which we are now deploring. Yet, in the face of
these obvious considerations, the friends of Mr. Canning,
or a large majority of them, are now charging his death
upon the opposition made to him in and out of Parliament, and the fury (as they choose to describe it,) of the
character which it has lately assumed. The journals of
this party, for the last week, and some at the very hour
of his death, teem with insolent complaints of insolence,
and ferocious denunciations of ferocity. Indeed, so rancor-
ous an *acharnement* of party rage, a fury so perfectly
rabid, we have not witnessed on any previous occasion.
And altogether we have the old case of the *Gracchi de
seditione querentes*[9] under a livelier form and illustration.
Now, it must be evident, one would imagine, to the most
thoughtless of these journalists, that no sort or degree
of hostility could be plausibly represented as affecting the
peace of a veteran politician, seasoned (as Mr. Canning
was) by more than thirty years' experience of party strife
and warfare, unless in so far as it met with a corresponding burthen of reproach from his own accusing heart. It
is true, undoubtedly, that calumnies of a *private* application do often inflict anguish as inevitable as if they were
truths; because the possibility of exposing their falsehood
is not always within our reach. But in *party* calumnies,

8 Probably Wordsworth (see p. 397 below) or John Wilson.
9 Adapted from Juvenal, II, 24: who would bear the Gracchi
complaining about sedition?

where the matter of the charge has relation to things and persons, words or deeds, of national notoriety, no such sting as this can ever lurk. The voice of the accuser is an idle sound, unless echoed from within; and no arrows can penetrate but those which are barbed by the attesting conscience. Most justly, therefore, may we *now* answer the clamorous complaints of Mr. Canning's friends, and their outcry of "*Pudet hæc opprobria dici,*" by the old retort of Junius, in the complement of that quotation,

"Et dici potuisse, et—non potuisse refelli."[10]

This is now become matter of inference from their own statements, and cannot be refused. For they will hardly wish it to be believed of their idol, that he was so deplorably wanting in strength of mind, as to surrender his peace and his life to a mere storm of words, and to charges that were palpably without foundation.

In what degree the taunts of his opponents, by continually reviving the reproaches of his own wounded conscience, may have co-operated with latent disease to prey upon his bodily strength, could not be determined, even by Mr. Canning himself: and so far the dispute amongst the newspapers is a most idle one. Holding those views, however, which, we *do* hold, of Mr. Canning's apostasy from the principles which had shed so much distinction on the first twenty-two years of his political life, we cannot at all doubt that it must have preyed deeply upon his mind. Mr. Canning's sense of honour was too nervously apprehensive, and his judgment too sound, to fail of coming to a true estimate of the whole evil involved in this apostasy. What that evil is, we are anxious to set in a just light; many of the newspapers on both sides having put the question upon a false and

[10] Adapted from Ovid, *Metamorphoses*, I, 758-59: it shames us that this insult could have been spoken and could not have been refuted. The reference to Junius is to the letter of Philo-Junius dated October 19, 1769.

dangerous issue. But this is a topic which, having already trespassed too much on the space disposable for such subjects, we must reserve for another occasion.

This is the first leader published on the fourth page of the *Post*, under the masthead; the leader in this position thereafter became a regular feature of the paper and De Quincey would seem to have been one of the chief writers of leaders.

The characterization of Canning here is similar to De Quincey's: showy, brilliant, generous, but unprincipled after he lost the guidance of Pitt. This article, written immediately after Canning's death, is relatively mild. Specifically, there are verbal similarities and identities between the passage here, on p. 78, about Canning in his earlier days combatting "social" anarchy by taking his place "in the ranks" of the " 'faithful armies,' " and the passage on p. 283 below, in the *Post* article of January 26, 1828; the latter was certainly written by De Quincey. The conjectures about Canning's troubled "conscience" after his apostacy (pp. 81-82) are repeated in the January 26 article (pp. 282-83). On "Mr. Canning's apostacy" see De Quincey's "French Revolution," *Blackwood's*, XXVIII (1830), 555, where the same phrase is used; also his "Present Cabinet in Relation to the Times," *Blackwood's*, XXIX (1831), 155, and "On the Approaching Revolution in Great Britain," *Blackwood's*, XXX (1831), 318. And for further references on De Quincey and "apostacy" see the notes to the article of November 24, 1827 (p. 208).

Better evidence, because more peculiar to De Quincey, are the concepts and the specific language used to describe Canning as orator (pp. 76-77). In the following year, in his article on "Rhetoric," De Quincey said that the admiration given to Canning's rhetorical display was like that given to a young lady rising from a "brilliant performance" on the pianoforte; Canning was one of the "ornamental performers" of his time (M., X, 120-21). In 1840 he said Canning was "a most accomplished orator . . . as a great *artist*, the first orator of our times," not a man of natural power (M., III, 125, a passage containing another important similarity to an article in the *Post*, p. 397 below). And in the article "Sir Robert Peel's Position on Next Resuming Power," *Blackwood's*, L (1841), 403n., he called Canning a great orator "in the class of artificial orators."

The one essential test-question of political honesty during the wars with France, "Will you fight?" (p. 77), is repeated in the same words, and in reference to the same period and for purposes of the same test, in De Quincey's "Mrs. Hannah More," *Tait's*, IV (1833), 305.

There is a further sign, as elsewhere in the *Post*, in the intimate knowledge of Wordsworth's poetry, evident in the adaptation here (p. 78) of two very appropriate lines from one of his lesser known sonnets.

There are also some minor verbal similarities with De Quincey's writings. "Acharnement" (p. 81) is one of his favorite words; he uses it more than fifteen times in essays before and after this one. For "onus" (p. 80) see the article of August 4 (p. 57) and the further references given there. The Latin tag *"ultimus Romanorum"* (p. 76) he used in two works written shortly after this: in "The Duke of Wellington and Mr. Peel," *Blackwood's*, XXV (1829), 294, also in a political context; and in *Klosterheim* (1832), M., XII, 37. *"Gracchi de seditione querentes"* (p. 81) turns up in one of his later essays (M., XIV, 296n.).

[The Nomination of Mr. Herries]

The death of Mr. Canning has been the signal for schisms between the parties in coalition, which have already gone near to dissolve their ill-assorted union. We shall briefly state their origin and cause. The immediate occasion of these schisms was the nomination of Mr. Herries as Chancellor of the Exchequer; a nomination which, we observed last week,[1] was, on several accounts, likely to be thrown void. Mr. Herries is supposed to be of the King's personal selection. On the other hand, Mr. Tierney, who is backed by the Whig part of the coalition, is known to have made this office, through life, the peculiar object of his ambition; and, in an article of the *Times* newspaper, supposed to be written, or instigated by that gentleman, it was announced, in words that rang ominously in the ears of the Whig party, "that nothing short of a conviction that they no longer possessed that share of influence over the determinations of the Sovereign, without which no Ministers can advantageously conduct the affairs of the state, could induce them to entertain any *intention of retiring from the posts assigned to them.*"[2] And, in a subsequent paper, after af-

---

[1] *Post*, August 25, p. 121, col. 1, an article perhaps written by De Quincey.

The new Prime Minister was Lord Goderich, who had been Secretary for War and Colonies in Canning's cabinet; before that, as Frederick Robinson, he had been Chancellor of the Exchequer in the last years of Liverpool's ministry. The King had not forgiven Wellington's and Peel's resignations and tried a more pliable man; Goderich was, as he was expected to be, a weak premier and he lasted only a few months. One of his first problems was the nomination of John Charles Herries as Chancellor of the Exchequer. Herries was the King's choice, not Goderich's, he himself did not want the Exchequer, and the Whigs were so opposed to him that the coalition was almost broken.

[2] *Times*, August 23 (p. 2, col. 2). George Tierney was one of the

fecting ignorance whether Mr. Herries were or were not "the King's candidate," this organ of the Whigs forgot its previous affectation so entirely, towards the conclusion, as to disclaim all certain knowledge of objections to Mr. Herries on the part of "a single individual in the cabinet, for any reason *beyond that* of being a responsible Minister* forced on the Government by the only member of it who himself is not responsible."[3] These, reader, are the words of those Whigs whose constitutional sensibilities were so much alarmed by the pretended dictation to the King on the part of the ex-ministers!—Meantime the intrigue against Mr. Herries was prosecuted by other weapons in another quarter. Reports had been noticed in the *Morning Herald*, as prevailing in certain circles, of too close a connection between Mr. Herries and the great loan-contractor of Europe, Mr. Rothschild: but in that instance these reports had been disarmed of their sting by the tone in which they were treated. Another journal, however, the *Morning Chronicle* (influenced, it is believed, by the friends of Mr. Brougham, whose exclusion from office is reported to have been made a *sine quâ non* by Mr. Herries,) caught eagerly at these calumnies, as we readily believe them to be, and conferred upon them a prominence and a credit which cannot but have given a serious shock to the pretensions of Mr. H. in the public estimation; especially for *this* office, in which,

---

* What the writer meant, or should have meant, by the course of his logic was,—"being a minister (no matter whether responsible or not,) forced upon a responsible government by the only member of it who is himself irresponsible."

Whigs in Canning's cabinet, as Master of the Mint, an office he retained in Goderich's cabinet. He was opposed to Herries but it is not true that he was himself the Whig candidate for the office. The Whigs opposed Herries because he was an ultra and for other reasons; and among these reasons was the attempt by the King to force appointment of a minister: this they thought an unconstitutional act by "4" (as they referred to him privately).

[3] *Times*, August 27 (p. 2, col. 2).

above all others, "clean hands" are a foremost qualification. The insinuation in these reports is twofold; first, that Mr. H. might be likely to assist his friend's views by occasional communications of state secrets, or by hints such as a man less sagacious than Mr. Rothschild would know how to improve. Secondly, that he might use his official knowledge for more selfish purposes, as a direct jobber in the funds on his own account.[4]

At this point of the drama, forth steps upon the stage Lord Goderich, the prime minister; and, in a little billet, as *amiable* and familiar as any novelist could wish, and dated officially from Downing Street, (*credite posteri!*) exonerates "his dear Herries," both on the original charge, (which unfortunately no individual friend of Mr. H. can be entitled to do, except as regards his own private belief,) and also, which Lord G.'s station enabled him to do with full authority, on the secondary imputation that this charge had been the bar in the Cabinet to his definitive appointment.[5]

On the monstrous indecorum of the conduct in Lord Goderich, no journal that we have seen, except one (*the Watchman*)[6] has animadverted at all; and *that* with no adequate severity. It is not in any spirit of party, but with sincere zeal for the honour of the English Government, that we blush to see its Prime Minister descending to a conflict with what he himself calls "a paragraph" of

[4] The suspicion that Herries had sold official information to Rothschild was another of the reasons for the Whigs' opposition to his appointment. The *Morning Herald* was a Tory paper opposed to the coalition. The *Morning Chronicle* was a Whig paper supporting the coalition; the article on Herries had appeared on August 24. But the rumor about Brougham would hardly seem to be true; though he thought Herries a brute and a man of bad principles he pressed the Whig leaders to acquiesce in the appointment rather than break up the coalition.

[5] Goderich's letter was said to have been written by Tierney. It is dated August 24, was published in the *New Times,* and was also in the *Times* of August 27 (p. 2, col. 2).

[6] A Tory opposition paper.

the *Morning Chronicle*. Think of William Pitt, not sub-pœnaed in a court of justice, not appealed to even, but as a volunteer entering the ring of newspaper warfare, against the anonymous author of a paragraph in the *Morning Chronicle*! The indignity which such an act puts upon the King's government is unspeakable. And, apart from *that*, we doubt exceedingly whether the duties and *solemn engagements* of a minister are compatible with any revelation to the public, even a negative one, of what is going on in the Cabinet.

The true bars to Mr. H's appointment are perhaps first his own disinclination to the office: the *latentis semita vitæ*[7] is said to have peculiar charms for him; and he is believed to feel heavily some disqualifications for the place; not moral (as pretended by the *Morning Chronicle*) but intellectual. Some of our contemporaries seem not fully to understand this—they allege that a Chancellor of the Exchequer cannot require much talent for public speaking. Perhaps not *as* Chancellor of the Exchequer; or, if even in that office, his duty were always confined to the exposition of the budget: but a Chancellor of the Exchequer is called upon to speak not merely in that distinct character, but also generally—both as a member of the House and as a minister of the Crown. And this call would be made, more especially at a period when, unfortunately for the public service, so large a proportion of the ministers belong to the other House.

But the main bar to Mr. H. is the determined hostility of the Whigs: and this is what makes the case important. It is a rehearsal in miniature of the whole issue between the two interests in the Cabinet. In our last paper we predicted a Premiership for Lord Goderich, co-extensive with the Administration; not intending, by any means, to augur a long course of office for his lordship, but a very

---

[7] Misquoted from Horace, *Epistles*, I, xviii, 103: the path of an obscure life.

short one for the Administration. If this should turn out otherwise, and the coalition should be longer-lived than we expect, in that case Lord G.'s maintenance of office will *not* be co-extensive with theirs. It is the fixed intention of the Whigs, and but thinly disguised at this moment, to "jockey" him. They had the same kind intention towards Mr. Canning, as opportunity might serve. But he was aware of them, and civilly designed that favour to themselves. Mr. Canning would perhaps have triumphed. But Lord Goderich will fall. Weak, and without disguise, he will be no match for the subtlety of the Whigs, their perseverance, and, above all, their *cohesion* as a party which supplies their want of individual respectability. Even the King's personal support will not sustain a Minister who wants energy, in his turn, to support the King. One intrigue, such as that we have here recorded, sufficiently attests the power and the disposition of the Whigs to avail themselves to the uttermost of this want in Lord Goderich. Meantime the *dénouement* of this particular intrigue awaits the presence of Mr. Huskisson, who has been anxiously looked for, since Mr. Canning's death, as a sort of *Deus ex machinâ,* and is at length arrived, but without that restoration to health, we are sorry to hear, which he went abroad to seek.[8]

ATTRIBUTION

This is one of several leaders written during the time when the new cabinet was being formed and it is likely that De Quincey wrote some of the others which are not

[8] Huskisson, a Canningite, President of the Board of Trade and Treasurer of the Navy in Canning's cabinet, had been traveling since the end of the session. When the King continued to insist upon Herries the Whigs decided (on the 22nd) to withdraw; but at Goderich's suggestion they agreed to shelve the problem until Huskisson's return. He was back in London on the 28th and the problem was resolved, after much maneuvering and dissatisfaction. Herries took the Exchequer.

reprinted here. This one I am going to assign to De Quincey because of the misquotation from Horace on p. 88, "latentis semita vitae" for "fallentis semita vitae." The slip is understandable since the two words mean the same and sound almost the same, but "latentis" is not in any text and cannot be a variant because it entails a false quantity. Since the author of the *Post* is quoting only the last part of the line the false quantity doesn't appear and doesn't bother him. Nor does it bother De Quincey, who twice makes the same misquotation of the half-line: in his article on "Shakspeare" (1838), M., IV, 43, and in "Introduction to the World of Strife" (1853 version), M., I, 59. On two other occasions, because either his memory or his editor was livelier, he quotes correctly: "Schiller" (1838), M., IV, 433, and "Notes on Gilfillan's Literary Portraits" (1845-46), M., XI, 341.

The other bits of Latin (or French) are commonplace and one can only point out that they are not negative evidence; De Quincey uses them too. For *sine qua non* (p. 86) see the article of November 17, p. 211 below, and the further references there. *Credite posteri* (p. 87) is in M., I, 158; X, 114; X, 258; XI, 27. *Dénouement* (p. 89) is in the article of December 29 (p. 237 below), which is certainly his; it is in M., IV, 408; IX, 314; X, 348 and 353; XI, 255; XII, 359; and in "Animal Magnetism," *Tait's*, IV (1834), 467; it is always italicized, as it is here. *Deus ex machina* (p. 89) is in M., II, 20, where the same phrase is used, "as a sort of *deus ex machina*"; VI, 387; XII, 352; *Blackwood's*, LIV (1843), 679.

The direct apostrophizing of the "reader" (p. 86), though again common, is one of De Quincey's habits.

September 1, 1827

West India Petition

A most important petition has recently been presented
to the King, (though dated so far back as last December 22,) from the House of Assembly in Jamaica; which,
after reciting a long series of aggressions on the rights of
the planters, prays, in conclusion, that, if these are to
be persisted in, they may be "accompanied by an act of
Parliament, to secure that ample compensation, without
which they can never consent to their adoption." We
have not room to speak at length, but we gladly take
the occasion, thus offered us, of declaring the course
which we mean to pursue on this most important question. Our opinion is, that the West India proprietors
have been long used with crying injustice. Myriads of
people in this country, for the sake of a cheap participation in the honours of sentimental philanthropy, have
signed petitions to the legislature, which went the length
(if acted upon,) of voting away the whole value of prop-
erties—held by as just and legal a title as any estate in
this country; which petitions never would have obtained
one-thousandth part of their support, if, with the liberty
of subscribing the name, had been coupled, as a *sine quâ
non* preliminary, the condition of subscribing also—one
shilling to the cause of negro emancipation. By far the
greater part of the subscribers knew not in fact what
they were doing; and, had the same outrageous attacks
been made upon any sort of private property familiar
to men's eyes in this country, and consecrated by old
habitual feelings, a perfect frenzy of reaction and national indignation would have been roused. The fact is,
that, to give any colour of justice to the sentimental
tricks and experiments which are now playing with the
West India property, the nation ought first of all to pur-

chase that property at a fair valuation; and, satisfied we
are, that a hint on the part of any Cabinet Minister that
such a plan was in agitation, would, at one blow, forever extinguish all attempts at getting up another petition. *That* bubble would never mount again. Make the
philanthropists sensible that sentiment was in future to
be paid for—keenly put it to them, that their own prop-
erties were to be touched in this cause, and they would
have their sensibility speedily quickened to the rights
of property in others.

In illustration of this position, we shall take the liberty of telling a little anecdote.—A short time back,
there happened to be a meeting in London of a certain
Joint-stock Company, who had a considerable interest
in South American mines. Some "curious impertinent,"
on this occasion, took it into his head to put a very ugly
question to the chairman. But first let us mention, that
amongst the share-holders were some who had more than
once flourished at public assemblies on the rights of "our
sable brethren," and so forth; and most of them perhaps
could be proved to have promoted petitions in that tendency. It may be judged then, how irritating and disgusting it must be to the very respectable assembly, to find
themselves abruptly asked—how many slaves they had
at the bottom of their mines? Dire was the wrath of the
company: the chairman, who was a discreet person, rose
and "deprecated" all such inquiries, as tending to disturb the "harmony" of the meeting; and the unfortunate
mover of the question was glad to go off without waiting
for his answer, under the probable alternative which he
anticipated, of being kicked out of the room.

On this occasion we are sorry to notice the very intemperate conduct of the *Standard*, which must have
given pain to all who, like ourselves, approve its general
line of politics.[1] We can explain it into nothing but per-

[1] The *Standard* was a London evening paper, which, like the

sonal pique interfering with the natural direction of the Editor's principles. He rates the House of Assembly *de haut en bas*; calls them "hounds," and recommends it to Government, in a summary way, to put an end to them and their petitions as equal nuisances. Though so far puerile in its manner, and detestable in its tone of feeling, the article was intelligible; but what are we to think of the sequel? The *Glasgow Courier*,[2] with just indignation, reproves the *Standard*, and what is the reply? In his paper of Tuesday last, the Editor, in a tone of affected good humour, carelessly tells the *Glasgow Courier*, not to mangle him, but, if he chooses to give one half of his doctrine on this matter, not to suppress the other. And what is this other, which he repeats in italics? *"There is not an honest man who would desire to see property, guaranteed, (no matter how or why) by us, destroyed, without* AMPLE *equivalent."* Well, this is just and rational; but why should the *Glasgow Courier* be bound to quote, or the *Standard* be entitled to repeat a passage which is in the teeth of every sentence, before or after, with which it stands connected? The whole purpose of the Jamaica petition was to pray for exactly such an "ample equivalent" as the *Standard* here recommends; and yet for this they are called "hounds," and, in the very act of explanation and apology, are a second time reviled as "nuisances to be repressed."

Our own sentiments we desire not to have misinterpreted. To the abolition of the Slave-*trade* we were

---

Post, had been started in May 1827. Like the *Post*, too, it was a Tory opposition paper, but its political economy, to De Quincey's eye, was not up to the standard of its politics.

The two articles in question here are in the *Standard* of August 21, p. 4, and August 28, p. 4; it had reprinted the petition of the Jamaican House of Assembly on August 21, p. 1.

[2] The *Glasgow Courier* was die-hard Tory, had long fought and continued to fight against abolition and in defense of the West Indian proprietors.

friendly, and to every *just* plan for improving the condition of the Slaves; but let not our pretended beneficence to the Blacks commence in monstrous injustice to our own countrymen.

ATTRIBUTION

Probably De Quincey's because the same ideas, though they are not distinctive, reappear in a couple of other *Post* articles which certainly are his. The argument that the abolitionist attack upon West Indian slavery is an attack upon property is restated on January 26, 1828, where there is a reference back to this article (pp. 290-91), and in the continuous article of June 14-28, 1828 (pp. 358ff.). And he presents the same argument in his known writings: in "France and England," *Blackwood's*, XXVIII (1830), 717, and in "Political Anticipations," also *Blackwood's*, XXVIII, 726-730; there is verbal identity between p. 91 here and p. 729 of "Political Anticipations," where he says that compensation is "*a sine qua non* among the preliminaries" of abolition. (For De Quincey's use of *sine qua non* see also p. 211, below, and the further references there.) There is further verbal identity between p. 91 here and De Quincey's *Logic of Political Economy* (1844), where he looks back to the "sentimental" folly of the "experiment" of sudden emancipation (M., IX, 215).

The distinction made in the last paragraph here, between the slave-*trade* and slavery, is made also in the articles of June 14 and June 28, 1828, and in his known writings: "Political Anticipations," p. 727n.; "Parentage and the Paternal Home" (1834), M. I., 18-19 and n.; "Conservative Prospects," *Blackwood's*, XLIX (1841), 417; "On Christianity" (1846), M. VIII, 233.

Blackwood's Magazine

N O . C X X X [1]

This is a good Number. Yet, in one thing, we find a want
—there is no politics. Conceive the disappointment of an
old thorough-paced connoisseur in executions, after paying overnight a guinea for a front seat, and leaving his
bed at six o'clock on a wintry morning, on finding all
hushed and silent in the Old Bailey, and no sign of any
'performance' at the Debtor's door. The old gentleman
pulls the check-string with agitation, and, stammering
with wrath, ("Why, why, why, coachman, I say, what's
the meaning of all this? are people to be ch-ch-ch-cheated
in this manner?") learns, with disgust, that a reprieve had
reached Newgate at midnight, and goes home muttering
something about "mere swindling on the part of government." Such feelings have we, or *had*; for perhaps
Christopher is in the right: he waits till the enemy have
got into line, and "dressed," before he will condescend
to open his fire upon them. There is also no "knouting"
in this Number; it is a maiden assize; which again seems
a pity, and rather inconsiderate in C. N. when one counts
over the thousands of kind souls that will thus be de-
frauded of their pleasure. C. N. we fear, gets old; that is,
he indulges the tender-heartedness of old age; for, as to
its weakness, he defies *that*; and, in spite of his omissions,
we repeat that this is really an excellent number.

ART. I. discusses the chances of any European armament, but especially of a Russian one, reaching our Indian empire overland.[2] For our enemies, the prospect is

[1] September 1827.

[2] By Sir John McNeill. Identification of authors in *Blackwood's*
is taken from the *Blackwood's Contributors' Book* in the National
Library of Scotland, corrected and supplemented by the publica-

not encouraging; it seems they must make up their minds
to a constant course of fighting over "at least two thousand miles," from the Russian to the Indian frontier, and
of starving for "eight or ten months;" and these are bad
preliminaries to offensive operations against an army
such as ours in India, with nine points of the law in
their favour, and seasoned to the climate. It is true,
there is a choice of four roads, which are here discussed;
but as all four are beset by the same dire necessities of
starving and fighting,—fighting and starving, it seems
an insult to talk of any choice, and a sort of "distinction
without a difference." Lord! how we should laugh to
hear of an enemy of ours floundering about in Bokhara
or Kharizm, whilst we sate eating "tiffin" at Moorshe-
dabad, or reading Blackwood over a bason of mulliga-
tawny at Calcutta. An old captain said to Shelvocke,[3]
who threatened to play h-ll with him when he got to
India, for his conduct on the west coast of South America, "Aye, Captain Shelvocke, but there's the Pacific to
be crossed yet; and, considering your condition, the child
that is now playing at Calicut will be a grey-haired man
by the time you reach India." Such a scoff would *we*
send to Bokhara. The whole article is interesting and
able; but, to understand it thoroughly, requires some
acquaintance with the geography of central Asia, a
knowledge which (the writer complains) is not rated
according to its proper value: "An obscure notice," says
he, "of an insignificant stream in central Africa excites
more attention than the discovery of a new nation in
central Asia." True: but he forgets the reason. There is
a riddle connected with the former case: Africa has al-

tions and courteous correspondence of Alan Lang Strout. Most of
those whose names are given here can be found in the *DNB*, and
and some of them were personally known to De Quincey.

[3] George Shelvocke, author of the *Voyage Round the World*
(1726); it was his second captain who shot the albatross.

ways been the mother of wonders: and, in modern times, a new wonder was imagined, viz. that the Niger had been detected doing a thing which no mathematics could reconcile—flowing in a mighty stream westwards and eastwards; and, if eastwards, where was its mouth? There was, besides, a great discovery anticipated of some central city, the asylum of fugitive Carthage, and the secret growth of two thousand years. So that, altogether, Africa has the advantage over Asia which romance has over history—alchemy over chemistry—astrology over astronomy.

ART. II.—*A Trip to Spa in* 1782, shews what marvels can be achieved merely by manner and style.[4] We may truly say, *materiam superabat opus.* Excepting the opening adventure of being chased by a French privateer, with the odd coincidence of afterwards meeting the owner at Spa, there is no incident which seems at all out of the high-road of every-day life—or, separately considered, worth recording; and yet merely from an impression, diffused over the whole, of extreme good sense and candour, and, above all, from the excellence of the style (for a narrative style) which is not bookish, but bespeaks a high-bred gentleman familiar with the best society, the whole is delightful to read.

ART. III.—*Horæ Germanicæ*, No. 24. We have the highest regard for the accomplished writer of these articles: but his subject is a bad one.[5] The Müllners, Oehlenschlägers, Grillparzers, and all those horrid people, are insufferable; and that they are wholly without power, is evident from this—that, after reading a bushel of their odious dramas, we remember no iota of any one. In the passage at p. 311—

[4] By the Rev. Horatio Townsend.
[5] De Quincey probably thought the author was Robert Pearse Gillies (see pp. 221n., 232 below); Gillies and Lockhart had been the regular authors of the *Horæ Germanicæ.* But this one was by Mrs. Mary Margaret Busk.

> Nations no longer burst, like snow *lawines*,
> On nations, &c.

the word *lawines* will be taken by most readers for a mere error of the press: it is pure German, and therefore inadmissible, not being naturalized amongst us, like the word *avalanche*.

ART. IV.—*A Subaltern in America* we read with less pleasure than usual; which we attribute in part to the disgust impressed upon us by the never-ending series of blunders which he records.[6] Take one as a specimen: Our engineers had "imprudently rolled into the parapets, barrels filled with sugar, under the impression that sugar would prove as effectual as sand in checking the progress of cannon balls." Lord bless their simpleness! would it have been one whit more absurd to have loaded their guns with black pepper, "under the impression" that in this way the enemy would have been peppered. And what became of this luscious muscovado-way of defending a battery? "The event shewed that we had been completely mistaken. The enemy's shot penetrated these sugar hogsheads as if they had been so many empty casks, dismounting our guns, and killing our artillery-men in the very centre of their works." Sweet engineering with a vengeance! as if any old woman who had ever poised a bag of sugar in her hand, and knew its slight cohesion, could have doubted of the result; or, as if the experiment, if it *were* doubtful, might not have been rehearsed before the battle!

ART. V. we have purposely avoided reading, that we might not make our own article too long, and its general complexion too laudatory: for laudatory, we are sure, it must have been from what we have seen heretofore from the same pen.[7]

---

[6] Part of a series that had been running in *Blackwood's*; by the Rev. George Robert Gleig.

[7] The reference is probably to Chap. XII of the "Chapters on

Art VI.—*Schlegel* v. *Campbell.*—A most awkward charge of plagiarism from the German critic, against Mr. Thomas Campbell, Lord Rector of the University of Glasgow, and also editor of the New Monthly Magazine,

————————that great god of war,
Lieutenant-General to the Earl of Mar.

What aggravates the ugliness of the charge is, that, on the single occasion where Mr. Campbell had referred to Mr. Schlegel, it was for the purpose of reproving him.[8]

Art. VII.—*The Marvellous Doctor.*—This story is built on the idea of a man's discovering an elixir, one drop of which will compel all whom he wishes to follow him—and sometimes rather more than he wishes. It is admirably comic: the original idea is perhaps suggested by the magic horn in the romance of Oberon, which sets all people a-dancing—kings, senators, judges, juries, executioners. But, from whatever quarter suggested, it is imagined, and told with the happiest effect. In particular, the pursuit of the old dowager, aunt to Donna Rashelli, and the whole affair with the Countess's bull, are irresistible. But why attribute it to the Ettrick Shepherd, of whose hand we cannot see a trace in any one sentence?[9]

Art. VIII.—*Leonarde Mayburn and Susan Hendrie.*—This is by the *Old Bachelor*, a former correspondent of Blackwood's. We like him better in prose than in verse.

Churchyards" by Caroline Bowles (later the second Mrs. Southey). But De Quincey has skipped an article and is out in his numbering from this point on.

[8] By Mr. [William?] Stenhouse. He is attacking the lectures on poetry published by Campbell in the *New Monthly Magazine* in 1821-22. On the same subject see also the letter of November 3, 1827 (p. 181 below). The quotation is an instance of anti-climax from the "Peri Bathous":

And thou *Dalhoussy* the great God of War,
Lieutenant Colonel to the Earl of Mar.

[9] Rightly or not, it is attributed to James Hogg.

His last paper (*De Omnibus Rebus et quibusdam aliis*) was, in parts, almost worthy of Sir Thomas Browne. But his verse is often attenuated, though many of the thoughts are beautiful. The description of a contested election for a county, and of the previous canvass, is vigorous: in particular, the following is a pretty periphrasis for expressing in verse the party colours:

> "Hark!—the loud war, proclaimed by drum and fife,
> And labell'd banners, that affront the sky
> With gaudy blazonry of factious hate,
> Turning the innocent hues of flower and field
> To party Shibboleths."

If, however, (as we have heard hinted) the particular election pointed at is that of Westmoreland, the colours are not historically true; not being blue and green, but blue and yellow. By the way, we congratulate our readers on the recent triumph of the yellow over the blue in the adjoining county. At Carlisle, the *blues* were beaten all to sticks. Mr. James Brougham was sent down to head the war:—whatever thumping could do, and kicking, with every sort of Kentuck ruffianism was tried: perjury, we hear, was not forgotten: but all was unavailing: they were smashed. Speaking of the Broughams, *John Bull* says that Mr. Henry goes about 'stretching' (as they call it in Westmoreland) and protesting that he *might* have been Master of the Rolls. Rolls! What Rolls? There are more sorts of Rolls than one; and more ways than one of being a 'Master of the Rolls.' To return to the Old Bachelor, we observe that he is prone to luxuriate on *la belle passion*; on which account, we are sorry to recollect his having said that his signature is irreversible.[10]

---

[10] The Old Bachelor was Hartley Coleridge. His earlier article referred to here had been in the July issue.

In the election at Carlisle Colonel Lushington, the Lowther can-

ART. IX. *Review of Moore's Epicurean.*—This article
is properly placed last, on the principle of concluding
con la bocca dolce. We are happy, for once, to agree with
the *Sun* newspaper, and to pronounce it the sovereign
flower of the garland. In saying this, we do not affect
to be in any doubt as to its author. That author is apt
to set his mark upon what he writes. In prodigality of
fancy applied to ludicrous subjects, and in general activity of mind to the very verge of a diseased activity,
he has no equal.

"Within that circle none durst walk but he."[11]

If there is any fault in the article, we would suggest that
the badgering of the unfortunate Alciphron for his gym-
nastics at the ring, is pursued too far, and too unmerci-
fully. As a whole, it is delightful, and exhibits every
mode of power. In particular, there are scattered up and
down some profound philosophical remarks, of which we
shall quote one, both for its importance, and for the
beauty of the illustration. Madame de Stael (and thousands of others,) had remarked that nothing so much
warps and disfigures a work of fiction *"que d'avoir un
but;"* meaning, by *"un but,"* a formal moral proposed to
the author's mind from the beginning, and giving an
unnatural bias to the whole movement of the story. In
this remark there was a great truth, but so expressed
as to include a great falsehood. Far more justly is the
doctrine on this head developed by the author before us
in the following beautiful passage:

---

didate, had been victorious. The *John Bull* was a disreputable
Tory weekly (in which De Quincey himself had been slandered);
the article referred to here was reprinted in the *Post* of September 1 (p. 130).

Master of the Rolls is explained below (p. 104).

11 The author was John Wilson. The quotation is from Dryden's
Prologue to *The Tempest.*

"The great moral of all works of fiction should permeate the whole living mass, not merely evolve itself in an unexpected, perhaps unaccountable corruscation at the close. At the catastrophe of a tragic tale must we lean our brow on our hands, and begin inquiring at the soul within us, what is the conclusion to be drawn from the acted agonies of all the phantoms that are now gone into darkness and dust? One continuous master emotion must have been with us from the uplifting to the letting down of the curtain, making us, if we have looked and listened aright, better because wiser men, with more power over the passions of our individual selves, because with more knowledge of the passions that belong to human nature at large. There can be no distinction between poetical justice, as it is dealt out by genius, to the creatures moving along Fancy's enchanted floor, and that justice, that from highest heaven, is, day and night, seen smiting the children of men. Have not all the events of real life, great or small, each its own moral—that speaks either with a still small voice, or trumpet-tongued, the whisper and the blast equally intelligible, and easy to be understood? How is this to end? is a question that, in reading any wise fiction, is seldom, if ever, distinctly put by the awakened mind to itself, but the passion with which it peruses continually involves the forward-looking hopes and fears, from which such a question would spring. Although clouds and thick darkness gather over the agents and events, and, as it were, shut up the prospect, as mists to a man walking among the mountains suddenly enshroud the scenery, that a moment before beheld its beauties close upon his eye, yet we read on, assured that the path of life will soon in light re-appear, just as we walk on not doubting that the wind, or the sunshine, will ere long reveal the landscape, with its torrents, its woods, and its rocks."

This fine remark, if applied to Mr. Beckford's *Vathek*,

reflects light on this writer's opinion of it—an opinion in which we heartily coincide. *Vathek* is a monstrous chaos of absurdities without drift or meaning; and it is a remarkable evidence to the truth of what we have just quoted—that, as on the one hand, there is no moral *à parte post*, so, on the other, there is no determining principle, *à parte ante*. Every incident has been separately and capriciously invented, under no impulse from what preceded it. In each defect (both of the moral, and of the governing principle in the succession of the incidents) there is an equal departure from the analogies of real life.

In conclusion, we regard Mr. Moore on this occasion as at once a fortunate and an unfortunate author; fortunate in finding a reviewer so capable of illustrating his merits, unfortunate in finding one so superior to himself in strength and versatility of power as to eclipse his own pretensions, and to draw off the attention from their inferior lustre.

ATTRIBUTION

De Quincey wrote several reviews of *Blackwood's* for the *Post* and always favorable reviews. John Wilson was a friend of his; he himself wrote a few articles for *Blackwood's* before and during the time he wrote for the *Post*, and after leaving the *Post* he wrote much for *Blackwood's*; it was a magazine whose politics and liveliness he admired.

The story told here of Shelvocke (p. 96) is told by De Quincey in the same context, where he again scoffs at the supposed danger of a Russian threat to India, in "Affghanistan," *Blackwood's*, LVI (1844), 137-38. (In that article Shelvocke's name does not appear; the story is said to be reported by Dampier.) De Quincey refers to Shelvocke, in his essay on Coleridge (1834), as one of the sources for the *Ancient Mariner* (M. II, 145).

The particular knowledge of Westmorland, its politics and its dialect (p. 100), points to De Quincey; both as resident and journalist of Westmorland he had been intimate with both subjects, especially during his editorship of the *Westmorland Gazette*. The colors of the parties make frequent appearances in the *Gazette*. The phrase "Kentuck ruffianism" in the same passage, used in a political context, and with particular reference to the Broughams, is strong evidence of De Quincey's authorship. In "Political Anticipations," an essay in which there are also similarities to the *Post* of the preceding week (p. 94), he uses the phrase "ruffianism . . . of Kentucky" in reference to politics (*Blackwood's*, XXVIII [1830], 725). In "The Present Cabinet," *Blackwood's*, XXIX (1831), 149, he writes of Henry Brougham and "Kentucky violence"; the same phrase, also in political reference, is in "Toryism, Whiggism, and Radicalism" (1835-36), M., IX, 346. For other references to Kentucky rough-and-tumble, etc., in other contexts, see "Mr. Schnackenberger" (1823), M., XII, 354; "Philosophy of Herodotus" (1842), M., VI, 135; the 1856 *Confessions*, M., III, 236 n.

The facetious play on "Master of the Rolls," in the same passage, is explained in the first of De Quincey's essays "On Murder Considered as One of the Fine Arts," published earlier in this year; there was a London baker who had distinguished himself in the ring and was known as the Master of the Rolls (M., XIII, 40). Speaking of murder, facetious play and other arts, the comic-macabre anecdote with which the present article opens sounds very De Quinceyan.

The Latin tags are common, but at least De Quincey did use them. *A parte ante . . . a parte post* (p. 103) are in "Paper of the Bank of England," *Westmorland Gazette*, April 3, 1819, p. 2; in the *Confessions*, both versions, M., III, 409; in "On Wordsworth's Poetry" (1845),

M., XI, 312; and in "Professor Wilson" (1850), M., V, 299; *a parte ante* appears in "Greece under the Romans" (1844), M., VII, 257 and "Joan of Arc (1847), M., V, 399; *a parte post* is in "Kant on the Age of the Earth" (1833), M., XIV, 73. *Materiam superabat opus* (p. 97) is also in "Dr. Samuel Parr" (1831), M., V, 117, and the *Posthumous Works* (1891), I, 157. *Con la bocca dolce* (p. 101) he used in his review of Carlyle's translation of *Wilhelm Meister* (1824), M., XI, 243.

September 15, 1827

Owen of Lanark

Mr. Owen, formerly of New Lanark, whom it would re-joice all rational friends of his to think insane, as *that* view of his case would acquit him of the obstinate *char-latanerie* and spirit of imposture which are else so dis-creditably attached to his name, has *again* abandoned his American settlements, and is once more at his old work in London. Outrageous thirst for notoriety, and bustling self-importance, which are the true keys to the whole of Mr. Owen's public life, can find no theatre of display in the wilderness. Indiana is but a dull region to him who sighs for the luxury of applause or the stimulus of opposition: and *New Harmony*, though plagued with discords enough of its own, produces none of a character in which it can flatter any man's vanity to participate.[1] Hence it is, that though Mr. Owen "often takes leave" of Europe,

> "Her fields of carnage and polluted air,"

he is exceedingly "loth to depart" in good earnest: and, like the hermit in Rasselas, lays hold of the first pretext for descending from the dignity of solitude to the abom-inations of artificial society.[2]

The place and the time of his public re-appearance in London, throw light upon each other. At a breakfast of the "Co-operative Society" it was, on *Sunday* morning

---

[1] Robert Owen's experimental colony at New Harmony, In-diana, had been in operation for over two years; Owen himself had just returned from it.

[2] "Her fields of carnage, and polluted air" is from the *Excur-sion*, III, 834; Wordsworth's Solitary had left Europe for a purer America only to return disappointed. "And often took Leave; but was loath to Depart" is from Prior's "The Thief and the Cordelier, a Ballad"; but the phrases were also familiar from an older song. The hermit is in Chap. XXI of *Rasselas*.

last, that Mr. Owen read and commented on an "address to the labouring classes of Great Britain and Ireland," which he had published in a London journal of that day.[3] Now, a public breakfast on a Sunday is, in this island, too extraordinary an occurrence to be interpreted by the world, or to be designed by the party assembled, in any other light, than as a most indecent affront to the religious institutions of the country. From the choice of the day, therefore, those who never before heard of the Co-operative Society, will draw their conclusions as to the character of the meeting. On the other hand, our private knowledge of the Co-operative Society, sufficiently explains their motive in choosing that day. The Co-operative Society, which we have kept our eye upon for about three years, is, indeed, neither more nor less than a nest of infidelity; [we may add—of *unlearned* infidelity,] and anxious to be known in that character so far as their prudent terrors of public opinion will allow them.[4] They now publish a journal of their own; and, from this and other signs, we are sorry to infer that their influence is extending.* We notice these circumstances, as illustra-

* Of the good sense which governs this body, some idea may be formed from the designation they have assumed. Other Societies seek a title expressing the particular feature which distinguishes them amongst the infinite crowd of their contemporaries. This Society describes itself by the only circumstance which must of necessity be common to all Societies whatever.

3 "To the Agriculturists, Mechanics, and Manufacturers, both Masters and Operatives, of Great Britain and Ireland," in *The Sphynx*, September 9, pp. 148-50; but De Quincey probably read the reprint in the *Standard* of September 11, which identifies its source only as "a Sunday paper." The quotations from Owen's address, later in the present article, are not always *verbatim* but they are substantially accurate.

4 (The brackets are in the original.) The London Co-operative Society was founded in 1824 to promote Owenite principles of co-operation. Young John Stuart Mill, as he tells us in his *Autobiography*, came to its meetings to do battle against it, in a friendly way, on behalf of political economy. The journal of the

ting Mr. Owen's connexions, and the final drift of his plans; which are, and have always been, desperately irreligious. With schemes addressed to the poor of earthly hope, too puerile and baseless, to deserve the name of *theories*, he is anxious to connect others for laying waste those grand and more affecting hopes, to which the humblest labourer looks for his final consolations: Of this design, indeed, we do not need the indirect evidence just cited: for many of our readers will recollect, that within the last year, Mr. Owen issued a formal manifesto in America, against the three pillars of social life, which he described as three desolating superstitions, viz. 1. Property; 2. The institution of marriage; 3. Public worship, and religious creeds.[5]

Anti-social principles of this desperate character, which rank Mr. Owen with the worst of the German *Illuminati*,[6] are not, however, quite safe in this country. Public opinion would be armed in a moment against an apostle of this quality, which, for the present slumbers, as regards Mr. Owen, or is languidly directed to him as one of the "quizzes" of the day, and a visionary too prosing to excite much interest. Mr. Owen is well aware of *that*. Probably he is not weak enough to calculate upon ever again getting up a public meeting under the *Royal* sanction:[7] those days are gone by: but to hold footing at all in decent society, he feels the necessity of keeping back his American doctrines. And hence it happens that, in the

---

Society, alluded to in the following sentence, was the *Co-operative Magazine*.

[5] Owen's "Declaration of Mental Independence," published on July 4, 1826.

[6] A late eighteenth-century movement, republican and freethinking.

[7] The Duke of Kent (Victoria's father) was a friend and patron of Owen, and Owen helped him with financial problems; after he died he communicated with Owen spiritually. The Duke of Sussex, mentioned below, was another son of George III, aberrant and a supporter of several humane causes.

address which he issued on the 9th of this month, we hear only the old story—the *crambe recocta* of that scheme for improving society, which originally led him to take up the trade of an itinerant philosopher.

The scheme moves on two hinges, one of morals, the other of political economy. We shall dispose of both in that order; for it is scandalous that such delusions should so long have insulted the knowledge and good sense of the age—with no examinations, or objection even that we are aware of, except the vague one, that they were "untried," and "hazardous:" that objection involves a falsehood; for it supposes that this is a case in which we need the aid of experience. But there can be no title, on Mr. Owen's part, to a tardy experimental refutation, (especially where no possible experiment could be exempt from the cavil of imperfect execution in some point or other,) when the very principles on which the whole speculation is bottomed, will be seen to contradict either our English notions of civil liberty, or the laws of political economy, the very instant that they are exposed.

First, then, one word upon the morals of Mr. Owen's scheme.—By way of giving to it a colour of philosophy, Mr. O. affected to lay, as the substratum of the whole, the doctrine of philosophical necessity, as revived in the middle of the last century, by David Hartley, and adopted from him by Dr. Priestley, and hundreds of others.[8] Not that Mr. Owen exactly comprehended that doctrine, or that in fact it had any particular connexion with his views. But these were points of no moment. For the practical mischief of the system lay elsewhere. Man, according to Mr. Owen's postulate, is passive to the influences by which he is surrounded. The great object then is,

[8] David Hartley's *Observations on Man* (1749) were abridged by Joseph Priestley in 1775 (with another edition in 1790); Priestley wrote several works on the doctrine of philosophical necessity. See Coleridge, *Biographia Literaria*, ed. J. Shawcross (Oxford, 1907), I, 76, among many other places in Coleridge.

that he should be surrounded from infancy, by none but such as are salutary. But how shall that be accomplished? By a society expressly organized with that view. And here, accordingly, commences a system of tyranny, and interference with *domestic* liberty, such as no nation has ever yet tolerated.

It strikes us as a matter of great astonishment, or, more properly, it may be taken as an evidence of the complete darkness in which all people were, on the nature of Mr. Owen's plans, that the Duke of Sussex, and others of his Royal Highness's party, should have patronized a single meeting for the forwarding of such views. Even Mr. Ricardo, on that occasion, gave the sanction of his presence, though speaking dubiously of the result to be anticipated: Mr. Ricardo! who, both as a Whig, and as a great economist, ought to have abhorred Mr. Owen; and would have done so, had he read enough of his accursed plans, to know the main-spring by which they move.[9] Drunkenness, for example, an evil in itself, and the parent of many more,—doubtless it were a fine thing, if that could be suppressed; but how? It needs no philosopher from Lanark to tell us—that, if the philosopher at the head of every settlement, is sole proprietor, and every man beside is a tenant at will under him, it will be easy for this philosopher to play the tyrant: Summary ejectments will put an end to all open displays of inebriety; and a system of domestic *espionage*, or public parades, at short intervals of three or four hours, might do much to repress it in private. This is not difficult either to plan or effect; but how to reconcile so base a despotism with our English ideas of civil liberty, or with good morals, that *is* difficult, and a task for subtler heads than Mr. Owen's. We, heaven knows! look with no fa-

[9] The reference is to a public meeting of June 1819. Ricardo could give no theoretical support to Owen, but he was willing to support some of Owen's practical work in model communities, for such good as it might produce.

vour on drunkenness; but far rather would we see a nation of drunkards, than know that the humblest man among us should not be at liberty to get drunk in his own house and castle, without suffering in the weightiest interests of his life. Nothing but feudal vassalage could result from this; and, having said *that*, we have said enough. Once put upon the right scent, the reader who is interested in the examination, will hunt out all the rest; and he will find that the influence by which Mr. Owen is to work all his marvels, does not flow from any legitimate course—not from subtlety of legislation—or from education more wisely conducted, but, in every instance, from blank tyranny; from so arranging the property of the settlement, as that the immediate interests of the settlers shall be arrayed against their most sacred rights.

Next, for Mr. Owen's Political Economy. His great bugbear is, and has always been, "over-production,"— or, as he elsewhere expresses it, "the dire effects of superabundance." But Mr. Owen shall speak for himself:— "The new powers of production created in Great Britain and Ireland since the days of Adam Smith, are now little, if any, short of the labour that could be obtained from 600 millions of active men previous to that period: or, the working classes of Great Britain and Ireland can now, aided by mechanical and chemical improvements, finish as much work as could be completed in the days of Adam Smith by *three times the whole manual power of the world.*"

Well, be it so: and what is Mr. Owen's exquisite conclusion? In general, the old objections to machinery, which, at this time of day, we need not tax ourselves to repeat; and more particularly the following theory of our present condition. In consequence of this over-production, "You," says he, addressing the labouring classes, "experienced the paralysing effects of a superabundance, for which the present organization of society does not admit of any other remedy than time,—to dissipate or waste, in foreign markets, the superabundance which you toiled to produce: while your labour for this period becomes of little, and, in many instances, of no value; and you are compelled, in consequence, to experience all the privations of famine, and evils of poverty; while yet you are surrounded with a superfluity of which the present arrangement of society in civilized life" (Bow Street, to wit) "forbids you to partake."

Now, as to the possibility of an over-production such as this, it must be recollected, that all production is limited, on the one hand, by the cost, and on the other by the demand. Nobody would produce even at the very lowest cost, against a continued defect of demand: but, waiving this, and supposing the rate of production to be governed by the single consideration of cost, Mr. Owen's political economy labours with this dilemma. The cost has, or has not, been reduced materially by machinery. If not, then how comes there to be any excess of production? If, on the contrary, the cost *has* been so materially reduced as proportionally to extend production, exactly in that degree must the price have fallen: so that, with falling wages,* there will be the simultaneous compensation to the poor of falling prices. But perhaps, (for this is part of Mr. Owen's hypothesis) production will be extended *more* than in proportion to the reduced cost. Well: but this case is still stronger against him. For thus, in addition to the lowering of *natural* price from the diminished cost of production, the poor would enjoy a lowering of *market* price also in consequence of an excess in the supply, and for as long a time as that excess should happen to last.

* Wages will *not* fall under the circumstances stated; but we are adopting Mr. Owen's premises.

Such is the truth: but, proceeding on his own delusions, Mr. Owen says—"I now request to ask our legislators, and political economists—why, in proportion as these new powers were brought to your aid, your labour did not gradually diminish from nine hours per day, to eight, to seven, to six, to five, to four, and to three; and why the three hours of labour per day, should not now be of more value to you, as they might easily be made more productive, than the nine were before the introduction of these enormous mechanical and chemical powers of production?"

"Gentle Shepherd, tell me why!"—The *why* is soon told by political economy. It is simply because a greater power of production in one direction has been balanced by a less in another. If shoes, by some new discovery should to-morrow be made with half the labour which is requisite to make them to-day, then, after allowing for the fixed capital in this trade (which will be unaffected by the discovery, and will maintain its old value,) shoes will to-morrow sink to half their former price. If muslins require one-fourth of the labour which was required twenty years ago, in that case (making the same allowance as before,) muslins will now be bought at one quarter of the old price. Thus far, therefore, when Mr. Owen asks why the labourer does not benefit by the increased powers of production? the answer to Mr. Owen is, that he *does* benefit, and by the whole value of that increase. "Why are not his ten hours reduced to five?" Answer: they *are* reduced in that proportion, as regards the shoes. "Why are not his five hours still further reduced to two and a half?" Answer: they *are* reduced in that proportion, as regards the muslins. Whether aware of it or not, the labourer works fewer hours for shoes and for muslins, unless he chuses to consume more shoes and muslins. And this he would not fail to know, if all other things continued as before. But it so happens that people consume food as well as clothes, furniture, &c. Now the machinery for producing food is a machinery of nature, which it is that makes the whole difference. For, whilst the machinery of art is always advancing from worse to better, the machinery of nature is constantly declining from better to worse. Not that the soil, which grows our corn and pastures our bullocks, is of necessity impoverished by use; but that, as population extends, the necessities of the case are continually carrying cultivation upon lower and lower qualities of land; soils of the first quality being insufficient, we are obliged to resort to soils of the second; those being all occupied, we must put up with No. 3,† and so on; in which declension it unfortunately happens, of necessity, that the lowest quality in use, (*i.e.* the one requiring the heaviest cost to produce a given quantity of food,) fixes the price for all the superior qualities. This is the foundation of the doctrine of rent. And here we see two great forces at work, in opposite directions; one tending eternally to diminish, the other eternally to increase the expenses of living. Food, and in general the raw material of all articles, are for ever tending to grow dearer, as the inferior powers of nature are resorted to, and very rapidly too, if it were not that continual improvements in agriculture, fishing, &c. enable us to make a better application of labour to these inferior powers. On the other hand, this great tendency in food and raw products is met by an opposite tendency in all manufacturing processes, which are continually abridged, and therefore made cheaper, by new discoveries in the arts. These two forces fortunately counteract each other, and, upon the whole, something like an equilibrium is maintained.

† By No. 3, &c. is meant that quality of soil which, with the same expense, will not produce the same quantity as No. 2; or which, in order to produce the same quantity, must be forced by a higher expense, and so of any other number.

Hence, when Mr. Owen, by way of proof that the labouring population have *not* benefited by the increased powers of production, argues that they now work as many hours as heretofore,—he is unconsciously, and from mere ignorance of the doctrine of rent, giving the strongest possible proof that they *have* benefited: to be stationary is, in this case, a demonstration of having advanced: for, had it not been through the continual movement upwards in the production of manufactures, they must have yielded to the continual movement downwards in the production of food: and, instead of working for the old period of ten hours, they would, from the increasing difficulty of obtaining food, have found it necessary to work 12, 13, 14, and so on. Not to have lost ground under a depressing force, is good evidence that they have benefited by an elevating force in counteraction.

From the quality of Mr. Owen's speculation on the evils which oppress us, the reader may guess at the value of his practical remedies. We know not that it can answer any purpose to pursue him into these, when his grounds are shown to be so palpably false and unscientific. But possibly, at a leisure moment, we may throw away a word on that part also of his blunders.

Note.—Mr. Owen contends, that the artizan now works even *more* than he did previously to the great manufacturing improvements. But the difference between the *as much* and the *more* is one of no consequence; and we have neglected it: because, even conceding the question of fact, (which it is his business to prove,) *that* would simply imply, that the two antagonist forces have not been exactly brought into equilibrium, so as to neutralize each other, and that there has been a positive excess of the depressing force: which may be very true, (and, in the various oscillations of these forces, sometimes will be true) without any prejudice to the principle insisted on—that the *whole* benefit of the elevating force has been reaped by the labouring population.[10]

[10] The next issue of the *Post* (September 22, p. 159) printed the following letter and reply. If, as seems certain, De Quincey wrote the present article then he probably wrote the reply to the letter. (Malthus' attack on Owen, the subject of the correspondence, was added to his edition of 1817.)

MR. OWEN OF LANARK.

TO THE EDITOR OF THE EDINBURGH SATURDAY POST

Sir,—I have read with pleasure the very able exposition, in your last paper, of the absurdities of Mr. Owen's speculations. Permit me, however, to express my surprise, that a person so well versed in the doctrines of political economy, as the writer evidently is, should assert that Mr. Owen's "delusions" have been hitherto subjected to no examination, nor been even objected to, but as "untried" and "hazardous." If the talented writer will examine the treatise on population, he will find that Mr. Malthus did summary justice on the doctrines in question long ago, and be disposed to conclude, that had Mr. Owen been accessible to the voice of reason, it would be unnecessary to urge him *now* to throw away the base dross which he has laboured so unweariedly to transmute into gold.

You, however, and Mr. Malthus, do not attack Mr. Owen from the same point, though it might, perhaps, be shewn, that your refutation is really comprehended in the other; and it may be remarked, that if Mr. Owen's plans be demonstrably absurd, in reference to a state where the antagonist principles of increasing mechanical skill, and decreasing fertility of soil, are nearly equally active—*a fortiori* must these plans be absurd, in reference to a state where the principle of population is feebly, or not at all opposed by increasing mechanical productiveness,—I am, etc.   B.

The reproof of our Correspondent is just; and his concluding remark is a weighty one, and capable of important applications to many other questions. In apology for our oversight, we must remind B, that we had not so far forgotten the prodigious extent of the *periodical* literature, (which makes it difficult to say what has and what has not been done), as not to qualify our censure by the words "that we are aware of." We have since heard that Mr. M'Culloch had formerly examined Mr. Owen's schemes on principles of political economy; but this being done in a newspaper, (as we understand) which is past and out of sight in a moment, we have no means of referring to it. As to Mr. Malthus's examination, our excuse

116

ATTRIBUTION

This is certainly De Quincey's. The main evidence is its several parallels, including some close verbal similarities, to an article on Owen in De Quincey's *Westmorland Gazette*, August 7, 1819, p. 3 (with a short sequel on August 14, p. 2). As in the first paragraph of the present article, he there attacks Owen as one of the "impostors and *charlatans*" of the day. Owen is both intellectually imbecile and morally under no other influence than that of an "outrageous vanity and a delirious thirst after notoriety and power." The immediate occasion of the 1819 article was Owen's success in "public meetings . . . sanctioned by the presence of a Royal Duke," referred to on p. 108 of the present article. Ricardo's presence at these meetings (p. 110 above) is also noted in the *Gazette* and with a similar comment. As in the latter part of the present article, the demonstration of Owen's false ideas on production and consumption invokes the "doctrine of rent" as unfolded by Ricardo: as additional corn is grown upon inferior lands of fifth or sixth-rate quality the price of corn rises generally, since it is corn from the "lowest quality of land, that regulates the price of the whole"; rent on all qualities of land will rise accordingly. Owen never answers this objection because he is simply unacquainted with it.

De Quincey refers to Owen again, briefly, in "Political Anticipations," *Blackwood's* XXVIII (1830), 725-26n.,

---

is a very simple one,—that the edition of his work which we have always used (we forget at this moment whether the 3d or the 4th) does not so much as mention Mr. Owen's name. Few persons can have read Mr. M.'s *other* works with more rigorous attention than ourselves; but, with respect to the Principle of Population, conceiving all the corollaries from it to be sufficiently obvious, we had not thought it necessary to recur to it in each successive edition. Upon B.'s information, we shall now make it a point of our duty to do so.

an essay in which there are several other parallels to these essays in the *Post* (pp. 94, 104 above). He doesn't seem to have known—at least he doesn't say—that Owen at one time lived at Greenhay, which had been De Quincey's boyhood home.

The "doctrine of rent" (pp. 113ff.), the phrase and the Ricardian teaching, reappears in a number of later essays in the *Post*: October 6, 13, 27, and November 10, 1827, and April 5, 1828 (pp. 149ff., 164ff., 341ff.); and of these the essay of October 27 (which is continued in the essay of November 10) seems certainly his. The same ideas, sometimes with verbal parallels, are also in his known writings. In "Dilemmas on the Corn Law Question," *Blackwood's*, XLV (1839), 172-76, he writes about the "doctrine of rent" and of how food and raw materials "are always growing dearer and dearer" because there is a natural movement "from good to worse," as "lower and lower" qualities of land ("No. 1," "No. 2," "No. 3") are brought into use, and the worst quality sets the price for all; and how, on the other hand, manufactures are "always growing cheaper" because human experience and "discovery" are forever at work; and how these "opposite and counteracting" causes restore an "equilibrium." His manuscript essay "The Corn Laws," now in the Berg collection of the New York Public Library, goes over the same ground: one must understand the "doctrine of rent"; the progress in manufacture is "from good to better," but the movement in the production of food and raw materials is "from good to worse" so that they are "continually growing dearer"; these two tendencies, proceeding by "opposite" and "counteracting" laws, maintain an "equilibrium"; land is a "machine"; as population expands "lower qualities" of soil (Nos. 1, 2, 3, etc.) are brought into use and the lowest sets the price for all. The same points and the same language are in his "Hints Towards an Appreciation of the Coming War with

China," *Titan*, XXV (1857), 72-73. Also on how the price of food is governed not by the best but by the worst "qualities of soil," a natural "machinery," see "Sir Robert Peel's Position on Next Resuming Power," *Blackwood's*, L (1841), 400. On the differences in "quality of soils," designated "No. 1," "No. 2," "No. 3," as the basis of rent, see *Logic of Political Economy* (1844), M., IX, 234ff. On how "raw materials . . . are constantly tending to grow dearer," as the expansion of population forces a descent through "soils Nos. 1, 2, 3, 4," and the lowest regulates the price of all, while "discoveries" in "manufacturing art" move the prices of manufactures in the opposite direction, see the note added in 1854 to "Dialogues of Three Templars," M., IX, 94-95n. On "the doctrine of Rent" and land "No. 1," "No. 2," "No. 3," see "California" (1852), M., IX, 405-07.

The distinction between market price and natural price is explained at greater length in the *Post* article of October 27, 1827, and its continuation of November 10, 1827 (pp. 165-67, 171-72); both of these, as we have seen, also discuss the "doctrine of rent" and both seem certainly De Quincey's. The article of December 1, 1827 (pp. 215-16) makes the same distinction and it too is certainly his. It is, further, the same distinction made in two of his works referred to above as having other parallels with this essay: "Dialogues of Three Templars" (1824), M., IX, 61, 71, and *Logic of Political Economy* (1844), M., IX, 121, 200-207.

The general point should also be made that although De Quincey's political economy and Ricardian language were not unusual, his combination of political economy and Toryism was unusual; and when the Tory *Standard* had this peculiarity of the *Edinburgh Saturday Post* forced into its notice it was surprised: "The *Edinburgh Saturday's Post* [sic] . . . is a clever paper, notwithstanding that it aims to be that most incomprehensible, and

preposterous of all things—a Tory political economist"
(October 9, 1827, p. 2); "The *Edinburgh Saturday Post*
[is] a paper with which we have no desire to quarrel, because, though strangely enough, it pretends to be a political economist, it is Tory" (October 17, 1827, p. 2).
This, then, establishes another point of identity between
De Quincey and the *Post*.

Also, the "antagonist forces" here (pp. 114-16) are pervasive in De Quincey, both in economic contexts and
many others, both in the *Post* and in his known writings,
both the specific phrase and many close variants. They
are in the article of October 13 (p. 153 below), which
also deals with an economic question and also has other
signs of his authorship; they run throughout the *Logic of
Political Economy*, chiefly in relation to problems of land
and rent: M., IX, 223, 248, 259, 284n., 293. They are
basic to the political questions argued in the article of
April 19, 1828 (p. 346 below), which is certainly his, and
in the Bodleian MS. (p. 353 below); references to similar
contexts in his other writings are given in the notes to
those articles. In still another context they are in the
article of December 15, 1827 (p. 227 below), which is certainly his. They can be found, in varied contexts, in M.,
I, 38; III, 344, 444; V, 350-51; VI, 249, 417; VI, 435; X,
49; X, 403-404; X, 436; "The Duke of Wellington and Mr.
Peel," *Blackwood's*, XXV (1829), 302; "French Revolution," *Blackwood's*, XXVIII (1830), 544. J. Hillis Miller,
in *The Disappearance of God* (Cambridge, Mass., 1963),
pp. 43-45, demonstrates the significance of the principle
of "antagonistic forces" in De Quincey's thought and
additional references can be found there; the list I have
given is limited to places where the actual phrase or a
close variant can be found.

The dilemma (p. 112), both as an argumentative
form and serving other purposes, both in economic contexts and others, is so frequent in De Quincey that it

may be offered as corroborative of other evidence of authorship. It appears often in the *Post*: October 6, 1827, November 24, 1827 (an essay which is certainly his), February 16, 1828, April 5, 1828 (pp. 149, 199, 314, 344 below). The references that follow include works written both before and after this date and works that have additional parallels to both this essay and others in the *Post*: M., III, 338, 399; IV, 100; VI, 392n.; VII, 128-29, 138-39; VII, 198, 227-28; VIII, 116; VIII, 284; IX, 109 (the "Dialogues of Three Templars"); IX, 420-21; X, 14-15; X, 280-81; X, 310; XI, 172n.; XI, 299; XIV, 168ff.; XIV, 241-42; "Immanuel Kant, and John Gottfried Herder," in the *Westmorland Gazette*, August 28, 1819, p. 3; the MS. published as *Dr. Johnson and Lord Chesterfield* (New York, 1945); the MS. essay on "The Corn Laws" in the Berg Collection of the New York Public Library, p. 13; and the following essays in *Blackwood's*: "Political Anticipations," XXVIII (1830), 727n.; "The Late Cabinet," XXVIII, 967; "Dilemmas on the Corn Law Question," XLV (1839), 170-76; "Hints for the Hustings," XLVIII (1840), 290, 305; "Conservative Prospects," XLIX (1841), 416-17n.

In the passage that follows (p. 113), the expository technique of asking a question and then announcing the "Answer:" (or "*Answer*—," etc.) is a De Quinceyan device. It is in economic contexts, as here, in *Logic of Political Economy* (1844), M., IX, 270, and the MS. "Corn Laws," p. 11; in other contexts it is in "Richard Bentley" (1830), M., IV, 216, and "Ireland," *Blackwood's*, LV (1844), 526; cf. also M., VII, 146. It appears in the *Post* a number of times, usually in articles on political economy and therefore in articles already cited in the present note: October 13, 1827 (p. 158), November 10, 1827, an article which is certainly his (pp. 172-73, 175), November 24, 1827, also certainly his (p. 198n.), December 29,

1827, and January 12, 1828, both also certainly his (pp. 241-44, 266), and April 5, 1828 (p. 344).

The very appropriate quotation from the 834th line of the third Book of *The Excursion* displays once again the *Post's* De Quinceyan intimacy with the poetry of Wordsworth.

The German *Illuminati* (p. 108) make several appearances in De Quincey's works, always with the same brief contempt: "Richard Bentley" (1830), M., IV, 211n.; "Kant in His Miscellaneous Essays" (1830), M., VIII, 114; the essay of London reminiscences in 1837, M., III, 25; "Secret Societies" (1847), M., VII, 179.

Charlatanerie (p. 106) is perhaps a sign of De Quincey's hand. The word is used in the *Post* essay of June 28, 1828, which is certainly his (p. 382n.); and he uses it in the *Westmorland Gazette*, April 17, 1819, p. 3, in "Rosicrucians and Free-Masons" (1824), M., XIII, 416, in "Animal Magnetism," *Tait's*, IV (1834), 475, and in "Plato's Republic" (1841), M., VIII, 46.

Mr. Canning and the Aristocracy

There is one point connected with the late changes of
Administration, which it is very important to place in a
just light, because it happens to have been strangely misrepresented. Immediately after the death of Mr. Canning, the *New Times*, insisting on the various claims
that pointed out Lord Goderich as his successor, urged
amongst them what that paper ludicrously denominated
'his *illustrious* descent;' an expression from which one
might have supposed that Lord Goderich was of the
house of Bourbon or Nassau, at least, that he had the
blood of all the Howards in his veins. Well: this descent,
the *New Times* argued, would protect Lord Goderich
from that objection which had weighed so much with the
aristocracy against Mr. Canning; affecting to suppose, or
perhaps being *bête* enough really to suppose, that the
fierce hostility of the aristocracy had been grounded on
the pretended low birth of Mr. Canning.[1] There never
was a grosser blunder. And desperately blind must that
man have been, who could fall into it. Mr. Canning's
family was upon the whole better than that of Lord
Goderich: the English family in Worcestershire, of which
Mr. Canning's first Irish ancestor was a cadet, is of much
greater antiquity than the Robinsons. And even the Irish
branch was quite as good. Lord Garvagh, it is true, is a
creation of Mr. Canning's; but it must be remembered,
that Mr. Canning found him in a condition to be en-
nobled, without which he could not have used his interest
in that way. As to the marriage connexions of Mr. Canning's family, the Bentincks, De Burghs, &c.; they were
superior to any which Lord Goderich gained by his mar-

---

[1] Probably the *New Times* of August 11, 1827, p. 2, col. 4; but
memory has much heightened the original.

riage with a Hobart. Lord Goderich's chief weight is derived from the great wealth of his brother Lord Grantham, who is fortunate enough to be heir to the vast estates of Miss Lawrence—a lady both old and infirm.[2]

But waiving any claim of precedency for Mr. Canning's family, and admitting that "between tweedledum and tweedledee," it may be difficult to find a difference: by what strange caprice could the British aristocracy have taken alarm at a defect of this nature for the first time in 1827? The Harley of Queen Anne's reign, the Walpole of George II.'s, the elder Pitt, were all of respectable families, and no more: each was the builder of his own fortune; and any splendour they could boast, came by recent marriages. Charles Fox, looking back two generations, was positively of base descent; Sir Stephen Fox being a thorough *terrae filius*. And, coming nearer to Mr. Canning, what was Mr. Addington? His father, a physician at Reading, did certainly become heard of—thanks to the soubriquet of '*the doctor*,' which settled on the son. But, as Sir Archy says in the play, we doubt whether he ever had a grandfather.[3]

[2] Canning's cousin, also George Canning, was created Baron Garvagh of Londonderry in the Irish peerage, in 1818. Canning was connected with the Bentincks through his wife's sister, who was married to William Henry Bentinck, Marquis of Titchfield, eldest son of the third Duke of Portland (the Prime Minister) and himself the fourth Duke in 1809. He was connected with the De Burghs (in the later nineteenth century they became the De Burgh-Cannings) through his daughter, who married Ulick John De Burgh, 14th Earl and then the first Marquis of Clanricarde.

Goderich's wife was the daughter of Robert Hobart, fourth Earl of Buckinghamshire. His elder brother was the third Baron Grantham. Miss Lawrence I fear I do not know.

[3] Sir Stephen Fox, who figures in Evelyn's and Pepys's diaries, had risen to high office and wealth from humble beginnings. Henry Addington, first Viscount Sidmouth, the Tory statesman, was the son of Dr. Anthony Addington.

Sir Archy is probably the character in Charles Macklin's *Love à la Mode*; though he has no line quite like this one it is very much in his style throughout the farce; and he is involved in an argument about the superior antiquity of his grandparents.

With these recollections before him, and scores of others, matters almost of historical notoriety; how could any blunderer, the most obtuse in his judgment on political affairs, go so far astray as to ascribe the opposition which confronted Mr. Canning, to any defect in his quarterings? But, doubtless, this is affectation: no man errs so extravagantly. It would, however, serve a great purpose of faction to have this believed; for it would arm against those who thought it their duty to oppose Mr. Canning, all the aspiring talent of Great Britain, and all its honest independence. The thing itself is a trifle; but "*hae nugae seria ducunt in mala.*"[4] It is on this consideration that we recal our readers to the true view of the case. The opposition of the aristocracy was not to Mr. Canning as himself wanting the ordinary claims of birth, (which he did not, and would not have suffered for if he had,) —but, *to Mr. Canning throwing himself, for revolutionary ends, upon a democratic support.*

---

[4] Horace, *Ars Poetica*, 451-52, adapted: these trifles lead to serious evils.

September 22, 1827

The Standard Newspaper

[a continuation of the preceding]

Our London friend, the *Standard*, if friend he will allow us to call him, for whose talents and various erudition we profess the highest respect, seems to be out of humour with us, and, in a particular instance, treats us with injustice. By detaching a single passage from the connection in which it stood, he gives to an article which we published last week on "Mr. Canning and the Aristocracy," the colour of extravagant genealogical purism, as though our object had been to make out a pedigree for Mr. Canning, longer and broader than that of Lord Goderich. "But, in fact," says the *Standard*, after spending a paragraph or so on this unaccountable misconstruction of our meaning, "in fact, the superior nobility of Messrs. Canning or Robinson is a question of small importance. It is not worth arranging the precedence between — — — — —. But in these nice times, we dare not always quote Swift."[1]

Stranger, indeed, must all this appear to those readers who happen to recollect that we ourselves dismissed the whole question between the Cannings and the Robinsons as one betwixt *tweedledum and tweedledee*, which we presume to be that dangerous quotation from Swift here alluded to.[2] The question about precedency, we think,

[1] *Standard*, September 18, p. 4. The *Standard* is really more vicious about Canning's ancestry than the quotation in the *Post* indicates: "It is a wise child, they say, that can tell its own father; and we were always in the habit of thinking that the paternity of Mr. Canning was one of those difficult questions which, like the birth-place of Homer, or the executioner of Charles I., will puzzle the curious."

[2] From the "Epigram, on the feuds about Handel and Bononcini," which was attributed to Swift; it was, however, the conclusion of a brief poem on the same subject by John Byrom.

126

and we then thought, to be as idle as the *Standard* represents it, but it was no question of ours. It was raised by
the *New Times,* who had described Lord Goderich in a
studious comparison with Mr. Canning, as of "illustrious
descent." This, though laughable, was no particular
business of ours. To describe a *parvenu* as illustrious, is
absurd undoubtedly; but absurdity is a thing we doat
upon. And so far all was right. But when the *New Times*
went on to insinuate that *thus* would Lord Goderich be
protected from that hostility of the Aristocracy to which
Mr. Canning had been liable, this worthy journal was
obviously building upon its first harmless error a second
which was *not* harmless. We thought it therefore right to
recal the true view of the case, which was thus artfully
obscured: not Mr. Canning, as himself a plebeian, we
contended, but Mr. Canning the courtier of plebeians,
that Mr. Canning who threw himself too ostentatiously
on a democratic support, was the object of hostility of
the Aristocracy. And to shew that this hostility could not
have been personal to Mr. C. as himself a plebeian, we
touched incidentally on Mr. Canning's family.

Such was our logic. But let our dear brother acknowledge, with his wonted candour, that he had not
read us, or had skipped three quarters or so. He has
much to read every day—too much,—and we forgive
him. And we heartily hope to see him soon occupying
that place on the tables of the worthy country gentlemen
throughout the island, from which the base rene-gado,
the *Courier,* has been so generally kicked out.[3]

ATTRIBUTION

These two, the original article and the reply to the
Standard, I think are De Quincey's because he goes out

---

[3] The *Courier* was a Tory journal now supporting the coalition.
The *Standard* carried regular reports of the reading-rooms from
which the apostate was being ejected and how the *Standard* was
replacing it.

of his way to make much the same point, about Canning's birth and his politics and English prime ministers in general, in "Sir Robert Peel's Position on Next Resuming Power," *Blackwood's*, L (1841), 403n.; this is a passage cited above (p. 84) because it is also very similar to the *Post* of August 18, 1827, in its characterization of Canning as orator. There are verbal as well as substantial similarities. De Quincey says, in 1841, that it is a misinterpretation, a delusion, a misconception to think that ministers in general, or Canning in particular, have been opposed because they have not been aristocrats. For one thing, Canning's origin was "not disrespectable"; in family he stood upon the same general level as Sir Robert Walpole. Canning was unacceptable to some of the aristocracy not because he was a *novus homo*—such a ground of opposition could not flourish in this country at this time; he was unacceptable because, being a *"parvenu,"* he was understood to have formed the plan of doing without the support of the aristocracy, "of dispensing with such support in an ostentatious spirit," and because he was a man who would have bent before "any revolution that borrowed strength from the democracy."

Charles Fox (p. 124) and the elevation of his family from a stock so modern as Sir Stephen Fox, who had an equivocal history, are also in a note to De Quincey's "France and England," *Blackwood's*, XXVIII (1830), 701. *"Terrae filius,"* in the same passage (p. 124), for what it is worth, appears about five times in De Quincey's works. And the line on tweedledum, etc., just above, is in a letter of 1810, in John E. Jordan, *De Quincey to Wordsworth* (Berkeley, 1962), p. 258.

September 29, 1827

Blackwood's Magazine

NO. CXXXI.[1]

This Number was published this morning.

ART. I. *The Faction* is a long article of 29 pages, on the Coalition and their pretensions, evidently from the same vigorous writer who has so often wielded the political scourge in this powerful journal.[2] It is elaborate, and yet *apparently* desultory. The stamp of energy is upon every thing he says—of indignation, and of fierce, intolerant scorn. These qualities make it pleasant to read; yet, from the want of breaks, or other palpable marks to point out the subdivisions into which the subject is thrown, many readers (we fear) will shrink from an article of this length. The leaders of the present Coalition, the Edinburgh Review and its contributors, are all called over the coals. Speaking of Mr. Brougham, he describes him as "a man of great talents and acquirements, the value of which is sadly impaired by a most blind and infirm judgment." But want of judgment is not the greatest drawback on that gentleman's power—a greater still is, his unmanageable temper, which would defeat the finest judgment in the world. He is at once insolent in excess, and childishly wanting in self-government. Mr. Brougham's article in the last Edinburgh Review, on the "Society for the diffusion of Useful Knowledge,"* is properly exposed.[3] To the claim made by Mr. B. for the

---

* On this subject we recommend to our readers a pamphlet just published, *On the Errors of a Big Wig.*

---

[1] October 1827.

[2] David Robinson; see also p. 215 below.

[3] On Brougham's article, see De Quincey's review of the same issue of the *Edinburgh*, p. 39 above. The pamphlet referred to in the footnote is *The Blunders of a Big-Wig; or, Paul Pry's peeps into sixpenny sciences. (Peep the first, into the Objects, Advan-*

little books issued by this Society, as distinguished by "the admirable union of plain and pure English diction," it is justly replied, "On this point we cannot take his word, for he is evidently no judge of pure English diction. His article before us ranks with the worst English that was ever placed before the public by a writer of any repute. It is disfigured by numberless grammatical errors; the construction of its sentences is exceedingly faulty, and a vicious impure use of terms pervades it throughout." The fact is, that public speakers have rarely any sense left for good composition; the rapidity, and the cadences of the voice, hide the unwieldiness of structure, to which oral sentences tend; but this becomes disgustingly obvious in written composition, to all who have a cultivated taste, unblunted by the noisy vulgarities of the Forum. The writer adds, with respect to Mr. Brougham, "Although he has lived so long in England, he never opens his lips without proving that he is a stranger to the English character," &c. From this we conclude that the writer has fallen into the common error of supposing Mr. Brougham to be a Scotchman. It was but the other day that, at a public dinner in Edinburgh, Mr. B's health was drunk as such. But this is a mistake. Mr. B. is an Englishman, of respectable family, seated for centuries in Westmoreland.

One thing we grieve for in this writer: being so excellent a politician, why should he obstinately adhere to false political economy? He is much mistaken if he thinks that all the measures, which he opposes, are countenanced by the Political Economy of David Ricardo; or, that this system of economy is countenanced by all the members of the Coalition. In fact, he has himself noticed,

---

tages and Pleasures of Science.) It was followed by another peep, into Brougham's *Hydrostatics.* The title is given correctly in the *Post* article of November 24, 1827, p. 200 below.

that "Lord Goderich now speaks of it with contempt; and Lord Holland speaks of it with greater contempt; and says he has not read a line of it." (Rather a lordly reason, by the way, for speaking of it with contempt.) Lord Lansdowne, too, it seems, protests that free trade in corn "would be vastly ruinous." As to Lords Holland and Lansdowne,[4] we do not remember; but poor Lord Goderich made a sad discovery of his ignorance; for he said, resolutely in the House, that he did not know but the 'Spectator' (*risum teneatis?*) might be a better authority in political economy than Mr. Ricardo, &c. Perhaps he thinks, with some learned men, that the Iliad contains the best system of chirurgery; and, with the Hutchinsonians,[5] that the Pentateuch is the completest Encyclopædia extant. We can add to the list of the heterodox in matters of political economy, the name of Mr. Henry Brougham: no man has distinguished more, or more often, between his regard for Mr. Ricardo, as a man of great speculative subtilty, and his confidence in him as a practical guide. Let not the able writer then be scared by the name of Mr. Brougham, as though Ricardianism were vitiated by Mr. Henry's countenance; it has *not* his countenance. Liberated from this prejudice, let him proceed to combine, with his excellent politics, a sounder knowledge of Ricardian Political Economy. He will then be armed in panoply: —

"Unum hoc doleo et maceror tibi deesse, Terenti."[6]

[4] Henry Petty, third Marquis of Lansdowne, Home Secretary, was the leader of the Whigs in the coalition. The King kept Holland out (see below, p. 317).

[5] Followers of John Hutchinson (1674-1737) in religious-scientific controversies of the eighteenth century.

[6] The order of words is not accurate, but it is the last line of Caesar's comment on Terence (from Suetonius' life of Terence): I am vexed and pained, Terence, that you lack this one thing.

ART. II. *Who can it be?*[7] Apparently this little sketch has arisen on the suggestion of Washington Irving's *Stout Gentleman*, a story much overpraised in our judgment. It is not, we think, very felicitous; or not *so* felicitous, however, as those which we have lately seen in Blackwood: Reverses and the Marvellous Doctor were admirable.

ART. III. *Letter from Lord Harris.* Lord H. is better known as that General Harris who commanded in the Mysore on the final war with Tippoo, the son of Hyder Ali. He here defends himself successfully, and with a soldierly warmth, against the charge inadvertently made in a former No. of having been "*assisted* in his command by a military council," ———————— "an arrangement," says he, "which, making me a commander without a command, would have degraded me as a soldier." We imagine that it will be long before Lord Harris will think it worth his while to correct a mistatement in any other Magazine.

ART. IV. *Lines to the memory of a favourite Dog.* This together with Art. X (*The Tomb of De Bruce*,) are from Delta;[8] but do not strike us as peculiarly effective. Some sonnets of his on Winter, &c. within the last year we remember as exquisite; the thoughts drawn from *original* inspiration, and most beautifully expressed.

ART. V. *The Devil's Dream on Mount Aksbeck.*[9] This is darkly, and in some instances sublimely conceived: but the dream of a spiritual being, one depth below another depth—a mystery within a mystery, is hardly to be imag-

[7] By Robert Macnish, who also wrote for *Blackwood's* a couple of other adaptations of the same story by Irving. "Reverses," in the August issue, was by William Harness; the "Marvellous Doctor," in September, was by James Hogg (see p. 99 above).

[8] David Macbeth Moir, who gained some celebrity as the Delta of *Blackwood's*. The sonnets referred to are probably those in the July issue.

[9] By Thomas Aird. For John Paul's dream see pp. 147-48 below.

ined. John Paul has attempted something of this kind in German: but even *his* angel's pinion to our feeling has flagged in that ascent. The dream itself is further objectionable—that it is not characteristic: it may suit the purposes of God indeed, which were "to plague him with a dream," that the Devil should dream of restoration, of forgiveness, and recovered innocence; and infancy,

> "That he should summer high in bliss upon the
> hills of God;"

but this does not suit the Devil's nature: it is not a dream growing out of himself, but a phantasma of alien origin impressed upon him; and would be better entitled *The Devil's Delirium.*

ART. VI. *The Traveller's Oracle.*[10] Of this most entertaining article we can give the best idea by specimens: it opens thus:—

"It greatly grieved us to think that Dr. Kitchiner should have died before our numerous avocations had allowed us an opportunity of dining with him, and subjecting to the test-act of our experienced palate his claims to immortality as a cook and a Christian. The Doctor had, we know, a dread of us,—not altogether unallayed by delight,—and on the dinner to us, which he had meditated for nearly a quarter of a century, he knew and felt must have hung his reputation with posterity—his posthumous fame. We understand that there is an unfinished sketch of that dinner among the Doctor's papers, and that the design is magnificent. Yet, perhaps, it is better for his glory that Kitchiner should have died without attempting to embody in form the idea of that dinner. It might have been a failure. How liable to

[10] A review by John Wilson of the book by Dr. William Kitchiner, recently deceased, a noted epicure and giver of dinners, author of books on cooking, digestion, telescopes, music, housekeeping, and many, many more. He appears in Carlyle too. The quotations from Wilson's article are not always accurate.

imperfection the material on which he would have had to work! How defective the instruments! Yes—yes—happier far was it for the good old man that he should have fallen asleep with the undimmed idea of that unattempted dinner in his imagination, than, vainly contending with the physical evil inherent in matter, have detected the Bishop's foot in the first course, and died of a broken heart!"

*

"The Doctor then treats of the best season for travelling, and very judiciously observes that it is during those months when there is no occasion for a fire, that is, just before and after the extreme heat. In winter, Dr. Kitchiner, who was a man of extraordinary powers of observation, observed "that the ways are generally bad, and often dangerous, especially in hilly countries, by reason of the snow and ice. The days are short—a traveller comes late to his lodging—and is often forced to rise before the sun in the morning—besides the country looks dismal—nature is, as it were, half dead. The summer corrects all these inconveniences." Paradoxical as this doctrine may at first sight appear, yet we have verified it by experience—having for many years found, without meeting with one single exception, that the fine, long, warm days of summer are a most agreeable and infallible corrective of the inconveniences attending the foul, short, cold days of winter—a season which is surly without being sincere, blustering rather than bold,—an intolerable bore—always pretending to be taking his leave, yet domiciliating himself in another man's house for weeks together,—and, to be plain, a season so regardless of truth, that nobody believes him till frost has hung an ice-padlock on his mouth, and his many-river'd voice is dumb under the wreathed snows."

*

134

"Above all things, continues Dr. Kitchiner, avoid traveling during the night, which, by interrupting sleep, and exposing the body to the night air, is always prejudicial, even in the mildest weather, and to the strongest constitutions. Pray, Doctor, what ails you at the night air? If the night air be, even in the mildest weather, prejudicial to the strongest constitutions, what do you think becomes of the cattle on a thousand hills? Why don't all the bulls in Bashan die of the asthma—or look interesting by moonlight in a galloping consumption? Nay, if the night air be so very fatal, how do you account for the longevity of owls? Have you ever read of the Chaldean shepherds watching the courses of the stars? Or, to come nearer to our own times, do you not know that every blessed night throughout the year, thousands of young lads and lasses meet, either beneath the milk-white thorn, or on the lea-rig, although the night be ne'er sae wet, and they be ne'er sae weary; or under a rock on the hill—or—no uncommon case—behind a frozen stack—not of chimneys, but of corn sheaves; or on a couch of snow; and that they are all as warm as so many pies—while, instead of feeling what you call "the lack of vigour attendant on the loss of sleep, which is as enfeebling and as distressing as the langour that attends the want of food," they are, to use a homely Scotch expression, "neither to haud nor bind;" the eyes of the young lads being all as brisk, bold, and bright as the stars in Charles's Wain, while those of the young lasses shine with a soft, faint, obscure, but beautiful lustre, like the dewy Pleiades over which nature has insensibly breathed a mist, almost waving and wavering into a veil of clouds?

"Have you, our dear Doctor, no compassion for those unfortunate blades, who, nolentes-volentes, must often remain out perennially all night, we mean the blades of grass, and also the flowers? Their constitutions are often far from strong—and shut your eyes on a frosty night, and you will hear them—we have done so many million times—shivering, ay, absolutely shivering under their coat of hoar-frost! If the night air be indeed what Dr. Kitchiner has declared it to be, Lord have mercy on the vegetable world! What agonies in that field of turnips! Alas! poor Swedes! The imagination recoils from the condition of that club of winter cabbages—and of what materials, pray, must the heart of that man be made, who could think but for a moment on the case of those carrots, without bursting into a flood of tears?"

Speaking of the interruptions to sound sleep in the country, the reviewer says, "Did we wish to be personal, we could name a single waterfall that, even in dry weather, keeps all the visitors from town awake within a circle of six miles diameter. Then, on another point, we are certain—namely, that rural thunder is many hundred times more powerful than villatic.* London porter is above admiration; but London thunder below contempt. An ordinary hackney coach beats it hollow."

Very true this is, and very odd. What scores of people are killed annually in the country by thunder storms! Every body recollects Pope's sentimental story, (or was it Gay's?) about two lovers killed under the hay-cock; and every year furnishes many such "green-gown" facts.[11] But who ever heard of a couple of lovers killed by lightning in Fleet Street or Houndsditch? Was ever bill at two months protested in consequence of the acceptor's being blasted in his road to Smith, Payne, and Smith's?[12] or ever handkerchief saved by Jove's thunderbolt smiting

---

* *Villatic* we object to as too near to *rural*.

[11] The poem is Pope's "On Two Lovers Struck Dead by Lightning." A "green-gown" is one that has been used for sporting in the grass.

[12] A banking firm, well known at the time. The head of it, Robert Smith (first Baron Carrington) had been a friend of Pitt's and had given money to Cowper.

the pick-pocket in the Poultry? We know what people will say—there are no trees in these places—as if the lightning descended nowhere but on trees. We answer that there *are* trees, to our knowledge, close to Cheapside; although we never saw, with Poor Susan, "twelve reapers at work in the Strand."[13] But look at St. James's Park—*there* are trees surely, and goodly ones; and when they were planted, poor Waller, the poet, prophesied of them that they should become the favourite resort of lovers. "Methinks," says he,

"Methinks I hear the love that shall be made," &c.[14]
We hope he did *not* hear. However, in some sense, his prophecy is accomplished,—sure enough there are "lovers," of one kind or other, beneath these trees at dusk; yet when have they suffered any terrors but those of a watchman's rattle, or the horse patrol? Yes; it is too clear, the very thunder grows dyspeptic in London. For it is too monstrous to suppose that it can stand in awe of Bow Street; though nearly as odd things have happened. For Charles Lamb remarks, that witches who "held the moon in fee," and even the infernal powers, were not at all the less afraid of the constable.[15]

By the way, we observe, that, at p. 461, the reviewer mentions, as belonging essentially to the establishment of an English inn, "the painter;" and, in a note, he explains

[13] Poor Susan is from Wordsworth's "Reverie of Poor Susan," who saw a river flow through the vale of Cheapside; but the quotation is from his "Farmer of Tilsbury Vale" (l. 72). The confusion is understandable; Wordsworth himself directed the reader to a comparison between the two poems, and in later years he said that their partial similarity required perhaps some apology. *Poetical Works,* ed. de Selincourt and Darbishire (Oxford, 1947), IV, 447.

[14] "On St. James's Park, as Lately Improved by His Majesty":
Methinks I see the love that shall be made . . .
Methinks I hear the Musick in the Boats . . .

[15] "Witches, and Other Night-Fears." But the quotation is adapted from Milton's sonnet "I did but prompt the age."

his functions as follows: "The painter is the artist who is employed in inns to paint the buttered toast. He always works in oils." Now this is misrepresentation; for which we appeal to Mr. Wordsworth. Twenty-one years ago, not having yet met Mr. W., but anxious to glean every particular about him, we happened to be talking with a boy, nine years old, (Hartley Coleridge, by the bye,) who had recently been travelling with his father and Mr. Wordsworth. "And what," we asked, "did the great man say? Could you recollect any of his remarks?" "Yes," said H. after a long pause, and very emphatically, "I can." "What was it?" "Why, when we came to Uxbridge, Mr. Wordsworth observed, that what they had the presumption to call buttered toast, was in fact dry toast dipped in hot water." Dire was the *bathos* to us, in our state of expectation at that time; but time teaches wisdom; and twenty-one years' experience has convinced us, that whatever this *propos* might want in brilliancy, it made up for in truth. We beg leave to say, therefore, that "the painter," according to our view of him, does *not* work in oils, but in water colours.*

Art. VII. *Miscellanea Critica*, &c. No. 2.[17]—This article presents us with some acute speculations, brief and elegant, on questions of philosophical criticism, often agitated. In saying *often*, we confine ourselves to the two first sections (5. and 6.) on Poetic Truth, and the Grounds of the pleasure derived from Metre. For, as to the last, (7.) it touches on a question, (viz. the possibil-

* At all events, whether in oils or water-colours, there is an end for ever of Mr. Mackenzie's jest, in the Mirror,[16] on a London tourist in Scotland, who disclaimed all "nationality," when he declared himself in conscience bound to say, that the only genuine buttered toast he had eaten in Scotland was at an inn kept by an Englishman.

[16] No. 41 (June 15, 1779). On Wordsworth and this anecdote, see below, pp. 145-46.
[17] By Alexander Blair.

ity of a legitimate poetic diction distinct from that of prose,) first raised by Mr. Wordsworth, and not since treated by any man of philosophic mind except Mr. Coleridge, in his "Biographia Literaria," in which work this discussion forms by much the ablest part. The whole argument against Mr. Wordsworth's theory both there, and in the article before us, rests on a confusion between the conception and the expression.

ART. IX. (which, that we may conclude with a *bonne bouche* from Art. VIII. we take out of its place,) *Montgomery's Pelican Island*.[18] Mr. Pollok, (whose death we are concerned to see announced in this week's papers,) and Mr. Montgomery, are the only writers who have for some time given us any valuable poem of considerable length. Writers are not always aware of the first hints which excited them; and this, in Mr. Montgomery's case, we take to have been a fine sonnet of Lord Thurlow's, the passage in Captain Flinders having afterwards matured this original germ.[19] We fully agree with this eloquent reviewer, that the Pelican Island is the finest of Mr. M.'s poems, and that the interest is derived chiefly from the Pelicans, what follows being in a lower key. But two things we quarrel with: first, the constant recurrence of the dissyllabic close, (as in dramatic blank verse,) which continually disturbs the metrical effect. Secondly, we complain heavily, that from such a lyre there should ever be heard the base drone of tabernacle

[18] A review of James Montgomery by John Wilson. The Pollok of the next sentence is Robert Pollok, young author of the *Course of Time* (1827), which went through many editions. It was published by Blackwood and praised in his magazine.

[19] In his preface Montgomery said that the subject of *Pelican Island* was suggested by a passage in Flinders' *Voyage to Terra Australis* (Matthew Flinders, whose book was published in 1814). The sonnet by Edward Thurlow, second Baron Thurlow (1781-1829), was "To a Bird that Haunted the Waters of Lacken in the Winter"; see below, p. 147.

superstition. Of religion a poet cannot have too much; but conventicle religion is an abomination.[20]

ART. VIII. *Schmelzle's Journey to Flätz*. The translation, made use of throughout this brilliant article, is Mr. Carlyle's, published in Edinburgh last winter.[21] Of John Paul, and his comic romance, it is not necessary to say any thing here; we shall gratify our readers much more by a specimen or two of the irresistible extravaganza which has been built upon it. The article opens thus:

"Most men are cowards; and that will be seen, felt, proved, and confessed, as soon as there have been a few centuries of universal peace. Of all the virtues, as they are called, courage is the most artificial. It is created and cockered up by war. Let all swords be once fairly converted into ploughshares, and spears into pruning hooks, and the natural cowardice of the human race will exhibit itself in an infinite variety of unexpected forms. It would be tedious to trace the causes which in our country have so long concealed, in some measure diminished,—but it is to be trusted, not destroyed, the cowardice of the people. Such an inquiry would lead us back to a period long antecedent to the Invasion of Great Britain by Julius Caesar; however cruel, wicked, and unnatural man has always been, war has still been at the bottom of the business; and if, instead of Whig or Tory, or Tory-Whig Administration, we could contrive to form and keep together for a few years, a Quaker Administration—a Drab Cabinet—cowards as we are bold enough to avow our-

[20] Montgomery was a Moravian.

[21] The article was by John Wilson, the translation from Carlyle's *Specimens of German Romance*. Wilson praises De Quincey's eulogy of Richter and the specimen translations in the *London Magazine*; in the next sentence he praises Carlyle's recent article on Richter in the *Edinburgh Review* but repeats De Quincey's stricture (p. 38 above) that it was injudicious not to provide translated extracts (p. 470 of *Blackwood's*). It is likely that Wilson had read the *Post* review of Carlyle and knew that De Quincey had written it (p. 9n. above).

selves to be, we should then fear not to wager all we might happen to be worth, that the natural character would soon re-appear in all its natural timidity, and that not a person in Great Britain would be found so valiant and irrational as to volunteer leading a forlorn hope.

"It is cheering to know, however, how much hypocrisy there is in what is called courage. Hypocrisy in a large congregation praying in a church is bad, but hypocrisy in two large armies fighting in a field is good. Were they really the blood-thirsty murderous ruffians, that to a shallow spectator of their conduct they appear to be, words would be wanting to express the abhorrence and detestation with which all good men must regard battalion, light infantry, and grenadiers. But it is refreshing and consolatory to reflect, that there are not above some score of men in either armament, who on the morning of the pitched battle, do not, half in fear, half in anger, curse the day on which they sold themselves for food to the cannon. Both armies are trembling from head to foot. What would not that fine Irish regiment give to be handling the useful spade on a lazy bed of potatoes, or flourishing the harmless shillela in a fight down at the Bridge? The brave Forty-Second, often as they have been cut in pieces, have never come to like it; and the heart of every true Gael is sighing for the still life of his Highland hills."

But the very sublime of fun is the following:—

"We cannot help, by way of contrast to the adventure which the Army chaplain is about to recount, describing, in a very few words, our sensations on one occasion, when we were run away with on horseback by a half-blood mare, who we verily believe must have been got by Satan out of Devil's Dam. We give our honour, and our name if desired, that the statement is verbatim and literatim true.

"We were sitting rather negligently on this infernal animal, which, up to that day, had seemed quiet as a

lamb—kissing our hand to Mrs. Davidson, then Miss
Duncan, and in the blaze of her fame, when a Highland
regiment, no doubt the Forty-Second, that had been
trudging down the Mound, so silently that we never
heard them, all at once, and without the slightest warning burst out, with all their bagpipes, into one pibroch!
The mare, to do her justice, had been bred in England,
and ridden as a charger, by an adjutant to an English
regiment. She was even fond of music, and delighted to
prance behind the band, unterrified by cymbals or great
drum. She never moved in a roar of artillery at reviews,
and, had the Castle of Edinburgh, Lord bless it, been
self-involved, at that moment, in a storm of thunder and
lightning round its entire circle of cannon, that mare
would not so much as have pricked up her ears, whisked
her tail, or lifted a hoof. But the pibroch was more than
horse-flesh and blood could endure, and off we two went
like a whirlwind. Where we went, that is to say, what
were the names of the few first streets along which we
were borne, is a question which, as a man of veracity, we
must positively decline answering. For some short space
of time, lines of houses reeled by without a single face at
the windows; and these, we have since conjectured, might
be North and South Hanover Street, and Queen Street.
By and by we surely were in something like a square;
could it be Charlotte Square? and round and round it
we flew—three, four, five, or six times, as horsemen do at
the Caledonian Amphitheatre; for the animal had got
blind with terror, and kept viciously reasoning in a circle.
What a show of faces at all the windows then! A shriek
still accompanied us as we clattered, and thundered, and
lightened along; and, unless our ears lied, there were occasional fits of stifled laughter, and once or twice a guf-
faw; for there was now a ringing of lost stirrups, and
much holding of the mane. One complete round was executed by us, first on the shoulder beyond the pommel;

142

secondly, on the neck; thirdly, between the ears; fourthly, between the forelegs, in a place called the counter, with our arms round the jugular veins of the flying phenomenon, and our toes in the air. That was, indeed, the crisis of our fever, but we made a wonderful recovery back into the saddle, righting like a boat capsized in a sudden squall at sea, and once more, with accelerated speed, away past the pillared front of St. George's Church!

The Castle and all its rocks, in peristrephic panorama, then floated cloudlike by—and we saw the whole mile-length of Prince's-Street stretched before us; studded with innumerable coaches, chaises, chariots, carts, waggons, drays, gigs, shandrydans, and wheel-barrows, through among which we dashed, as if they had been as much gingerbread, while men on horseback were seen flinging themselves off, and drivers dismounting in all directions, making their escape up flights of steps and common stairs—mothers or nurses with broods of young children flying hither and thither in distraction, or standing on the very crown of the causeway, wringing their hands in despair. The wheel-barrows were easily disposed of, nor was there much greater difficulty with the gigs and shandrydans. But the hackney-coaches stood confoundedly in the way—and a waggon, drawn by four horses, and heaped up to the very sky with beer-barrels, like the Tower of Babel or Babylon, did indeed give us pause—but ere we had leisure to ruminate on the shortness of human life, we broke through between the leaders and the wheels with a crash of leathern breeching, dismounted collars, riven harness, and tumbling of enormous horses that was perilous to hear; when, as Sin and Satan would have it—would you believe it, there, twenty kilts deep at the least, was the same accursed Highland regiment, the Forty-second, with fixed bayonets, and all its pipers in the van, the pibroch yelling, squeaking, squeal-

ing, grunting, growling, roaring, as if it had only that
very instant broken out; so, suddenly to the right-about
went the bag-pipe-haunted mare, and away up the
Mound, past the pictures of Irish Giants, Female Dwarfs,
Albinos, an Elephant indorsed with towers, Tigers and
Lions of all sorts, and a large wooden building, like a
pyramid, in which there was a thundering of cannon—for
the battle, we rather think, of Camperdown was going
on—the Bank of Scotland seemed to sink into the North-
Loch—one gleam through the window of the eyes of the
Director-General—and to be sure how we did make the
street-stalls of the Lawn-market spin! The man in St.
Giles's steeple was playing his One o'Clock Tune on the
bells, heedless in that elevation of our career—in less
than no time John Knox, preaching from a house half-
way down the Canongate, gave us the go-by—and down
through one long wide sprawl of men, women, and children, we wheeled past the Gothic front, and round the
south angle of Holyrood, and across the King's Park,
where wan and withered sporting debtors held up their
hands, and cried, Hurra, hurra—hurra—without stop or
stay, up the rocky way that leads to St. Anthony's Well
and Chapel—and now it was manifest that we were
bound for the summit of Arthur's Seat. We hope that we
were sufficiently thankful that a direction was not taken
towards Salisbury Crags, where we should have been
dashed into many million pieces,—in which case this
Magazine "must have slept in uncreated dust." Free now
from even the slightest suburban impediment, obstacle,
or interruption, we began to eye our gradually rising situation in life—and looking over our shoulder, the sight
of city and sea was indeed magnificent. There in the distance rose North Berwick Law—but though we have
plenty of time now for description, we had scant time
then for beholding perhaps the noblest scenery in Scotland. Up with us—up with us into the clouds—and just

144

as St. Giles's bells ceased to jingle, and both girths broke, we crowned the summit, and sat on horseback like King Arthur himself, eight hundred feet above the level of the sea!*

ATTRIBUTION

This is certainly De Quincey's. The anecdote about Wordsworth and the buttered toast (p. 138) is also told by De Quincey in "William Wordsworth and Robert Southey" (1839), M., II, 314-15. In both instances the author hears the story before he has met Wordsworth, is eager to gain first-hand information about the great man and is, of course, baffled by the anticlimax. In both instances the evidence of the London tourist, from Mackenzie's *Mirror*, is cited in the footnote. There are also verbal identities.

The date of the experience given here in the *Post*, twenty-one years ago, would be 1806; Hartley is said to have been nine years old at the time and that would be 1805-06; the article of 1839 gives the year as 1805 and says it was probably a year before he met Wordsworth; in fact it must have been 1807, because that was the year he met the Coleridges and traveled with Mrs. Coleridge, Hartley, and two other young Coleridges to his first meeting with Wordsworth.

A more important difference is the difference in tone in the two tellings of the story. Here it is light and amusing; in 1839 there is an animus: the anecdote confirms the commonplace quality of Wordsworth; De Quincey's in-

---

* It is right to mention, that our mare had, a few weeks before, (ridden by Colonel Leigh, then in the Castle) performed a match against time, (we forget the number of minutes,) from the drawbridge of the esplanade to the summit of Arthur's Seat. As her confusion subsided, she naturally enough conceived that she was engaged in doing the match over again—and the fact, therefore independently of its merits as a mere sporting achievement, is valuable also as a "psychological curiosity," in the philosophy of the Horse.

formant is not young Hartley but an unidentified gentleman who is a "donkey." The 1839 version is altogether
heavier and less pleasant. The changes in De Quincey's
relations with Wordsworth and his circle are traced in
detail by John E. Jordan, *De Quincey to Wordsworth*
(Berkeley, 1962); the material in the *Post* adds a bit to
that story. It was in the *Post* that De Quincey began to
exploit his friendship with Wordsworth, but in a friendly
way. Here he is friendly to Hartley, too, both in the
present anecdote and in the remarks on his writing (pp.
99-100 above). When De Quincey began writing about
Coleridge (1834), Hartley was angered and was egged
on by Southey (Jordan, p. 336). He was further infuri-
ated by the articles on the Wordsworths (Charles Mac-
Farlane, *Reminiscences of a Literary Life* [New York,
1917], pp. 81-82); the reference to himself as a donkey
could not have helped.

The author of this review has also an acquaintance
with the writings of Wordsworth and Coleridge. He remembers a line from a minor poem like "The Farmer of
Tilsbury Vale," and even the confusion with "Poor
Susan" is further evidence of that acquaintance (p. 137).
When he reads a brief discussion of the language of
poetry as distinct from prose, he thinks immediately of
Wordsworth's Preface, as the place where the question of
"poetic diction" was first raised, and of Coleridge's reply
in the *Biographia*; neither the names nor the term appears in the article in *Blackwood's*, which refers only to
"some discussion" of late. In an early paper De Quincey
defended Wordsworth, on the diction of poetry, against
Coleridge (*Posthumous Works*, ed. Alexander H. Japp
[1893], II, 210, and see also 205-06); in a late paper he
criticized him ("On Wordsworth's Poetry" [1845], M.,
XI, 296-300).

The author would seem to have known Lamb, too. To
begin with, the allusion to the second paragraph of

"Witches, and Other Night-Fears" (p. 137) is evidence
of De Quincey's authorship. He alludes to the same passage in "Modern Superstition" (1840), M., VIII, 444;
and, as here, there is a combination of witch and moon,
a "constable," and the witches' fear of the constable,
though none of these are in Lamb: Lamb's point is that
no simple Justice of the Peace seems to have scrupled in
issuing a warrant against those hags in league with
Satan. The reference to Lord Thurlow's fine sonnet (p.
139) is perhaps evidence of personal acquaintance with
Lamb. The poem was obscure, the reference to it here is
not too pertinent, and neither it nor its author seems to
have been much praised: on the contrary, the poet was
ridiculed. But the poem was, as De Quincey tells us, a
favorite with Lamb: Lamb delighted to read it to friends,
as well because of its beauty as because it was written
by one who had been unworthily treated, and so far
resembled himself; De Quincey, who knew nothing else
of Thurlow's work, agreed that the sonnet was most
beautiful ("Recollections of Charles Lamb" [1838], M.,
III, 81, 84). In his second essay on Lamb (1848), De
Quincey tells again how Lamb read the very beautiful
sonnet to him and says of himself that he could almost
repeat it verbatim, twenty-seven years afterwards (M.,
V, 254). Lamb had quoted the sonnet in a footnote to
his essay on Sir Philip Sidney in the *London Magazine*
(September 1823), when he and De Quincey were fellow-contributors. For other evidence of Lamb's enthusiasm for the poem see E. V. Lucas' edition of Lamb's
Works (1903-05), II, 438-39, and his biography of Lamb
(1905), II, 296; also George L. Barnett, *Charles Lamb*
(Bloomington, 1964), p. 248.

The acquaintance with the works of Richter also points
to De Quincey. The anglicizing of Jean Paul (pp. 133,
140) is an excellent indicator; see p. 55 above. The
work referred to on p. 133 may be the second "Blumen-

stück" of *Blumen- Frucht- und Dornenstücke*. It may be, however, the selection translated by De Quincey as "Dream upon the Universe," in the *London Magazine* of 1824 (M., XI, 290-93), where, within a dream the dreamer has a further revelation of depth upon depth; in "System of the Heavens" (1846), De Quincey returned to Richter's dream-vision and there, as here, criticized its partial lack of success (M., VIII, 33 and n.).

On Brougham's unmanageable temper (p. 129) see November 24, 1827 (pp. 201-203), in another article certainly written by De Quincey; also De Quincey's article "The Present Cabinet in Relation to the Times," *Blackwood's*, XXIX (1831), 148, where he talks of Brougham's "natural infirmity of overmastering violence of temper." Brougham's Westmorland and Scottish origin would be well known to De Quincey (cf. November 24, p. 199). Brougham's attempt to magnify his Westmorland connection had annoyed De Quincey in 1818 (Jordan, *De Quincey to Wordsworth*, pp. 321-22); but he knew, when he edited the *Westmorland Gazette* (January 2, 1819, p. 3) that Brougham's station in Westmorland was "respectable," though not more so than that occupied by the editor's family in their part of England.

Among the odds and ends, "bonne bouche" (p. 139) is used a few times by De Quincey: M., V, 329; *Hogg's Instructor*, XIV (1852), 273; a letter of September 1824 (Axon, *Library*, N. S., VIII [1907], 268), where, as here, the reference is to the concluding article in a magazine. And it was a draft upon Smith, Payne, and Smith (p. 136) that De Quincey received, fatefully, in the revised *Confessions* (M., III, 286, 309).

October 6, 1827

Waste Lands and Emigration

We are grieved to see the amount of ignorance which still prevails on the plainest topics of Political Economy. The *Morning Herald* has for years been the depositary of speculations in this department, opposed to the elementary principles of the science; and opposed, not in any spirit of perverse ingenuity, but of downright illiterate ignorance. Of late, it has been advocating the old plan of waste land improvement, against the new one of emigration defrayed by Government. And on Monday last, this paper took occasion, from the Emigration Report, to return to the old theme of its ignorant declamation.[1] From the year 1815, in which Sir Edward West discovered the law of rent,[2] its application to the question of waste lands has been too obvious to leave any room for dispute amongst those who are acquainted with that law. To meet every revival of exploded errors with the refutations due only to those which are very plausible, or very original, is too much to expect. Yet, as we observe the enlightened *Standard*,[3] in this instance, adopting the ignorance of the *Herald*, we shall just remind any reader, who may find himself at a loss on this question, of a few old truths (as, fortunately, they may now be called,) thrown into a dilemma shaped to meet this particular version of obsolete follies.

[1] *Morning Herald*, October 1, p. 2. The Emigration Report was the Third Parliamentary Report on Emigration, written by Robert John Wilmot-Horton, vice-president of the Board of Trade. The report recommended loans for emigration, to solve the problem of "redundancy of population." The *Herald* wanted the loans to be made to enable the "surplus poor" to cultivate waste lands at home.

[2] In his *Essay on the Application of Capital to Land*.

[3] *Standard*, October 2, p. 2, and other relevant leaders on October 1, 4, and 5, all on p. 2.

The waste lands may be cultivated either at an equal cost with that already in use, or at a greater. If at an equal, undoubtedly there is no objection; and the only task which remains for the writer is, to explain how it can have happened that this land has hitherto been neglected. If at a greater, then all the consequences take place which are so well known to those who are acquainted with the doctrine of rent: land, which is now last in the scale, will then become last but one, or (to express it in one word,) the penultimate land; rent immediately commences upon this land, and a series of additions to the rent upon all higher qualities, which will permanently establish a higher price upon the produce of *every* quality of land, rob us therefore, virtually, *pro tanto*, of the natural fertility upon the best soils, and inflict the greatest curse upon this nation which it is in the power of ignorance to devise.

But possibly the argument of the *Standard* is simply this: that, supposing land to require draining, for instance, but *being* drained to have the same advantages as other land now in use, then the *extra* expense will be confined to the first outlay; which expense may fairly be balanced against the proposed national expense of emigration. To this the answer is obvious. If the *extra* expense will not raise it after all above the lowest quality of land now in cultivation, then there is a loss by the whole amount of this expense, and the former argument takes place. If, on the other hand, the *extra* expense will do more than this, how happens it, with the excess of capital in this country seeking employment at the lowest rate of profit, that such a measure should await the suggestions of the *Herald* or the *Standard*? Land there may be, under the circumstances here supposed; but such land must form a very small proportion of the lands about which the question was raised—viz. the waste lands in general of Great Britain and Ireland.

With respect to the comparison between absolute loss on the emigration scheme, and the other absolute loss on the waste-land scheme, the main difference is overlooked by the *Standard*, viz. that the first is a national subscription or tax for that one year in which it is paid, and no more: the other is a permanent tax—and upon that commodity which, in this country, will least bear to be taxed.

Finally, we will trouble the *Herald* and the *Standard* with one little question, which really is of some importance:—to meet the new supply created by (suppose, we say,) six millions of acres added to our present productive powers, there must of course be a new demand in the same proportion; from what quarter is it proposed that this demand should arise? From the *Herald* office, or the *Standard* office?

Heavens! that men cannot be content to apply their talents to those subjects with which their studies and researches have fitted them to deal!

October 13, 1827

Emigration Report

[a continuation of the preceding]

Though pretty firm in our opinions, we are not obstinate
in the manner of defending them; and can cheerfully
submit to be found in the wrong, as well when we are so,
(which we remember to have happened once or twice
in our lives,) as when most undeniably we are not. It is,
therefore, with no sort of ambition for the 'last word'
that we make our rejoinder to an article in the *Standard*,
of Tuesday last, on the emigration-scheme, as compared
with the waste-land improvement scheme. In this article,
the *Standard* replies to the comments we took the liberty
of making last week, on the opinions with regard to that
question, avowed by itself and other journals; and describes us, though certainly in obliging terms, as "imposed upon by a delusion."[1] On a matter of pure political
economy, we know not that it would be becoming in us,
who are veteran economists, to decline the attack of one
who resolutely defies the science, and all its lofty pretensions. But this consideration singly, perhaps, might
have failed to warrant us in prolonging the discussion,
had we not perceived some misconception of our meaning
on the part of the *Standard*; and misconceptions, it is
always pleasant, and, at the same time, easy to remove.

I. The *Standard* seems to suppose us friendly to the
emigration-scheme of the Report. We are not. Our purpose was not at all to plead *for* the emigration-scheme,
which is liable to weighty objections, but *against* the
waste-land scheme: by others, these two schemes had
been contradistinguished in point of policy; but not by

[1] *Standard*, October 9, p. 2: "we feel that a delusion which im-
poses upon a mind as acute as his, may easily enough succeed with
the vulgar, and therefore that it ought to be dispelled at once."

us, who place them in the same category of false measures—though, in our apprehension, not equally false.

II. Even the Report itself seems to be misconceived by
the *Standard*, with regard to the nature and limitations
of the emigration proposed. Apparently, by the *Standard*,
this proposal is understood as a plan of redressing, generally, the evil of a redundant population. If this were
so, the Committee must have been in a midsummer
madness:[2] and really, with all the extravagant illogicalities of Mr. Malthus, we can hardly suppose him to go
this length in self-contradiction.[3] For no man has dwelt
more on the tendency of all abrupt and violent depopu-
lations, (as by war, by pestilence, by famine, and, therefore, by emigrations,) to stimulate population in the
opposite direction; and as the reaction (according to
him) always exceeds the antagonist force which calls it
out, manifestly the proposed remedy of emigration would
have to go on, not only *ad infinitum*, but also against a
resistance continually growing in magnitude,—and growing (which is worse) by means of the remedy itself.
Certainly Mr. Malthus has written himself down the
worst logician extant in his "Principles of Political Economy;" but such sublime blundering as this, we must have
leave to doubt even in a Malthus, unless backed by an
affadavit before three justices of the peace. As *we* understand this Third Report, the emigration-scheme is shaped
to meet the evil of an excess in one particular part of
the Irish rural population, not an absolute excess, but
an excess relatively to the estates on which it is settled.
Every body has heard of the *Squatters*, as they are
called, who form the advanced guard, or pioneers, of
American civilization. They are a sort of sturdy beggars,
who cannot be reached by the Yankee Chancery, and

[2] *Twelfth Night*, III, iv, 62.
[3] Malthus had been questioned by the parliamentary committee
and had favored emigration.

will hear no reason except from a field-piece. Equally restive, but much more mischievous to the national progress, and the rights of the land-proprietors, are the Irish Squatters, on innumerable estates, who draw from the soil a most miserable subsistence for themselves, and, with respect to the landlord, are a mere nuisance, and the sole insurmountable bar to those improvements of estates, which the advanced state of Ireland would now make possible. The very same state of things grew up in the Scotch Highlands, after the extinction of the Rebellion in 1745. The numerous tenantries, who could no longer be used as feudal retainers, were now felt as a burthen on the land. That same estate which had hitherto carried fifty head of human beings, necessarily consuming upon themselves the whole produce of the soil might, when thrown into a sheep-farm, not require more than one family of five persons, who left a surplus equal to the consumption of the 45 supernumeraries, as a rent to the landlord. These Gaelic squatters, accordingly, were gradually dislodged; and, as many will remember, were making loud outcries at the beginning of the present century: Some of them the late Lord Selkirk carried off to Prince Edward Island, in the Gulf of St. Lawrence;—(see his very sensible book on that subject,) [4]—others went to the Canadas; others to Nova Scotia; others to the United States; and they are now pretty generally squatting upon lands of their own. This same happy consummation it is the object of the Report to secure by national bounty for the Irish squatters: emigration is recommended as a more feasible mode of ejectment, pleasant to the squatter, and safe to the rest

[4] Thomas Douglas, fifth Earl of Selkirk, who carried out successful emigration of highlanders in 1803. His book is *Observations on the Present State of the Highlands of Scotland, with a View of the Causes and Probable Consequences of Emigration* (1805); it is given favorable notice in the Postscript to *Waverley*.

154

of the community. For it is well known that ejectment unqualified, in its naked legal shape, is sure to drive the Irish squatter into insurrection, and every other mode— public and secret—of desperate revenge. Under the limitation here explained, the Committee seem to talk reasonably in recommending emigration. But why at the national expense? This is what we cannot understand. To eject nineteen thousand families of squatters, or ninety-five thousand individual squatters, is well: but why must we purchase this benefit at the rate of £.12 per squatter, from the public purse, or £.60 per family of squatters? The profit will be private: why not the cost? And, above all, why must England and Scotland subscribe to this expense of eleven hundred and forty thousand pounds, and subscribe by far the greatest share? For, as to the repayment anticipated by the Committee, *that* is quite an Irish calculation.

III. If we are right in this way of reading the drift of the report (which is justified by the examination we have hitherto made,) we easily reconcile ourselves with the *Standard* upon a point where else we seem to be in utter contradiction. Comparing the expense on the emigration-scheme with the other on the waste-land scheme, we had said "that the first is a national subscription or tax for that one year in which it is paid, and no more: the other is a permanent tax—and upon that commodity which, in this country, will least bear to be taxed." To which the *Standard* replies bluntly—"The reverse of what is here stated is the truth. Land, once well reclaimed, *is reclaimed for ever.* While money expended upon emigration is so far from obviating the necessity for a future similar expenditure, that it actually stimulates the increase of population." True. And that, which *we* said, is also true. The moment we understand each other, our difference disappears. The *Standard* speaks of an emigration continually renewed, in order to meet a continual growth of redundant population: we speak of one single emigration, between this and 1831, once for all to eject 95 thousand squatters. Then, as to the other case of the waste-land, we were assuming the land *when* reclaimed to be of worse quality than any now under cultivation; in which case, as the lowest quality of land fixes the price for the whole (since there can be but one price at one time, and that price must be such as to enable the *worst* circumstanced to be brought to market,) it would follow, agreeably to our assertion, that the reclaiming of this worst soil would *permanently* raise the price of corn. On the other hand, arguing (*as the Standard does*) from the opposite assumption, viz. that the land, when reclaimed, might be superior in quality, we shall come to the opposite inference; and the only question is about the probability of this assumption: and, undoubtedly, the *Standard* offers a very colourable reason why an Irish bog of 100 or 150 miles long, may have remained hitherto unreclaimed in spite of superior natural capacities—viz. the impossibility, in default of government interference, that any "combined effort" should take place in so great a division of property. Whether this probability ought also to be received as a fact, is more than we can say: the *Standard*, who has the best information upon Irish affairs, is likely to know far better than ourselves. The fact, however, *if* a fact, is certainly one which the writers on the doctrine of rent are apt to omit in their list of cases; and, on their account, we shall take a note of the *Standard's* hypothesis. But we must add, that once let this hypothetic case be established as a real one, and the reasoning, which we and every other political economist would build upon it, is precisely that of the *Standard*: and the *Standard* must not flatter himself, in this instance, that he is at war with Mr. Ricardo.

IV. In answering our final question, however, the

Standard has that good fortune. Here we do not disguise from ourselves, that the difference between us is substantial. Anticipating the great increase of produce which must accrue from any great addition to the land now in use, we required to know how this produce was to be disposed of? For a new supply so enormous, whence was to come the proportionate new demand? Who shall be the purchasers?—"We answer this question," says the *Standard,* "we answer it readily—*the occupants.*" And we, on our parts, expected this answer; but it will not do. To say of any land, that its whole produce is consumed by the occupant—is to describe a worse quality of land than any which has been, or could be cultivated in a civilized state. Even in the most abject condition of society, part of the produce, (say x,) must be reserved as a fund for purchasing manufactured articles, as clothes, tools, furniture, &c.; where is the new demand for x? The labourer wants the manufactures, but the manufacturer does not want x; for, no case has been made out to show that x was previously deficient. Next, because the labourer on this reclaimed land cannot be better off than the labourer on the old, (the law of competition will prevent *that*,) he must reserve another part (y) of the produce, to pay the profits of the capital which reclaims it: where is the new demand for y? He will be glad to pay with y; but the capitalist will have no motive for taking what is in no demand. Lastly, because much of the land (as in the Irish bogs for example) is, by the supposition, not the worst under cultivation, then, upon this land, there will arise rent; to meet which, another part of the produce (z) must be set aside: where is the new demand for z?

V. *Finally*, in what follows, we cannot suppose the *Standard* itself to be the dupe of its own statement. "If those who now go naked were to wear clothes—would not *that* create a demand for manufactures?" Doubtless:

but what fund is to enable the naked to wear clothes? Wages, perhaps? But the rationale of all wages is this— that, out of what the labourer produces for others, part (or its equivalent) is deducted as a remuneration for himself: now, if there are no 'others' demanding the products of his labour, which is exactly what the *Standard* acknowledges, in representing the 'occupant' of the soil as the sole demander of its products, where is the fund out of which wages are to come? The labourer's own demand cannot, even in Babel, be the fund out of which his own wages are to be deducted.

Again, "What is the meaning of the cry against the corn laws, if a new supply of corn is a thing to be dreaded?" Answer, A new supply of corn, that is not wanted, is to be dreaded only by the growers of the corn. By the consumer, it is *not* dreaded, except in so far as every fresh growth of corn throws us, or tends to throw us, upon the inferior qualities of soil; and the evils of *that* are exactly these two, which should seem intelligible enough; that, this new supply, if grown on worse soils, must itself cost more. Secondly, that, by a necessary consequence, it raises all other corn, even of the best soils, to the same level; all the differences of cost passing into rent, according to the well-known law on that head.

ATTRIBUTION

These two articles, both by the same man, seem very probably to be De Quincey's. For one thing, both of them deal with the "doctrine of rent"; see the article of September 15, pp. 118-19 above, and the further references given there. One of these references, the essay on the "Hints Towards an Appreciation," applies the doctrine to the particular question of cultivating waste lands, with the same result; another, the "Dilemmas on the Corn Law Question," uses the expression "penultimate land," used here (p. 150). The use of the argument thrown into a dilemma, in the same passage, is again characteristic of De Quincey; see the article of September 15 (pp. 120-21 above) for references, and they include some of his essays cited elsewhere in the present note. On Sir Edward West as the discoverer of the law of rent, also in the same passage, see De Quincey's "Ricardo and Adam Smith," *Blackwood's*, LII (1842), 349-50, his *Logic of Political Economy* (1844), M., IX, 237n., and the manuscript essay on "The Corn Laws" in the Berg collection of the New York Public Library, p. 13; also the article of November 10, p. 173 below.

On the extravagant illogicalities of Malthus, who has written himself down the worst logician extant in his *Principles of Political Economy* (p. 153), see De Quincey's "Malthus on Population" (1823), M., IX, 14-16, 28-29, where he points to the "greatest logical oversight" that has ever escaped any author of respectability; his "Malthus on the Measure of Value" (1823), M., IX, 32-36, on the "illogical structure" of Malthus' understanding; his "Dialogues of Three Templars" (1824), M., IX, 47, where it is impossible to conceive any person below Malthus in logic, and again on IX, 68, where Malthus is "eminently illogical"; his *Logic of Political Economy*, M., IX, 292, on Malthus' "clouded logic."

The reference to the "antagonist force" in the passage on Malthus is most characteristic; see the article of September 15, p. 120 above, and the further references there.

Other signs of De Quincey's ways of expressing himself include the use of algebraic symbols, x, y, etc. (p. 157); they turn up on more than a dozen occasions in his writings, before and after this date, in his essays on political economy and in other essays cited elsewhere in this note. The question-answer form (p. 158) has been noted above (p. 121). The facetious use of the affidavit (p. 153) is in the revised *Confessions* (M., III, 307) in almost the same words: "affadavit made before two justices of the peace"; cf. also the article of January 5, 1828, p. 253 n. †, below.

Lord Selkirk's book and the emigration of Highlanders to Prince Edward Island in the Gulf of St. Lawrence after the rebellion of 1745 (p. 154) are also in De Quincey's "Tory's Account," etc. (1835), M., IX, 322-23n.; see too "M'Gregor's British America," *Blackwood's*, XXXI (1832), 920. In 1809 De Quincey had sent Wordsworth another of Selkirk's publications; Jordan, *De Quincey to Wordsworth*, pp. 190, 201, 356. "Squatters," in the same passage on p. 154 appear in De Quincey's "Dourranee Empire," *Blackwood's* XLIX (1841), 301, and "Milton *versus* Southey and Landor" (1847), M., XI, 457.

Among phrases, "midsummer madness" (p. 153), from *Twelfth Night*, may also be a sign of De Quincey; he uses it in the "Letters to a Young Man" (1823), M., X, 40, in "Sir Robert Peel's Position on Next Resuming Power," *Blackwood's*, L (1841), 399, in "Affghanistan," *Blackwood's*, LVI (1844), 149 and in "Notes on Gilfillan's Literary Portraits" (1845-46), M., XI, 359, 389; see also the article of February 9, 1828 (p. 305 below). *Pro tanto* (p. 150), though it can't prove much, he does use several times in the *Logic of Political Economy* and also in other economic contexts when, as here, he is discussing movements in price and quality; and he uses it in a variety of contexts, fifteen to twenty times.

October 20, 1827

Disciples of Mr. Malthus

Accident has driven us of late to the necessity of too
often differing with the *Standard*, whose politics, however, (as separated from Political Economy,) are, at all
points, our own politics. On this account we shall, for
the present, notice only that opinion of the *Standard*, on
the newest versions of Malthusianism, which commands
our unqualified assent, omitting those which do not.
There never was a conceit more entirely worthy of Laputa, or more ripe to be bottled up for the Limbo of
Vanity, than the scheme of Mr. Malthus for checking
population by appealing to the prudential feelings of
ploughmen and the lowest artizans, in charges to be delivered *at the altar*, on the impropriety of lowering wages
by contracting early marriages. Addressed to the species,
such dehortations might have a show of sense; practical
effect they could have none. But as to the individual of a
vast nation, whose single act of self-denial must perish
and be confounded in the mighty tendencies of the whole
community, no less utterly than a bucket of water in the
tides of the Atlantic, he would laugh at such insanities as
heartily, if he were a philosopher, as he will inevitably
laugh, being what he is, Hodge the clod-hopper, or Dick
the scavenger. The ridicule of this proposal has been felt
by the later Malthusians; and some of them have suggested other remedies for redundant populations. Mr.
Godwin's is now forgotten;[1] but there have been others

[1] Godwin had listed, among the various methods by which population may be checked, exposure of children, abortion, promiscuous
intercourse ("which is found extremely hostile to the multiplica-
tion of the species") and systematical abstinence; but he was not
advocating any of these, or any express institution, feeling that
the same intelligence that could bring about the improvement of
the state of man could find remedies to over-population if that

161

even more unutterable to Christian ears. To these the *Standard* has twice alluded of late with energetic and becoming abhorrence.[2] The particular parties, at whom the indignation of this journal is pointed, are not mentioned: and some readers may suppose the whole to be a fiction of an anti-Malthusian. Such persons we would advise to inquire amongst the *camarilla* of the Westminster (or, as it used to be called in allusion to Mr. Place, the *breeches*) Review.[3] More particularly we refer them to the last edition of Mr. Mill's Political Economy, where there is a cryptical passage on this subject, which may exercise their talents at decyphering one of those riddles, which, if clearly expressed, might chance to be obnoxious to the criticism of Bow Street. No reader, whom we have consulted, has found it possible to explain the passage but in one way; and, supposing that interpretation to be just, we can only say that the author of such a suggestion should be sent to graze amongst the beasts of the field. We cannot contaminate our pages by speaking out, in plain English; but, if it should be called for, we shall briefly explain our allusion in Latin.[4]

---

ever became a real problem (*Enquiry concerning Political Justice,* VIII, vii in the 1793 edition, VIII, ix in 1798).

[2] *Standard*, October 8, p. 2, October 16, p. 2.

[3] Francis Place, the radical and Benthamite, started life as a leather-breeches maker; he wrote for the Benthamite *Westminster Review*, though he was not a major contributor to it nor was it a major part of his activity. He is relevant here, with his breeches, because he was an advocate of birth control.

[4] The reference is probably to this passage in James Mill's *Elements of Political Economy* (II, ii, 4): "The result to be aimed at is, to secure to the great body of the people all the happiness which is capable of being derived from the matrimonial union, without the evils which a too rapid increase of their numbers involves. The progress of legislation, the improvement of the education of the people, and the decay of superstition, will, in time, it may be hoped, accomplish the difficult task of reconciling these important objects." But the same passage is in the first edition (1821) and the "last" (the third, 1826).

This one is included because it is part of the series on political economy and redundant population and agreements and disagreements with the *Standard*: De Quincey was certainly the author of the others in the series and so was probably also the author of this.

The only other signs of his authorship are commonplaces: the use of *camarilla*, which is also in the Bodleian MS. (p. 352 below) and a couple of other places in De Quincey; the allusion to Laputa, which is a special favorite with De Quincey, who uses it eight times; cf. p. 276 below.

Quarterly Review, No. 72, and the Standard Newspaper—on the Doctrine of Rent

There is an old saying—that, "between the cradle and the grave, a man must eat a peck of dirt." And a story is told of the last Lord Grosvenor[1] (perhaps of a thousand others) that, being urged with the authority of this proverb by an inn-keeper, as a reason for submitting quietly to some very uncleanly accommodations, he replied—"True, Mr. Boniface,—what you say is just; and I admit the necessity you speak of: but what I object to—is the eating my whole peck at once. For that, I think, you have no proverb." We also, who spend our lives in communicating between the writing public and the reading public, are aware of the necessity that, in the course of our ministrations for 20 years,[2] we should read a boat-load of ignorance—and some of presumptuous ignorance. But we anticipated no necessity for reading our whole boat-load in one season. However, *Diis aliter visum est*:[3] Jove in his anger, and the host of paralogicians, who style themselves Anti-economists, have decreed, that not a journal shall appear, literary or political, (unless expressly conducted by a sound economist) which does not teem with attacks upon the reformed doctrines of Political Economy—and issuing from those who, if put upon the rack, could not state any one of those doctrines in terms which would be endured by men who understand them. The first duty of a disputant is to make himself master of what it is that his antagonist says: and, therefore, in the old discipline of the logical

[1] Richard Grosvenor, first Earl Grosvenor, who had died in 1802.

[2] Beginning, presumably, with his contributions to Wordsworth's *Convention of Cintra*.

[3] *Aeneid*, II, 428, adapted: it was seen (i.e., fated) differently by the gods.

schools, it was wisely provided that the opponent should repeat every proposition of the respondent before he presumed to contradict it. Well would it be, if such a law prevailed at present: since, in every instance, the opposition would be stifled in its birth by a loud outcry from the Ricardians—*That* is not Mr. Ricardo's proposition.

Two prominent illustrations of what we are saying, amongst scores of others less noticeable, are forced upon us in the present week: we shall briefly notice both.

First comes the *Standard,* (Oct. 20,) and quotes "the prodigious paradox of a Scotch newspaper—*the more corn, the dearer*—as a reason for not answering it."[4] That is to say, in the view of the *Standard,* this proposition deserved no answer, being self-refuted. A paradox, by the way, is not necessarily untrue. But, waiving *that,* how sublime must be the ignorance of the *Standard* on the new doctrine of rent, when he can fancy that this proposition is something new and startling—some audacious *bravura* of extravagance peculiar to an individual Scotch newspaper, whereas, in the sense in which it could ever have been uttered, it is adopted of necessity by *every* man who adopts the new doctrine of rent—being in fact an inevitable and immediate corollary from that doctrine. But the secret of the matter is this—the *Standard* is so entire a novice in these matters, that it has not yet learned to distinguish between *market* price and *natural* price. Hence its denunciation of a paradox in what will appear to be the simplest of truths, though a very important one, the moment it is explained. Listen, *Standard*!

Given the quantity of land cultivated, no man says that the more its produce the higher its price. On the contrary, all people that on earth do dwell—Rics, and

[4] *Standard,* October 20, p. 2; see also October 17, p. 2.

anti-Rics—with one voice, agree, that the more its produce the cheaper. Again:

Given the quality of land under cultivation, assuming (that is to say,) that, in extending the quantity of the land, you shall not be obliged to have recourse to a worse quality of land, (land that will require a greater expense,) no man says that *the more corn the dearer.* On the contrary, all men agree, that *the more corn the cheaper.* The Scotch newspaper, whatever be its name, will, in this point, assuredly agree with the *Standard.*

But then, my *Standard!* whom we would willingly inoculate with the first elements of economy, this cheapness is cheapness of *market* price—*i.e.* cheapness arising out of quantity in relation to demand: the supply is supposed to increase, without any condition in the hypothesis that the demand is to increase in proportion: and such cheapness is good only for the buyer, but ruinous (if it were to continue,) to the seller.

Now the dearness, spoken of in the paradox, is dearness of *natural* price; dearness arising out of increased cost. The case supposed is this—that, in order to extend cultivation, we are obliged to descend upon inferior soils. Now, inferior soils, *vi termini,* mean soils which cost more to make them yield the same produce; else, in what sense *are* they inferior? If, therefore, they cost more, the produce must sell for more. And, because there can be but one price of equal corn in the same market, the produce of the worst soil regulates the price of the whole; which is, in other words, saying, that the produce of the best soil becomes dearer in consequence of an additional quantity raised from inferior soils. And this, we take it, is the very paradox in question: the more you increase the quantity of corn, the dearer it shall become.

For example: we grow corn for 3d.: in order to increase it, we are forced upon soils which will not produce the same corn (quality and quantity) for less than 4d. What follows? Even the three-penny corn will now rise to 4d.; and the consequence of adding to the quantity of corn is, that we pay, *universally*, a penny more: for there cannot be two prices. What becomes of the penny? Answer: It constitutes rent.

Here then is a big, thrasonic, attack upon Mr. Ricardo, which turns out to be a pure tyro's confusion between *market* and *natural* price: and yet this distinction is quite as essential to Adam Smith as to David Ricardo; and in fact no coherent thinking, on *any* system of economy, can go on without it.

*

Next comes the *Quarterly Review*, infamous for its dotage in Political Economy, even more than it is celebrated for the excellence of its geographical articles. In an article of 46 pp., entitled *Agriculture and Rent*, it undertakes roundly to *settle Mr. Ricardo's hash*. We borrow from the vulgar dialect, in speaking of a vulgar and most ignorant writer.—The index of the *Quarterly Review* is an important part of that journal; for by means of this index, it was once convicted of a libel.[5] This index, therefore let us consult for an analysis of this pretty piece of Anti-Ricardianism.

"Rents and prices, remarks on certain modern theories respecting, 391.—Examination of the opinion of some theorists, that no rent can accrue from land, so long as the best soils only are cultivated, 406-408.—*Proofs, that the whole of such theory is a delusion, &c.*"

Quid dignum tanto feret hic promissor hiatu?[6]

[5] *Quarterly Review*, October 1827. The *Quarterly's* excellent geographical articles were written by John Barrow, as De Quincey knew; see *Walladmor* (1825), I, xiii. The author of the article on agriculture and rent in this issue was the Rev. Edward Edwards; for this information I am indebted to the kindness of Sir John Murray. I do not know the incident in which the *Quarterly* was convicted of a libel because of its index.

[6] Horace, *Ars Poetica*, l. 138: what will this boaster bring forth

This week our limits forbid us to proceed.—Meantime we shall anticipate so much as to give our readers the key to these 46 pages of conceited Anti-Ricardianism. The whole hinges upon a confusion between profit and rent; not, understand us, ingeniously imbroiled or mystified, but so used as to shew that the writer never heard of a distinction between them. With the uttermost self-complacency he is shewing us how *rent* will arise; and, in fact, is all the while shewing how *profit* will arise. The words, "it is evident," "it is quite evident," "it is self-evident," are glittering in every page, and there chiefly where his own confusion and self-distrust, in the midst of his vapouring, are most apparent. And this writer, who should be ordered back to school, is to step forward as a master in Israel! A champion is to be paraded against David Ricardo, who has not yet learned the difference between the functions and the laws, and the definitions of rent and of profit!!—But scorn and just disdain close our mouths.

---

that is worthy of such a big mouth? (The next line is the one about the mountains laboring for the birth of the absurd mouse.)

November 10, 1827

Political Economy
The Standard and the
Edinburgh Saturday Post

[a continuation of the preceding]

On Saturday, October 27, we published an article, reflecting on the Political Economy of the *Standard,* and the *Quarterly Review, No.* 72. Last Sat., Nov. 3, the *Standard* does us the honour to publish something, by way of reply.[1] "We are not the men" say they, "to turn our backs upon any challenger;" and they "are not quite sure whether, after the severe turn-ups they have had with Whigs and apostates during the summer, they should not rather like a little light play with a Tory antagonist." We are glad to hear this, because it would vex us to do any thing that a journal, generally so worthy of admiration, did *not* like. Yet, with submission, the *Standard* estimates the severity of the two cases upon a false scale: political polemics, especially with a party that have, now, not a word to throw at a dog, cannot be supposed to cost much effort of thought; labour undoubtedly there is in that sort of warfare, and room for great variety of display—reading, eloquence, power of illustration, &c. (as the readers of the *Standard* in particular must have daily proof,) but of direct difficulty and perplexity, such as occurs in intellectual problems, absolutely none at all. Nothing in the shape of a logical *nodus* can ever occur in mere politics; consequently no room for subtlety of solution, or of evolution from a remote *à priori* grounds. In Political Economy, on the other hand, properly so called, and kept apart from mere empirical statistics, there is

1 November 3, p. 3.

169

nothing else. And that the *Standard* should account such a science a mere relaxation, may be one reason why that journal succeeds in it so ill.

As to not "turning their backs upon any challenger," we doubt how far that assumption is realized: not to reply would surely be to turn one's back; but to detach parts from their connexion, to select, to garble, or to evade, is in effect the same thing, for the boldness of the matter, as making no reply at all; for the justice of it, much worse. However, if the *Standard* would, in earnest, resolve upon shewing fight in future, perhaps, with the other conditions of the ring, it will submit to that of keeping time. A turn-up between two parties as staunch and immoveable as a *Standard* and a *Post*, should in all reason be a fair stand-up-fight at half-minute time. We publish on Saturday night, and reach London on Tuesday morning. By replying on that night, or Wednesday, the *Standard* will give us the advantage of meeting it whilst our blood is up, and our readers the advantage of understanding both parties. So mind, *Standard*, in future always to come to time.

Now for the arguments on this occasion, which ought to be excellent in quality, being slender in quantity—indirectly presented by way of apologue and interrogation—and dispersed through a great over-proportion of wit and other extra-essential matter.

*

I.—The *Standard* tells a story from the Hebrew, the moral of which is this: That those who clamour for a revolution, especially upon points affecting the great interests of the species, and the feelings which (well or ill-founded) are apt to be regarded as sacred guides, ought, at least, to be agreed among themselves. But Say,[2] Mill, Ricardo, &c. are not agreed: *ergo*, &c. ANSWER.—This

[2] Jean Baptiste Say, the French economist, still living at the time.

argument would be a good one against the writers in question, supposing that they urged their collective authority, or built any thing upon the pretence of unanimity. But this they do not. In the Hebrew tale, the argument of the pagan had been *ad verecundiam*; he had pressed the Jew with the authority of nearly all mankind,—Greeks,—Romans,—Barbarians, as opposed to "a small fraction of the human race." And it was therefore a good answer, in point of logic, (however little made out as a matter of fact,) that the Jew should object to the internal dissensions of this large majority: because, had these dissensions respected the capital, and not the secondary points of the pagan creed, such an argument would have been fatal to the pretence of an unequivocal majority for paganism. The supposed majority might have turned out to be a mere aggregate of minorities in relation to the number of the Jewish people. But what parity is there between this and the case of Mr. Ricardo? In the particular question before the *Standard*, the question of rent, some of the alleged contradictions are apparent only, and have imposed on the *Standard* simply because the *Standard* is not master of the doctrine: others are really contradictions, but then from persons who avow and profess themselves to be opponents of Mr. Ricardo. The argument from supposed concurrence, had *that* been relied upon by Mr. R., would very pertinently have been met by proofs of real disagreement: but how can it affect a writer who relies on no such extrinsic or collateral support, but exclusively on the direct force of his principles, and the intrinsic evidence of his demonstrations?

II. The distinction between natural price and market price, is characterised by the *Standard* as "trashy," "absurd," and "nonsense,"—stigmas in which we have no separate or peculiar interest. We claim the merit of applying this distinction to the solution of a particular error: but the distinction itself is Adam Smith's, and adopted (in profession at least,) by every writer of note since his day—though it is true that in the practical application of it they are too often at a loss.

III. The *Standard* "begs to ask us, what we mean by two prices, where we say there can be but one price!" ANSWER.—The confusion in this question is so enormous, that we must suppose the *Standard* to be designedly muddying the waters, in order to darken the subject and confound the reader. Without going into the *entire* exposure of this confusion, three words will suffice to clear ourselves of the pretended contradiction. We never spoke of two prices,—we spoke of two *laws* of price, two different principles which govern price. And we presume there is no contradiction in saying, that the one sole price, for which, at any one time and place, corn of the same quality must always sell, may to-day be determined by one of those principles, and to-morrow by the other. What is called *natural price*, is price governed by the single consideration of cost; and it takes place undisturbed when the supply happens to be just equal to the demand, neither more nor less. What is called *market* price, is price governed by the cost complicated with the quantity, and never takes place, (to speak with a strictness which all writers have occasionally lost sight of,) except when the quantity in the market is above or below the demand.*

---

*The reason for insisting on the fact, that corn of the same quality, and in the same market, cannot fetch two prices, and the relation which it bears to rent, is this:—If it were possible that corn grown on three-penny land could sell for threepence, whilst corn of the very same quality sold at the same time and place for fourpence, upon the allegation that it was grown upon worse, (*i.e.* four-penny) land, rent could never arise. But because, when 4d. land is resorted to, corn will *universally* rise to 4d. (that is to say, not upon the 4d. land only, but also on the 3d. land), there arises immediately upon this last land an extra penny available as rent. For, by the supposition, the 3d. land *originally* afforded the

IV. The *Standard* "wishes us to explain, why an inferior soil, paying *less* rent, may not be cultivated with as much advantage to the farmer, as a richer soil paying more rent." ANSWER.—This is a question which could not have been put by a person in possession of the doctrine. No Ricardian has ever denied, that inferior soils, by paying *less* rent, might be cultivated with as much advantage,† &c.; and on the contrary, the whole doctrine of rent proceeds on such a graduation of soils, connected with such a graduation of rents. What the Ricardians *do* assert, is, that the *lowest* soil of all in the scale cannot be cultivated on these terms. Now, after this corrected version of our doctrine, if the *Standard* thinks fit to press its question, and "wishes us to explain why the lowest soil of the whole gradation, by paying *less* rent, may not be cultivated with as much advantage," &c.; our answer is, because it could not be cultivated with as much advantage, if it paid any rent at all; *a fortiori*, therefore, not merely by paying "less" rent. The doctrine is, that the worst soil in cultivation, will, in every case, pay no rent. And, if the *Standard* demands the reason of *that*, we refer him to the existing expositions of that doctrine,—Sir Edward West's, and above all, Mr. Ricardo's. Or, as this part of the theory may be explained in a word or two, let him look back to the case already stated, of three-penny

---

common rate of profit; it will certainly afford no less *now*, in consequence of 4d. land being used. *Ergo*, the penny is so much beyond the universal rate of profit; and whatsoever is beyond *that*—is rent, no matter by whom pocketed—whether by a capitalist cultivating his own land, or by a landlord distinct from the farmer.

† i.e. In the case of an effectual demand existing for these inferior soils: otherwise, and supposing the proprietor of the inferior soil to imagine that he will create a market for himself by driving out the produce of superior soils, and that he will accomplish this by sacrificing part of his rent,—he will find this impossible; for upon his land, as the worst by the terms of the hypothesis, there will at any rate be no rent to sacrifice.

and four-penny land, which has the advantage of being
exceedingly free of all needless complexities. Now then,
when the 3d. land became insufficient, and a growing
population made it necessary to resort to 4d. land, (i.e.
land whose produce costs 4d., instead of 3d.,) it is evident, for the following reason, that no rent could exist on
this latter land: suppose a landlord to ask a halfpenny
rent, of necessity he will be unable to support a competition with any man who is in a condition to forego the
halfpenny,—i.e. to content himself with *profits minus*
rent; but every landlord is in that condition, who chooses
to take upon himself the functions of the capitalist;‡ and
this he will always choose, when such a competition as is
here described would be available. For there can be
no reason why a proprietor of land, more than other men,
should not *always* be content with the universal rate of
profits, *minus* rent, provided it would be available as a
measure of competition. But this is impossible on any
other land than the lowest.†

‡ And he has precisely the same adequate inducement to do so
that any man has to carry his capital into trade. It is true that,
as soon as rent rises, this enables the landlord, by ceding profits
to the farmer, to live a life of leisure. And this only it is which
hides from the novice that the customary rate of profit without
rent is exactly the same bounty upon the cultivation of land that
it is upon the exercise of any trade whatever.

† It will strike some readers, that the same renunciation of rent,
which is here described as taking place by the compulsion of competition on the lowest quality, might also take place on the higher
qualities. But this is impossible; since there is no motive for such
a renunciation. The whole *rationale* may be briefly stated thus: No
man will be satisfied to obtain profits only, without rent, who has
it in his power to obtain both. Both, however, he cannot have,
wherever he is exposed to the competition of those who will be
satisfied with one. But to this competition he is of necessity exposed on the lowest quality of land, and on this quality only. Why?
Because there only can a competition be available. For the
object of all competition is to drive a rival out of the market, and
to step into his place. We underbid another only with this view.
But if both must of necessity find a place in the market, all motive for underbidding him ceases. Now a necessity of this kind exists

V. The *Standard* demands of us, "whether, if population, and therefore consumption be increasing, it will not be necessary to bring more of the inferior land into cultivation, (which, in that case, may clearly be done without disturbing the rents or profits of richer lands) in order to secure the nation from that most awful of all calamities—a dependence upon foreigners for subsistence." ANSWER. —To speak first to the matter in the parenthesis, the culture of inferior soils *will* disturb the rents of richer soils by raising them, and *will* disturb the profits of richer soils by sinking them: for the proof of which, we refer the reader to the Ricardian laws of rent and profit.

Secondly, to the rest of the demand we answer—like Thomas Diafoirus—by distinguishing.[3] The best writers on this question, forget that, in some cases, political economy says one thing, and larger considerations of general political prudence another. For example, WAR—what says political economy to *that?* Does any man imagine—that,

---

for the higher qualities of land, so long as an acre of a lower quality is in cultivation; because *that* implies all the higher quality to have been taken up, and all competition at an end, therefore, between land which possesses equal advantages for competition.

For example, when 4d. land is called into the market, it is because the 3d. land is all taken up already. The price now becomes 4d.; and this makes room for a rent of 1d. (*i.e.* the difference between 3d. and 4d.) on the 3d. land. Now it is clear that, by exacting the whole of this penny, without any abatement whatsoever, the land proprietor will not raise any effectual competition against himself; since by the supposition 4d. is now the lowest price in the market; and his rent therefore adds nothing to the price which must at any rate take place. But in the case, argued above, of an attempt to levy one halfpenny rent on the *lowest* quality of land, it was seen that this would raise the price by its own entire amount; so that the price would be 4½d., which immediately opens the door wide to the competition of all who can sell for 4d.: And this is what every body can do; the 3d. people of course, even retaining their rent; and the 4d. people, by renouncing rent, and contenting themselves with the ordinary profits of stock. And thus the very first attempt to raise rent on the lowest quality of land, is constantly met and baffled in its birth.

---

[3] Molière's *Le Malade Imaginaire*, II, vi.

simply as a question of the purse, simply on considerations of political economy, we can ever find it advisable to go to war? It would be folly to think it. But what then? Shall we lay down, as an unconditional rule, that we will in no case have war? God forbid! We will go to war, please heaven, at an enormous loss—a ruinous loss, viz. upon considerations transcendant to all that political economy can offer; in behalf of our national honour, outraged by insult or aggression, in behalf of the same honour pledged by treaties, in behalf of interests paramount to those of the purse. The same distinction applies to the corn question: treated merely as a question of political economy, it must obey the voice of the modern economist; else it has not a leg to stand upon. Viewing it in exclusive reference to the purse, it would be irrational for us to struggle with a continual descent upon inferior soils in England, whilst soils in a high degree superior are offered to us in Poland: upon a bare question of profit and loss, it would be as absurd to deny the policy of growing our corn upon our Polish farm, as the policy of growing our wine in French or Portuguese vineyards, rather than in English hot-houses. The sole demur on this side of the case is—that remotely, though much more slowly, the same developement of inferior resources will take place in Poland. But, to retard our descent by some generations, would be argument enough with political economy. On the other hand, political expedience, of a much higher character than any which belongs to political economy, raises doubts upon this question, both in reference to the dependence upon foreigners, and also to the injurious changes* which any considerable transfer

* It is true that these changes would be less than is imagined by those who, knowing nothing of the law of rent and the principles which determine the price of landed produce, imagine that, if British corn were exposed to an unfettered competition with Polish, *all* the British would be driven out of the market, if *any* were. But, it is clear, that the price of the higher soils is hidden from

of our agriculture to the continent would impress upon the structure of English society, substituting a race of vicious manufacturers, (we regard not the denial of the Edinburgh Review)[4] for some part of our honest rural population, and also crippling in a still greater degree the invaluable class of our landed proprietors.

These are our distinctions with regard to the last question put to us by the *Standard*; and on the whole, we presume, that, on this topic, there is not much difference between ourselves and that journal.

Finally, the *Standard* puts an end to the discussion in these words—*ad colophonem duximus*: *Vale, Economia Politica*! If this is meant to announce an eternal adieu, we know not whether to be glad or sorry. On the one hand, it would please us to have a round with the *Standard* every fortnight or so, on subjects of this nature; because in that case, within six revolving moons, we should infallibly "mill" him into a good Political Economist. Yet, on the other, it would gratify us, that he would abstain from Political Economy, because, by keeping off the only ground on which he betrays ignorance, he

---

us by the regulating price of the lower. Suppose the lowest quality in use to be in extent but a thousand acres, this trifling quantity raises the price of every acre in the kingdom: consequently, knock but this trifling quantity off, and the price is universally lowered, and probably a very few of the lowest quantities knocked off, would bring our British corn on a level with Polish; because, it must not be forgotten, that, whilst this change was lowering our British corn, *pari passu* the Polish corn would be mounting from the *immediate* necessity there would be in Poland for resorting to worse soils in order to furnish the increased growth. A motion of this kind on *both* sides would speedily bring them to a level; and less changes, of every kind, would take place than is apprehended. But still the changes would be for the worse, in every sense, but a pecuniary one.

---

[4] In the conclusion of M'Culloch's article on the "Rise, Progress, Present State, and Prospects of the British Cotton Manufacture," *Edinburgh Review* of June 1827, pp. 32–39. The article had been reviewed in the *Post* of July 28, pp. 32–34 above; see also December 15, p. 230 below.

would then become entitled to that undivided admiration which we would willingly pay to his conspicuous merits.

*

We notice, with some surprise, that the maxim of— *The more corn the dearer*, which the *Standard* had previously cited generally as the "paradox of a Scotch paper," and which we justified a fortnight ago, without any knowledge that we had a peculiar interest in doing so, is now charged by the *Standard* upon the *Post*. We have no remembrance of having either written or read such a passage in this paper.

ATTRIBUTION

This pair of articles, by the same man, certainly seems to be De Quincey's work.

On the "doctrine of rent" and on the distinction between market and natural price see the article of September 15, 1827 (pp. 118-19) and the further references there. On Sir Edward West (p. 173) see the article of October 6 (p. 159) and the references there. On the specific argument here (pp. 176-77), based on the law of rent, that if Polish corn were freely imported the prices of Polish and British corn would soon meet at a level, see De Quincey's "Dilemmas on the Corn Law Question," *Blackwood's*, XLV (1839), 174-76, and "Sir Robert Peel's Position on Next Resuming Power," *Blackwood's*, L (1841), 400-401. The argument here in the *Post* and in the *Blackwood* articles is that in Poland there would be a descent upon inferior soils to meet the increased demand, while in Britain the lowest quality of soils would no longer be cultivated, and a trifling change in the quantity of soil cultivated makes a large difference in price because it affects the price of every other degree of soil; and such a change would have bad consequences other than economic, on the balance

178

of the classes in England and on national independence. Also on the large effect upon prices of a small change in the quantity of soil in culture see "Canton Expedition and Convention," *Blackwood's*, L (1841), 685, and "The Opium and the China Question," (1840), M., XIV, 182-83.

The example of the logical schools (pp. 164-65) had been used earlier by De Quincey, also in the context of political economy, in his "Malthus on Population" (1823), M., IX, 17: a critic must be able to present a just analysis of the doctrine he is attacking and this must be demanded of him "for the same reason that in the old schools of disputation the respondent was expected to repeat the syllogism of his opponent before he undertook to answer it." He had used the same example, with the same verbal similarities, in the *Westmorland Gazette*, September 19, 1818, p. 3.

On the expository device of the question and answer (pp. 172-73, 175), see the article of September 15, 1827, and the references there (p. 121 above).

That a paradox is not necessarily untrue (p. 165) is a point De Quincey makes at greater length several times, both before and after this date: in "Dialogues of Three Templars" (1824), M., IX, 48, 81, where the context is political economy, and in *Logic of Political Economy* (1844), M., IX, 136-37, again in the same context, and, in other contexts, in M., I, 97; I, 199; VII, 205-06; also "Passing Notices of Indian Affairs," *Titan*, XXV (1857), 504.

The use of boxing slang (pp. 170, 177) is characteristic of De Quincey; it appears twenty different times in essays before and after this date, including some of those on political economy already referred to. The particular term "turn-up" he had used earlier this year in the first of the papers on "Murder as One of the Fine Arts," M., XIII, 33; it is also in "Aelius Lamia" (1856), M., VI,

425; "turn-up" and "stand-up fights" and "milling" are all in "A Brief Appraisal of the Greek Literature" (1838-39), M., X, 291, 303.

Several of the common Latin phrases or words are used by De Quincey. *Diis aliter visum est* (p. 164) is in M., I, 403; III, 55; IV, 151; VI, 329; VII, 445; "Dr. Parr," *Blackwood's*, XXIX (1831), 71; "Animal Magnetism," *Tait's*, IV (1834), 471. *Vi termini* (p. 166) is in M., V, 358; IX, 15; XIV, 82. *Nodus* (p. 169), in both logical and economic contexts, is in M., II, 291; V, 65; V, 328; IX, 120; X, 263. Even *a priori* (p. 169), common as it is, is some evidence because of its unusual frequency in De Quincey (see also February 9, 1828, p. 311, below); he uses it sixty or more times. More specifically, he uses it frequently in economic contexts. His enthusiasm for Ricardo and political economy, when he discovered Ricardo, was that where other political economists had been crushed by the enormous weight of facts and documents Ricardo had deduced *a priori* the laws of that science (*Confessions*, both versions, M., III, 432; see also "Ricardo and Adam Smith," *Blackwood's*, LII [1842], 349). "Ad verecundiam" (p. 171) is in M., II, 345; VIII, 120n. On his use of *a fortiori* (p. 173) see the article of August 4, 1827, p. 59, and the further references given there.

November 3, 1827

Plagiarism

SIR,—I am concerned to see your able correspondent W. H. throwing away his valuable time on so threadbare a topic as that of Plagiarism, treated in the common-place way.[1] I might add, that I am still more concerned to see him attempting to screen as well-attested a case of Plagiarism as ever was committed: but this I cannot allow myself to say, for I am persuaded that the circumstances of the case must have dropped out of his recollection. It is undeniable, that thousands of feeble writers are constantly at work, who subsist by Plagiarism, more or less covert. It is equally undeniable, as W. H. alleges, and partly it arises out of this very fact, partly also to shew their reading, and partly because it is the cheapest way of writing criticism, without any expense of thought, that thousands of feeble critics (such as Todd on Spenser, Dean Milles on Chatterton, &c. &c.)[2] subsist by detecting plagiarisms or imitations, real or supposed. This general disposition to commit thefts on the one hand, and to imagine them on the other, leaves us without any grounds of presumption for or against a particular person charged as a delinquent, until we have heard his case: the circumstances ought all to be *en évidence*, before we are

[1] W. H. had written a letter to the *Post*, October 27, p. 199, defending Campbell against the charge of plagiarism; see the review of the issue of *Blackwood's*, where the charge had appeared, p. 99 above.

[2] Henry John Todd, better known as an editor of Milton; his variorum edition of Spenser (1805) was criticized for its "learned lumber," by Scott in the *Edinburgh* (October 1805). Jeremiah Milles' edition of the Rowley poems was published 1782; he attempted to prove the authenticity of the poems, by supposed similarities to other medieval poems, and made himself ridiculous; he was also denounced as a calumniator of Chatterton.

entitled to any opinion. To shew, therefore, that others have been falsely accused of Plagiarism, which is the line of argument taken by W. H., does not at all assist us in judging of Mr. Campbell. The charge against him ought to have been specifically stated, and the defence adapted to that circumstantial charge. This charge I presume to be the same which was brought forward a month or two ago in Blackwood's Magazine. If so, it cannot be met by any defence whatever. The Plagiarism is brought home by a little circumstance which no art and no friendship can evade. The writer (whose name I have since heard,[3] with an assurance that he is an accomplished scholar, incapable of any malignity to Mr. Campbell,) does not argue that Mr. C. has a certain thought in common with Schlegel, and therefore had probably been reading Schlegel. No: he brings proof that Mr. C. acknowledges to have been reading Schlegel, for Mr. C. had referred to him *with blame.* And that the criticism was originally Schlegel's property, is proved by this fact, that a mistake occurs in it, which is very naturally explained by reference to the German passage, but which could have no foundation except in such a mis-translation.

There is a quality of criticism on this subject of plagiarism, in which the taste of W. H. might do signal service; pointing out the limits, for example, which distinguish a just imitation conceived in the spirit of originality, and in which the thought borrowed receives a new life from the class of base plagiarisms: or, again, on the other side, detecting those real plagiarisms of a subtler kind, which shroud themselves in disguises that deceive the injudicious, or which, according to Sheridan's illustration, disfigure, like gypsies, the children which they have stolen.[4] Many a book has caught the whole

3 See p. 99n. above.
4 Sir Fretful Plagiary in *The Critic*, I, i.

spirit of its life and movement from another, and would not have been written but for that other, although no particular phrase or passage might argue to an unlearned eye any direct or conscious robbery.

But all this by the way. In conclusion, let me say, that I am sure I speak the sentiments of many of your readers in wishing that *W. H.*, whose translation of the Latin epitaph from the *Nugæ Venales** proves his identity with the admirable translator from Buchanan in former papers, would favour us with further specimens of his extraordinary ability in that department.[5] I must not take the liberty of pointing out a subject to a stranger; else I would say that, with the single exception of Mr. Cary, the translator of Dante,[6] whose versions of the old French poets, are equal to any thing in translated literature, I know of no writer of this day so capable as *W. H.* of building a lasting name for himself by a translation of what is excellent in the Greek Anthology; which, of all parts of Greek literature, is that which best unveils the domestic affections of the ancients. I doubt whether even Mr. Cary's style of translation is so well adapted to this task as that of W. H. I am, Sir, Your constant Reader,

X. Y. Z.

---

* The reference to this work, which is one of the old *Facetiae,* does not of necessity acquit Burns of obligation for his *Wee Johnnie*; on the one hand, the thought is sufficiently obvious to have occurred to multitudes; yet, on the other, for the questions of fact, it must not be overlooked, that the best part of the *Facetiae* has been long ago transplanted into every EUROPEAN language.

---

5 W. H. had been contributing translations and original poems to the *Post*; translations from Buchanan are in the issues of September 29, p. 167, October 20, p. 191.

In his letter of October 27, W. H. had pointed out the similarity of Burns's poem to the Latin poem (a similarity later noted also by Robert Chambers, the editor of Burns); the point he hoped to make was that the similarity could not have been a plagiarism.

6 Henry Francis Cary, who, with Lamb, Hazlitt and De Quincey, had been one of the contributors to the *London Magazine.*

ATTRIBUTION

Probably De Quincey's: first because of the "X. Y. Z." signature (for which see the article of August 11, 1827, p. 73, and the further references there); secondly because De Quincey had already noted and supported the charge against Campbell, in the *Post* article of September 8, 1827, p. 99 above, an article that is certainly his. The very complimentary references to Cary also point to De Quincey: they had been colleagues on the *London Magazine* and in his reminiscences of that publication De Quincey refers to Cary as the unrivalled translator of Dante (1840), M., III, 143; elsewhere he calls him the best translator of any age (1838-39), M., X, 314. For "en évidence" (p. 181) see the article of July 28 (p. 59 above).

[The Battle of Navarino]

In another page our readers will find the official account of the sanguinary and destructive battle of Navarin:[1] an event which we do not view entirely in the same light as *any* of our contemporaries. As a martial achievement, all of them seem disposed to regard it as very brilliant,— very complete it certainly was, in a degree which is rarely witnessed; and this arose from the position of the Christian fleets, which intercepted all escape. But, considering the relations of force and skill on each side, and the total inexperience of our enemy, we should not have expected that Great Britain would have numbered this amongst her distinguished victories. It is true, that Sir Edward Codrington speaks of the "excessive number" opposed to the allies; but this expression has been taken in a larger sense than could have been designed, in consequence of an absurd error, which has run through all the public journals,—assigning to the Mahometan fleet, the enormous disproportion of *forty-seven* frigates,—a force "to dream of, not to tell,"[2] and never assembled in one action,

[1] The Greek attempt to gain independence from the Turks made the English worry that the Russians would exploit the opportunity to extend their own power. By the Treaty of Armed Mediation, signed in London on July 6, 1827, England, Russia and France agreed to act together to gain an armistice and to prevent further clashes between the Greeks and Turks. Sir Edward Codrington, as commander-in-chief of the combined allied fleets, blockaded the Turkish fleet in Navarino; on October 20, 1827, he entered the bay itself, presumably to anchor, but an incident followed, then a battle, and the Turkish fleet was destroyed. In England the supporters of Greek independence were pleased and those who regarded the battle as a great feat of arms were pleased; but those who were not enthusiastic about the success of revolutions and those who feared that the Turkish defeat meant Russian success, or that a general war might begin, were not happy. Codrington was a philhellene and his motives and responsibility for bringing on the battle were questioned.

[2] "Christabel," l. 253.

even by the gigantic naval power of this country. The truth is, as the sequel of the battle shews, that the *maximum* of the enemy's strength in frigates, could not have exceeded *nineteen*,—i.e. was not quite double that of the allies; whilst, on the other hand, the superiority in the line of battle was more than triple in favour of the Christians. In reality, what is most worthy of attention in the *military* character of the battle, is the length and severity of the resistance; and, in order to explain it, we are obliged to recollect, that absolute desperation is a formidable quality, even when possessing an undisciplined force; and secondly, that Christian skill was undoubtedly at work, and perhaps, in effect, presided on board the navy of the Crescent.

With respect to the political aspects of the battle, we find ourselves more in agreement with others. But here we desire to speak with caution and reserve, for as yet we write in the dark. Even the ministerial journals, however, by their apologetic tone, manifestly confess that the grounds of a full justification for this violent and bloody course, are not as yet apparent. The British Admiral has been understood to say, in his despatches, that the battle "was brought on entirely by our opponents:" but, on examining his words more closely, we find Sir Edward "consoling himself with the reflection"—not that the battle—but that "the measure which *produced* the battle," was absolutely necessary;—i.e. the measure of "taking up a position" in the harbour of Navarin. Now, in the first place, this will call for an inquiry into the intermediate occurrences which connected this measure with the battle. If the one step led *necessarily* to the other, then Sir Edward is loaded with a greater responsibility than he has acknowledged: if, on the other hand, they were only *accidentally* connected by the intemperate conduct of two Mahometan ships, it will require to be known in what degree these acts of hostility might reasonably be supposed authorized, and likely to be avowed by the Mahometan commanders. Secondly, "the measure which led to the battle was absolutely necessary"—for what? "For obtaining the results," says Sir Edward, "contemplated by the treaty." This is no question of fact, but of opinion, and may lead to two inquiries—first, on the part of ministers into the soundness of the British Admiral's decision in this question of necessity: and, secondly, supposing the Admiral were to be borne out in his judgment on what the treaty demanded, a more general inquiry on the part of the nation into the merits of this treaty itself.

On any of these questions, no light has yet been thrown. The Paris papers received in London by express on Tuesday night, and which come down to the 12th, (Monday last) affirm, that the Sultan had positively directed Ibrahim[3] to repel force by force. This account, if true, throws an unpleasant light on the ulterior question of peace or war, but none at all upon the immediate question before us: a determination "to repel force by force," still leaves the inquiry open—from what quarter came the first act of *authorized force?*

We wish not to pre-judge: but the consequences of this one bloody day may eventually prove awful for Christendom at large, considering how speedily any spark of war mounts into a general conflagration, from the intricacy of interests which bind together the European system of politics: a burthen, therefore, of solemn responsibility rests upon ministers at home, no less than upon their agents abroad.*

* A correspondent of the *Standard*, (Tuesday last,) amongst other ingenious arguments upon the conduct of the allies, suggests, that Sir Edward C. could not have acted upon the protocol which he assigns as the ground of his hostile movement upon Navarin, from a comparison of dates.[4] But on this point we feel satisfied, that the Admiral will acquit himself of all blame: probably

[3] Ibrahim Pasha, commanding the Turkish forces.

ATTRIBUTION

There is a series of articles on the battle of Navarino, written as more details become available and retrospection and prognostication increased. De Quincey, it is my guess, wrote most or all of them, but solid evidence is lacking. This, the first of the series, is given as a sample. The fragment of the line from "Christabel," in a publication where De Quincey elsewhere makes use of his knowledge of Coleridge, is perhaps a sign of his authorship. He later quoted the same portion of the line, again adapting it to his own purposes, in "Hurried Notices of Indian Affairs," *Titan*, XXV (1857), 345.

the information, which governed him, was oral, and not formally reduced to a protocol until it was wanted for an official purpose.

[4] The excerpt from the *Standard* is reprinted in this issue of the *Post*, on p. 218.

November 17, 1827

Edinburgh Review

No. 92.

The old medical experiment of the transfusion of blood, to which Dr. Darwin recalled the attention of modern times,[1] is loudly demanded by the condition of the two great Reviews. *Great* we style them, not in acknowledgment of any claims they ever had to the reputation which attended them, but solely with reference to that reputation. A commanding intellect, it is certain, never came forward in either; not one that could overrule the public taste, or write effectually in defiance of public errors and the prejudices of the age: on the contrary, the very best papers in both were most conspicuous for the talent of a clever advocate, availing himself, designedly, of the ignorance or half-knowledge, which exists in his audience, for the purpose of a momentary effect. Both Reviews wrote *ex professo* in that spirit of submission to all popular abuses of the times, and to the idols of the human intellect, at that time enthroned, which a well-bred man justly adopts in company, and in assemblies of people convened only for purposes of pleasure. Wisdom, by an unseasonable intrusion, would here show like folly. Had the purposes of the two journals been loftier and more permanent, this could not have been. Even to make himself understood upon any great question, merely that he may not talk in an unknown tongue, an original thinker must begin by reforming (and, in some degree, by shocking) his audience: for a long time at least he must, in Milton's words, be an utterer of "odious truth."[2]

---

[1] Erasmus Darwin in his *Zoonomia* (1796), I, 377; II, 120-21, 605. In one of the cases cited by Darwin the transfusion is used to keep an old man alive.

[2] *Paradise Lost*, XI, 704.

For example, in the two transcendant walks of the mind
—Poetry and Philosophy,—had the Edinburgh Review
been conscious of any power or vocation to speak profit-
ably, or with lasting authority, it would not from the
first have offered homage to the spirit of the world, which,
in all shapes of society, is at war with the grander modes
of enthusiasm, whether taking the shape of religion, of
patriotism, of intense passion for beauty, severe dedication to truth, or fervent striving after the indefinite and
the ideal. To the spirit of the world, nothing is acceptable
but the ungenial and the sarcastic,—or, amongst the
serious and the real, it is sure to be duped by the spurious.
At the commencement of the Edinburgh Review, Kant,
and his colossal scheme of thinking, presented one of the
great phenomena of the age, as much so as the French
revolution. Yet, to understand this, was a work of great
labour and difficulty; to communicate it with effect to a
nation, whose intense habits of business make it intolerant
of all the profounder studies, a work of even greater. Far
easier it was, and for immediate ends more useful, to fall
in with the national infirmity, to profess a total ignorance
even of the German language, and, upon the authority
of a French trifler, to treat a great scheme of philosophic
truth, which had agitated and divided the great central
nations of Europe, as a momentary candidate for half
an hour's jesting and buffoonery—fitted to take its
turn in one evening's amusements with Matthews or
Grimaldi.[3]

This sketch of the plan on which the two Reviews
moved, is bare truth. We do not say that it is a bad plan.
People have a right to choose their *rôle* in life and in
literature. But let us not forget what *that* plan was, and
measure our praises accordingly. As lights of the age, let

[3] Charles Mathews and Joseph Grimaldi, both comic performers
of great reputation. On the *Edinburgh*'s early article on Kant
(January 1803), see below, p. 209.

it be acknowledged that their pretensions were ridiculous: but, for the transient topics of the day, the fugitive
interests of party, person, time, and place, their authority was deservedly great: considered as fasciculi of lively,
stinging, sarcastic pamphlets, or (as might happen) of
libels or lampoons,—they were, indeed, a happy innovation upon the comatose dulness of the old booksellers'
hacks—monthly or critical. The world thought so: and
within its own province, the world is a judge, from whose
sentence *de jure*, as well as *de facto*, there lies no appeal,
however great a fool the world is, and ever will be, in the
highest walks of human intellect.

But, even for this limited merit, we must now say—
Fuit Ilium. In literature we have no party: and we do no
more than give voice to a general feeling, when we say,
that for some years back both the Quarterly and the
Edinburgh Review, like the Archbishop of Grenada's
sermons, have had a "furious scent about them of
apoplexy."[4] The cause of this lies in what originally constituted their merit: both Reviews had connexions with
the great parties in the state: this was the ground of
their advantage over the old journals; and hence, knowing where their strength lay, they were naturally anxious
to lay a greater stress, than strictly belonged to their
functions as *literary* journals, upon politics; or, in literature, allowably so called, to concede an undue proportion
of culture to that which partakes of a political interest,—
memoirs, for instance, of courtiers and statesmen, political economy, statistics, or science, so far as it is immediately applicable to state purposes,—making room
for literature κατ' εξοχην,[5] or for abstract science, just in
that proportion which might be useful to liberalize and

[4] Le Sage's *Gil Blas*, VII, iv (but not an exact quotation); the
symptoms of apoplexy in his sermons were the result of advancing
dotage.

[5] Pre-eminently, or par excellence.

elevate the general character of the work. Hence, arose a danger, now fully realized, that the preponderant department of these journals, and that from which they consciously drew the weightiest part of their support, would absorb all the rest. For some years back, the Quarterly Review has been almost exclusively a political journal, and having little or no connexion with any thing that can even by courtesy be called literature: nay, which is worse, not even political in the large and liberal sense of that term; but grovelling in downright *vestry* politics, roads, bridges, canals, jails, Mr. M'Adam, poor rates, houses of correction, and such branches of the fine arts. Even in Mr. Gifford's time, who was superannuated and inactive, this was rather surprising; but under the present editor,[6] whose disgust to such lore is as well known as the earnestness of his dedication to literature upon a scale of extent unknown to his predecessor,—we have reason for great astonishment, and for some complaint. The Edinburgh Review is fast verging to the same consummation. *Plausuque sui gaudere theatri*, must always have been true of partizan journals; but we have *now* reason to complain, that another feature of Pompey's character, as sketched by Lucan, applies to both,—viz. that they are content to repose upon their past laurels.[7] Certainly their characteristic merits, such as they were, have almost forsaken them. Hardly a plank remains of the old ship: and, were it not for the difficulties of a competition with works so long established, youthful rivals would ere this have exploded the two quarterly dotards—building upon the same superiority of vigour, and alacrity, which originally drew favour upon *them*. It cannot be supposed, that the editor of the

6 John Gibson Lockhart.

7 Lucan, I, 133: he rejoiced in the applause of his theater. This is the passage in which Lucan contrasts the older Pompey's contentment with his past achievements and Caesar's youthful vigor.

Edinburgh (confining ourselves to that journal) is insensible to this state of things: but his very attempts to
infuse new blood into the old lady's circulation, demonstrate the torpor of his management, and the very lan-
guid interest with which he *now* regards the whole
concern. Hazlitt, the misanthrope, and not a misanthrope
in a noble style, the Apemantus, and not the Timon of
modern life, is the only considerable performer whom he
has added to his *corps* for years: and the tone of that
gentleman's writings was not harmonized with the general key in which the Review is set. To say nothing of
eternal paradoxes, without even a momentary consistency amongst each other, shifting, collapsing, moulding,
and unmoulding themselves like the dancing pillars of
sand on the deserts,—a mode of composition with which
levity itself can be pleased only as with a single exhibi-
tion on the tight rope,—it must be a still greater offence
in the eyes of many readers of the Edinburgh, that the
style and manner of Mr. H. argue a low-bred person.
Some people very disobligingly describe Mr. Hazlitt by
the emphatic word—*Scamp.*[8] To the full extent of that
reproach, as applicable to any man of so much talent,
we should be sorry to subscribe; but certainly the tang
of low society, which is one elements of a 'Scamp', is
painfully odorous about his writings. He dogmatizes at
will about high life, and people of rank; but manifestly
never had any introduction into that sort of society. And
if by accident he had, we all feel that either he would
behave with a painful want of gentlemanly ease and self-
possession, or with a jacobin insolence—according to his
temper and his spirits. Mr. Carlyle, a very recent ally,
for a different reason, is still more out of keeping with
the prevailing style of this Review. Writing with much
originality, and originality more in alliance with truth

[8] *Blackwood's* had done this, XVII (1825), 363, in a review of
Spirit of the Age written possibly by Lockhart.

than that of Mr. Hazlitt, writing also in a more amiable
and philanthropic spirit, at times we may even say in a
noble spirit, not a querulous and disappointed egotist,
but a young and hopeful enthusiast, reverencing the as-
pirations and the destiny of human nature; he is a most
agreeable companion to those who estimate the matter
and the manner of a writer according to their just pro-
portions. But in the drawing rooms and boudoirs, to
which the Edinburgh Review will find its way, so long
as it continues to be the organ of the Whigs, it cannot
but be a stone of offence, that the style and the mode of
presenting his thoughts are not according to the polished
standard of the times—do not win their way gracefully
and with ease—but have a repulsive air of quaintness
and austerity like those of a recluse, and (which is worse)
of a sectarian recluse. In Mr. Irving,* the friend of Mr.
Carlyle, who went up to London as a prophet of wrath
to that mighty Nineveh, such a style was in its place: to
be rude, harsh, and *incondite* in the uttermost degree,
was in him not unbecoming: sackcloth and ashes even
were looked for as his appropriate costume: nobody
would have been surprised if he had dined on locusts and
wild honey; and no small part of the public admiration
did, in fact, settle upon the savagery and hirsute aspect
of his exterior. But for him, who comes forward to the
beau monde, in the uninspired character of an Edinburgh
reviewer, it is indispensable to adopt the common earthly
means for making that character respectable. We shall
dismiss these topics, by suggesting to all persons whom
it concerns, that, although the two leading Reviews were
originally raised to the position which they now occupy

* *Brandy* Irving, as he is usually called,[9] in contradistinction to
Washington Irving, whose effeminate sentimentality has gained for
him the unlucky nick-name of *Washy* Irving.

[9] And more usually, Edward Irving, the celebrated preacher of
Hatton Garden.

in the highest society, chiefly by means of their *political* connexions,—yet this was not effected, nor could have been, by politics alone uncombined with literature,— nor by literature in any combination, unless presented with the ordinary attractions of style. These concessions, as to matter and style, must be made to the female part of families at any rate. On their present apoplectic system, the two reviews will soon cease to have any interest for *them*; and once let that judgment upon them be ratified, let the Edinburgh and Quarterly Reviews be banished from the drawing-room, which inevitably they will be as soon as their present infamous dulness is understood to be incorrigible, and their banishment from the library will not be long in following. To be talked about is the *sine quâ non* condition for the vitality of a journal: let their names be unheard of in the *circles* of the saloons, and farewell to the Quarterly and Edinburgh.

These remarks, due for a long time back to the two journals, are more immediately called forth by No. 92. of the Edinburgh, concerning which No. 92. we cannot possibly say a severer thing, than that it is almost as dull as No. 72. of the Quarterly: as, on the other hand, of that No. 72. the harshest word we shall ever be drawn to utter, is, that it is positively worse than this No. 92. The only articles of the least general interest, are the first, the second, and the sixth.[10] Mere dulness it is degrading even to notice; and therefore, we shall beg permission to decline noticing, even by name, any other of the articles, except two,—one (the fifth) on Retrench-

---

[10] No. 92 is the issue of October 1827. The first article is by Brougham, on Burke's letters; see Chester W. New, *The Life of Henry Brougham to 1830* (Oxford, 1961), p. 443, where the title of the article is mangled, but the evidence of attribution is strong. The sixth, "State of Parties," is also probably Brougham's, though with less certainty (New, p. 443). De Quincey attributes both to Brougham in the subsequent discussion, thereby offering contemporary corroboration of the evidence. The second is Carlyle's "State of German Literature."

ment, which is respectable for its execution in defiance of its subject, being both sound in point of political economy, moderate in its tone, and reasonable in the expectations it encourages: [11] the other (in order the *eighth*) on the *Record Commission,* which, on account of its subject, and its unparalleled importance to the historical literature of the country, we beg to point out to our readers' attention, in defiance of its rather somnolent execution. [12] There is a paper somewhere in the posthumous works of Gibbon, sketching a plan for the publication of the early English records, in the way of a counterpart to Muratori's great works for the Italian history of the correlative periods, which may serve to give any reader, as yet uninformed on this subject, some idea of its importance. [13] But, alas! of what avail is all this? What are materials, what but chaos upon chaos—anarchy below anarchy, unless some organizing mind arise to shape out of this blind abyss a world of life and light? Let us hope that there will appear some creative intellect to call up from these dry bones and mouldering relics, a form of life and historic beauty worthy of the mighty island to whose glory they are consecrated by the wise munificence of her senate!

(To be concluded in our next.)

[11] By John Ramsay M'Culloch; see Fetter, *Journal of Political Economy,* LXI, 252.

[12] Attributed to John Allen in William Young, *The History of Dulwich College* (1889), II, 419. Information from Esther Rhoads Houghton of *The Wellesley Index.*

Of the articles not even named, because they are so dull, one is Thomas Moore's "Private Theatricals" and another is Jeffrey's "O'Driscol's *History of Ireland.*"

[13] "An Address, &c.," in Vol. II of Gibbon's *Miscellaneous Works* (1796).

November 24, 1827

Edinburgh Review

No. 92.

(concluded from our last.)

Art. VI. *On the State of Parties*, makes a curious confession. We guessed what would come of *ducal horse-
whippings*.[1] It seems that young Mr. Macaulay's article
had been misunderstood even by "our own peoples," as
well as misrepresented by Gentiles like ourselves; and it
was thought necessary to call in Mr. Brougham to doctor
the wounds of the party. A more laughable case was
never heard of, nor a sadder; and the last state of that
party appears to us to be worse than the first. For the
young gentleman's article, though a miracle of coxcombry, was for that very reason as brisk as quicksilver;
whereas the old orthodox doctor, with his big wig, is not
at all clearer of blunders for being dull as ditch water.
He shakes his ambrosial curls like νεφεληγερετα Ζευς,[2]—
night-shade and poppies descend at every shake; and, as
for us, who were nearly poisoned when this subject was
discussed four months ago, we are obliged to keep at a
distance. But one little item we descry in the lawyer's
special pleading, which calls for notice: It relates to
Coalitions, and the principles on which they may be
varnished. Now, if a man will say, that, for the sake of
some transcendant points in which they agree, two
parties may, under conceivable circumstances, be entitled to merge those upon which they differ, this man
speaks plausibly; what he says is *primâ facie* endurable.
For it cannot be denied, that differences, which can

[1] See above, p. 44.
[2] Zeus the cloud-gatherer; the Homeric epithet, as in the *Iliad*,
A, 511.

never be extinguished, may yet be of diminished importance in relation to the age generally, or to other great questions then pressing. But, if a man will tell us that the characteristic doctrines of Whigs and Tories have grown, or ever can grow, obsolete,—we turn upon our heel from that man as from one who prattles childishly; because the two creeds, Whig and Tory, whose synthesis* composes the total thing called the British Constitution, can be obsolete only when *that* is obsolete. But suppose we indulge him in his chimera that such a thing *could* be, as matter of principle, let us next ask at what time it began to be as matter of fact? Since *when* were these differences of Whig and Tory to be regarded as idle distinctions? This is no trifling question at this moment, and to this particular writer (supposing him to be Mr. Henry Brougham). For it is the cue of the Whigs at this moment, *i.e.* since their coalition, to insist on the superannuation of the division by Whigs and Tories. This idea was thrown out by the President of the York Whig Club; again at the Cheshire Club of the same denomination;[3] and here again in the Edinburgh Review, p. 431,—"the distinctions, and almost the names of Loyalist and Jacobin, Whig and Tory, Court and Country faction, are fast wearing away. Two great divisions of the community will, in all likelihood, soon be far more generally known—the *Liberal* and the *Illiberal*." Happy

---

* It is a false, though universal notion, that the Whig and Tory creed exclude each other,—as though, if a Whig, then no Tory, if Tory, then no Whig. On the contrary, they are the two hemispheres of the total truth;—the true theory of our Constitution being equally mutilated if either be wanting. Why then oppose the Whigs? *Answer*—Not for the principles properly belonging to them *as* Whigs, but for others, arbitrarily assumed; and for *conduct* during half a century opposed to all constitutional principles whatever,—Whig as much as Tory. But all this requires a separate essay; and the argument in the text applies equally under the false or the true idea of Whigs and Tories.

---

[3] Reported in the *Standard*, October 2, p. 3, col. 4, and October 12, p. 2, col. 3.

doctrine for the parties to the Coalition; that change would cloak their apostacy! and with respect to Mr. Henry Brougham, in particular, the policy of such a change is specially urgent. For a certain period (hour and place can be sworn to) there is good evidence that he and Mr. Canning were in fierce hostility night after night. It will not be said that they were disputing about nothing; *that* would criminate both. About what, then? Now from this question there is no issue but into the following dilemma: Either it must be argued that *all* the subjects of dispute not in a course of years, but suddenly and *per saltum*, exploded like a rocket; or that the whole *materia litis* still subsists in full force, but that one of the disputants has suddenly seen cause to alter his opinions; and that, wherever he before said *No*, (unless in those cases where the two agreed to divide the apostacy) he now says *Yes*. In the first case of the dilemma, there is a miracle; in the second certainly no miracle at all. But there is an awkward question annexed to it—viz. which of the disputants it is that puts the *Yes* where heretofore he put the *No?* Both factions will be silent so long as they are allowed to interpret this silence each in their own favour. But let either speak out what both insinuate, and there goes to the winds the whole harmony between Mr. Brougham and the party of Mr. Canning. Their harmony, real or unreal, is built, in any case, on apostacy; and even such a harmony, it seems, is supported only by concealment and reciprocal imposture! One word of truth, and it is dissolved.

But the two articles which, on different accounts, are likely to interest the most, are the first and second; and these we must despatch more briefly than we could wish.

Art. I. *Burke's Letters.* No doubt it was imagined that *Brougham upon Burke* would be a taking invitation. Mr. Brougham, though an Englishman, was educated in Edinburgh, and has some friends here—some proneurs—some toad-eaters. From all these there is a chance for more or less flattery, to Mr. Brougham personally, as well as to Mr. Brougham the partizan. But every neutral person of judgment will tell Mr. Brougham, that a more unfortunate collision of names for himself could not have been suggested. Burke, the philosopher, on the one hand, with the finest and subtlest understanding that appeared in the eighteenth century, whose works are one galaxy of original and profound thoughts;—on the other Mr. Brougham, the man-of-business, with the plain matter-of-fact understanding, from whose whole speeches and writings not one remarkable or brilliant sentiment can be cited. Literature is overrun with the words of Burke: Where did any man ever read a quotation from Mr. Brougham, for any separate value that even a parasite could attach to the thought? But the question of Mr. Brougham's pretensions to a superior understanding, we conceive to be finally settled by his Glasgow Inaugural Discourse, and above all by his Discourse on the Objects, &c. of Science. Not, reader, by the innumerable blunders which it contains in matters of science, as exposed in the 6d. pamphlet called the *Blunders of a Big Wig*;[4] for these affect his pretensions directly only as a man of science; although, indirectly, no doubt, they extend further, by calling in question the good sense of one who, being so utterly unprepared as a learner, could think it his vocation to step forward as a national teacher. But the point we would insist on, as indicating a coarse and vulgar cast of intellect, is the style of wonder-making, in which Mr. Brougham brings forward the great laws and phenomena of nature. The selection is itself vulgar, being generally of things odd and singular—rather than of

[4] Brougham had been elected Lord Rector of the University of Glasgow; his Inaugural Discourse (April 6, 1825) is in his *Speeches* (Edinburgh, 1838), III, 69-98. On his scientific discourse and the *Blunders of a Big Wig* see above, p. 129.

those which move by the grandeur of simplicity: Just as a sailor, who forgets every thing of interest in the high road of nature, will be sure to remember that he boiled an egg in a spring of hot water, that he saw a black swan, &c. And the style of wonderment in which these wonders are related, is still more revolting: Everywhere we seem to hear one of Mr. Pidcock's showmen,—"Step in, gentlemen and ladies, only 6d. a-piece; all for the small sum of 6d.* Here's the wonderful system of Copernicus! with Jupiter—that Royal Bengal planet. And here are the little Asteroids! And here's a pound of butter, which perhaps you think is a pound everywhere—Bless your souls! if it were taken to the sun, it would weigh 22 lb. odd,"—and so forth.

But amongst all the evidences which Mr. Brougham has given that his understanding is any thing but a fine or subtile one, we rely most upon this attempt to characterise Burke. People will only smile good-naturedly when they read from the pen of Mr. Brougham that Edmund

* "*All for the small sum of sixpence:*" This is no joke, as the reader may suppose, but sober earnest. In the last Number of the Edinburgh, there was a downright tradesman's attack, and one which no honourable tradesman would condescend to, on the rivals of Mr. Brougham's *Library of Useful Knowledge.* This present Number contains another, insisting at great length that Mr. Brougham's Firm gives more print, paper, &c. for the money than one Mr. Paxton does, who never apparently meditated the least opposition to Mr. Brougham. Both articles are attributed to Mr. Brougham.[5]

5 Pidcock had been the proprietor of a Wild Beast Show. There is a reference to him near the beginning of Chap. XXIII of *Biographia Literaria.*

On Brougham's article in the last number of the *Edinburgh* see pp. 39, 129-30 above. His article in the present number is the eleventh, on an edition of Paley's *Natural Theology*, with plates and notes by James Paxton, and on *Animal Mechanics*, published by the Society for the Diffusion of Useful Knowledge; see New, p. 443, for other evidence of his authorship. Brougham praises Paxton's edition but points out vigorously how much more for the money is given by the Society.

Burke laboured under the "infirmity of a judgment weakened by his *temper*;" but, whosoever has any knowledge of the human mind, will smile disdainfully when he reads the old hack opinion promulgated for the thousandth time—that his judgment was vitiated by his fancy, or that fancy was the distinguishing faculty of Edmund Burke. Judgment vitiated by fancy! Paltry style of thinking!—Fancy the antagonist of the judgment!—Poor, hackneyed, inane philosophy! As if the fancy were not the best ally of the judgment, or in fact its only one. For that would be no judgment at all, in any commendable sense, which represented only the narrow field of absolute experience. Experience can be applied analogously only by the fancy. So much a man *conceives*, as he is able to represent by his fancy; so much he judges, as he conceives. The fancy is the express organ of the judgment. But if by *fancy* is meant this faculty, as actuated by the inspiration of vanity, and luxuriating in its own activities beyond the necessities of the understanding,—to no human being is fancy, under this modification, less attributable than to Edmund Burke. There is a description of ornamented composition, which, in popular criticism, is expressed by the term 'flowery,' meaning excess of figurativeness sought for its own sake, and not spontaneously prompted. To poor understandings, caught only by the surfaces of things, no two writers that have ever existed, are more liable to this stigma of floweriness, than Jeremy Taylor and Edmund Burke; whilst, in fact, none are less so. In some writers, celebrated for the brilliancy of their embellishments, as, for example, Foster the Baptist clergyman, (author of the Essays,) [6] the figure, metaphors, &c. appear to have been laid on separately, and artificially, as so much embroidery, and to have a distinct substance from the tex-

[6] John Foster, whose *Essays* were published in 1805.

ture of the ground. Now, on the contrary, in Taylor and
in Burke, every thing figurative is part and parcel of the
process of thinking, and incarnated with the thought; it
is not a separable descant *on* what they think, but a part
of the organ *by* which they think,—for we will take upon
us to affirm, that no passage can be produced from either
of them, in which the imagery does no more than repeat
and reflect the naked unillustrated thought, but that
always there is some latent feature, or relation of the
truth revealed by the imagery, which could not have
been revealed without it. Burke, overmastered by the
weight of the truth he was communicating, was the last
man in the world to court ornaments of boyish rhetoric.
A man who builds for a purpose of utility, supposing
that he builds with a view to the accidents of climate in
a mountainous country, will probably build pictur-
esquely; but this is the last of his thoughts. His pic-
turesqueness is not an end, though it may seem such to
a spectator; but a means, and, in relation to his intentions, an accident. So of Burke,—it was the necessity of
his understanding, dealing with subtle truths, that required a perpetual light of analogy, (the *idem in altero*)
for making them apprehensible,—to write by the organ
of a figured diction, which, yet, for a purpose of display
and rhetorical effect, he would have despised. And what
came of it? Why, this,—that he wrote a thousand times
more philosophically, and with a wider compass of
thought, than plain straight-forward understandings like
those of the Broughams, &c. on this earth, can at all
measure or comprehend. Away then with this old doctrine of Mr. Burke's 'fancy;' as to that about his 'temper,'
coming (as it does) from Mr. Brougham, we say nothing,
but willingly resign it to the laughter of the world.

In regard to the second Article, *(German Literature)*
which is all that now remains for us to notice, it is by so
many degrees the weightiest in the Review, that we

cannot, within the short limits assigned to us, render any justice to its merits. We prefer, therefore, to an inadequate account of this article, the plan of passing it entirely *sub silentio*. One word only, by way of apostrophe to the writer, on a particular subject introduced into it. You, Reviewer, are not merely a man of genius and original mind, but also a man of honour. Say not, therefore, (though from friendly motives) what hereafter it may give you pain to find untenable. Dugald Stewart is *not* a preparation for reading Kant. No man is more entirely ignorant of Kant, and of the spirit of Kant's writings, or boasts more of his ignorance, than Mr. Stewart. One work only of Kant's (*De Principiis et Formâ Mundi Intelligibilis*) did he ever look into, and one expounder (Schmidt Phiseldek) for they were both in Latin. Even these he did not read; and in the former he ridiculed, as "jargon," the thoughts of Newton and of Leibnitz, which he mistook for those of Kant. This suggestion we take the liberty of making as one lover of truth to another.[7]

ATTRIBUTION

This review, in two parts, of the *Edinburgh Review* for October 1827 is certainly De Quincey's. Carlyle, a good witness here, says it is (pp. 5-8 above). And there are several pieces of internal evidence strong

[7] The author of the article was Carlyle. Dugald Stewart's confession of his ignorance of Kant and his dependence on secondary sources is in his *Philosophical Essays* (1810), *Collected Works*, ed. Sir William Hamilton (Edinburgh, 1854-60), V, 117-18n., and the Second Part of his *Dissertation* (1821), *Works*, I, 389n. His correspondence with Thomas Wirgman on the same subject (see p. 339 below) was in the *Encyclopaedia Londiniensis* (1823). Schmidt Phiseldek is Konrad Friedrich von Schmidt-Phiseldeck and his book is *Philosophiae criticae secundum Kantium expositio systematica* (Copenhagen, 1796-98). The title of the work by Kant should be *De mundi sensibilis atque intelligibilis forma et principiis.*

enough to enable us to attribute this to De Quincey even apart from Carlyle's testimony.

The characterization of Hazlitt here (pp. 193-94), that he was a misanthrope but not a "noble" misanthrope, not Timon but Apemantus, is repeated, with the same names, in De Quincey's "Recollections of Charles Lamb" (1838), M., III, 82. Also on Hazlitt's misanthropy see "Notes on Gilfillan's Literary Portraits" (1845-46), M., XI, 341-42, 353. On Hazlitt's "mode of composition," its discontinuity and splinters and flashes, but with the qualification that he was a man of "splendid talents," see "Charles Lamb" (1848), M., V, 231-32, 236-37.

The account of Burke's mind and style (pp. 201-203) is very close, both in ideas and language, to the account in De Quincey's "Rhetoric," published in the following year (1828), M., X, 114-15. Burke there is called the supreme writer of his century, the man of "the largest and finest understanding." De Quincey emphasizes *understanding* because, he says, for one-third of a century donkeys have been braying about what they are pleased to call Burke's "fancy," and he replies with the same exclamatory, contemptuous excitement apparent here. Burke's fancy is not employed for "separable ornament"; he is a man of fancy only in the sense in which Jeremy Taylor and all larger and discursive thinkers are; he apprehends many and complex relations of objects, as one must, by physical "analogies"; he is "figurative," meaning "thinking in and by his figures," not "laying them on" by way of enamel or "after-ornament" but *"incarnating . . .* his thoughts in imagery." De Quincey continues the comparison of Burke and Taylor a few pages later in the essay on "Rhetoric," M., X, 125: in Burke and Taylor the imagery never "does no more than echo and repeat what is already said in the thought which it is brought to illustrate," but it extends and amplifies or fortifies the thought. (In several other essays De Quincey characterizes Taylor as an author of gorgeous imagery and gigantic thinking.) The reference to Foster in this context also has its parallel in the essay on "Rhetoric," a few pages earlier (M., X, 110): Foster's imagery and ornaments have evidently not grown up in the loom and concurrently with the "texture" of the thoughts but have been "separately" added afterwards, "as so much embroidery." He says much the same of Foster in "Gilfillan's Literary Portraits," M., XI, 337: Foster's images are "embroidered" upon the "ground" of his text; they are not "spontaneous" and do not grow up as part of the "texture" but are as extraneous to the "substance" as "flowers" chalked on a ballroom floor. Also on the commonplace notion of Burke's imagination and on Burke as the very "finest, subtlest" intellect see "Dr. Samuel Parr" (1831), M., V, 74, 115-16; on Burke's "philosophic understanding," see "On the Political Parties of Modern England" (written 1837), M., IX, 372; on Burke's "fineness of understanding" see "A Brief Appraisal of the Greek Literature" (1838-39), M., X, 339.

There is additional evidence of authorship in the use of the figure of incarnation (p. 203) to express the union of thought and image. Not only does De Quincey apply the same figure to the same effect in the same author, as pointed out in the previous paragraph, but he also says elsewhere that he learned the figure from Wordsworth, having heard him use it; see "Style" (1840-41), M., X, 229-30. The figure is also in "Language" (first known publication 1858), M., X, 262, and it is in the 1850 "Professor Wilson," M., V, 301, where, as here, the reference is to the thought of Burke and Taylor. Wordsworth had used the figure to express the relationship of words and thought, in his essay "Upon Epitaphs," written for the *Friend*; but the portion of the essay in which it appeared was not published until 1876 in A. B. Grosart's edition of Wordsworth's *Prose Works* (II, 65). We have already had occasion to note De Quincey's association with Wordsworth and Coleridge at the time of the *Friend* (pp. 71-72 above). The author in the *Post*, then, like De Quincey, employs a strikingly original, Wordsworthian, critical term and principle, which had not been published; and, like De Quincey, he extends the principle from the relationship of thoughts and words to the relationship of thoughts and images and, like De Quincey, applies it to Burke.

On the relationship of Whig and Tory (pp. 198-99) as essential complementary halves of the British constitution see the later article written for the *Post*, the Bodleian MS., pp. 356-57 below, where the same idea and some of the same language reappears: the distinction between the parties cannot become "obsolete," as some now pretend; it is the "synthesis" of the two that forms the "total truth" of the constitution; the argument there too is directed against Brougham and his attempt to cloak apostacy by new and absurd combinations of *liberal* and *illiberal*; see also De Quincey's article in *Blackwood's*, XXX (1831), 318, on *liberal* and *illiberal*. And the same identities of thought and word are repeated several times in De Quincey's other essays. In "A Tory's Account of Toryism, Whiggism, and Radicalism" (1835-36), M., IX, 331-32, Whig and Tory, so far from "excluding each other" are both essential: "they represent the total sphere of the constitution, each representing one hemisphere . . . they make up the total truth." In the sequel to that article, "On the Political Parties of Modern England" (written 1837), M., IX, 373, "each party forms one hemisphere; jointly they make up the total sphere." In the Preface to one of the volumes of his collected works, a volume published in 1857, he says once more that Whigs and Tories form "the two hemispheres which jointly compose the total truth," the "synthesis which realizes and embodies the total constitutional truth" (M., V, 129-30). The same ideas and some of the same language are also in his article "French Revolution," written for *Blackwood's* a few years after this one, XXVIII (1830), 556-57: only fools think that Whig and Tory can be extinguished when both together make up the total constitution; there too the argument is connected with the apostacy of the Canning coalition. There too he makes the distinction between the original principles of a political party and its secondary and arbitrary characteristics, as he does again in "The Late Cabinet," *Blackwood's*, XXVIII (1830), 960, 975; and that point is made also in a cancelled passage in the Bodleian MS. (pp. 352-53).

On "apostacy," incidentally, see the article of August 18, 1827 (p. 83, above) and the references given there. It is a common word in the Tory vocabulary at this time, but we can note that it runs through all De Quincey's political writings of the period. E.g., "The Duke of Wellington and Mr. Peel," *Blackwood's*, XXV (1829), 294, 295; "France and England," *Blackwood's*, XXVIII (1830), 710; "Political Anticipations," *ibid.*, 734. It was in the *Westmorland Gazette*, May 29, 1819, p. 3, in reference to one of Fox's coalitions. It is also in some of the subsequent articles written for the *Post*, including the one of January 26, 1828 (p. 285), which is certainly his, and the article of February 9, 1828 (p. 305).

To return to the specifically De Quinceyan: on popular journals (pp. 189-92), including the *Edinburgh*, which make it their ambition not to lead but to follow the public mind in its opinions on poetry, see his "Oxford" (1835), M., II, 60. The *Post* article of June 14, 1828 (p. 363n.), which is certainly his, refers back to the comment in the present article on the servility of the journals. The same unfavourable characterization of the

Edinburgh and the *Quarterly*, that they are primarily political and not literary, appears in a manuscript written by De Quincey for the *London Magazine* in 1821 but not published; the MS. is now in the Pierpont Morgan Library, M. A. 1225. The article of December 1, 1827 (p. 213), which is also certainly De Quincey's, refers back to the present article and repeats the comment that the two Reviews have ceased to be literary and are only political; see also the article of March 8, 1828 (p. 338).

The attack on the *Edinburgh's* early account of Kant, in this same passage, is one De Quincey had made earlier, in his "Letters to a Young Man" (1823), M., X, 68-69; there too he had said that the author of the article (whom he identified as Thomas Brown) had drawn his information from imbecile, childish French books. A few years after the present attack, in "Kant in His Miscellaneous Essays" (1830), M., VIII, 87, he said that Brown, in an early number of the *Edinburgh Review*, had written "mere nonsense, in a degree possible only to utter and determined ignorance of the German language." In "Professor Wilson" (1850), M., V, 297, he returned once more to Brown's preposterous paper on Kant in an early number of the *Edinburgh*; Brown hadn't even mastered the German language but was indebted to a Frenchman for the monstrous conceits imputed to Kant. See also M., XIV, 127.

Dugald Stewart and his ignorance of Kant (p. 204) also had been attacked by De Quincey in the "Letters to a Young Man," in the same passage (M., X, 68-72); there, however, Stewart's main source is said to have been a French book, though he had also looked into Phiseldek. See too Richard Woodhouse's "Notes of Conversations with Thomas De Quincey," in Richard Garnett's edition of the *Confessions* (1885), p. 197. De Quincey also refers to Phiseldek in his "Immanuel Kant, and John Gottfried Herder," *Westmorland Gazette*, August 28, 1819, p. 3; in "German Studies and Kant in Particular" (1836), M., II, 89n.; and in "The Last Days of Immanuel Kant" (1854 version), M., IV, 324n. He gives the title of Kant's Latin work in "The Last Days of Immanuel Kant" (1827 and 1854 versions), M., IV, 328.

The weakness of Brougham's inaugural address at Glasgow (p. 200) is attacked by De Quincey on other occasions: "Oxford" (1835), M., II, 64ff.; "On Wordsworth's Poetry" (1845), M., XI, 297. On Brougham's temper (pp. 201-203) see the article of September 29, 1827 (p. 148), and the reference there; that article too is certainly his.

On the dilemma as a form of argument (p. 199) see the article of September 15, 1827, and on the device of the question and answer (p. 198n.), see the same article (pp. 120-22) and the references there.

Of the Greek phrases used in this article, νεφεληγερετα Ζευς (p. 197) is common but it is worth pointing out that De Quincey does use it (M., I, 58) and νεφελγερερετα (M., XII, 359), before and after the date of this article. κατ᾽ ἐξοχήν (p. 191) is more unusual, it is a favorite phrase with De Quincey, and the specific phrase "literature κατ᾽ ἐξοχήν" he later used in "The Poetry of Pope" (1848), M., XI, 59, to designate the literature of power. In a couple of other essays of earlier date he had referred to "poetry κατ᾽ ἐξοχήν": in the "Letters to a Young Man" (1823), which has other similarities with the present article, M., X, 54, and in "False Distinctions" (1824), M., X, 442; "poetic κατ᾽ ἐξοχήν" is in a note to "Lessing's Laocoon" (1826-27), M., XI, 206. In an earlier, private, criticism of the *Edinburgh Review* he had denounced its feebleness in philosophy and esthetics and similar "indefinite" subjects, the only class where any truly great and "κατ᾽ ἐξοχήν" intellectual power can be manifested;

Illustrations

The illustrations are reproduced from prints in the British Museum and are published here with the permission of the Trustees. They are described in the *Catalogue of Political and Personal Satires* in the Department of Prints and Drawings of the Museum, by M. Dorothy George, vols. X (1952) and XI (1954), a work that has been most valuable to me. The *Catalogue* numbers are given in the parentheses, after the date of publication and the artist; some dates are taken from the prints themselves, others are approximate.

The prints are directly illustrative of the text, where it deals with the political events and personalities of 1827-1828, often of specific passages, and they are chosen, therefore, for their content rather than their formal qualities. Frequently hasty, misprinted, even illiterate, cluttered and clumsy, they can be, moreover, terribly violent and cruel. But in their best moments the play is exciting, or they cut wittily, or the wild passion becomes a unifying and designing force.

1. *The Rising Sun or Faction Defeated* (May 10, 1827; Henry Heath; 15390).

The rising sun is Canning, now prime minister, encircled by the motto *Astra Castra—Numen Lumen* (the stars are my camp, the deity my light), and radiating *Liberalism, Independence, Loyalty, Patriotism, Magnanimity, Sincerity*. This is the earliest appearance of "Liberalism" in the political prints at the British Museum and, in its context, it still seems to be as much a moral virtue as a political principle. (See the articles of November 24, 1827, pp. 198, 207, and May 31, 1828, p. 353). The sun is dispelling the *Cloud of Ignorance* and driving off the Tories who had resigned from the cabinet; he is aided by the thunderbolts of the King, who is exercising his royal *Prerogative* to choose his own minister, in defiance of Tory attempts to dictate. The leading Tories are Wellington, who says, "I smell *Gunpowder*, where shall I *march* to this *light* blinds me," and Eldon, who answers, "I smell *Coke*—never mind Gunpowder my Lord. I'll introduce you to my Old Friend. he'll find places for us both." His old friend is the Devil, who invites them, "Pop into this Bag my Lords and Gentlemen—I'll take care of you all," and collects them in his *Old Bags*, which was the King's nickname for Eldon, used derisively by his enemies. Behind Eldon is Bathurst, saying, "I smell a Rat," and Bexley, who says nothing. Peel is on his knees, crying, "This blaze of Light is more than I can bear." He is identified by the *Orange Peel* on the ground beside him, indicating his anti-Catholicism (after 1829, when he supported the Catholic Emancipation, he became Lemon Peel). The others are Westmorland: "I am Thunderstruck"; and Melville, a Scot with an itch and in need of a cure: "I smell Brimstone." In the background the *Holy Alliance*, too, is reacting to the new liberal sun. *France* is falling on its back; *Russia* swaggers; *Austria* is kicking *Spain*. Meanwhile revolutionary *Greece* is plucking *Turkey* by the beard.

Cabnet IN's and OUT's. No.3.

The RISING SUN or FACTION DEFEATED.

Ecod they have zaun vound, him out
Ha! ha! ha! they wont leave him a feather
to fly with!!!

Catholic Emancipation

Free Trade

Foreign Wonders

The CROWING JACKDAW & the PEACOCKS.— A Sketch from St Stephens Furmyend. 2 June 1827

An ambitious Jackdaw having picked up some feathers which fell from the Peacocks, and stuck them in his own tail, endeavoured to pass for one of those noble birds; they however were not to be so easily cheated, but found him out, strip him of his borrowed plumes, and punished him as his presumption deserved.— Upon this he again wished to flock with his old companions, but they knowing his late duplicity turned their backs upon him and refused to admit him into their company.—— Thus having attempted to deceive his neighbours, and having feathered his nest with their goods he had nothing to expect when found out but to be stript of his plunder and used like a felonious Rogue into the bargain—Vide Æsops Fable.

2. The Cu̇nning Jackdaw & the Peacocks.—A Sketch from St Stephens Farm-yard (June 2, 1827; Thomas Howell Jones; 15402).

"An ambitious Jackdaw having picked up some feathers which fell from the Peacocks, and stuck them in his own tail, endeavoured to pass for one of those *noble* birds; they however were not to be so easily cheated, but found him out, stript him of his borrowed plumes, and punished him as his presumption deserved.—Upon this he again wished to flock with his *old* companions, but they knowing his late duplicity turned their backs upon him and refused to admit him into their company.—Thus having attempted to deceive his neighbours, and having feathered his *nest* with their goods he had nothing to expect when *found out* but to be stript of his plunder and used like a felonious Rogue into the bargain.—Vide Æsops Fables."

Canning is the jackdaw who moves from party to party and who claims credit for what he has not originated. The false feathers being plucked from him are *Free Trade, Foreign Policy, South America, Catholic Emancipation*. (See the articles of August 4 and August 18, 1827, pp. 49-51, 78-80.) Immediately to his left is Grey and to his right is Wellington, the leading Whig and the leading Tory opposing his coalition. In the background John Bull enjoys the spectacle: "E'cod they have zuun vound him out, Ha! ha! ha! they won't leave him a feather to fly with!!"

3. *The Pilot Lost and the National Steamboat in Danger* (August 1827; Charles Williams; 15423).

Canning has just died (article of August 18, 1827), and without her pilot *The Britannia*, flying her ensign upside down to signal *Distress*, is in danger of going on the *Rocks of Tory Island*. The Tories who had left the cabinet are now attempting to board the ship again, but John Bull calls to them: "Stand off you set of lubberly Pirates d'ye think I'll suffer such mutinous dogs to come on board? No! although our poor Pilot is overboard our Captain is strong in heart and hand, and will get safe into port without your assistance for which you want such enormous Salvage so back water you dogs or I'll sink you—!" The Captain, George IV, cheers him on: "Bravo John

rake them fore and aft let them know that depending on you I have never been de-cieved!!" And the Tories are forced to hold back. A belligerent Wellington is advised, "Fair and softly Mates she makes a strong swell and may upset us, who would hav though he would have been so obstinate, we must persuade him he is in great danger and get the honor of saveing him." Eldon, in the bow of the boat, says characteristically, "I think we had better *Hesitate!*" To the right are two sailors who recognize the unsuccessful boarders: "I'll be d——d Tom if thes arnt the wery same lubberly crew as wanted to capsize our Pilot ven he first com'd aboard us!!"; "I'll be D——d if it arnt Ben!" George's choice of Goderich as the new prime minister kept the Tories out.

THE PILOT LOST and THE NATIONAL STEAMBOAT in DANGER.

4. *Old Harry looking out for a Warm Birth or a Peep in to the Oven!!!* (October, 1827; William Heath; 15431).

Brougham is dressed as one of the German broom-girls who sold their wares in the streets of London. A broom was also, when tied to the mast of a ship, a sign that the ship could be bought. Brougham, in the eyes of his enemies, had sold himself to Canning and the Canningites and wanted to be rewarded, in his barrister's wig, with the Mastership of the Rolls. (See the article of September 8, 1827, pp. 100, 104.) Peeping greedily into the oven marked *Rolls* Brougham declares, "I should like to *Master* this *batch*—there are so many

Crumbs to pick up—besides it does not take away one's *eyes*
or one's *nose*—like some of the tit bits—this would realy be
a *prime* little *Crust*—." Unlike some other lucrative offices,
including that of Chief Baron of the Exchequer, which he
had refused, the Mastership did not require that he give up
his seat in the House of Commons.

5. *A Change in the Head of Affairs* (January, 1828; William
Heath; 15498).

Goderich has resigned and Wellington is now prime minister. (See the article of January 26, 1828.) The King, using
tongs, hands his old wig to Wellington: "Throw it away. I
can't get any of them to suit me." Wellington replies, "Happy
I am to see the Whig discarded—I'll try and Administer
something that shall fit your M——— better."

THE ROYAL SPEECH

6. *The Royal Speech* (February, 1828; Robert Seymour, later of *Pickwick* fame; 15511).

On the King's speech which had declared the Battle of Navarino an "untoward event." (See the articles of November 17, 1827, and February 2, 1828.) Jack the tar addresses Sir Edward Codrington: "Please Your Honor's Glory there's something wrong in the wind, for they've clapt a Marine at the Helme of Old England, and He and other lob lollies have made Sombody (God bless Him) to call our Glorious Victory an UNTOWARD EVENT And when they where told to belay their jawing tackel they shifted the wind and began to blow another way." Codrington agrees: "Aye Aye Jack they or we must be fools." In his left hand is the *Treaty of London*, in his right a sword inscribed *England expects every Man to do his Duty* (Codrington had led a squadron at Trafalgar). In the background between the two speakers is a cliff overlooking the sea with the face of Wellington, the "Marine"; a Wellington boot caps the flagstaff.

7. *Druming Out. Or Making an Example of a Mutineer* (May, 1828; William Heath; 15531).

Wellington kicking Huskisson out of the cabinet. (See the article of May 31, 1828.) Wellington: "What? encourage *Mutiny*—no no, *decision* is my motto come turn out you shall not stay in my *corps discipline* must be kept up—Attention there in the Ranks Attention—let this be a warning to you—." The ranks behind him are the *Proposed new Administration*. Huskisson, stripped of his coat and insignia, his wig reversed, and placarded *East Retford*, laments: "Oh that foolish vote— and worse than all the cursed *Letter*—resign I never thought of such a *measure*." At his feet is a version of the unfortunate letter: *If after taking such a step my holding office should be felt embarrassing to the Administration I'm ready to Resign.* In the background the King is fishing (as he liked to do in Virginia Water), encouraging Wellington: "Take him at his word A———r let him go——." To the left is Liverpool, Huskisson's constituency, declaring, "we shall turn our backs on him." (For Huskisson's troubles in Liverpool see the articles of February 2, 16 and 23, 1828.)

DRUMING OUT - OR MAKING AN EXAMPLE OF A MUTINEER.

O Connell for ever and a day after
be der mighty powers but we'll be getting emancipation and whiskey galore
for nothing, bltherumskite blarney an botheration entirely
well all be Gentlemen this time aney how at all

AN **INDEPENDANT FREEHOLDER** rejoicing at the **TRIUMPH** of the **MAN** of the **PAPAL**.

July 1828

8. *An Independant Freeholder rejoicing at the Triumph of the Man of the Papal* (July, 1828; William Heath; 15539).

An Irish forty-shilling freeholder celebrating O'Connell's election at Clare. (See the article of July 12, 1828.) He has speared an orange with his weapon, a fork tied to a shillelagh, and rants: "O'Connell for ever and a day after be der mighty powers but we'll be getting *mancipation* and *whiskeypation* for nothing. bletherumskite blarney an botheration intirely we'll all be Gintlemen this time aney how at all." In the background church and country burn.

letter to Henry De Quincey, June 8, 1811, in *De Quincey Memorials*, ed. Alexander H. Japp (1891), II, 158. The same Greek phrase in other contexts is in "The Present Cabinet in Relation to the Times," *Blackwood's*, XXIX (1831), 147, "Dr. Parr," *Blackwood's*, XXIX, 781, and again in "The Poetry of Pope," M., XI, 81.

To take up, in the order of their appearance, the Latin phrases, some of which do not offer much evidence, but others of which are more impressive. *De jure . . . de facto* (p. 191) De Quincey uses several times (M., VI, 96; XI, 6; XII, 87); and he uses them individually (M., VI, 237, 297; VIII, 253n.; XI, 99). *Sine qua non* (p. 195), the most commonplace of phrases, is, surprisingly, rather good evidence here. First of all, it is pervasive in De Quincey; he uses it about three dozen times and it turns up in some of the other articles in the *Post* (pp. 86, 91, 318). But more to the point, the particular usage "*sine qua non* condition" is less usual and it is De Quinceyan: M., VII, 269; IX, 154, 193; X, 232; and on fifteen to twenty other occasions he writes "*conditio sine qua non.*" For *prima facie* (p. 197) see the article of August 11, 1827 (p. 73) and the further references there. *Per saltum* (p. 199) he uses in twenty different places, including "A Tory's Account of Toryism," etc., where there are other parallels to the same passage in the present article; J. Hillis Miller, *The Disappearance of God* (Cambridge, 1963), p. 38, has noted the characteristic quality of the phrase in De Quincey's thought. "Materia litis" (p. 199) is in M., IV, 125; *Blackwood's*, XLVIII (1840), 300; and *Posthumous Works* (1891), II, 121.

December 1, 1827

Blackwood's Magazine

No. 133.

(December, 1827.)

Every body remembers the old story of Themistocles—
Because *all* his fellow generals allowed him the second
place, disinterested judges presumed him entitled to the
first.[1] On this argument, combined with others, we regard Blackwood's Magazine as the first, in point of
talent, amongst the journals of the present day: certainly
none would collect so many suffrages, if it were a candidate for the second place; and therefore, it is presumable,
that, considering the present execution of the two leading
reviews, nothing stands in the way of its claim to the
first, excepting only the name of *Magazine*. According to
the feeling of the world, undoubtedly the name *Review*
has the advantage in point of dignity. For *Magazine* was
a name which Blackwood found already degraded to the
dust, when he planned his memorable revolution in that
department of literature; and it would be too much to
expect, that ten years of brilliant writing should dissolve
the inveterate associations which almost a century of
dulness had gathered about that title. Notwithstanding
this, in a philosophical estimate of things, the Magazine
is entitled to the precedency. In the Review, as related
to the current needs of society, there is a defect of the
same description as that which affects English law. In
this we are reminded often of the narrow basis out of
which it has grown, by the multitudes of fictions which
time has rendered necessary for bringing the expanded
interests of social life within the field of its original rules.

[1] Herodotus, VIII, 123, and repeated by Plutarch in his life of
Themistocles.

The same error in the first model, appears in the practice
of Reviews. Fictions of the grossest kind, down even to
absolute lies, and the forging titles of pamphlets that
have never existed, are at present found necessary, in
order to furnish an excuse for bringing topics of immediate interest before their bar, and connecting themselves with the shifting passions of the day. Now in
Magazines, all this is effected naturally, and in consistency with their plan and professions. They profess to be a
general *depôt*, a πανδοχειον,[2] both for life and literature;
this they profess to be,—and this they are. It is melancholy to see an old tiger of a reviewer grinding his teeth
and lashing his tail, at a man whom he longs to tear limb
from limb, but can find no pretence for getting at him,
because the fellow has not written a book. Mr. O'Connel
for instance,[3] or Mr. Brougham, makes a treasonable
speech; but, because it is no where to be found, excepting
in the columns of a newspaper,—the learned gentlemen
defy you, and snap their fingers at you scornfully, just
as a man hisses a bull, and insults him by the cruelest
and most barbarous personalities, after he has once
climbed up a tree, to a prudent elevation above his
horns. But now let your gay magazines be slipped at
them,—he soon takes the conceit out of the O'C., or the
B., that is sitting up a-loft in the tree, by showing himself to be a snake who can climb trees as fast as they,—
and chase them through earth, air, and water, alike.

But of this enough: for the plan and conception,
whether better or worse, is, in anybody's account, of less
consequence than the execution: and here at least, if
there be any truth in what we said a fortnight ago on
the mismanagement of the two leading Reviews, Blackwood undoubtedly has the advantage. For one thing

[2] A house for the reception of strangers, an inn.
[3] Daniel O'Connell, the Irish Catholic leader, the subject of
other attacks in the *Post* and in De Quincey's other political writing; see below pp. 291-92, 388ff.

there is which in this point is remarkable as to Blackwood, viz., that upon a comparison of any triennium with the preceding one, he has upon the whole continued to improve; whereas the general tendency of such undertakings is downwards, whether by a rapid descent as in the majority, or a gradual and lingering one, as in the Edinburgh and Quarterly Reviews.

These two Reviews, by the way, (as we observed in our last notice of the Edinburgh) have altogether ceased to be *literary* journals, and perhaps wish to have it understood that they decline any connexion with the literature of the country, as a subject out of their department. They confine themselves apparently to committees of the House of Commons, to Quarter Sessions, and Select Vestries. This derelict, therefore, or waif of literature has lapsed to Blackwood, the only journal that has for years back made itself felt or feared in literature. But even Blackwood has been latterly disposed to allow an undue preponderance to politics; and another thing we hear whispered, viz., that an amiable weakness begins to manifest itself in Christopher North, as in the late King during his latter years,—an unwillingness to sign death-warrants, and a general indisposition to any act of criminal justice. Amiable, but wrong! Impunity will produce a great crop of crime; which is a sad alliteration. So that it will be real mercy in Mr. North to assume the fatal velvet, and make a few examples in his Lent circuit. For felons begin to abound in literature; and we hear continually of honest authors that are hustled, and robbed in open day-light.

But to come now to the particular No. before us, it is a respectable, but (for Blackwood) not a splendid one. There is no thunder and lightning: the whole lies in a middle region, and a climate of serenity, which is pleasant to wander through, but less suited to purposes of effect and powerful impression.

On this account we take leave to notice only the first article (*Game-laws,*) and the last (*Country Banks*); which, from the distinguished excellence of their morality and their politics, as well as from the distinguished badness of their Political Economy, we presume to come from the same person; and that person to be the celebrated writer of politics in Blackwood.[4] Luckily, both the questions here treated, and especially the first, belong only in a small proportion to the Political Economist; and hence the general excellence of these papers in spite of the writer's weakness in that one particular character. It is not perhaps very fair to select the little which is bad, in preference to the much which is good; but, as the following case presents an easy illustration of a blunder, the commonest that occurs in Political Economy, and the most *productive* of all in false corollaries, we shall adduce it. He affirms that the sale of game makes butcher's meat cheaper: we deny it.

But here there is the usual confusion of market and natural price. For think a moment in what way it is that game can diminish the price of butcher's meat: Supposing the butcher's supply to be calculated upon the assumption that there will be no game, and, that unexpectedly a large supply of game enters the market,— under these circumstances, would not the game affect the price of butcher's meat? True: it would do so: it would affect the market price, i. e., that mode of price which represents the mixt considerations of cost, modified by the quantity. Such a result would benefit the purchaser, at the expence of the butcher, by robbing him of a portion of the common rate of profit. But surely the writer in Blackwood is not prepared to say, that this effect could, in the first place, be a permanent effect; or, in the second place, that, if it were so, it would be a

4 David Robinson, praised also in an earlier review of *Blackwood's,* p. 129 above.

desirable one. A strange subject of congratulation it would be to society in general—that, by the ruin or oppression of one class amongst them, they would get their butcher's meat cheaper! No: plain good sense will lead a man to the very same conclusion as Political Economy, viz. that a reduction of price, to be a beneficial one, must not arise from a special taxation of the butcher, by reducing his profits below the general level, but from a change somewhere or other in the cost of production: *i. e.* not by any accidental disturbance of *market* price, but by a regular change in the *natural* price. Now, here, we have the writer in a noose fast as ever hangman knotted. For, tell us, great anarch of Political Economy, how shall the cost of producing a sirloin of beef be affected one way or the other, because there is a ship load of grouse in the market? The *price* may be so, because that may be the market price (which we have discussed:) but how shall the natural price, or cost, of a bullock, be effected by the more or the less influx of hares and birds? To make the cost of a bullock depend on the success of a sportsman, is like the old Cambridge problem, *given the latitude of a ship to determine the captain's name.* Yet, it is true that one mode there is by which this strange connexion may be accomplished; but, then, it is such a one as barely to whisper in this writer's ear, will make him throw up his heels, and bolt from the course in a panic. Suppose the supply of game to be steady, and in some considerable proportion to the entire consumption of animal food; in that case, the demand for butcher's meat would be seriously and permanently diminished. Now this would dispense with that part of the supply which was obtained from the *worst* grazing lands; and, by thus throwing the growth of butcher's meat upon superior soils, would diminish the cost of the whole—according to the known law of rent. But *law of rent* is as startling a word to some writers in Blackwood as the name of *Cœur de Lion* whispered to a Mameluke's horse.[5]

To have done with economy, however, in all other respects the article is excellent. We heartily agree with the writer, in thinking that the ordinary objections to game, as property, stand on no other footing than all Jacobinism, and the whole levelling philosophy. It is not that this sort of property is less really sacred, or at all less entitled to the protection of the law—this is not what suggests the attacks upon it—but a feeling on the part of those who would willingly attack *all* property that the attacks upon this in particular are more popular, and find a welcome which they should *not* find amongst respectable people who do not see the final tendencies of what they so thoughtlessly encourage. To what degree, however, the unquestionable evils under the present system of the game laws, might be remedied, this writer does not very closely discuss. The following, however, are some of his excellent suggestions:—

1st, To compel the owners of game-preserves to protect their property more effectually: "the mode not to be left to their own discretion, but to be defined by law." He justly insists, that "a man ought to protect his property as far as possible from theft—to have a fair claim on the law for the punishment of those who may steal it." This is the principle on which linen-drapers, mercers, &c. have recently been fined in London for exposing their goods too much. No man has a right to tempt others too heavily, or beyond the necessities of his own rights.

2d, To make the punishment for killing game unlawfully "more discriminating." "Labourers who occasionally

---

[5] A tremendous name used among the Syrians (and no doubt Mamelukes too), by mothers to silence their infants and riders their horses; see Gibbon, *Decline and Fall*, Chap. LIX (ed. J. B. Bury, VI [1898], 350), who cites Joinville. Scott used the same story in *Ivanhoe* and *The Talisman*.

kill a hare when it is thrown in their way, while they are following their occupation, but who do not make a practice of it, or for profit, ought to be dealt with leniently. In a case like this, he should only be called on for a small fine within his power to pay. Such a fine would do little injury to his character, and none to his morals. But to impose a fine on him which he could not pay, would be in reality to send him to prison; and this, in all probability, would make him a confirmed poacher."[6]

3dly, To throw the punishment more upon the trespass than upon the killing of the game, as a means of more directly reconciling the punishment to the general feeling; the rights of land proprietors being in this point more in coincidence with the popular notions than his right over the game.

But want of room obliges us to pass to the last article, which the same cause obliges us unwillingly to dismiss with a word. The uses of country banks are here most clearly and comprehensively stated: Now what we miss is this,—a proof sufficiently circumstantial, that the branch banks could not meet these uses. We do not by this mean to express any dissent from the general conclusion of this writer. On the contrary, we are altogether hostile to the branch banks; for no matter whether they could or could not discharge the functions of the country banks, it is manifestly contrary to every principle of fair competition that they should be enabled to do so, and to attack vested interests by means of extraordinary state privileges granted by Parliament with no view of that kind. This writer's belief is, that the branch banks would be banks only for the rich; and that the far greater advantages which the country banks now yield to the national prosperity by assisting the humbler traders, which advantages are here most ably developed, would

6 As usual, the quotations are not exact.

mainly be lost. We are disposed to think so too; but should be glad to have the point more entirely cleared up.*

ATTRIBUTION

This article, which continues the criticism of the leading journals begun in the article of November 17 (pp. 189ff.), and which twice refers the reader back to that article, is also certainly De Quincey's. De Quincey had already compared magazines and reviews, to the advantage of magazines (pp. 212-14), in an article written in 1821 for the *London Magazine*; this is the unpublished manuscript referred to above in the notes to the article of November 17 (p. 209), and the fact that it was unpublished makes it, of course, especially good evidence. In that manuscript he made the same comparison between reviews and the law; reviews are forced to resort to "fictions" to bring particular cases "before their bar," and sometimes these are purely verbal fictions (Morgan Library MS. M. A. 1225, pp. 4-5).

The anecdote about Themistocles, in the same passage (p. 212), is one De Quincey used in "The Caesars" (1832), M., VI, 267.

The "Cambridge problem" (p. 216) is a favorite with De Quincey. It was in his "Letters to a Young Man" (1823), M., X, 75, and his "Memorial Chronology" (written c. 1850), M., XIV, 319. He uses it, as here, in the context of political economy, in "Ricardo and Adam

---

* One mistake, no ways affecting the argument, however, we observe at p. 752, where it is said,—"In and about London, Manchester, and Liverpool, the notes of the Bank of England have brought the notes of the country banks into such discredit, that they will only be accepted from necessity." But the fact is, that there are no such notes to accept. Lancashire has no bank for issuing notes; and the case of London, and the Bank of England *preserve* around it, is notorious. Notes of other provinces, *if payable in London*, are occasionally found, but only as Bank of England notes at Paris—with no general currency.

Smith," *Blackwood's*, LII (1842), 728, and in the revision of that article in *Logic of Political Economy* (1844), M., IX, 189, where also he makes the distinction made here between market price and natural price (M., IX, 121, 200-207). See also the article of September 15, 1827 (p. 119) for further references on this distinction.

Foreign Quarterly Review

In common with the rest of the literary world, we were acquainted,—it may be supposed,—with the dispute between the *Foreign Quarterly Review* and the *Foreign Review*,—and with somewhat more of its details than have been published to the world. But we forbear to take any part in it; because it would be difficult for us to speak in the character of a neutral. Connected by ties of old friendship with the Editor of the Foreign Quarterly, it is natural that we should wish success in the first place to that; but it will give us pleasure to find that the interest in Foreign literature is so much more extended than we had supposed, as to be capable of supporting two journals.[1]

This number is better than the last.

Art. I. is on *Daru's History of Brittany*. Of a nation like the Bretons, expressly described as one

'Prodiga verborum sed non et prodiga facti,'

it cannot be expected that mere political annals should

---

[1] This was the second number of the *Foreign Quarterly Review* (November 1827). There had been attack and counterattack by it and its rival, the *Foreign Review*, in newspaper advertisements; the *Foreign Review* began publication the following year but didn't last long. The editor of the *Foreign Quarterly Review* was hapless Robert Pearse Gillies, who made himself and his review a chronic pest and a burden upon poor Sir Walter Scott, and who enters the literary history of the first half of the century in a number of other capacities. His own account of the war between the publishers of the two foreign reviews is in his *Memoirs of a Literary Veteran* (1851), III, 169-70. For Gillies' connection with De Quincey see p. 232 below.

The following identification of contributors to the *Foreign Quarterly Review* is taken from the article by John Macray in *Notes and Queries*, 2nd ser., VIII (1859), 124-27, and from the excellent dissertation by Eileen Mary Curran, "The *Foreign Quarterly Review* (1827-1846)" (Cornell, 1958). Most of the contributors have entries in the *DNB*; Miss Curran has some material on the others.

be a very attractive subject.[2] M. Daru is pretty well
known in this country by his researches into the history
of Venice: but there, and it seems also in the work
before us, he is generally taxed with an enmity to what
is called "Philosophical History" in an excess that would
make the most interesting series of events but the dry
bones of a history, stripped (as they are in his hands)
of their coherency and the general tendencies which
construct them into any tolerable unity: for some unity,
or some analogon of unity, is always necessary to support
a continuous interest. Mr. Southey is an example in this
country of the anti-philosophical historian. But the fact
is, that by "philosophical history," Mr. Southey means
history written upon preconceived theories to which the
facts are made to bend;[3] and moreover being himself
a man of high moral feelings, he gives to his narrative an
interest of another and a universal kind, which in some
degree supplies a more philosophical character: so that
he is quite as far removed as the most transcendental of
theorists from the mere annalist. M. Daru comes nearer
to the ideal of that dull and respectable character. However, it was impossible for him to "make a silk purse out
of a sow's ear:" and to write a readable book on any
thing Armoric, unless indeed on the Armoric literature
we hold to be much beyond the power of any man who
confines himself to facts. Still for the service of universal

[2] The review is by Herman Merivale. The book is the *Histoire
de Bretagne* (Paris, 1826) by Pierre Antoine Daru, who had been
a soldier and administrator under Napoleon; his history of Venice,
referred to below, had been published in 1819. The Latin quotation (big talkers but not big doers) is from a chronicle cited by
Merivale.

[3] See Southey's review of Henry Hallam's *Constitutional History
of England*, in the *Quarterly Review* of January 1828 (XXXVII,
195). This issue of the *Quarterly* was published January 7. Either
the *Post* had an advance copy (as it had of the *Edinburgh*, p. 30
above), or De Quincey had private knowledge of Southey's opinion,
or Southey had said the same thing in an earlier publication I
haven't seen.

history, all parts of which throw light upon each other, the annals even of stocks and stones (where they happen to have any) ought to be written: and, with this explanation, we are glad that such a subject has been treated by a writer whose known accuracy of research justifies the student in relying upon him as a final authority.

Art. II.—*Life and Writings of Ernest Schulze,*[4] confers an importance on the subject (and especially by the excellence of the translation) which does not properly belong to it. Schulze is described as "a name of some note in the martyrology of love;" but considering the time he took to die of love, and also that the proximate cause of his death was confessedly *phthisis pulmonalis,* we cannot forbear smiling when we read this, and involuntarily recal a little story once told to us by a gallant old Scotch officer. He was narrating the unfortunate history of an early friend, who had been jilted by a fickle beauty of that age, in favour of the Duke of A———; and he concluded the story thus, in a tone of much emotion:— "poor fellow, he never got over it; no! Sir, it was the death of him;" and then, after a pause of much pathos, with a faultering voice, he added,—"*He did not live above fifteen years after it;*" a consummation which seemed to us so comical a way of dying for love, that, if our eyes filled with tears, undoubtedly they were tears of a merrier birth than altogether suited with our excellent friend's view of the case.

Art. III.—*Cousin's Fragmens Philosophiques.*[5]—Professor Cousin is one of the most interesting phenomena of modern France: his activity, even apart from its direction, is itself portentous; and his own writings, together with those of many of his disciples for the last three years in the literary journal entitled *Le Globe*, are indeed

[4] Review by George Moir. Schulze was a German poet who had died in 1817 at the age of 28.

[5] Review by Dr. Robert Ferguson.

remarkable: the increasing subtilty and more exalted tendency of their philosophy, and (speaking more generally) the enlarged compass of the French taste and sensibilities in literature, as evidenced by their growing capacity for Shakspeare, and, in general, for the poetry of passion, English and German,—are all so many evidences that the great political convulsions of France have been followed by intellectual ones still more important, and affecting far weightier interests. On this account we looked with more anxiety to this article than to any other in the No.: but we acknowledge that we have been disappointed. The writer is a man of talents; but talents in a general sense are not enough: philosophic talent, and philosophic knowledge in a large range, together with the particular talent for communicating it, are here indispensable: and of these we find some want. The account of Kant is peculiarly defective; and it augurs ill to find him joining at the outset in the ignorant clamour against Kant's Terminology. Without that organ we maintain firmly that Kant's scheme of philosophy would have been incommunicable. Deny to an Algebraist the use of such terms as *roots, powers, exponents, negative exponents, co-efficients*, &c. and his labours must terminate from the mere cumbrousness and unwieldiness of the periphrases that would become necessary. But philosophic terminology, unless guarded by severer restraints than it is possible to impose upon a diction already used and abused, is liable to a much heavier danger than that of cumbrousness. Of mere necessity it must mislead: old associations will triumph; and the student will halt between the equivocal use of the word, even where a double sense is known and apprehended; much more in cases where the new sense is itself a problem, to which attention is perpetually to be solicited by a name that will not suffer the most negligent reader to slide *insensibly* into a misconception. "The

German metaphysics," says he, "afford a most eminent example of that dialect, which Swift calls the *Babylonic*." It was not Swift, but the author of Hudibras, who talked of a "Babylonish" dialect;[6] and the opinion of neither Swift nor Butler is here relevant, the course of their studies not having fitted either one or the other for judging of the necessities which in this and other cases justify a departure from the universal dialect.

At the latter part of the following passage we could not but smile: "To such" [*i.e.* a particular class amongst the followers of Schelling,] "it is in vain to say, that a power which is unconscious of its own existence" [*i.e.* the unconscious reason][7] "until it knows itself in *man*, is not and cannot be an object of adoration to the conscious reason. We feel that our consciousness is a higher faculty than that unconscious power; which, after all, is a phantasy of the mind."

This, beside [*sic*] the pleasant dogmatism of the concluding words, is to us like putting the case that the centripetal and centrifugal forces should happen both to be invited to the Lord Mayor's dinner, and then demanding which of the two would be invited to dance first with the Lady Mayoress! From the nature of the case, there is no such *before* or *after* the other as is here supposed. The unconscious reason is striving through all worlds after that organization into consciousness, which *itself* partially and imperfectly attains in man. And hence it is that some of this school have affirmed that it is not so true to say of God that he *is*, as that he *will be* hereafter,—and is in a perpetual nisus to be. We are not defending this mode of thinking; but certainly it is not liable to the inconsistency of calling upon us to adore a God inferior to ourselves.

6 *Hudibras*, I, i, 93.
7 The brackets are De Quincey's.

ART. IV.—*Balbi's Classification of Languages.*[8]—Three sorts of people have reason to despair,—naturalists, for every Humboldt or Bonpland discovers new genera by hundreds, and new species by thousands;[9]—astronomers, for every improvement in the telescope reaps new harvests in the starry heavens; and, finally, linguists,—for at every fresh attempt of a learned philologist to number their tribes and affiliations, "another and another still succeeds," until the line appears likely "to stretch even to the crack of doom." Adelung, in his *Mithridates*,[10] enumerated 3064 languages and dialects; but M. Balbi reports a total of 860 distinct languages and more than 5000 dialects. "Of the 860 languages—153 belong to Asia, 53 to Europe, 114 to Africa, 117 to Oceania, and 423 to America." And this number M. Balbi expects to see increased by more accurate researches in Africa and America.

It is remarked by the reviewer and M. Balbi, as an interesting phenomenon in the history of the human species, that originally languages were few—afterwards, in the middle period, they multiplied prodigiously: and now again are, (and long have been,) rapidly declining,—the more civilized languages, like Aaron's rod, eating up the others.

This tendency, setting in at different periods, in such opposite directions, has often struck us; and the philosophy of it we believe to be this:—Languages, like rivers, mountains, religions, &c. are designed as barriers of separation: the effect of which is to throw the species into the greatest possible variety of conditions, and to subject

[8] Review by T[homas?] Hodgkin of Adrien Balbi's *Atlas Ethnographique du Globe* (Paris, 1826).

[9] Alexander Humboldt, the naturalist and explorer; he and Aimé Bonpland, a botanist, had gone to South America together in the late 1790's and early 1800's.

[10] Johann Christoph Adelung; his *Mithridates, oder allgemeine Sprachenkunde* was published, after his death, 1806-17.

them to the widest compass of influences—the final purpose being the developement of human nature in its
greatest latitude. Afterwards, when this developement is
secured and *radicated* by long transmission, and when
further purposes require that the species should now
tend to fusion and amalgamation, as much as formerly
to repulsion, this great end is gained—that the unity of
the species rests upon a basis of the widest expansion,
and the uniformity, from the final amalgamation, is met
by an antagonist force of multiformity from the previous
separation.*

ART. V.—*De Bausset—Memoirs of Napoleon.*[11] De
Bausset was prefect of the palace to Napoleon, *i.e.* (as
he himself acknowledges) in effect *chef de cuisine.* The
article is very amusing, as 'anecdotage,' (to borrow
John Wilkes's expression,) [12] usually is; but, according to
the common practice of anecdote-mongers, M. Bausset
is manifestly a great liar. The following are much too
good to be true:—1. The late King of Spain, when playing concerted pieces on the violin with M. Boucher,
"would often begin *alone*; and, when the artist remon-
strated, he would reply, *that he was not made to wait
for him.*"* 2. On the day of the battle of the Moscowa,

* It is pretended, (p. 385) that the Mexican name for a *kiss,*
(that very simple and monosyllabic act) is the following sesqui-
pedalian polysyllable—*Tetenamiquilitzli.* But this must be a mistake
of the same kind as that which ascribes to the Arabic language,
500 synonymes for a lion. These are not names, but schematisms.
A kiss may be schematized under a thousand notions, as a lion
under the notion of King of the Forests, Lord of the Deserts,
Terror of the Antelope, &c. &c.

* In fact we remember this, or something very like it, as an old
friend in Joe Miller: A rich but ignorant man gave a concert; and
observing one of the orchestra at a particular moment not playing, he went up and taxed him with idleness. "Sir," said the mu-

11 Review by B[enjamin?] Keene of L. F. J. de Bausset, *Memoires Anecdotiques* (Paris, 1827).

12 Traditionally attributed to Wilkes, but, so far as I know, it
has never been traced. See pp. 234-35 below.

M. de B. says—"At 12 o'clock I asked Napoleon whether he would breakfast? the battle was not yet gained, and he signified his refusal by a gesture. I had the imprudence to say, that there was no reason in the world which ought to prevent a man from breakfasting when he had the opportunity. Upon which he dismissed me in a way sufficiently unceremonious." That is to say, kicked the prefect (we presume) out of the tent. The sentiment about breakfast is certainly worthy of a *chef de cuisine*; and the whole story reminds one of Falstaff's presenting the prince, in the heat of battle, with a bottle of sack by way of a pistol. But, unfortunately for the prefect's veracity, Count Ségur[13] (whose authority all the world will prefer) contradicts him, not only generally as to Buonaparte's habits for the last years of his European life, but particularly as to this very day of the Moscowa, on which it is expressly recorded, that he took large doses of his then favourite beverage, a strong infusion of tea with a very large proportion of brandy. Of this the Reviewer seems unaware, when he elsewhere (p. 401) compliments the prefect for having refuted the 'ridiculous' fables circulated about Buonaparte's diet, &c.

Napoleon's superstitions, in connexion with Mademoiselle Le Normand, whose publication of the Secret Memoirs of Josephine, by herself, is noticed at the end of this article, will be read with great interest.[14]

Art. VI.—*On the Achromatic Telescope, &c.* relates to

---

sician, "there is a rest in my part for several bars." "Rest," replied the angry Crœsus, "I do not pay you for resting, but for working as hard as you can."

[13] Philippe Paul, Comte de Ségur, a general on Napoleon's staff; his *Histoire de Napoleon et de la grande armée pendant l'année 1812* (Paris, 1824) had given an unfavorable account of Napoleon; Hazlitt used it as a source of his life of Napoleon.

[14] M. A. Le Normand, *Memoires historiques et secrets de l'Imperatrice Josephine,* 2nd ed. (Paris, 1827).

Fraunhofer,[15] the great discoverer in flint-glass,—and has no general interest.

ART. VII.—*Southern Germany*, is little more than an abstract of two German works, describing the present condition of Upper Germany and Vienna.[16]

ART. VIII.—*Von Hammer's History of the Assassins*, is a good article on a good book, which ought not to have remained so long unknown.[17] Some readers will be surprised to hear that, upon a collation of all the evidence, Von Hammer pronounces Cœur de Lion guilty, in the case of the assassination of Conrad, marquis of Montferrat. There is much arrear of argument still on the other side; but it is unfortunate for Richard, that presumptions of his general tyranny and baseness crowd upon us at this moment from other quarters. Even this very review furnishes two,—in the 1st art. (p. 329.) it is said of him: "This prince, remembered among ourselves chiefly for his chivalrous and warlike generosity, appears in the Breton annals a treacherous and rapacious tyrant." And in the Literary Notices, under the head of *Austria* (p. 647.) is an account of a MS. account of the crusade of 1190, by an Austrian monk, recently discovered at Prague, which, though a biassed testimony, tends to swell the probabilities of Richard's guilt.—In this, there is nothing which surprises ourselves, who lay it down as a fixed rule—that all heroes are scoundrels; the only difference being that some are, and some are not, finally detected.

15 Joseph Fraunhofer, the German optician and physicist, who had died recently. The review was by Dr. (later Sir David) Brewster.

16 Review by William Taylor of Norwich. The two books were anonymous: *Deutschland; oder Briefe eines in Deutschland reisenden Deutschen* (Stuttgart, 1826-27) and *Wien, wie es ist* (Leipzig, 1827).

17 Review by Thomas Keightley. The book is by Joseph von Hammer (Hammer-Purgstall, the orientalist), *Die Geschichte der Assassinen* (Stuttgart and Tübingen, 1818).

ART. IX.—Dupin—*Productive and Commercial Powers of France*.[18]—This, as a statistical article, and crowded with details, admits of no circumstantial notice: but one statement we must correct. About 1-13th part of all the children born in France, it seems, are illegitimate; but for Paris this proportion is much higher, being one-third (as all readers must have seen often repeated in our journals); so that, says M. Dupin, "amongst every three little Parisians that you look at, one, upon an average, will be a bastard." Now, in the year 1793, "when Mr. Burke supposed morals to be in the most relaxed state," the proportion was lower; upon which an inference is grounded to the advantage of that year. But here the mistake is the same as that which has been exposed in Mr. M'Culloch's comparison of the manufacturing and rural populations:[19] A smaller number of illegitimate births does not of necessity argue a diminished licentiousness; to say nothing of the infanticides, direct and indirect, which are likely to have followed so bloody a period as that of 1791-2,—luxury of all kinds is unfavourable to child-bearing, and excess of licentiousness in this way tends to defeat its own natural exposure.

An ingenious speculation is added by the Reviewer on the supposed declension of stature in Revolutionary France. Of one million and upwards of young men, called before the Council of Revision for military service, considerably above one-third were rejected because they did not reach the stature of 5 feet $1\frac{7}{8}$ inches, (*English* measure;) thirty-seven in the hundred, of those admitted, are below 5 feet 5 inches, English; and only forty-five in the hundred exceed 5 feet $6\frac{1}{8}$ inches. This Dupin attributes partly, if not entirely, to the conscription—

[18] Review by C[harles?] Maclaren. The book is by Baron Charles Dupin, the mathematician and economist, *Forces Productives et Commerciales de la France* (Paris, 1827).

[19] See the article of November 10, p. 177 above.

draining off the finest specimens of the species and leaving the weak, old, and deformed, as the fathers of the succeeding generation. And the Reviewer ingeniously supposes that the excessive cultivation of war in a nation tends, in this way, to defeat itself, by gradually impoverishing the physical qualities of the soldier. For an illustration, he refers us to the Romans, who were ridiculed for their short stature by the Gauls, and, we add, by the Germans. But this superiority of stature, it should be remembered, in the first place, belonged only to the *Northern* enemies of the Romans; and, in the second place, that these Northerns were precisely the most warlike nations they had to contend with: whilst the unwarlike Syrians of Antiochus, &c., had no such physical superiority. So much for the theory: but we doubt the whole fact of any deterioration in the French; what they are now, *that* they were, very probably, in 1789.

Art. X.—*The Betrothed*,[20] a Romance from Manzoni, is the most interesting article in the Number; the specimens are translated with great elegance; and, if our limits allowed us any extracts, it is from this article that we should take them. But we are obliged to conclude.

Of the five remaining articles—*Catholicism in Silesia*, (an excellent paper,) *Modern German Tragedy, Russian Literature, De Lambris' History of the Astronomy of the Eighteenth Century*, and the *German Pocket Book for 1828*;[21] the 2d is the only one of any general interest, or which we regret that we cannot notice more particularly. The last is manifestly from the pen of the accomplished Editor; and, being so, very much disappoints us that it should be no more than an index to their contents.

[20] A less than favorable review of *I Promessi Sposi*; by George Moir.

[21] The first is by the Rev. Hugh James Rose; the second by Gillies; the third by John George Cochrane and W. Smirnove; the fourth by the Rev. Thomas James Hussey; the fifth by Gillies.

ATTRIBUTION

This certainly seems to be De Quincey's, on several counts.

The editor of the *Foreign Quarterly Review* is said here to be an old friend and Gillies was one of De Quincey's friends. His name appears in De Quincey's letters and their relation can be followed in Horace Eaton's biography of De Quincey (New York, 1936). They had been fellow-contributors to *Blackwood's*. De Quincey reviewed favorably Gillies' *German Stories* in 1826 (*Blackwood's*, XX, 844-58) and he later wrote about their acquaintance in "Sir William Hamilton" (1852), M., V, 322. Gillies too wrote about it, at greater length, in his *Memoirs*, II, 218-21 (and see II, 162); he also says that he had conferred with De Quincey, among others, and De Quincey was to have been a contributor to the *Foreign Quarterly* (*Memoirs*, III, 145). His account is corroborated by a letter of De Quincey's, written on Gillies' behalf, soliciting contributions to a new journal of foreign literature; in it De Quincey says that he himself will write for the journal (letter of January 9, 1827, now in the Harvard library). In fact De Quincey never did contribute, but that would be characteristic.

The point made here about Southey and philosophic history (p. 222) is made also in De Quincey's "Charlemagne" (1832), M., V, 354-55: because "Philosophic History" has been abused and "the truth of facts has been so much forced to bend before preconceived theories" Southey and others have opposed the whole class; but Southey himself, with his interest in morality, among other things, writes a type of philosophic history. Also on Southey's opposition to philosophic history, see "A Brief Appraisal of the Greek Literature" (1838-39), M., X, 317; and on "What is called *Philosophical History*," see "Greece Under the Romans" (1844), M., VII, 250.

De Quincey had already defended (pp. 224-25) "Kant's terminology" against commonplace attacks upon its barbarousness; it is, among other things, essential to the distinctions Kant had to make; and it is "organic" in his system: "Letters to a Young Man" (1823), M., X, 72-77. He defends it again in "German Studies and Kant in Particular" (1836), M., II, 88.

Adelung's *Mithridates* (p. 226) appears several times in De Quincey's writings, before and after this date. He had referred to the book and to the three thousand languages of the earth in the "Letters to a Young Man" (1823), M., X, 33; there too he had said that the European languages will destroy the barbarous languages. He had also referred to the book in the original version of the *Confessions* (repeated in the revised version, M., III, 404), and he returned to it and to the number of languages on earth in "The Antigone of Sophocles" (1846), M., X, 362. See, too, M., II, 65. In "The Lake Poets: William Wordsworth" (1854 version), M., II, 251, he says that the English language is "eating up, like Aaron's rod, all other languages."

On the importance of the "antagonist force" which appears in this same section (p. 227), see the article of September 15, p. 120 above, and the further references there.

The similar figure of centrifugal and centripetal forces (p. 225) is a favorite with De Quincey, to illustrate forces which are not exclusive opposites but which exist only as paired antagonists. He uses it in the Bodleian MS. and further references are given there (p. 357 below).

There is evidence, too, of De Quincey's acquaintance with several of the foreign scholars noted here. Most important is Cousin (p. 223). In "French Revolution," *Blackwood's*, XXVIII (1830), 551, as here, "Professor Cousin" and the journal, the *Globe*, conducted by his pupils, are "evidences of increasing depth" in French character, consequent upon great political struggles; the French have been "growing . . . in their literary sensibilities" because of the "exalting tendency" of the age; proof of "the great enlargement in the French intellectual tastes" is in their new taste for English drama and in "the general toleration, of foreign poetry appealing to the higher passions," both English and German. There is more on Cousin, the only great name in philosophy in modern France, and on his efforts to naturalize Kant in France, in "German Studies and Kant in Particular," M., II, 88; this is in a passage cited just above because, there, as here, the name is coupled with a defense of Kant's terminology.

The other names of foreign scholars are less important, but Humboldt and Bonpland (p. 226) are reviewed in De Quincey's *Westmorland Gazette*, March 27, 1819, p. 4; he refers to Fraunhofer (p. 229) and the making of glasses for telescopes in "System of the Heavens" (1846), M., VIII, 27; and, more interestingly, Von Hammer and his history (p. 229) are one of the toasts of the Society of Connoisseurs in Murder, in the second essay on "Murder as One of the Fine Arts" (1839), M., XIII, 62.

The word "nisus" (p. 225) is also a favorite of his. He uses it in the "Letters to a Young Man," in the same passage in which he defends Kant's terminology, M., X, 73. The specific phrase "a perpetual nisus" he had used in "Malthus on the Measure of Value" (1823), M., IX, 32 and 33n. The word is also in a dozen other essays he wrote.

"Anecdotage" (p. 227), too, is probably a sign of his authorship. At least the earliest example of the word in the *OED* is the title of De Quincey's article in the *London Magazine* of 1823 (M., V, 146); and the second earliest is in one of his articles on "The Caesars" in *Blackwood's* in 1832 (M., VI, 244). It is also in his "Philosophy of Roman History" (1839), M., VI, 438, 440, and "On War," M., VIII, 375. Furthermore, an editorial note in the *London Magazine* of 1823 (VII, [244]), at the beginning of the issue in which De Quincey's article appeared, says of him: "He had imagined himself to be the author of this term . . . But he afterwards found that the word had been already invented by John Wilkes."

Letters of Junius

TO THE EDITOR OF THE POST

MR. EDITOR,—Of all the problems in history, which have stimulated the curiosity of inquirers by their mysteriousness connected with the belief that they were not altogether hopeless of solution, none whatever, no, not even the question of Mary and Darnley, of Perkin Warbeck, of the Ruthvens, of the Iron Masque,[1] &c.—has attracted one quarter of the notice given to a question of the last generation, viz. *Who wrote the Letters of Junius*? I know a man who has a *Chatterton library* made up entirely of books, tracts, &c. on the Rowley controversy: another perhaps still larger might be formed on the question of Junius.

In my opinion, this question was for ever laid at rest by the work published in 1816, under the title of *Junius Identified*, which traced the authorship to Sir Philip Francis:[2] and many others, lawyers of great experience in weighing the value of evidence, agree with me in that

[1] Darnley, the second husband of Mary Queen of Scots, was murdered in 1567; three months later Mary married Bothwell, who had been tried for the murder. Perkin Warbeck claimed the throne from Henry VII; according to his story he was one of the young princes thought to have been murdered in the Tower by order of their uncle (who had become Richard III). Ruthven was the family name of the third Earl of Gowrie; he and his brother were killed in 1600 at Gowrie house, in Scotland, by attendants of James VI; according to James the Gowries had lured him to the house in a conspiracy against his person, but his story was widely disbelieved. The man in the iron mask was a prisoner, held masked and anonymous in the Bastille, in the reign of Louis XIV; it was Voltaire who said that the mask was iron and the man a natural brother of the king (which made him useful later to Dumas).

[2] The author was John Taylor, best known to literary history as Keats's publisher. The book was *The Identity of Junius with a Distinguished Living Character Established*; it was followed by *A Supplement to Junius Identified*, in 1817; and both were pub-

judgment. In particular, I have reason to know that
Chief-Justice Dallas (late of the Common Pleas) was
pleased to say that he would cheerfully have hanged Sir
Philip upon the evidence there accumulated—supposing
the authorship of Junius to have been a hanging matter.[3]

Yet, I know not how, the most complete solution of
historical doubts never has a complete success. Partly
perhaps the reason is—that, whilst all are acquainted
with the mystery, few have a circumstantial knowledge
of the explanation; partly, that mystery for its own sake
is agreeable—and no thanks are given to him who dis-
perses it; and, partly, also (which was the case of old
Woodfall)[4] a sort of bathos is felt in a *dénouement* of no
great lustre where a magnificent one has been long anticipated. It cannot be from any one of these reasons,
yet so the fact is, that Mr. Ellis of the British Museum
still speaks distrustfully of Perkin Warbeck's pretensions,
in spite of Malcolm Laing's dissertation upon that question, at the end of Henry's History of Great Britain:[5]

---

lished together in a second edition, corrected and enlarged, in
1818. It had been preceded in 1813 by *A Discovery of the Author
of the Letters of Junius*, in which Taylor had argued the authorship of Sir Philip and his father, Dr. Francis, before finding additional evidence that led him to decide for Sir Philip solus.

[3] Sir Robert Dallas, who had died in 1824; he had participated,
as counsel or judge, in a number of famous trials, including those
of Warren Hastings, the Luddites, and the Cato Street con-
spirators.

[4] Henry Sampson Woodfall, conductor of the *Public Advertiser*,
in which the Junius letters had been published; according to his
son he said that Francis never wrote a line of Junius. He is called
"old" Woodfall here to distinguish him from his son, George, who
published the three-volume 1812 edition of Junius.

[5] Henry (later Sir Henry) Ellis had just become principal
librarian of the British Museum; on Perkin Warbeck see his
Original Letters, Illustrative of English History (1824), I, 18.
Malcolm Laing had completed Robert Henry's *History of Great
Britain*, Vol. VI (1793); in an appended dissertation he argued
that Warbeck was a genuine Plantagenet and Richard III no
tyrant stained with the blood of his kinsmen.

Sir Walter Scott, again, in his little sketch of the Gowrie conspiracy, just now published in his Tales of a Grandfather, seems to have forgotten the discussion of this case printed in the appendix to Laing's History of Scotland;[6] and we doubt whether one person in a hundred is satisfied with Mr. Agar Ellis's account of the Iron Masque—however probable and simple.[7]

In the same way multitudes are found who still affect to speak sceptically on the question of Junius. Amongst these Dr. Parr has attracted a fresh attention to the discussion by a memorandum printed since his death in the *Bibliotheca Parriana*.[8] I forget the Doctor's words, which are indeed of no consequence; for the worthy Doctor's opinion was of little value on any subject; and upon this in particular he discovers a remarkable ignorance of every thing in the situation of Sir Philip Francis that bore upon the case. A doubter of more weight is Sir Walter Scott, who (in the preface to his *Fortunes of Nigel*)[9] seems to take it for granted that a momentary impression made by the "*Junius Identified*" had been entirely effaced.

[6] Laing's *History of Scotland* was 1800; John Pinkerton's dissertation, appended to Vol. I, argued that the conspirator was the Earl's brother, a favorite of the queen, Anne of Denmark. Scott's account of the Gowrie conspiracy is at the end of Chap. XXXIV of *Tales of a Grandfather*, first series, which had just been published in Edinburgh, December 1827; an excerpt from it was given in the *Post* of December 15.

[7] George Agar Ellis, later first Baron Dover, an M.P., a distinguished public servant of the arts and scholarship, and himself an author. The work referred to here is *The True History of the State Prisoner, commonly called the Iron Mask* (1826, with a second edition in 1827). Following a French source he tried to identify the prisoner as Hercules Anthony Matthioli, an Italian diplomat.

[8] This catalogue of Parr's library (1827) printed one of his marginalia (p. 407), in which Parr said that the author of Junius was Charles Lloyd, private secretary to George Grenville; see also Parr's *Works* (1828), VII, 677-80.

[9] Actually the "Introductory Epistle" to Scott's novel (1822).

From the terms in which Sir Walter has conveyed his opinion, (or, speaking accurately, his impression with regard to the opinion of others) I collect two inferences —1st, That Sir Walter builds chiefly on the *supposed* disavowal of Junius, by Sir. P. F. in his answer to Sir Richard Philips's most audacious application;[10] 2dly, That Sir Walter has not himself read the book which argues Sir Philip's claim. In fact, most people will be disposed to take their account of such a book upon trust, rather than be at the trouble of reading 366 octavo pages, and a supplement of 36 more.

On this account, I make sure of doing a general service, by abstracting into a short compass, the evidence brought forward in this work. I shall omit nothing of importance; and I shall place the argument perhaps in a clearer light, as there is a remarkable obscurity in the management of it through two or three chapters: and another objection to the original work is, that it weakens the force of the evidence, by relying sometimes upon slight presumptions; apparently acting upon the principle of—*Si non pondere, at numero*—which, in this case at least, is a very bad principle.

If the reader finds any thing in my statement, for which there is no authority in the book itself, he must understand, that in these instances I am indebted to several private conversations with Mr. Taylor, the ingenious author of the book.

I.—Whosoever wrote the letters of Junius, it is clear beyond all doubt, must have had a close connexion with

10 After Taylor's publication of 1813 Sir Richard Phillips (as the name should be spelled) wrote to Francis, asking whether Taylor was right in his conjecture. Francis replied with a letter which Phillips understood as a denial (*Monthly Magazine*, XXXV [1813], 532-33), but which Taylor said was deliberately evasive (*Identity of Junius*, 2nd. ed., pp. 7ff.). The third of the articles in the *Post* returns to this point and promises that it will be taken up in a following article (p. 270 below), which never appeared.

the WAR-OFFICE. This has struck many people; and it was in fact the clue to the whole discovery. The dismissal of Sir Jeffrey Amherst from the government of Virginia, —the arrest and rescue of General Gansell,—the preferment of General Burgoyne,—the appointment of Sir William Draper to a regiment out of his turn, with the terms on which he sold it,—the secret and incomplete promotion of Colonel Luttrell to be Adjutant-General in Ireland, to which "very few forms concurred except *private commissions*,"—together with the conduct of Lord Granby, and many other military cases, are treated with a circumstantial knowledge of the facts that could belong only to a person having access to private documents, and enjoying a confidential connexion with the office through which all these cases had passed.

This, indeed, it was amongst other presumptions, upon which was built the hypothesis of Lord George Germaine's having written the letters.

A still stronger proof of the connexion between Junius and the War-office, is found in the malignity with which he pursued Lord Barrington, the War-Secretary, in his *official capacity.**

Universally, therefore, in every attempt to identify Junius, it is an unconditional postulate that this connexion shall be established.—Now, then, for Sir Philip Francis: what was *his* connexion with the War-Office? *Answer*: That *he was a principal clerk in that office.*[12]

* See Woodfall's edit. of Junius, vol. III., for the letters which he wrote under the signature of *Veteran.*[11]

[11] This is the 1812 edition by George Woodfall. It included not only the Junius letters from the *Public Advertiser* but many private letters and many public letters published under different pseudonyms, attributing them to Junius; it was the text that inspired Taylor's "discovery."

[12] The material is presented more economically and dramatically than it is in Taylor's book, but the substance is taken from it. For the details of section I see the *Identity of Junius*, 2nd ed., Chap. VI. The names in the Junius story are so many and the details so

II.—Early in 1772 the Letters of Junius cease. Is there any incident in the life of Francis which would account for this cessation? *Answer*: In March 1772, Francis was dismissed from his office by Lord Barrington. This is sufficiently remarkable; the letters cease at the moment when the sources of secret information are closed; and it becomes more so when connected with another circumstance—viz. that in all probability the dismissal of Francis arose out of the letters of *Veteran*. Lord B., there is reason to think, suspected him of being *Veteran*; now, as *Veteran* is *now* known to have been Junius, if Francis were *Veteran*—it follows that Francis was Junius. And hence we see the reason why Junius was so urgent with Woodfall (in his private notes) to conceal the identity of Veteran and Junius. To be detected as *Veteran*— simply affected him at the War-office; and not in any aggravated way either; because under that signature he had done no more than expose a personal injury to himself in the partial treatment of Mr. Chamier. But, in his character of *Junius,* he had committed an enormous breach of trust; having violated the confidence reposed in him as an official servant—and no doubt in some instances the confidences, extra-official, which he had conciliated by his gentlemanly qualities.†

† By the way, the letters of *Veteran* (acknowledged privately by Junius) prove to demonstration that connexion of Junius with the War-Office, which, in No. I., had been insisted on by way of inference only, and presumptively. For no man could pretend to be believed in his account of a quarrel at the War-Office, unless upon a private and personal knowledge of what passed in that office. From the letters of Veteran, therefore, *taken alone*, it is possible to establish the identity of Junius and Francis. And a further ground for this identity appears in the coincidence (in point of time) of Francis's dismissal from the War-Office, with

complex that annotation will be limited to these references to Taylor's book, the immediate source. (Taylor sometimes repeats himself, and at the end of the book he summarizes his main points; here, and in the following notes, the major references are given.)

III.—It is a very remarkable circumstance about Junius, especially connecting it with his known admiration of Lord Chatham, that he practises a uniform forbearance towards Lord Holland. This forbearance, towards a public man, so obnoxious to censure, cannot be an accident. All observing judges have felt that it was intentional, and grounded in some private connexion with that nobleman; and have endeavoured to find, in this circumstance, some clue to the real Junius. Horace Walpole, in particular, builds upon it an argument in favour of "Single-Speech" Hamilton: "Hamilton," says he, "was brought forward by Lord Holland; and it is remarkable, that Lord Holland, though very open to censure, is not once mentioned."

This, then, is one of the great outstanding phenomena about Junius to be accounted for; and what solution of it do we find in the history of the Francis family?— *Answer*: Dr. Francis, the translator of Horace, father to Sir Philip, lived in great intimacy with Lord Holland, was his domestic chaplain, was tutor also to his second son—the late Charles Fox, dedicated to Lord Holland, as his patron, his translation of Demosthenes; and obtained, through the interest of that nobleman, all the church preferment which he held,—viz. the living of Barrow, in Suffolk, and the Chaplaincy of Chelsea Hospital. These were strong obligations to self-restraint in a writer who certainly did not flatter himself with any security against *immediate* detection: witness the anxious arrangements which he concerted with Woodfall, for maintaining his incognito. But, over and above these family obligations, Sir Philip Francis was checked by very weighty ones in his own person. In the year 1756, when

the earnest request to Woodfall, on the part of Junius, that his identity with Veteran might not be made known.[13]

---

[13] *Identity of Junius,* Chap. VI.

he was about 16 years old, we find, from the account of his life, that "Mr. Henry Fox, afterwards Lord Holland, gave him a little place in the Secretary of State's Office;" and this little place was his first introduction into political life.[14]

IV.—Junius, who in other instances was tolerably careless about the risks into which he might lead his publishers, uniformly showed a lively concern for the welfare of Woodfall. "If your affair should come to a trial," says he, (in a private letter,) "and you should be found guilty, you will then let me know what expense falls *particularly on yourself*, for I understand you are engaged with other proprietors. Some way or other *you* shall be reimbursed." Now, is there any circumstance in the history of Sir Philip Francis which will explain this exclusive, and almost unfair regard to the interests of Woodfall?—*Answer*: Francis and Woodfall were schoolfellows, of pretty nearly the same standing, at St. Paul's School; and, upon the authority of Woodfall, the younger, "formed an acquaintance there, which caused them through life to regard each other with particular kindness; and though various circumstances soon dissolved that early connexion, yet the remembrance of it was ever after kept up between them, by some friendly token of acknowledgement whenever they met."‡

The Rev. Philip Rosenhagen was also a school-fellow

‡ Careless readers will be apt to say that, on the supposition of Junius having been the school-fellow of Woodfall, the latter ought to have know his hand-writing.—*Answer*: And so he probably did; and for that reason, apparently, Francis disguised his hand. But, be that as it may, the fac-similes of the hand-writing of Francis and Junius, clearly show, that the latter was an attempt to masque the former: Of this, now that both are published, every one is as good a judge as Woodfall could be; and so much the better, as Mr. W. was acquainted only with the boyish hand of Francis—and with that only by recollection at a distance of twelve or fourteen years.

---

[14] *Ibid.*, Chap. VIII.

and a common friend of Francis and Woodfall: of him it is recorded, that he gave occasional assistance to the latter in the composition of his *Public Advertiser*; and this again strengthens the presumption that Francis would throw his political essays into that channel.[15]

V.—Woodfall, among the publishers of the day, stood first in the regard of Junius, and we have seen that he stood high in the regard of Francis. Was there any other publisher to whom Junius resorted in cases where Woodfall declined to come forward? There was; and this publisher was Almon.

Now, then, can any connexion be traced between Almon and Francis?—*Answer*: Yes; Francis communicated to Almon two speeches of Lord Chatham, and other speeches reported by himself.

Here is an odd coincidence; both have a friend who is a printer; and both resort occasionally to another printer, *not* a friend; and this other is in both cases the same.[16]

VI.—Upon learning that David Garrick was busying himself in tracing the author of the letters, Junius falls into a perfect panic; passionately exclaims (private letter to Woodfall) "I am sure I should not survive a discovery three days,"—meaning that he should be assassinated; and, to prevent that catastrophe, writes a private note hinting, that he would cause Garrick to be assassinated if he did not immediately desist from his "impertinent inquiries:"—"I desire you will tell him" (says he to Woodfall) "that I am aware of his practices, and will certainly be revenged if he does not desist."—Wherefore all this wrath and agitation? Why in this taking? Thousands, besides Garrick, were hunting upon the trail of Junius. True: but Garrick had special advantages for this chase, supposing Francis to be Junius; for Garrick, was on a familiar footing in the family. Of this, by the

[15] *Ibid.*   [16] *Ibid.*, Chap. IX.

merest accident, we have full proof: Francis, the father, tells us in the preface to his play of Eugenia, that he was well acquainted with Garrick, who enjoyed "his friendship and esteem." Hence the danger: knowing the father thus intimately, Garrick of course knew the son—and probably his hand-writing; or, if not, upon any suspicion arising, he soon *would* know it. Now, it appeared that Garrick had been in personal conference with the printer —and, as Junius expresses it, *pumping* him: and he had only to obtain a sight of one MS. of Junius, either by the indulgence of Woodfall, or the accidents of a printing-office, and all his suspicions would have been instantly verified. And this explains the earnestness of Junius in desiring of Woodfall, that a threatening note, which he had addressed to Garrick, might be copied out before it was despatched to him. Hence, also we explain the immediate alteration which Junius made in the place for depositing his packets: "Change," says he, "to the Somerset coffeehouse; and let no mortal know the alteration." He found that, under Garrick's "pumping," Woodfall might inadvertently have suffered the name of the coffee-house to escape him: in which case David would be in ambush; and, supposing (as there is good reason to suppose) that Junius was the bearer of his own packets, instant detection would ensue.[17]

VII.—Was Junius a Member of Parliament? This question has been repeatedly agitated, and upon a vigilant examination of his letters, it is clear that he was *not*. But there is evidence from himself that he often attended as an auditor in both houses, and took notes of important debates, or of single speeches that were particularly interesting. There is also proof that Francis did exactly the same thing at exactly the same period. Further, it is remarkable that two speeches of Lord Chatham, which

[17] *Ibid.*, Chap. VIII.

are known to have been reported by Francis, were precisely those speeches to which Junius had declared that he looked with particular anxiety, as likely to be most important and critical in the circumstances of the existing administration.[18]

(To be concluded in our next.)

[18] *Ibid.*, Chap. IX. The article was not in fact concluded in our next but continued for two more issues.

Letters of Junius

[*cont.*]

TO THE EDITOR OF THE POST

MR. EDITOR,—My first letter ended with insisting on the presumption (No. VII.) arising out of the common relation in which Junius and Francis stand to Lord Chatham, particularly in regard to two memorable speeches of that nobleman's in 1770. But here I scarcely did justice to the case, which is a good deal perplexed in Mr. Taylor's statement of it, and requires some care to present it so as to make its full force apprehensible. The tenor of the argument is this:—In the letters of Junius are several passages, which are *now* known to have been borrowed in substance from speeches delivered by Lord Chatham; but at that time, as the passages in question were not marked as citations, there was no reason to suppose them other than what they appear to be, viz. the thoughts and words of Junius. For in those days, when as yet reporting was not a regular and authorised practice, it happened that no account was published of the particular speeches in question; *nor indeed until twenty years afterwards.* Mark this, reader, well. About that distance of time from the letters of Junius, appeared a report of several speeches of Lord Chatham, particularly of the two very remarkable ones delivered on the 9th and 22d of January, 1770, a period at which we know that Junius (both in his public letters and his private ones to Woodfall) manifested the highest agitations of hope for some imminent change which was likely to replace Mr. Grenville and Lord Chatham in power. Nearly thirty years after the publication of these reports, i. e. nearly 50 years from the period of Junius, it happened that Mr. Taylor, upon examining them, was so struck with the coincidences in these speeches with certain passages in Junius, as to be forced into the conclusion that either Lord Chatham must be the author of Junius, or Junius the reporter of Lord Chatham.

That the reader may judge of this point for himself, I shall here interrupt the argument to make a few extracts; premising that the first of these very memorable speeches was delivered at the opening of the Session (Jan. 9, 1770,) on a motion for an address by the Duke of Ancaster, seconded by Lord Dunmore.

1. LORD CHATHAM:—"That he had himself advised a measure which he knew was *not strictly legal*; but he had recommended it as *a measure of necessity to save a starving people from famine; and had submitted to the judgment of his country.*"

JUNIUS (about 21 months afterwards, but still 18 years before the above sentence was published)—"Instead of asserting that the proclamation was legal, he (Lord Camden) should have said, My Lords, *I know the proclamation was illegal, but I advised it because it was indispensably necessary to save the kingdom from famine*: *and I submit myself to the justice and mercy of my country.*"

*   *   *   *   *

2. LORD CHATHAM:—"What security would they have for their rights, if a court of judicature might determine every question, *not by any known positive law*, but by the vague, indeterminate, arbitrary rule of what the noble Lord (Mansfield) is pleased to call the *Wisdom of the Court?*"

JUNIUS, addressing the same Lord Mansfield:—"Instead of those *certain, positive, rules*, by which the judgment of a court of law should be invariably determined, the judge refers only to the *wisdom of the court.*"

*   *   *   *   *

3. LORD CHATHAM:—"It" (the decision of the House of Commons upon the Middlesex election) "is not supported by a single precedent: for the case of Sir R. Walpole is but *a half precedent*; and even that half is imperfect."

JUNIUS, writing of the same transaction: "the author has *divided his precedent*; for he knew that, if taken together," &c.

*　　*　　*　　*　　*

4. LORD CHATHAM:—"That the Americans had purchased their liberty at a dear rate, since they *had quitted their native country, and gone in search of freedom to a desert*."

JUNIUS, speaking of the same people:—"They *left their native land in search of freedom, and found it in a desert*."

*　　*　　*　　*　　*

5. LORD CHATHAM:—"Is this a false fact, my Lords?"

For this strange phrase of "*a false fact*," which is what the logicians call a *contradictio in adjecto*, see Junius and Sir Philip Francis, who (and who only of all the sons of Adam) both use it continually.

*　　*　　*　　*　　*

And now let me resume the argument: From these instances of parallelism between Junius and a speech of Lord Chatham not published until 20 years after, the reader will understand that there must have been some connexion between Junius and the reporter: but when he further understands that, as in some of these instances the letters of Junius are indebted to the speech, so in others the speech is indebted to the Letters,—he will easily admit that this system of lending and borrowing cannot possibly be explained on any other hypothesis than that of Junius and the Reporter being one and the same person.

Here is the first stage of the argument. The Reporter being now shown to be Junius, we have only in the next place to find out this Reporter's name, and Junius is at once detected. Of this the Reporter was evidently aware himself; and being sensible that, if ever the coincidences should come to be observed, a key would be obtained to his secret, he had taken every precaution to throw obstacles in the way of a pursuit. For when Mr. Taylor came to inquire upon whose authority this speech was given, he found that, whereas for most of the other speeches acknowledgments were made to different persons expressly *by name*, in this instance the name of the contributor was suppressed, and he was simply described, in general terms, as "*a gentleman, who afterwards made a distinguished figure in the House of Commons.*" So much it was useful to say, in order to authenticate the report of so important a debate: but beyond this it was clearly the design of the Reporter to furnish no clue to the public or to posterity for tracing him. However, as more than 25 years had now elapsed from the publication of the speech, and nearly 50 from the time of Junius, it seemed probable that the secret would at this time be less vigilantly guarded. Mr. Taylor, therefore, applied to the publisher, and begged to know—supposing it to be no intrusion into a private affair—whether Sir Philip Francis were not the gentleman designed in the above description; *the publisher answered that he was.* Now then, what do you think of *that*, sceptic? Here is Sir Philip confessedly the reporter of a speech, which Junius quotes, and otherwise uses, 20 years before it was printed!

After this, it is not necessary to go at length into a second case of the same kind, viz. that of the speech delivered by Lord Chatham on the 22d of the same January, 1770. The evidence in this case takes precisely the same course: here again we have Junius borrowing from the speech, although it remained in manuscript for a period of 20 years after; and here again we have an anonymous Report of the Speech containing the very words borrowed by Junius, which report is traced to Sir Philip Francis. Indeed, besides the publisher's acknowledgment that Sir Philip was the reporter, we find that fact sufficiently made out by Sir Philip's repeated quotations from these speeches in his *avowed* works: thus, for example:

1. LORD CHATHAM:—"Power without right is the most odious and detestable object that can be offered to the human imagination: it is not only pernicious to those who are subject to it, but tends to its own destruction. It is what my noble friend (Lord Lyttleton) has truly described it,—*Res detestabilis et caduca.*"

SIR P. FRANCIS, (*Essay on the Regency*):—"I HEARD IT from Lord Chatham, that power without right is the most odious and detestable object that can be offered to the human imagination. It is at once *res detestabilis et caduca.*"

*   *   *   *   *

2. LORD CHATHAM:—"That it was a maxim he had observed through life, when he had lost his way, to stop short; lest by proceeding without knowledge, and advancing from one false step to another, he should wind himself into an inextricable labyrinth, and never be able to recover the right road again."

Sir P. Francis, (Paper Currency, p. 1.)—"It was said by William Earl of Chatham, forty years ago, *or somebody has recorded it for him,** That it was a maxim he

* This *'somebody'* we now know to be Sir Philip himself: But the expression is remarkable, both as another evidence to Sir Philip's shyness of acknowledging himself the reporter, (for which he could have only one reason), and also as betraying in its latter part—'*has recorded it for him,*' that he was well aware of that system of lending and borrowing pursued by Junius, which makes it difficult to know when it is the reporter that speaks, and when Lord Chatham. That Lord Chatham is indebted to Junius, we

had observed through life, when he had lost his way," &c.
—and so on to the end.

*   *   *   *   *

3. LORD CHATHAM:—"If the breach in the constitution
be effectually repaired, the people will of themselves
return to a state of tranquillity: if not, *May Discord
Prevail for ever!*"

FRANCIS, 40 years after:—"Let the war take its course;
or, as *I heard* Lord Chatham declare in the House of
Lords with a monarch's voice, *Let Discord prevail for
ever!*"

*   *   *   *   *

If the argument in this No. pointed only to one speech
of Lord Chatham's, there is a bare possibility that the
coincidences between Junius and Francis might arise
from the circumstance of both being indebted to a common source; both, that is to say, having been present in
the House of Lords, both having selected the same parts
of the speech, and both having happened to express them
in pretty nearly the same words. But, when the reader
understands that the argument refers to several speeches
of Lord Chatham's, and in two different years, which
speeches are all reported by Francis and all used by
Junius twenty years before the reports were made public,
he will perceive that, if it were possible for Francis and
Junius to be different persons, they must in that case
have acted under a blind sympathy which only Animal
Magnetism could explain, and which would make one of
these persons but the *doppelganger* (as the Germans call
it) or *double* of the other. Speaking seriously, however,

---

are sure; because he is made to say things which Junius had
actually printed several months before the speech was delivered:
But that Junius is indebted to Lord Chatham, we cannot be
equally sure; because, in the cases where he seems to be so, we
do not know but he might be merely resuming sentiments which
he had gratuitously imputed to Lord Chatham.

252

as this explanation would be a greater mystery than any
it is called to solve, so in this case it happens that a single
consideration makes it impossible: for, though we should
thus understand how Junius might be indebted to the
speeches of Lord Chatham, it would through this very
explanation become an impossibility to explain how the
speeches happened to be indebted to Junius; which they
clearly *are* in the reports of Francis, since particular
sentences in those reports were written and published
by Junius not merely 20 years before the reports, but
some months before even the speech itself was itself
delivered.†

† The question of Junius has afforded an arena for some of the
ability of this age, but also for much of its absurdity, which has
happily escaped in this direction, rather than in the more costly
one of attempting to extract sunbeams from cucumbers. Human
folly cannot go lower than it has done in some of the guesses. One
elaborate guess in 8vo, within the last five years, which cost me 5s,
fixes upon Lord Chesterfield as Junius. The main argument, which
rests upon my memory at present, is—that Lord Chesterfield was
not dead at the time. And certainly that is something, for I agree
with the writer that it is altogether indispensable, and a thing
not to be excused in any man, commoner or peer, who is a candidate for this honour, that he shall adduce most satisfactory vouchers for his existence: Living a few years before, or a few years
after, will not do; he must give as a reference to two "respectable
householders" at the least—that he was "in the flesh" then and
there. Now, as to poor Lord Chesterfield, most undeniably he was
breathing at the time of Junius; but whether in a full sense *living*,
or what the vivacious Junius would call so, may be questioned by
those who recollect some of his posthumous letters written about
that time. If ever man was all alive with the fever of hope and
personal schemes of ambition, it was Junius; if ever man not
actually under a mortification, was in the last stage of decay and
listless indifference to the strife of parties, it was the Lord Chesterfield of that day, to whom the mere act of getting out of his
carriage had become a work of labour and anxiety. Lord Chesterfield retained, indeed, even at these years, the brilliant polish of
his manners, and the grace of his epistolary style; but at no
period of his life could he have endured the effort necessary to the
artist-like precision, and sustained elegance of Junius; nor would
his particular taste, sensible only to a happy spontaneous elegance
and the grace of unelaborate ease, have been peculiarly pleased

VIII.—There were five persons in the War-Office, whom Sir Philip Francis regarded with a friendly or unfriendly interest: there were five persons in the War-Office, who were objects of applause, or of malignant persecution to Junius. The five persons in Sir Philip's

---

with a style of composition so artificial, and in some degree scholastic. However, he was alive; and there is the first stone of a new hypothesis laid, for any man who may be disposed to build further upon so desperate a foundation. Yet even this claim for Lord Chesterfield, or that for Edmund Burke, is not more unhappy as regards the *internal* evidence, than the one brought forward for Hugh M'Aulay Boyd, by Almon, George Chalmers, &c. I mention it here, because it is connected with this point of the inquiry, from the circumstances of Hugh Boyd having also taken notes and afterwards published them, of the two speeches of Lord Chatham. These, as Mr. Taylor remarks, have no resemblance to the style of Junius; which is the more remarkable, as the anxiety of Boyd to pass for Junius is notorious. Mr. Taylor might have said more: They are altogether destructive of Mr. Boyd's pretensions, had those pretensions been otherwise much better than they are. No differences in the kind of style, so long as the kind is legitimate, can ever be conclusive against such a claim; because there is no setting limits beforehand to the versatility of human talent. But the least touch of the *spurious* and the *falsetto*, is fatal in this case. The style of Junius, though formed upon a narrow model, and fitted only to a peculiar range of thought, is severe and sparing of ornament; whilst that of Boyd is tawdry, false, and affectedly rhetorical. Junius, besides, is felt to be a gentleman, and writes in the style of good society; which Boyd does not. But one argument, and one specimen, will for ever put an extinguisher on Mr. Boyd: Is it in human nature, I ask, that a man like Junius, originally of arrogant, and even insolent temper, elated, too, as he must have been, with his prodigious success upon the greatest stage of the empire, should, twenty years after, offer himself, with the deprecating air of a conscious underling, to the notice of a colonial audience? Yet listen to this Hugh Boyd, when propitiating the public of Madras, in the first number of his *Indian Observer*, (Sept. 1793): "The present writer regards, with a most respectful eye, the interval between *his* humble essay, and the excellence of periodical publication; which, for an Augustan century, has been the ornament and instruction of his country." Faugh! Did ever any Christian, since the days of ancient Pistol, deliver himself in that sort of fustian? "*The excellence of periodical publication,*" put for "the excellent periodical literature!" And this rag finery,

case were himself (then Mr. Francis,) Mr. D'Oyley, Mr.
Bradshaw, Mr. Chamier, and Lord Barrington: the five
persons in the case of Junius, were Mr. Francis, Mr.
D'Oyley, Mr. Bradshaw, Mr. Chamier, and Lord Barrington. What do you think of *that*, skeptic? And their

delivered, too, with the airs of a haberdasher suing for custom, to
pass for the work of the brilliant and haughty Junius! Junius left
India about the time that Boyd reached it, (1781); but had he
foreseen the possibility that such a monster would ever be mistaken
for himself, he would have gone back and strangled him.

Mr. Chalmers's arguments for Boyd are truely comical. One, and
I believe *that* one upon which he most relies, is—that some light-
horseman or other, when drunk, was told by Boyd himself, (being
also drunk), that he (Boyd) was the real Junius; and he didn't
care who knew it. But a second argument, still more facetious, is—
that in Mr. Chalmers's opinion, Junius could not write English:
Now, says he, as Boyd could not write English, (though otherwise, he thinks an eloquent man), it is clear that Boyd and Junius
are one and the same person. But this is by no means clear: For
not writing English is no such rare accomplishment as Mr. Chalmers seems to imagine. Upon that foundation Mr. Chalmers might
set up for Junius himself. Since, not content with rating Junius for
supposed bad English, in a passage selected as a specimen, Mr.
Chalmers has the honesty to write it over again himself, in what
he considers unexceptionable language; and *such* language as ir-
resistibly recals the humorous old ballad, in which a miller takes
his son to task for speaking indecorously before the king,—
    "Speak clean to our king, or else —————,"[1]
but the rest is too gross to quote. However, most assuredly, with
his English, Mr. Chalmers has only to confess to some light-
horseman, and he will then himself have pretty nearly *all* the pretensions to be Junius, which he has been able to discover in Hugh
M'Aulay Boyd.[2]

[1] The old ballad is "The King and the Miller of Mansfield,"
reprinted by Percy:
    Thou whore-son unhappy knave, then quoth the knight,
    Speake cleanly to our king, or else go shite.

[2] For the substance of section VII see Taylor's book, Chaps. IX,
XV. But this long footnote is not from Taylor. The reference to
the guess at Chesterfield is probably to William Cramp, *The Author of Junius Discovered in the Person of the Celebrated Earl of
Chesterfield* (1821); followed by *The Claims of Sir Philip Francis
Refuted; with a Supplement to "Junius Discovered"* (1822). Taylor does deny the possibility of Boyd's authorship (pp. 351-52),

love and their hatred were distributed in the same way. To take the names in their order, Francis had a supreme regard for Philip Francis in the first place, and next for Mr. D'Oyley, as united in a common misfortune with himself, and what *he* regarded as a common injury: Junius never mentions these two persons without expressions of sympathy and respect. "I think," says he, under his signature of Veteran, "the public have a right to call upon Mr. D'Oyley, and Mr. Francis, to declare their reasons for quitting the War-Office. Men of their unblemished character do not resign lucrative employments without sufficient reasons. The conduct of these gentlemen has always been approved of; and I know that they stand as well in the esteem of the army, as any persons in their station ever did. They have too much honour, I suppose, to do some certain business by *commission*. They have not been educated in the conversation of Jews and gamblers; and therefore, Lord B. drives them out of the War-Office." In the word *commission*, and what follows, Junius alludes to Chamier the stockbroker, who was the successful rival of Francis. Again, "The army is come to a fine pass, with a gambling broker at the head of it! What signifies ability, or integrity or practice, or experience in business. Lord Barrington wants nothing in his office but ignorance, impudence, pertness, and servility. Of these commodities he has laid in a plentiful stock, that ought to last him as long as he is Secretary at war," &c. &c.

Secondly, for Bradshaw and his brother-in-law Chamier, Francis owed to them the loss of his place; and Junius overwhelms these two persons with ridicule. Brad-

---

as the footnote says, but only briefly. Chalmers is George Chalmers, whose case for Boyd is in *An Appendix to the Supplemental Apology*, etc. (1800) and *The Author of Junius Ascertained* (1817), the last with a new edition in 1819 opposing the claim for Francis.

shaw he calls a *"cherub,"* and never mentions, but with the ludicrous epithet of *"cream-coloured,"* and pursues him even after he became secretary to the Duke of Grafton, and had no longer any connexion with the War-Office. As to Chamier, he calls him *"Mr. Shammy"*— *"little Waddlewell"*—*"little three per cents. reduced"*— *"an omnium of all that's genteel, the activity of a broker, the politeness of a hair-dresser,"* &c. &c. And he even takes the trouble to draw up a ludicrous scene between a General officer and Chamier, who are described at cross purposes, the General talking of military matters, the private secretary understanding him of the stock exchange:—

"Lieut.-General.—Sir, the Secretary at War refers me to you for an account of what was done?

Waddlewell.—Done, Sir!—Closed at three-eighths! Looked flat, I must own; but to-morrow, my dear sir, I hope to see a more lively appearance.

Lieut.-General.—Sir, I really don't understand you. Lord Barrington says my regiment may possibly be thought of for India.

Waddlewell.—India, my dear sir! Strange fluctuation! from 14½ to 22; never stood a moment; but ended cheerful: no mortal can account for it.

Lieut.-General.—Damn your stocks, sir; tell me whether the commission—

Waddlewell.—As for commission, my dear sir, I'll venture to say that no gentleman in the alley does business upon easier terms. I never take less than an eighth—" and so on. "After such a scene as this," adds Junius, "do you think that any man of rank or consequence in the army will ever apply to you or your deputy again? Will any officer of rank condescend to receive orders from a little whiffling brother [broker?]; to whom he may formerly perhaps have given half a crown for negociating a hundred pound stock, or sixpence for a lottery ticket?"

Lastly, with regard to Lord Barrington, Francis viewed him as his oppressor, and the organ by whom his rivals triumphed. In what light Junius viewed him, cannot *now* be a secret, when it is known (from the private letters to Woodfall) that it was Junius who wrote under the signature of *Veteran*: in truth, the "hell" of malignity, in which Junius habitually lived, "grows darker with his frown," whenever Lord Barrington happens to cross his path.[3]

IX.—Hitherto I have used the materials of Mr. Taylor, giving to them only a new arrangement which (I hope) makes the logic more apparent. But here, I separate from Mr. Taylor altogether, who, in what follows, has let a most important argument slip through his fingers in a way that I cannot comprehend. At the end of his preface, Mr. Taylor asserts, that, in the character of Junius, Sir P. Francis "has additional claims to gratitude and admiration: " and, in the same spirit he says at the end of his Supplement, that "now, having ably and consistently performed his part, Sir Philip appears in his natural character before the curtain drops, and will retire amid the plaudits of an admiring people." What infatuation could possess a man of sense and right feeling to talk in such language, I pretend not to guess: but, for my part, I mean to place this matter in a very different light; and, from *my* view of it, I shall show that a most powerful argument is deducible in favour of the present hypothesis. Mr. Taylor himself must acknowledge, as soon as he is reminded of it, that, if the sole effect of the detection was to give Sir Philip "additional claims to gratitude," undoubtedly Sir Philip would not have waited until some random accident revealed him. And this argument applies in any case to the true Junius, be he who he may. Some most extraordinary motive he must have had for his

---

[3] *Identity of Junius*, Chaps. V, VI. "Grows darker with his frown" is adapted from *Paradise Lost*, II, 720.

obstinate concealment. Indeed there are two mysteries about Junius; one which has always existed—*who is he?* And another, which has begun to press heavily within the last thirty years—*What could be his motive for concealment after his own generation had passed away?* FEAR might be a sufficient answer to this question for one generation; and doubtless for 20 or 30 good years Junius had before him a constant vision of daggers, pistols, cudgels, attorneys, according to the variety of tastes in vengeance. But this motive must have ceased to operate long ago. The hand, that should have stabbed Junius (see his letters to Sir W. Draper and Woodfall,) is dust and ashes: the chief-justice, whom he affronted to his teeth, is "at supper—not where he eats, but where he is eaten:"[4] the House of Commons, that he defied, has "adjourned" to Plato's year; the speaker, whom he scowled upon, has "quitted the chair" for ever; the king, whom he insulted, has descended to the grave full of years and honours; even "cream-coloured" Bradshaw has long since had his complexion spoiled; and "little 3 per cents," if he still "waddles" in the alley, waddles there in the person of his posterity of the third generation. I contend therefore, that fear is *not* the motive, nor can be, to the concealment. What then? GUILT, I answer, GUILT: the consciousness that, by claiming his literary honours, he should cover himself with infamy as a man. This, and nothing *but* this, can be the cause that Junius has not long ago—either by himself, or by his representatives—come forward to claim his rights. And I contend that to this, as one of the tests, the true and very Junius must answer wherever he lies hid.

With this preface, let us now turn to Sir P. Francis: and here we have the man. If Francis, the clerk of the War-Office, were Junius, then was Junius a traitor to his duties—a thief, a spy, and the vilest of eaves-droppers;

[4] *Hamlet,* IV, iii, 18ff.

and the letters of Junius, considering the secret information they contain, whence, and how it was obtained, were
one long act of systematic perfidy. Doubtless the tempta-
tion to confess was great, for it is not often that honour
of any kind is to be had from confessing an enormous
crime. The laurel, which awaited Junius, was, no doubt,
in Sir Philip's eyes, a radiant prize: but, to claim it, he
must begin by making shipwreck of his good name. The
first sentiment in reflecting men upon Sir Philip's avow-
ing himself, would have been—*In that case you are a
very brilliant writer*; but the second—*And a very pros-
perous knave*. Hence it is that no confession has been
made; and hence, in spite of the foolish paragraph,* now
running the circle of the newspapers, the reader may rely
upon it, that, unless on that day when the secrets of all
hearts shall be made known, no confession ever *will* be
made.

Neither is this all:—Sir P. Francis, supposing him to
be Junius, was a Janus of perfidy, committing a double
breach of faith—in two opposite directions. First, by
revealing the secrets of office—he had sold the Court to
the people; afterwards, by selling himself, he had sold the
people to the Court. And here it is remarkable that, as

---

* This paragraph, as given in the *Morning Post*, of Wednesday
January 2, is as follows:—

"JUNIUS.—Five letters are deposited in the archives of the
GRENVILLE family at Stow, which are said to establish, beyond the
possibility of doubt, the real author of *Junius*. This eminent individual was politically connected with Mr. GEORGE GRENVILLE, the
grandfather of the present Duke of BUCKINGHAM, from whom
these autograph proofs have descended to the present possessor.
The venerable Statesman, nearly allied to the Duke of BUCKING-
HAM, has requested the discovery should not be published during
his lifetime."

Now one letter from Junius to Mr. G. Grenville, with whom, by
the way, he was *not* "connected" in any sense, has been mentioned
in print several years ago, as deposited at Stow; but of a very
different tenor, viz. exhorting Mr. Grenville to forbear seeking to

the situation of Sir P. F. has enabled me to explain a
mystery about Junius, viz. his continued silence; so, on
the other hand, the situation of Junius, in relation to the
Court, throws light on a mystery in the life of Francis,
viz. his sudden and else unaccountable elevation. A discarded clerk, with a salary of £.400, is at one step raised
to a seat in the Supreme Council of Bengal, and made an
assessor to the Governor General of India, with an allowance of £.10,000 per annum! Here is a *salto mortale* in the
history of Sir Philip, which his nearest friends have
found it impossible to explain. Even to *them* it was a
mystery. But the guilty secret is now apparent: Upon
one treason Sir Philip founded a second. First, he sold
the secrets of the king to the public; and, by these, united
with his own talents, having raised himself into a formidable seditious power—next he carried himself into the
market, and made his bargain accordingly. And those
solemn vows, by which he had bound himself to the
English nation in his dedication, to continue to keep
watch and ward over their rights and interests, were paid

know him, as an attempt which could lead to no good.[5] But, supposing that account to be erroneous, let the reader observe the
absurdities in the present one. First, the discovery is kept back
at the request of a "venerable statesman," *i. e.* of Lord Grenville,
as though *he* could have any separate interest in the matter. Secondly, the discovery is "beyond the possibility of doubt:" But how?
What more can a man do on a sheet of paper than assert, (as
others have done before him), that he is Junius? But he may argue
his claim on circumstantial evidence. True: and *that* is just what
I have been doing with the help of Mr. Taylor; and what others
have done. And the whole turns on a comparison of probabilities.
But as to any proof that can exclude the possibility of doubt, all
that is quite out of the question, when every body is dead that
could confirm the presumption by positive testimony.

[5] *Identity of Junius*, p. 398.
The *Literary Gazette* of January 12, p. 29n., in its discussion of
the newly reported material on Junius, cites the "very able article"
in the *Edinburgh Saturday Post*; but it does not believe Francis
was Junius. The *Post* reprinted the *Gazette's* comment on January
19, p. 295.

down as *his* part of the contract: And thus did the patriotism of the immortal Junius Brutus expire in ten thousand a year, and the reversion of a red ribbon!

But I have already, Mr. Editor, occupied so unreasonable a space, that I must defer what else I have to say until next week.—Yours, &c.—X. Y. Z.

January 12, 1828

Letters of Junius

[cont.]

TO THE EDITOR OF THE POST

X. Junius ceased to write in the spring of 1772—having then written under that signature for three years and a quarter.* I have already noticed, that, in the spring of 1772, Francis was dismissed from the War-Office. The two facts sufficiently illustrate each other: the cessation, and the reason for it, are thus brought out in their true relations. The secret opportunities of Junius were over; and nothing remained for him but to go immediately into the market, and drive the very best possible bargain for himself, before it should become suspected that he was now shorn of his Sampson locks, that Junius was indeed no more than a *"nominis umbra,"*[1] and his thunders but a *brutum fulmen*. In the course of 1772, therefore, the bargain was made. It has been shown that he was upon sale in that year; and it is equally evident, that in that year he must have been bought, if bought he was to be, from the absolute necessity of making hay whilst the sun shone. Now, it is a remarkable confirmation of these views, that his late Majesty, upon the authority of Sir N. Wraxall,[2] when riding out with General Desaguliers, in the year 1772, said to that officer, "We know who Junius is; and" (he added significantly) "he will write no more."† The reader must not confound, with this positive assertion of the King's, a report of the previous year, 1771, (noticed in the excellent little edition of Junius

* He began to write in January 1769.
† This information came to Sir Nathaniel through the daughter of Gen. Desaguliers, and was not therefore obtained circuitously.

1 "Stat nominis umbra" (Lucan, I, 135) was Junius' epigraph.
2 See *Identity of Junius*, pp. 398-401.

263

published by Oliver and Boyd, Edinburgh) ³ that Junius
had ceased to write. *That* report was premature;‡ but the
King's declaration to General D. was confirmed by the
fact; and was illustrated a few months afterwards, upon a
vacancy occurring, by the circumstance of Francis's
obtaining a place in the council of Bengal,—i.e. his pur-
chase-money.||

XI. As to political principles,—both Sir Philip Francis
and Junius were uncommitted to any known party for
systematic purposes, but differed occasionally with all.

‡ And probably had arisen with Garrick; for Junius himself
says to Woodfall that Garrick, after the *pumping* scene, went immediately to the king, and reported that Junius would write no
more.

|| It is a remarkable attestation to the truth of this secret his-
tory, that the *private* notes of Junius to Woodfall cease in May
1772, viz. till about the time when Francis went abroad, and are
resumed and finally concluded early in 1773, viz.— about the time
when Francis is known to have returned. No doubt it was from the
security of his residence on the continent that he conducted his
negociation. And my own opinion is that, besides the secret of
Junius and the covenant to write no more under that signature,
Mr. Francis in all probability sold other valuable considerations to
the court. In particular the reader must remember a memorable
passage, in which Junius obscurely intimates a storm within his
power to raise against the Duke of Bedford, that would "shake
him in his grave."⁴ This must allude to the case of the peace of
Paris. Now, when it is recollected *who* were the parties implicated
in that transaction, viz.—the king's mother and his nearest friends,
(Lord Bute, &c.); it cannot surprise us that Francis, who by his
own account held a situation "of great trust" in the War-Office,
and previously in the Foreign-Office, should have possessed himself
on that or other secret transactions of some discoveries that would
be alarming to the court in the hands of an incendiary like Junius.
It is true that Dr. Musgrave's evidence, in that particular affair,
was received slightingly at the bar of the House of Commons; but
there still remains something obscure about it, and the charges are
not wholly disposed of: *aliquid haeret*: and we may be assured
that all obscurities in this or any other case that passed through
the public offices during Mr. Francis's confidential connexion with
them, would be clear enough to him, and known in all its circumstances.

³ 1822.   ⁴ *Identity of Junius*, pp. 105-09.

Sir Philip surprised every body, by voting against a reform bill, which had the support of the whole Whig party: and he said of himself, in 1784, "I am not a party man on this or any other question." Junius, on the other hand, declares himself to be "disowned as a dangerous auxiliary by every person in the kingdom."[5] In fact, no person familiar with his letters, and with the history of those times, can fail to know, that, in some important particular or other, Junius differed with every one of those whom he most approved. Probably, this arose as much from the unhappy temper with which Sir Philip is known to have been cursed, as from any conscientious exercise of judgment. It was a necessary consolation to such an irritable nature, as appears in the works both of Francis and Junius, that the writer should believe nobody to be altogether in the right except himself.

XII. Differing, however, from every body else, Junius and Sir Philip might also differ from each other; but they do *not*. These eternal dissenters, as compared with every body else, are here in most unaccountable harmony; nor is it possible to allege any particular, either as to things or persons, with one single exception, on which they are known to have thought differently. Both have a vehement admiration of Lord Chatham,¶—but an admiration tempered with some disapprobation. Francis describes him as "a great, illustrious, faulty, human being." Junius throughout treats him in that spirit. Both approve of Mr. Grenville's politics upon the whole. Both take the same remarkable view of the American question, asserting (that is to say) an abstract right *in posse* in the British Parliament to tax the colonies; but denying the right *in*

¶An admiration probably sincere enough, but not likely to be the less ardent for the fact that Lord Chatham had recommended Francis as Secretary to General Bligh, and afterwards to Lord Kinnoul, when ambassador to the court of Lisbon.

5 *Identity of Junius*, p. 354.

esse, until the colonies were represented: both agree in their earnest attachment to triennial Parliaments: both agree in their abhorrence of annual and septennial Parliaments: both question the competency of Parliament to disfranchise the rotten boroughs, either by a direct act of power, or by way of purchase: both reprobate the extension of the elective franchise to the great trading towns; and in short, not to weary the reader, on every question common to the period of Junius and Francis, there is a complete uniformity of opinion in the two sets of writings—one question only (as I said before) excepted.[6]

XIII. Does not this one, however, in its degree, weaken the argument? No; but, on the contrary, greatly strengthens it. For, in bringing forward this one discordant opinion, Sir Philip Francis declared that *he had once thought otherwise*.[7]

XIV. Of what country was Junius? He has been pronounced an Irishman by Lord Temple (Mr. Grenville), by Mr. Dempster, by an Irish nobleman, by an anonymous writer, (Modestus), whom he himself replied to under his signature of Philo-Junius, by Almon, and by several others, upon various grounds, the most forcible of which is his peculiar use of certain words. In particular, when Junius says—"I will not descend to answer the little sneering sophistries of a *collegian*,"—it is justly contended that this word is below the society in which Junius must have mixed, and positively vulgar according to the usage of England, though not according to that of Ireland, nor perhaps of Scotland. Now then, of what country was Sir Philip Francis? *Answer*: an Irishman, and educated in Ireland until his tenth year. This however will not go so far in accounting for his Hibernicisms, as the fact that his father, with whom, as a literary man,

6 Ibid., pp. 95-104, 201-08, Chap. XII.
7 Ibid., pp. 190ff. of Chap. XII.

he must have associated a good deal, was an Irishman—
son to the Dean of Lismore, and grandson to the Dean
of Leighlin.[8]

XV. Have the *acknowledged* works of Sir Philip
Francis any resemblance to those of Junius? *Answer*: in
a question of style, let a man's natural taste be what it
may, I would not entirely rely upon it—unless he were
himself practised in composition; to such a person, in so
clear a case, I would confidently leave the decision. For
my own part, upon this one point of the comparison,
taken singly, I should at once decide for the identity of
Junius and Sir Philip; not only in the style, but in the
whole colour of the sentiments, in the brilliancy of the
treatment, in the mode of presenting and connecting
thoughts, in the expression of the moral temper,—
worldly, malignant, contemptuous, and eternally fretful,
in the unrivalled keenness of the sarcasm, in the tendency
to personality,* and a thousand other characteristics, Sir
Philip Francis is the twin brother, or mere *double* of
Junius. In fact, the same ideal is in all things contemplated by both, though naturally more nearly realized
by Junius—a young man in his prime, animated by hope,
and writing a very little for a particular purpose of the
last importance to his own success in life, than by Sir
Philip Francis elderly, or in decay, and writing a good
deal with no specific object of much value to himself, but
pretty generally under the mere impulse of restless constitutional irritability.[9]

* This is one of the many qualities which peremptorily excludes
Edmund Burke, beyond all other claimants ever brought forward,
from every sort of pretension to be Junius. It was the degrading
necessity of Sir P. F.'s mind to lower the universal to the particular: it was the honourable necessity of Edmund Burke's to
exalt the individual and the personal into the general and the
philosophic.

---

[8] Ibid., pp. 161-63.

[9] Taylor, too, thinks the style of Junius and Francis are similar,
but the argument here is not his.

XVI. *Phraseology*—Junius has some striking peculiarities of phrase. All these are common to Sir P. Francis.

1. '*A false fact*' has been noticed already: this is continually used by both: Lord North also uses it, but only when speaking of Junius.

2. "*Of* our (his, their, &c.) side" instead of *on* our side; *passim* in both: thus JUNIUS "We have the laws *of* our side:"

FRANCIS—"He who knows that he has the law *of* his side," &c.

3.-----"So far forth," an antiquated and somewhat pedantic expression, but very common in both.

4. "Examinable," which is Irish, and adopted by both.

5. Peculiar use of the verb *mean*: JUNIUS—"I meant the cause and the public."

FRANCIS employs the word in exactly the same way.[10]

XVII. *Spelling.*—Junius has some peculiarities, all of which are found in Francis. *Though* he always writes in the abbreviated form (tho'); so does Francis. The words *Enhance,* — *Engross,* — *Entire,* — *Enforce,* — *Enslave,* — *Entrust,* he uniformly spells with an *I*; so does Francis. Another peculiarity is still more remarkable: the modern substitution of the termination *or* for *our* in such words as *honor, labor,* &c. had not commenced in the time of Junius; and even now it is always confined to words of Latin origin; but Junius, by a singular caprice, universally writes even the Saxon word *endeavour* with a final *or*: so does Francis. Both also agree in the singularity of spelling the word practice when used as a noun in the way that other people spell it when used as a verb, i.e. prac*ti*se with an *s*.[11]

XVIII. *Handwriting.*—This is exactly the same in the MSS. of both, allowing a very little for the attempt on the part of Junius to disguise it. *These be his Ps*, we may

[10] *Identity of Junius,* Chap. XIV.
[11] For sections XVII-XX, see *Identity of Junius,* pp. 373-83.

say with Malvolio, *and so maketh he his Qs.* The hand-
writing of Junius is remarkably elegant; and so is that
of Sir Philip in that table of specimens commencing with
the words "*My, Mr., Friendship, Quarter,*" &c. But latterly, Sir Philip wrote carelessly, and as if with a bad
pen,—blunted, restive, and superannuated like himself.

XIX. *Correction of Proofs.*—Junius had this peculiarity in his correction of Proofs, that instead of the customary mark of deletion used by authors, which resembles
one of the small forms of the Greek theta, he chooses to
employ a symbol of his own, viz. a small Greek delta. Sir
P. F., in *his* Proofs, employs the very same peculiar mark.

XX. *Punctuation.*—Junius and Sir Philip were both
very "peevish" (to borrow a word from Hostess Quickly)
in the matter of punctuation: neither of them neglecting
to point the most trivial of his notes with the utmost
precision, according to his peculiar notions of punctuation, which system is exactly the same in the MS. of both.
1. For the *inverted commas*, which distinguish quotations, both writers substitute two *straight strokes.* 2. This
mode of marking quotations, Junius occasionally varies
by another, viz. that of *underscoring the words*: So does
Sir P. F.: but Junius never uses both modes together, as
some authors do; neither does Sir Philip. 3. Junius has a
peculiar and most absurd *mark of interrogation*: the same
identical mark, which one might swear to as absolutely
unique, is used by Sir Philip. 4. Both have the same
peculiarity in marking a *parenthesis.* 5. Both place a
grave accent ' over the small *i* more frequently than a dot.
6. Both have the same singularity with regard to the
division of words. "They very seldom divide a word,"
says Mr. Taylor, "at the end of a line, preferring in the
place of it to leave a great space which is often filled up
by an extended flourish of the pen, as is the case in law
writings." 7. But, when they *do* condescend to divide a
word, both use the same mark for connecting the syl-

lables, viz. a *colon* instead of a *hyphen*; and, not content with this colon at the end of the line, both writers repeat it at the beginning of the succeeding one. 8. Both have the same singularity in writing the common abbreviation (&) for *and*; the singularity consisting in this that the depending tail never drops below the line. Both have the same peculiarity in writing the abbreviation of *et cætera*; which peculiarity consists in writing an *a* over it, i.e. &c.ᵃ instead of the common form, *&c.*

Many other eccentricities common to the two hand-writings might be pointed out; but I content myself with an abstract of those which have been so diligently collected by Mr. Taylor.

* * * * *

Such then is the amount of evidence for the identity of Sir P. Francis and Junius. And to meet the force of these overwhelming proofs, what is the solitary argument that has since been put forward by way of counterpoise? Simply the allegation that Sir Philip, when questioned on the point by a man who had no right to question him, intimated that he was *not* Junius.

The reader, who *now* understands what commanding motives Sir Philip had for throwing a veil over that trans-action of his life, will smile in pity at the desperate credulity which could be duped by any denial, the most solemn and the most unequivocal that words could frame, coming from that quarter. But *did* Sir Philip deny it?

On this question, which yields a final and very important argument to convict Sir Philip, I will trouble you, Mr. Editor, with a few concluding words next week. If the one sole argument, for acquitting Sir Philip, can be placed in such a light as more than any other to convict him,—I fancy that there is at once and for ever an end to the dispute.[12]

---

[12] The concluding words promised for next week never appeared.

270

After this case is disposed of,—if your readers should take an interest in the solution of these historical riddles, I will briefly argue the question of the *Gipsies*, of the *Freemasons*, of the *Iron Masque*, and of the *Eikon Basilike*; which last has this peculiar interest about it—that, although now agitated (and very ably and most passionately agitated) for a space of 179 years, it still subsists like a Spanish game of chess transmitted as an heirloom from generation to generation; and, since the very able and minute researches of the Master of Trinity, Cambridge, is more than ever involved in a cloud of doubt and mystery.[13]

X. Y. Z.

ATTRIBUTION

On December 22, 1827, the *Post* announced: "We can promise next week a very interesting article from a most valuable Contributor on the subject of JUNIUS." The three installments that followed were certainly by De Quincey.

The author says he has had several private conversations with Taylor (p. 239). De Quincey had known Taylor when he was a contributor to the *London Magazine* and Taylor was one of the proprietors and editor. De Quincey wrote an article on the *London Magazine* and some of the people connected with it, in *Tait's* in

---

For the point that would have been made see p. 239 n.10 above. De Quincey, incidentally, does make the point in his 1840 article (M., III, 135-37), discussed below in the evidence for attribution.

[13] The Master of Trinity was Christopher Wordsworth, the poet's brother. In *Who Wrote* ΕΙΚΩΝ ΒΑΣΙΛΙΚΗ? (1824) and its *Documentary Supplement* (1825) he argued for the authorship of Charles and against the attribution to Gauden. In the controversy that followed he replied with *King Charles the First, the Author of Icôn Basilikè* (1828).

1840, including an account of Taylor's identification of Junius very similar to this one in the *Post* (M., III, 132-43); he says there that he had written a private letter to Taylor on the Junius question. He returned to the same subject of Taylor and Junius in *Tait's* in 1847, in "Schlosser's Literary History" (M., XI, 41-49). Those points which are common to De Quincey and the author of the *Post* articles and which are not in Taylor's book are conclusive evidence.

The comparisons between the Junius mystery and other mysteries of identification, made at the beginning and the end of the *Post* articles (pp. 236-38, 271), are also in De Quincey's "Historico-Critical Inquiry into the Origin of the Rosicrucians and the Free-Masons," published in the *London Magazine* in 1824 (M., XIII, 384-85): he had included there, among a number of "problems in history" that rouse the "curiosity," the questions of the Gypsies, Mary Stuart, the Ruthvens, the man in the Iron Mask, Perkin Warbeck, the author of the *Eikon Basilike* and Junius. In the same article (XIII, 388) he says that two of these problems have been conclusively settled by triumphant "dissertations": one of these dissertations is "Malcolm Laing's upon Perkin Warbeck (published by Dr. Henry in his *History of Great Britain*)" and the other Taylor's upon Junius. There is a brief reference to Laing's dissertations on Perkin Warbeck and the Gowrie conspiracy in "Charlemagne" (1832), M., V, 355n., and Laing's name is in "Schlosser's Literary History," M., XI, 41n. Henry the historian is in "Modern Superstition" (1840), M., VIII, 445. De Quincey also refers to Christopher Wordsworth's "research" on the *Eikon* (p. 271) in 1839 (M., II, 256-57), saying there that the question is still unsettled but much nearer settlement after his work; see too M., VIII, 148. De Quincey had met Dr. Wordsworth, perhaps in 1827, when Dr. Wordsworth settled a small dispute between De

Quincey and William Wordsworth, on a question of Anglican doctrine, ruling against De Quincey ("Protestantism" [1847-48], M., VIII, 290-92). Dr. Wordsworth probably sent De Quincey a copy of his 1828 book on the *Eikon*; see John E. Jordan, *De Quincey to Wordsworth*, p. 298.

Several of the other flourishes with which the author of these articles surrounds his subject are very like De Quincey's. That a library might be formed on the question of Junius (p. 236) is repeated in De Quincey's article of 1840, where he has heard of several persons projecting a Bibliotheca Juniana (M., III, 133). The authority of Chief Justice Dallas (p. 237) is invoked again in the 1840 article (M., III, 132), to demonstrate that the evidence gathered by Taylor is enough for a lawyer: "Chief Justice Dallas, of the Common Pleas, was wont to say that" a man arraigned as Junius "upon the evidence here accumulated" against Francis would be convicted by any court. And again in De Quincey's article of 1847, and picking up more of the language of the *Post*, Chief Justice Dallas has said that if Taylor was not right, and Francis was not Junius, no man was ever yet "hanged" on sufficient "evidence" (M., XI, 44-45). A reason why the identification of Junius has not been accepted, in spite of the evidence (p. 237), is repeated in the 1840 article (M., III, 134-35): some people have expected a greater name than Francis and the revelation is mortifying to that expectation; Woodfall is the particular instance cited.

The most significant departure from Taylor made by the author of the articles in the *Post* is his argument that Francis never revealed himself because to have done so would have been to reveal his guilt (pp. 258ff.). The same is true of De Quincey and it was on this point that De Quincey had written his private letter to Taylor (M., III, 135-40). Taylor does say that if Francis was

Junius and was discovered in 1772 then there is a reason
for the otherwise inexplicable sudden promotion of Francis to high position in India. But he talks of that as the
"honourable mode of banishing" Francis adopted by the
King's friends, not as proof of Francis' perfidy, not a
reason why Francis will not reveal his authorship. Besides, Taylor doesn't pursue the argument, being desirous
of restricting himself to documents and avoiding any
breach of delicacy (*Identity of Junius*, 2nd ed., pp. 309-
401). Both the arguments and the language used by the
author of the *Post* and by De Quincey are very close.
Fear, De Quincey says, could not have been a reason for
secrecy extending beyond Junius' own term of life.
Francis had stronger motives. He was a "thief," "traitor,"
"spy," "eavesdropper," a man of "perfidy," one who
committed a great "crime." Having obtained power like
a thief he sold it like a traitor; having first made himself
formidable to the King and Cabinet, he "brought himself . . . into the market for sale . . . by a double treachery"; having stolen ministerial secrets to become Junius
he then betrayed his principles *as* Junius by selling himself to the ministry for position and wealth. This explanation unlocks what had been something of a "mystery" to
his "friends": how Francis "the obscure clerk of the War-
Office . . . shot up all at once" into money and position,
became, among other things, one of the "Supreme Council in Bengal." It was this history that kept Francis from
claiming his "prize" of being known as the author of the
letters. If he had made any "avowal" that he was Junius
it would have been said to him, " '*Why, then, you are a
very brilliant fellow.*' That would be the first reflection;
but then would come a second on the heels of *that:* —
'*And a most unprincipled knave. . . .*' " De Quincey's 1847
article contains some of the same and some additional
identities with the *Post* articles (M., XI, 42-43, 47-49):
Francis was a man of "infamy," of "perfidy," of "crime,"

a "knave," a "thief" who stole secrets and "sold himself," obtaining in the bargain a position in the Council in Bengal and eventually a "red riband"; the identification of Junius and Francis not only clears up the mystery of Junius but also the "sudden and unaccountable" Indian appointment of Francis; had he revealed himself he would have been congratulated for his cleverness and condemned as a scoundrel.

The same ridicule of newspaper reports about Grenville and the Duke of Buckingham (pp. 260-61n.) is in De Quincey's 1840 article (M., III, 134); and besides, he says there too, even if such a piece of paper as has been reported should be discovered, it would not be evidence that no one could gainsay: "what more could [a dead man] possibly do than leave behind him a writing" making an assertion? And the utmost result would be one more rival case to be argued.

For the comparison between Burke and Junius (p. 267n.) see De Quincey's "Rhetoric," published later in the same year of 1828 (M., X, 117-20), where he again identifies the treacherous Francis with Junius and quickly disposes of the hypothesis that Burke was Junius: there is an absurd difference between Burke, "who exalted the merest personal themes into the dignity of philosophic speculations, and Junius, in whose hands the very loftiest dwindled into questions of person and party" or "individuality," not "general" ideas. Also on Burke's ability to "generalize what is personal," see "A Brief Appraisal of the Greek Literature" (1838-39), M., X, 334; and on Junius' inability, see the letter of 1842 in Alexander H. Japp, *Thomas De Quincey*, new ed. (1890), p. 240.

On the signature of "X. Y. Z." (pp. 262, 271), see the article of August 11, 1827 and the further references given there (p. 73).

On the style of question and answer (pp. 240-44, 266-

67) see the article of September 15, 1827 (pp. 121-22) and the references there.

The Laputan folly of extracting sunbeams from cucumbers (p. 253n.) is an illustration also used by De Quincey: "Shakspeare" (1838), M., IV, 51; *Logic of Political Economy* (1844), M., IX, 135.

Several of the foreign words and phrases, common and not so common, also appear in De Quincey's writings. "Doppelganger" (p. 252), perhaps not too common at this date, is in De Quincey's "Gillies's German Stories," *Blackwood's*, XX (1826), 853, and also in "Modern Superstition" (1840), M., VIII, 440, and "Milton *versus* Southey and Landor" (1847), M., XI, 461. "Brutum fulmen" (p. 263) he uses before and after this date about six times. "In posse . . . in esse" (pp. 265-66) he uses about the same number of times, in this combination, and he uses them individually; see also the article of July 12, 1828 (p. 390). A variation of "Si non pondere at numero" (p. 239) is in two of his essays, M., IV, 135 and X, 134.

January 19, 1828

[The End of the Coalition]

The Coalition—a name abominable to British ears—is
dissolved; and, through their several partizans in the
London journals, the different members of it have been
furiously assailing each other, criminating and recrimi-
nating, during the whole of the last week. Mr. Herries,
it seems to be resolved, shall be made the scape-goat for
the late administration; and the sycophants of Mr.
Huskisson are attempting to colour *his* share in the general discord by putting forward the odious falsehood that
he goes out of office a martyr to his plans of retrenchment.[1] *Retrenchment!* although, on the part of this very
Mr. Huskisson, a paper was inserted in the Edinburgh
Review for October last, having, for it's sole object, to
shew that no retrenchments of any consequence were
possible; that our several establishments were brought as
low as was adviseable; and that the sole alleviations to
the national burthens were now to be sought in paying
off the national debt, (or one half of it at least) and in
a better system of political economy.[2] The same sycophants are not ashamed to assert, roundly, that Mr.
Huskisson, the *ci-devant* sansculotte member of sansculotte clubs,[3] has refused the situation of Prime Minis-

[1] Goderich's brief administration, without leadership or unity,
had had difficulties with the King, with the problem of Navarino,
and with internal problems of personality and principle. Goderich
made a couple of attempts to resign and finally succeeded. The immediate cause was a quarrel between Herries and Huskisson over
an appointment to a finance committee. Subsequent articles (February 16, 23) deal with differing explanations that were given
for the fall of the coalition.

[2] Article V, by M'Culloch; see pp. 195-96 above.

[3] As a boy and young man, from 1783 to 1792, Huskisson had
lived in France. He was at the fall of the Bastille and he had
joined the moderate "Club of 1789," which supported the monarchy
as limited by the new constitution; in fact, he had, in the club,

ter!!* Mr. Huskisson, with the qualifications of a book-keeper, without talents, without rank, without wealth, without connexions—Prime Minister of England!

Meantime, to dismiss these extravagancies, the probability is—that Mr. Peel will be the efficient (if not the nominal) head of the new administration. More than this is not conjectured upon any grounds which would warrant our repeating it. The fact is, that the newspapers, in the eagerness of their impatience, are not willing to allow time for maturing the arrangements. Some *ratting* has been talked of; and such a thing is certainly probable enough in the desperate and ridiculous situation of the Whigs—banished from hope at the very moment when it was again dawning upon them. Indeed, generally, it may be laid down as a rule, that he who will *coalesce* will *rat*; for, though men will sometimes preserve their personal engagements, after they have forfeited their principles, yet undoubtedly, in politics, the one step leads naturally to the other. Whether, however, the Whigs will rat, and how many of them, is yet uncertain. In reality, except the one great fact of Tory supremacy, everything is yet uncertain, and probably will remain so for a week longer. To that time we reserve ourselves.

ATTRIBUTION

I think this is De Quincey's, though not much specific evidence can be offered. It is preliminary to the leader

*By the way, we observe the old hackneyed blunder still current, though so often exposed, that the Premiership is attached of necessity to any particular office: in an Edinburgh paper of this morning we find it said—that Mr. Peel's friends wished him to be "both Prime Minister and Chancellor of the Exchequer;" as though *Prime Minister* were but a variety of expression for *First Lord of the Treasury*!

argued against paper money, to protect property. The charge here, that he really had been a sansculotte, or a Jacobin, he had met in the past.

of the following week (January 26), which is certainly his. Like that (p. 287), it insists upon Huskisson's "sans-culotte" phase. And like the review in the *Post* of November 17, 1827, which is certainly De Quincey's, it approves of the political economy of the article on retrenchment in the *Edinburgh Review*; this sort of approval is unusual in the *Post*.

The series "without talents, without rank, without wealth, without connexions" (p. 278) is perhaps a sign of authorship; "The Duke of Wellington and Mr. Peel," *Blackwood's*, XXV (1829), 294, an article of his frequently cited in these notes because of similarities to material in the *Post*, has "without property, connexions, or remarkable talents."

The use of "rat," and its derivatives, in the political sense, is the language of the day, but it is De Quincey's language too. He uses it in next week's leader, in the same passage just cited (p. 287); it is also in the leader of February 9 (pp. 303, 305), which is probably his; and he uses it half a dozen times in his known works: "The Duke of Wellington and Mr. Peel," p. 296n.; "Dr. Samuel Parr" (1831), M., V, 37, 45; "Samuel Taylor Coleridge" (1835), M., II, 224; "Lord Carlisle on Pope" (1851), M., XI, 119; "The Anti-Papal Movement," *Posthumous Works* (1893), II, 176. "Ci-devant," used here with "sansculotte," is also perhaps a sign of De Quincey: letter to Wordsworth, April 4, 1818, in Jordan, *De Quincey to Wordsworth*, p. 309; "Mr. Schnackenberger" (1823), M., XII, 327; "Goethe's Wilhelm Meister" (1824), M., XI, 255; "Schlosser's Literary History" (1847), M., XI, 9.

The footnote on the hackneyed blunder has a characteristic De Quinceyan delight in precision of terminology and small detail.

The Ministry

Since this journal began, we have had little room for the language of pleasure and congratulation: The composition of government, and it's acts, were alike odious to men of our principles; and we found ourselves yoked to the ungenial duty of continual opposition. But at length, for the universal good, and pretty nearly for the universal joy, the scene changes; at length the morning of a new æra appears to dawn upon us; a Tory government is formed, with no more alloy than it will always be strong enough to purge off: We, from being of the party militant, suddenly find ourselves in the ranks of the party triumphant; the Whigs, or *soi-disant* Whigs, with the scowl of baffled hope, are fled and vanished; the nation exults; and (in the words of the old ballad) "The King enjoys his own again."[1]

Such have been the revolutions in our domestic politics within the last twelve months,—so many and so rapid— chasing each other with the passionate flight of a musical fugue, and with the monstrous surprizes of a pantomime, —that we shall pause a moment to review them.

At this time last year, we find at the head of the national councils a nobleman with more of the qualifications for a great *peace* minister of this country, than perhaps have met in any one man of our times: Eloquence suf-

[1] After Goderich's resignation the King asked Wellington to form a government, so the Tories seemed to have good cause to rejoice; Huskisson and a few other Canningites retained office, but not for long. The depth of De Quincey's pleasure is expressed in song—"When the King Enjoys His Own Again." Written in 1643 by Martin Parker, "to support the declining interest of the Royal Martyr," Ritson says, it served afterwards "with more success" to animate the Cavaliers, and to promote and celebrate the Restoration; it later became a Jacobite song. Ritson reprinted it in his *Ancient Songs* (1790), pp. 229-35, citing earlier versions.

ficient for all purposes of use, talents for business, much practical wisdom, political principles of the soundest character, modelled and trained to their application in the school of Mr. Pitt, a station of high personal favour with his Sovereign, balanced, however, by an original sympathy with popular feelings, and, finally, an irreproachable private life—which is absolutely necessary in a British minister to conciliate the entire confidence of his nation, and which is the best pledge of public integrity. No quality seemed wanting in this accomplished minister, except perhaps firmness and commanding energy. Latterly, at least, he was led astray, and insensibly to himself, by the glozing tempters who besieged his ear—to countenance a class of measures very alien from his own policy, and the principles on which it rested. His last three or four years (comparatively speaking) were imbecile and contradictory; and they paved the way for much of the confusions which followed.[2]

In a moment of time this great servant of the Crown, full of honours—in the plenitude of his power—and beloved in a degree which has rarely been indulged to that station, was smitten and laid prostrate by the hand of Providence; and forth stepped, as his successor, a gay rhetorician, armed at all points to dazzle and mislead—but, as a statesman, hollow and more shifting than a quicksand. A golden bribe was held forth, irresistible to *his* ambition, connected with *his* laxity of principle; and, at the price of fidelity to his party, and fidelity to his whole political creed, in an evil hour for himself, he be-

[2] In the last years of Liverpool's administration, after the suicide of Castlereagh, Canning and his "liberal" foreign policy and Huskisson and his "free trade" had become powerful forces within the government. And, as the last part of the present article indicates, the Catholic cause, after the foundation of the Catholic Association in 1823, had gained great strength.

came Prime Minister of Great Britain. From that moment there is no doubt that his peace of mind forsook him; and from the very day when he accomplished his utmost schemes of personal advancement, he bade adieu for ever to the luxury of an untroubled conscience. Historical readers will be reminded of the case of the unfortunate Charles Yorke; but the parallel is not complete. Charles Yorke, in accepting the Chancellorship, broke his personal engagements; and, wanting firmness to face the reproaches which he anticipated, destroyed himself.[3] But personal engagements, in matters of political party, resemble debts of honour in this—that they press rather on the sense of shame, than on the conscience; and belong to that species of imperfect obligations, the violation of which, when committed for any commensurate purpose, is in some degree lost and obscured in a very triumphant success, and to the worldly eye is justified by that success. Had Mr. Canning, therefore, broke faith *only* with his party, his sense of honour was not perhaps so sensitive, nor the particular circumstances of his case so much beyond the palliations of casuistry, nor unfortunately so entirely without the countenance of respectable authorities, and even of respectable accomplices, as very materially to disturb the enjoyment of his new honours. He would have said, possibly would have thought, that his party had forsaken him rather than he his party. But there were other and deeper compunctions peculiar to Mr. Canning's case, which gnawed at his heart, and could not be laid asleep by any sophistry. He had broken faith with his own conscience, and with every principle by which he had been meritoriously made known to Europe.

[3] Yorke, offered the great seal by Grafton in 1770, in an attempt to strengthen a dying administration, was urged by his brother and by Rockingham, leader of his party, not to accept; he refused office, was pressed by the King, who told him that the offer would never be repeated, then accepted, was reproached by his friends, and died three days later, perhaps by suicide; the cabinet fell.

He had broken faith with his great leader in the grave—with that William Pitt, whose memory and example he still continued to idolize. For what had been the characteristic glory of Mr. Canning's life, for which—or for nothing—he was to receive honour from history? What but this—that in the great Crusade which for five-and-twenty years had been maintained by "the faithful armies"[4] in every part of Europe, chiefly in Great Britain, against Jacobinism, against the spirit of disorganizing innovation, and against the desolating principles of the anti-social philosophy,—he had fought in the foremost ranks, and (when his age and weight of authority allowed it) as a conspicuous leader. Yet this—for the 'whistling of a name,'[5] for what, by comparison, must have appeared to him but as a baby's rattle—for a little perishable power—place and precedency—he had ignobly bartered for ever, and by one false step, irretrievably taken, had cancelled the merits of a life! Wheresoever, in whatsoever language, the history of that immortal crusade should be written with truth and knowledge, Mr. Canning felt that his long services—being by his own act virtually retracted, disavowed, abolished—must, henceforward, be recited with scorn; and that, from the roll of faithful champions, who had persevered to the end—in defence of social order, *his* honours must be "blotted out and razed, and of his name be no remembrance!"* These were the pangs which embittered the few and agitated months of his triumph; their sting was the deeper in proportion to the sensibility and goodness of his nature; and these it was, there can be no doubt, united to the other perplexities of his situation, to the persecutions of hungry

---

* Paradise Lost.[6]

[4] See August 18, 1827, p. 78 above.

[5] . . . ravish'd with the whistling of a Name,
    See Cromwell, damn'd to everlasting fame!
Pope, *Essay on Man*, IV, 283-84.

[6] I, 361-62, much misquoted.

expectants, and the mortifications inflicted by the formidable hostility of the aristocracy, which promoted that
irritation already established in his constitution, and
strengthened him in those habits, which led to his unhappy end.

That end made room for a third Premier, who did not
come in (like Mr. Canning) by breaking his political
engagements; for he had some months before left himself
with none to break. He had been foremost, and even
ostentatiously unscrupulous in proclaiming his unhal-
lowed league with Whiggism, falsely so called, that is
with all the jacobinism, lawless innovation, and moody
sedition in the land. He, like Mr. Canning, was seen arm
and arm with the *boutefeus* and incendiaries of the times,
with Sir ———, and ———, and ———, with the sower
of seditious speeches, with the venomous lampooner of
his King, with the man who stood up in his place in the
House of Commons, resolutely and formally to insult and
to spurn the Irish nation for wanting the spirit to rebel;[7]
and, through these worshipful associates, he, like Mr.
Canning, was justly held by inference and construction
to have connected himself with all the allies of those
associates in every station, who, though muzzled for the
present by the dire necessities of Newgate, and the gal-
lows, yet even at this time through the W—— Review,[8]
or other journals of that stamp, publish to the world
their grim Septembrizing instincts, and their appetites
for anarchy and spoliation. This third minister, however,
as compared with his predecessor, was altogether a person
minorum gentium; and, having none of Mr. Canning's

---

[7] The first is probably Sir Francis Burdett. The second is certainly Brougham. The third I do not know: Parliamentary supporters of the Catholic claims were always careful to advise the
Irish to advance their cause by peaceful means; the sentiments
reported here may be a deliberate distortion of remarks like those
of William Plunket on May 26, 1825 (Hansard, 2nd ser., XIII, 887).

[8] The *Westminster*.

JANUARY 26, 1828

high pretensions, naturally atoned for his apostacy by less exalted sufferings. Yet even he, according to his degree, illustrated, in his altered habits and broken spirits, the inevitable retribution which awaits the political renegade. Whilst yet true to his engagements and his principles, no man so cheerful as Mr. Robinson: He was the most sanguine of the sanguine; and his gay but somewhat thoughtless tone of confidence had gained him the nickname of *Prosperity Fred.*[9] Turn to him as Lord Goderich, and what a revolution! Timid, irresolute, gloomy, and torpid—who would suspect in this shrunken pantaloon his old jovial and bustling acquaintance *Prosperity Fred?* But the case tells it's own history: He also had been made familiar with the woes of apostacy: He had been worried by famished Whigs, "more fell than hunger, or the sea,"[10] with entrails raging from an abstinence of half a century (for their few months' taste of office 20 years back had but sharpened their appetites): he also had been summoned to set his seal to measures which possibly *he only* at the council-board disapproved, whilst, yet for these very measures, he chiefly from his fatal pre-eminence of place, would hereafter be held responsible. Hence would arise frequent misgivings in the mind of the unhappy Minister; self-reproaches, self-conflicts, agitations, distraction of purpose, and finally from over-excitement almost paralytic imbecility. Twice, it is believed, that the King absolutely refused to accept his resignation, not out of any wish that he should continue his services, but simply from a gracious regard to his minister's reputation: it was almost humiliating to his Majesty that any man, whom he, could for one mo-

[9] Conferred by Cobbett (see below, p. 294): as Chancellor of the Exchequer in the last years of Liverpool's administration Robinson had congratulated the House on the permanent prosperity of the country and continued hopeful while the economy declined.
[10] Misquoted from the last speech in *Othello.*

285

ment have selected as his first minister, should so little justify that mark of confidence as to slink feebly from the responsibility he had undertaken before he had (though but for a month or for a week) faced the terrors of Parliament. But such are the penalties of violated faith; such, even in political creeds, are the avenging terrors which haunt the steps of apostacy! Roused at last, and shocked by the spectacle of paralytic incapacity, the King was forced to say in effect—Take him away, and bring me a man who at any rate is no apostate, who is single-minded, and has established a character for energy and decision.

Answering to this summons came forward the Duke of Wellington, *'exortus uti ætherius sol;'*[11] and, at once, the owls, bats, vampires, and other Whig nuisances, fled before him like vapours. The reign of Chaos and old Night[12] is at an end: Of the storms which have swept over us in such furious succession, no memorials now remain but a few wrecks hulling about; and a general persuasion prevails—that out of the anarchy of darkness, in which we have been tossing for the last 10 months, has arisen, at last, a system of light and order—and under auguries which promise to that system a durable supremacy.

Now then, as an appropriate conclusion to this review of the year which is gone by, let us throw our eyes over the new Cabinet, constructed by the noble Duke, and from its general complexion endeavour to forecast the main features of its policy, during the year which will commence with the approaching Session of Parliament. The following is the cast of parts, on the authority of the London Journals, though not yet gazetted:—1, *First Lord of the Treasury*, Duke of Wellington; 2, *Chancellor*, Lord Lyndhurst; 3, *President of the Council*, Lord Bath-

---

[11] From Lucretius, III, 1044: as the ethereal sun when it rises.
[12] *Paradise Lost*, I, 543.

urst; 4, *Privy Seal*, Lord Ellenborough; 5, *Home Secretary*, Mr. Peel; 6, *Foreign Secretary*, Lord Dudley; 7, *Colonial Secretary*, Mr. Huskisson; 8, *Chancellor of the Exchequer*, Mr. Goulbourn; 9, *High Admiral, Duke of Clarence*;[13] 10, *President of the Board of Control*, Lord Melville; 11, *Chancellor of the Duchy of Lancaster*, Lord Aberdeen; 12, *President of the Board of Trade*, Mr. C. Grant; 13, *Master of the Mint*, Mr. Herries. The *Ordnance* is not filled up; and some other appointments which give no seat in the Cabinet, (*Commander-in-Chief, Attorney General, &c.*) are yet in suspence.

Such is the new Cabinet; and speaking as reasonable men, who take their station of view, as *in fæce Romuli*, and not as *in republicâ Platonis*,[14] we do maintain that it is a most hopeful (because, in the main, a coherent) one. Undoubtedly an experienced rat-catcher would, on reviewing this Cabinet, object loudly to No. 7, as a vicious subject and a rat; indeed, if we may be allowed that expression, a rat with three tails; first he ratted from his original friends, the *Sansculottes*, through some unknown varieties of more decent people, all the way up to the Tories; next he ratted, with Mr. Canning, from the Tories to the Whigs; and now again we find his friends in the *Times* newspaper, of Tuesday last, most clamorously charging him with having ratted back again from the Whigs to the Tories.[15] To all this we subscribe: but

13 Now heir to the throne, since the recent death of the Duke of York, and soon to become William IV, he was not actually in the cabinet; but he was Lord High Admiral and a burden to his colleagues by his assertion of authority he wasn't supposed to have.
14 From Cicero's letters to Atticus, II, 1, where Cato's opinions are said to be more appropriate in Plato's ideal state than in actual Rome (the dregs of Romulus).
15 For Huskisson and the sansculottes see above, p. 277. The reference to the *Times* should be Wednesday, January 23, p. 2; but the language of the *Times* is much milder than it is reported to be here.

the whole weight of the objection depends on the temper and character which preside in the Administration; and so long as the reins are in the hands of No. 1, we have no fears, except it were for the modesty which may too often lead him to distrust his own judgment. In all cases, however, where the D. of Wellington sees his way clearly, he will act firmly; and, with regard to No. 7, in particular, his Grace knows him too well not to keep a tight hand over him. About three years ago, in an action brought against a mail-coachman for overturning the Liverpool mail, it was stated by Mr. Brougham for the defence, that this mail had been long used as a *break* for vicious horses, a coachman being always selected who realized in a more than usual degree the Homeric description of Hector Ἑκτορος Ἱπποδαμοιο—Hector the tamer of horses; and all the unruly subjects on the road were regularly *civilized* in the Liverpool mail. Just such a break will be the present Cabinet under the firm hands of the D. of W. He will keep a tight "bearing-rein" upon any dangerous subject like No. 7; and, if No. 7 should "jib," or plunge, or shew any vice, he will speedily be taught who it is that holds the "ribbons," and will be brought into a beautiful state of civilisation.

Dismissing, however, any individual examination of the Cabinet, until the distribution of the several parts is finally and circumstantially made known,—let us endeavour to collect from its general complexion a few anticipations of the great outline of their policy on the main questions, foreign or domestic, pending at this moment.

First, with respect to the only great question of foreign policy which presses at this moment, viz. the terms on which we are to place our relations with the Porte, we are surprised to see it made a question by the *Standard*, whether the new Administration will retrace the steps of the last.[16] The doubt, if doubt there is, we presume to have taken its rise from the awkwardness anticipated in making Lord Dudley or the Duke of Clarence, as members of the present Cabinet, parties to any censure the most oblique, or to any disavowal the most general, of transactions, which, in two different stages, they as members of the last Cabinet, are supposed severally to have ratified with their *peculiar* approbation. But a little explanation will clear away this difficulty. Lord Dudley, it is very true, as Foreign Secretary, was a *special* party to the Treaty of Armed Mediation: and the Duke of Clarence again, supposing it to be a fact, (as alleged in some circles) that by prematurely obtaining a red ribbon for Sir Edward Codrington, he forestalled and fettered the free discussion of that Admiral's conduct (which could not with decency be very scrupulously pursued, after receiving so august a sanction) has certainly made himself a *special* party to the battle of Navarino: These are circumstances which, in point of form and delicacy, may be embarrassing to the new Cabinet; but else, and for the substantial question at issue, they can occasion no serious difficulty. For the case is thus—neither the treaty nor the battle can now be recalled. Hence it happens that no *practical*

---

[16] *Standard*, January 23, p. 2.

This picks up again the problem of British relations with the Ottoman Porte; see the article of November 17, 1827, and its notes (pp. 184-87 above). If the new Tory government was to get out of the difficulty created by the battle of Navarino it had to move delicately; its Foreign Secretary, Dudley, had been Foreign Secretary in Canning's cabinet, when the Treaty of Armed Mediation had been signed, and in Goderich's, when the battle had been fought. Furthermore, the Duke of Clarence was supposed to have urged Codrington to battle ("Go in, my dear Ned, and smash those damned Turks"), and though there is no evidence to show he actually did that, he certainly had many awards bestowed upon those who had fought; for Codrington there was a red ribbon (Grand Cross of the Bath).

question arises on either of those transactions; and the present administration will have it in their option to wave any formal expression of opinion upon their merits; although, in fact, we have little doubt that the debates in both houses will draw from them a pretty distinct censure of the battle. But the only *practical* question regards the mode and the extent of our interposition at this crisis between Turkey and her only enemy, that is more than nominally such: and this interposition, we cannot doubt, will be prosecuted in a much more effectual way under the new Cabinet; and accordingly we look upon it as very probable that to them we shall be indebted for our escape from war; which, however remote and nominal as regards ourselves, would doubtless—from the contagiousness of such convulsions—on one pretext or other, soon draw into it's vortex all the great powers of Europe.

Secondly, with regard to our domestic disputes, from the straight forward good sense and natural equity of the Duke of Wellington, we anticipate the dawn of a new system for regulating our interference with the rights of West India proprietors. On this subject we cannot here enlarge: We shall content ourselves with repeating what we have heretofore endeavoured to illustrate[17]— that, in a nation jealous beyond all others of the rights of property, this particular case of West India property has been treated with a reckless disregard of those rights which we believe to have no parallel unless in the dens of pirates, or in the councils of the French Revolutionary Convention. But this system, we have reason to think, has now reached that extremity, at which it must alter for the better; and we say so in defiance of the else ominous fact, that, according to the arrangements of the new Cabinet, that same Mr. Huskisson, who has just

[17] On September 1, 1827 (pp. 91-94 above).

thrown Jamaica into a flame by his letter to the Lieutenant Governor, is appointed Colonial Secretary.[18]

Thirdly, and above all, from the energy and decision
of a cabinet moving under the influence of the Duke of
Wellington, we anticipate a new set of measures in relation to the *Irish* management of the Catholic question.
Let it not be said that on this question we, the Tories,
are divided amongst ourselves: We know it, and deplore
it: We are so, but not in the point to which we are now
speaking: Upon *that* there is the most entire harmony
amongst all, but downright incendiaries on both sides:
We speak of the Popish Convention of Ireland, as con-
voked and managed by Messrs. O'Connell, Shiel, &c.[19]
This remains a monument of that imbecility which we
charged upon the latter years of Lord Liverpool's Administration, and most justly we may add of the imbe-

[18] Since 1823 (see the article of June 28, p. 378 below) the colonial legislatures had been under an obligation to take measures
improving the lot of their slaves and were subject to the super-
vision of the home government in discharging the obligation. Huskisson recently had written a letter to the Lieutenant-Governor of
Jamaica, Major-General Sir John Keane, disallowing an act passed
by the Assembly of Jamaica which changed the laws governing
slaves: it fell short of the recommendations made by the home government; it placed restrictions on the religious liberty of the
slaves; its regulation of the punishments of slaves was inadequate.
Huskisson's letter, reprinted from a Jamaican source, is in the
Times of January 19, p. 2.

[19] The highly successful Catholic Association, to the ultras "the
Popish Parliament," etc., was founded in Ireland in 1823 by Daniel
O'Connell and Richard Sheil; its purpose was to obtain, by legal
and constitutional means, Catholic Emancipation. Its enemies insisted that in effect it had become the government of Ireland,
adopting Parliamentary forms and levying a revenue; the "revenue" was the "Catholic Rent," a subscription of a penny a month
O'Connell asked every Irish Catholic to contribute, which made the
Association a genuine mass movement. Attempts by the English
government to outlaw the Association were ineffective because it
maneuvered legally around the laws and because it was simply too
powerful to contain.

See also the article of July 12, 1828, pp. 388ff. below.

cility of Parliament when left to itself with no leader of conspicuous authority. We all remember the bill brought forward for extinguishing this audacious usurpation: We remember the Catholic mission to London for the purpose of averting it—how they prayed for inquiry and delay:[20] We remember the becoming conduct of the House of Commons—refusing even to hear, and insisting upon unconditional submission. In spite of clamours, prayers, and threats, the bill passed. What followed? Simply this—that in utter mockery of the whole authority of the land, legislative and executive, the Popish Convention has since gone on to exercise all former acts of sovereignty, and others beside—to convoke innumerable tributary assemblies, to levy a revenue, to apply it most seditiously, and to fulminate speeches and manifestos against the British Government, as some alien and rival potentate. Oh for one hour of Chatham, or the son of Chatham, to deal with the brood of O'Connells that thus insult our imbecility!—William Pitt would not have tasted sleep before he had "scotched them in Corioli."[21] Yet, as no William Pitt survives, possibly in a case so plain as this, the decrees of a Wellington Cabinet, executed by an Angelsea,[22] may suffice for the occasion.

These are amongst the earliest benefits which we expect to reap from the happy revolution in our politics.

ATTRIBUTION

This one is identified as De Quincey's by the quotation of it in the Bodleian MS. (pp. 349-50 below); the relish

[20] In 1825.   [21] Misquoted from *Coriolanus*, IV, v.

[22] Henry William Paget, the Earl of Uxbridge whose leg had been buried in a garden at Waterloo and who was then created Marquis of Anglesey; he was now, in Wellington's cabinet, Lord-Lieutenant in Ireland. De Quincey's expectations were not fulfilled; though Anglesey hated giving in to the Catholic demagogues he saw the need for concession and in 1829 he was recalled for taking this stand.

with which he there repeats and extends the metaphor of the English mail-coach displays a personal pride in the foresight and pungency of the original. (He uses a similar extended coaching figure, with "jib" and "plunge," again in a political context, in "Hints for the Hustings," *Blackwood's*, XLVIII [1840], 296.) The present article itself (p. 290) refers back to an earlier article in the *Post*, September 1, 1827 (pp. 91-94), which in turn contains evidence of De Quincey's authorship. And within the present article there is further evidence.

"Chasing each other with the passionate flight of a musical fugue" (p. 280) is a most De Quinceyan idea and expression. Later in this year, in his "Rhetoric," M., X, 105, we have "chasing and chased, as in a fugue"; and in "Protestantism" (1847-48), M., VIII, 281, there is "chasing each other, like the parts of a fugue." "Musical fugue," which to others might be pleonastic, is in his 1854 Preface, M., XIII, 329, where he discusses his own "Dream-Fugue."

The characterization of Canning (pp. 281-84) is specifically De Quinceyan both in ideas and vocabulary. On Canning as a "gay rhetorician" who could be "bribed" into compromising any "principle," see De Quincey's "Sir Robert Peel's Position on Next Resuming Power," *Blackwood's*, L (1841), 403n.; and also on Canning as a "gay" and "dazzling" rhetorician, see "Rhetoric" (1828), M., X, 120-21. On Canning's "ambition" and "laxity of principle," and how he in one hour renounced the principle of his whole life, and for the sake of a glittering distinction allied himself with the enemy of Pitt the great anti-Jacobin, Pitt whom he had worshipped, see "The Present Cabinet in Relation to the Times," *Blackwood's*, XXIX (1831), 155. With the same quotation from Pope, "for a bauble of office, and for the whistling of a name, the all-accomplished disciple of Mr. Pitt" turned perfidious; "The Duke of Wellington and Mr. Peel," *Blackwood's*,

XXV (1829), 295 (in "The Present Cabinet," p. 156, he applied the same quotation to Brougham). The most brilliant of orators, for a dazzling bait that too powerfully tempted his ambition, in a single hour perjured himself to all posterity and turned his whole life into a lie, breaking faith with those whom since his youth he had honored as saints; since then all fidelity to party has been lost; "On the Approaching Revolution in Great Britain," *Blackwood's*, XXX (1831), 318.

The lament that no Chatham or Pitt is now at hand to guide us (p. 292) is in De Quincey's "French Revolution," *Blackwood's*, XXVIII (1830), 555, and, in a similar context of Irish problems, with verbal identities, in "The Repeal Agitation," *Blackwood's*, LIV (1843), 264: "we invoke the memories of Pitt and of Chatham: 'oh, for one hour,' we exclaim, of those great *executive* statesmen," etc.

On "apostacy" (pp. 285-86) see the article of November 24, 1827 (p. 208) and the further references given there, and the article of August 18, 1827 on Canning (p. 83) and the references there. On the apostacy of Goderich in particular, see once again "The Duke of Wellington and Mr. Peel," *Blackwood's*, XXV (1829), 295. In that same article, p. 296n., De Quincey uses "ratted" (p. 287 of this article) in the same sense; and he uses it, or variant forms in several of his other essays: references are given above, in the notes to last week's article (p. 279).

Cobbett's nickname for Goderich, when he was still Frederick Robinson (p. 285), is in a letter by De Quincey (1859), reprinted in James Hogg's *De Quincey and His Friends* (1895), pp. 160-61; both there and in the present article the name is "Prosperity Fred." Actually, though Cobbett worked, without mercy, many variations—Mr. Frederick Prosperity, Frederick Prosperity Robinson, Mr. Robinson (Prosperity), Prosperity Robinson, etc.,

etc.—he doesn't seem to have tried this particular one; or, if he did use it, it must be infrequent in appearance. This increases a bit the value of the coincidence between the *Post* and De Quincey.

Some of the foreign words and phrases appear elsewhere in De Quincey. For "*soi-disant* Whigs" (p. 280) see the article of August 4, 1827 (pp. 57-58) and the further references there. "*Boutefeu*" (p. 284) is also in the article of July 12, 1828 (p. 390), which has other evidence of De Quincey's authorship. "In fæce Romuli" (p. 287) is in "A Brief Appraisal of the Greek Literature" (1838-39), M., X, 336. "Ἕκτορος ἱπποδαμοιο" (p. 288) he had used in "Mr. Schnackenberger" (1823), M., XII, 363; it is also in his *Posthumous Works* (1891), I, 95n.

February 2, 1828

[The King's Speech]

About the middle of last month the official journal of the Whigs delivered its judgment with great confidence upon the prorogation of Parliament to the 29th of January—as an arrangement in itself nugatory and self-defeated: for, (said the *Times*) the 29th of January, as the anniversary of the King's accession, is a national holiday.[1] And upon premises as frail as these the factious journal went on to found a very unfavourable construction of the manner in which the public business is managed.

For the credit of the Whig oracles, and to illustrate the manner in which *their* business is managed, we think it right to place this demonstration of absolute inability on the part of Parliament to obey the King's summons in close juxta-position with our record of the fact, that the King's summons was after all obeyed. No doubt it was impossible for Parliament to meet on the 29th of January: but great men (according to Lord Chatham's saying) trample upon impossibilities: and so it happened, that both Houses did in fact meet on that day; heard the King's speech; and afterwards debated it at leisure.

The King's speech is more circumstantial, and more definite than usual; and two points in it are especially remarkable, viz. the terms in which it speaks, 1st, Of the treaty of July 6th; and 2dly, Of the battle of Navarino. Last week, when anticipating the course likely to be pursued by Government, we observed that, as no *practical* necessity arose for a formal opinion upon either of those measures (both being now past recal,) Ministers would have it in their power to evade it or not, according to the state of feeling with which they regarded their prede-

---

[1] *Times*, January 18, p. 2.

cessors; but that in all probability they would be drawn into some censure of the battle.[2] This is pretty much what we find. The Treaty is not disavowed: it is simply placed upon a different foundation: hitherto it was made to rest upon the hollow and irrelevant plea of the piracies in the Levant, but now upon the more pertinent but certainly not less unjust basis of "earnest entreaties" on the part of the Greeks for the interposition of this country. Had it been the duty of this country to interfere, (a question which we desire to leave untouched in this place,) it was so—apart from Greek entreaties and before them. Nothing has happened in the seventh year of the war different from what happened in the first, excepting only as to degree; nor, as to degree, different in any way from what was easily foreseen. The fact is, that the Treaty is in the teeth not only of that Circular Despatch from the Congress of Vienna [*for* Verona] which we cited on a former occasion,[3] (and to which both England and Russia were parties,) but also of the whole policy avowed by the British Government within the walls of Parliament, and acted upon without. What the policy was, may be seen by looking back to the Parliamentary debates; and in what spirit it was acted upon, will be sufficiently illustrated to our readers' recollection by the case of Colonel Stanhope and others who stood in his predicament.[4] To look on with inexorable neutrality as a passive spectator of a *Bellum internecinum* carried

2 See pp. 288-90 above.

3 In the *Post* of January 12, 1828; the Despatch, 1822, had denounced the Greek revolt and the principle of revolt.

4 Colonel Leicester Stanhope, agent of the London Greek Committee. One of his problems was the English navy, which was trying to control some of the local activity on the water; this led Stanhope into quarrels with Byron about how to handle English naval officers (which quickly became quarrels about Bentham's personality and principles). Stanhope published his account in *Greece, in 1823 and 1824* (1824).

through every stage, and at length when the whole land is swept as by the Destroying Angel, and nothing remains to contend about except the reversion of an Aceldama, to step forward with a pretence that merciful consideration for both parties will not allow of our further indifference, labours with too much of inherent contradiction to work much persuasion with the most indulgent audience. But a Treaty is too solemn and deliberate an act wholly to be disavowed; and the utmost that can be done for it—it is to varnish it with a new set of pleas and justifications; and this in effect it is that the King's Speech attempts.

With respect to the battle of Navarin, however, which some people would represent as the inevitable product of the Treaty, the speech goes further: It describes it as an 'untoward' event, as 'wholly unexpected,' and as one which his Majesty 'deeply laments.' This language cannot be misunderstood. Undoubtedly the language of the debate in both houses was more guarded and ambiguous; and the reason for *that* is—that naturally no individual wishes to take upon himself any conspicuous share of a censure which indirectly extends to the Royal Personage who stands next to the throne; but it is very evident from the soreness of Opposition in calling for explanations upon the word '*untoward*,' and from the little satisfaction they find in those which are offered, in what light the terms of the King's Speech are generally understood, and in what light they were meant to be understood. Speaking in their collective capacity, the ministers clearly design to authorize a censure, which very reasonably, and out of respect to the King's brother, they decline under the invidious condition of a separate and personal responsibility.

Here, then, we have the unique case of an administration publicly disavowed by the King. The late faction were in power only for about half a year; and in that period their single act of foreign policy has been of a nature to call down an expression of emphatic regret from the crown, upon an occasion the most solemn which the forms of our government offer, and to which the nature of the case attaches the weight of an historical testimony. In the heavy records of Whig demerits, let not this memorable fact ever be forgotten.

ATTRIBUTION

This may be De Quincey's, and it sounds like him; the one substantial piece of evidence is that it continues the subject of the leader of the preceding week, which is certainly his, and which it cites for the prediction of the new government's policy, now fulfilled by the speech from the throne. The quotation from Chatham (p. 296) is in De Quincey's "Repeal Agitation," *Blackwood's*, LIV (1843), 264, in the same sentence cited in the notes to last week's article (p. 294) because of a verbal identity: "those great *executive* statesmen—who 'trampled upon impossibilities.' "

The use of "bellum internecinum" and "Aceldama" in combination with one another (pp. 297-98) is repeated in his "Kant in His Miscellaneous Essays" (1830), VIII, 124. This is in a translation from Kant, but Kant does not use "Aceldama." De Quincey uses the word on other occasions, in "The Late Cabinet," *Blackwood's*, XXVIII (1830), 963; "The Prospects of Britain," *Blackwood's*, XXXI (1832), 589; "The Revolution of Greece" (1833), M., VII, 317; "The Caesars" (1834), M., VI, 368; "Story of a Libel" (1841), M., III, 173; "The English Mail-Coach" (1849), M., XIII, 299. "Bellum internecinum" is in the *Confessions* (both versions), M., III, 408.

Mr. Huskisson's Re-Election

On Tuesday last, Feb. 5, Mr. Huskisson was re-elected for Liverpool. On accepting the place of Colonial Secretary, under the new Administration, it had, of course, become necessary for him to vacate his seat; and he was thus thrown back upon an ordeal, which (well managed) might have proved a severe purgatory to himself, and have forced him into some discoveries interesting to the country. As it was, the whole examination fell into hands which either made it a collusive or a mock one, or else directed it to questions that were generally wide of the true ones. The three persons, (a *fourth* being incapacitated as no freeman of Liverpool) who were either put forward by their several parties, or put themselves forward, to cross-examine Mr. Huskisson, were Mr. Wallace Currie, who pretends to be a Whig; the Rev. Mr. Shepherd, who pretends to be a radical; and Col. Williams, that venerable and resolute old Jacobin, who has no pretence about him; but keeps true to the thing of his desires,—a system of Reform and levelling, without turning one inch to the right or to the left, out of compliment to any man, party, interest, or connexion, whatsoever.[1]

[1] William Wallace Currie was a Liverpool Whig (later the mayor) who favored all the causes—anti-slavery, free trade, Catholic emancipation, reform—that would make him despised by the *Post;* he had supported Canning. The Rev. William Shepherd was a Unitarian and in the dissenting tradition of politics. He was a friend of Brougham, who wrote his epitaph, a supporter of Sir Francis Burdett, a member of the Liverpool Concentric Society of Reformers, and a noted local public speaker. He had opposed Canning until the coalition of 1827. Colonel George Williams was, with Shepherd, the leading local reformer in Liverpool and had a long reputation as a crusty opponent of the Regent, a defender of habeas corpus, a condemner of Peterloo, and so forth. The names of all three appear together frequently in the annals of Liverpool,

The first gentleman opened the business. He is one of those Whigs who have ceased to be truly Whigs, for the purpose of "splitting the difference" with Tories who have ceased to be Tories. Accordingly, *his* part in the play was a mere juggle, and rather gave Mr. Huskisson an opportunity for a panegyric upon himself, than threw him on his defence. Mr. Currie absolutely set out by hoping, that "the Right Honourable Secretary would give such explanations on several points,"—*not* as the case demanded, but "*as he* (Mr. Huskisson) *thought fit to do*; explanations which he had no doubt would be satisfactory." And so anxious was this most gentle of operators to spare his patient all fear of being put to any pain by the *lene tormentum*[2] of his probings, that, in any case where Mr. H. might fail to make a satisfactory explanation, he anticipates for him this pleasant escape,— that his situation as a Cabinet Minister prevented his speaking explicitly. In this way of treating matters, there was an *à priori* necessity that Mr. Huskisson should justify himself: Explain, and he does so of course: Refuse to explain, and *à fortiori* he does so, because he is then supposed to be sacrificing his own personal interests to his public duties. Setting out in this spirit, Mr. Currie does not at all surprize us by declaring, after he has done

sharing the platform at election contests or meetings of reform groups.

Huskisson's problem was to explain how a Canningite, and one whose disagreements with Tories had helped break the coalition, could accept office under such Tories as Wellington and Peel, such opponents of Canning and his policies. The Whigs who had supported Canning had left office. Huskisson replied that he had "guarantees" that Canning's policies, domestic and foreign, would be secure. This only got him into further trouble, because Wellington, of course, had to deny that he had given such guarantees. The resulting confusion is the subject of leaders in the next two issues of the *Post*. In fact Huskisson's place in the cabinet was impossible and he didn't last long.

2 Horace, *Odes*, III, xxi, 13.

his worst in the way of questioning that "whatever Mr. Huskisson's explanation might be as to the recent change, he should, most assuredly, not oppose his re-election, but hoped rather to give him his vote." One passage only in Mr. Currie's speech *does* surprize us: it is this, which comes so near the brink of all which Mr. Huskisson hates, that we think *that* right honourable gentleman must have looked rather upbraidingly at him, considering the extent of his promises.

"Mr. Currie felt, in the first place, anxious to know, as far as the right honourable secretary could disclose them, the reasons why the Whigs, to use the term sanctioned by custom, who had come forward to support the late lamented and illustrious Premier, Mr. Canning, at a time when it was notorious that a government could not otherwise have been formed; why the Whigs, who, for years before their adoption, had supported those liberal measures on which the right honourable gentleman before them might rest his reputation as a statesman; why the Whigs who, to the very last, in the recent differences which were understood to have existed in the Cabinet, *stood* by the right honourable gentleman, pledging themselves to stand or fall with him: he was at a loss to know why *they* were now abandoned, and why the country saw the right honourable secretary united with those men, who had been most adverse to his enlightened measures, and had been the bitter enemies of his deceased and lamented friend. Mr. Currie could not help regretting that Mr. Huskisson had not retired with his late colleagues. Had he known his strength, that all parties confessed that he was essential to the formation of any administration,—that to him all eyes were turned, he would have stood on a proud pre-eminence, from which he would, no doubt, shortly have been recalled to assume his proper place, upon his own terms. It may be said,

that, provided the right honourable gentleman has secured pledges that his liberal measures, and the foreign
and domestic policy of the country shall go on as they
have till this moment done, it is enough, as far as the
country is concerned, and that, though the Whig members may complain, it is more a matter of personal
feeling than one in which the country is interested, and
that all the country has to look to is, that there is no
change of measures. Still he (Mr. Currie) could not but
deeply regret the retirement of the Whigs."

This, from a friend, is a somewhat of a home-thrust:
how does Mr. Huskisson parry it? "I wish we could
forget those terms, Whig and Tory;" (no doubt, rats always wish so; but it is the business of others to take care
that they are *not forgotten*;) "but, as I never did belong
of that party which is called Whig; and, as Lord Carlisle[3]
had been all his life a steady adherent to that party, he
retired because the Whigs retired. That could form no
reason for my retirement." And he then goes on to say,
that, had he retired, he "should have been identified
himself with a party to which he did not belong, and
should have separated himself from men with whom he
had acted throughout his political life." Now, let us stop
here, to admire the logic of Mr. H., in offering such an
answer; and the logic of Mr. Currie, in accepting it:—so
dazzled, apparently, is Mr. C. by the honour of drawing
an elaborate explanation from a Cabinet Minister,
(though, in fact, no more than a necessary concession to
any freeman of Liverpool, who appears to put questions
upon the hustings) that he swallows it with the most
gracious acceptance, as he would, no doubt, have swallowed any other explanation whatever; for it is scarcely

[3] George Howard, sixth Earl of Carlisle, a Whig who had been
in Canning's cabinet, as First Commissioner of Woods and Forests
and then as Lord Privy Seal, and in Goderich's cabinet, as Lord
Privy Seal.

possible to imagine one that more distinctly admits the whole of the charge which it is replying to. "My party," says Mr. Currie, in effect, "my party, the Whigs, came to the help of you and your friend Canning, at the very moment when, but for them, you must have sunk: by them only you kept afloat. Now comes a time, when it is *their* turn to be sent adrift; and in what way have you requited their kindness? Have you, or have you not, left them to their fate, and united with those by whom your benefactors are forced into exile?" Mr. Huskisson's answer amounts to this: "I have done so; but had I done otherwise, I must have quitted the Tories." Exactly so,—he must have quitted them; but *that* is the very thing which Mr. Currie's objection, shaped as it was, and unless contradicted, made it his bounden duty to have done. He had formed new ties; and was not to disown their obligation as soon as they enjoined a sacrifice. But, perhaps, he had other and paramount ties binding him to the Tories. Even if it were so, it would only prove that he had played a most double part by connecting himself with two parties in such a way as to lay himself under irreconcileable obligations, and to make it indispensible for him to practise treachery to one. But, on the contrary, he disowns any force (or any which is applicable to these times) in the distinctions of Whig and Tory. Thus far, therefore, he is free as air from any transcendant obligations, and quite at liberty to have followed the call of gratitude. True, it may be said; but perhaps the men, the individual persons, who compose the present Ministry, without reference to their Toryism, enjoyed Mr. Huskisson's confidence and approbation. No doubt; but so do the Whigs who are opposed to them; higher and more approving sentiments it is impossible that Mr. Huskisson should entertain of any men in existence, than those which he professes of Lord Lansdowne, Lord Car-

lisle, and Mr. Tierney.[4] Hear him!—"Men of more spotless integrity and high honour, of more moderate and
consistent principles, more straight-forward and honourable, than Lord Lansdowne, Lord Carlisle, and Mr.
Tierney, I have never met with in the discussion and
management of public affairs;"* and again, "at the same
time I must say that there are not two men in the
country with whom I should feel more proud and happy
to act with than Lord Lansdowne and Lord Carlisle."

What is this but the very midsummer madness of
apostacy? the act of ratting he makes its own justification, and ingratitude its own apology. Nay in the very
moment of pleading for past cases of that sort, he lays
a foundation for others: and the only words, that by any
construction can meet Mr. Currie's complaint, are those
in which he insinuates a promise to rat again in favour of
Lords Lansdowne and Carlisle, supposing that any turn
of the wheel should ever again bring them up into the
Cabinet.

However every thing must be measured, for its immediate effect, by the entertainment it finds in the ear
of him to whom it is addressed. Mr. Currie was satisfied;
and that is every thing. If ever it should happen to a
friend of ours to be tied to a post, and publicly rubbed

* As to the *"principles"* of these eminent persons, whether consistent or not, and how far moderate, we surely, who have their
Parliamentary conduct for many a year before us, can make up our
judgments upon as good grounds as any that are open to Mr. Huskisson. But, with regard to their *"spotless integrity and high honour,"* our readers must remember that these praises are wholly
irrelevant: They are neither the qualities which we of the opposite
party question, nor the qualities which could be adequately put to
the test in the cabinet, if we did. Nobody supposes Lord Lansdowne, for instance, would embezzle the public money, or that Mr.
Tierney would propose to do so at the Council-board.

4 Lansdowne and Tierney too were Whigs who had been in Canning's and in Goderich's cabinets and had now left office. Lansdowne had been in the coalition cabinets at first without office,
then as Home Secretary; Tierney had been Master of the Mint.

down for his misdoings, may the Gods allot him no harsher a currycomb!†

Next, and we may say—last, comes forward the Rev. Mr. Shepherd; for, as to Col. Williams, the gallant old jacobin is so habitually occupied with his own *chateaux en espagne*, raving about Magna Charta, Runnymead, the Bill of Rights, and "all that sort of thing," that he soars far out of sight of the particular case before him. Not so the *reverend* politician: he is apt to be keen and personal: and the biographer of Poggio,‡ having besides long had the benefit of radical connexions, for the improvement of his manners, is not much given to lay himself under any restraints from considerations of pro-

† Mr. Currie's valedictory prayer for Mr. Huskisson is—that, in case he should find his policy thwarted by the new Premier, he may consult his dignity, by withdrawing "to the classic retirement of Eartham:" *classic* no doubt, being once the abode of a tenth-rate poet, and at present of a tenth-rate Statesman. But we must tell Mr. Currie, that Eartham is connected with recollections of something besides bad verses. It was the scene of some naughty transactions (as he will find by inquiring into Mr. Hayley's life,) such as we hope he does not mean to recommend to an elderly gentleman like the Colonial Secretary.[5]

‡ In what degree, Mr. Shepherd's reputation as an Italian *literator*, was indebted to the time at which he first became known, is now well understood. Yet in the speech now before us, he practises the airs and condescensions of a great scholar—translating all his scraps of Latin, with the most insolent and personal applications of himself to the Mayor in particular. Yet, everybody, who knows what the general course of education is in this country, must be aware, that the first magistrates of great towns among us, can rarely be incapable of understanding such exceedingly trite quotations as *Ex pede Herculem*, or

> ————*Incedis per ignes*
> *Suppositos cineri doloso.*[6]

In reality, the man, who uses such quotations, is the most liable to suspicion on the score of scholarship.

[5] Huskisson had been a friend of William Hayley's, at one time addressing the older man as "father"; he had bought Hayley's home at Eartham in 1800, when Hayley went to Felpham to patronize Blake. As for the naughty transactions, Hayley's posthumous memoirs had been published in 1823; they partly revealed and

priety. The oddest circumstance about this gentleman's
speech is—that he actually appears as the eulogist of Mr.
Canning: and surely no better illustration can be had of
the degree in which Mr. Canning had revolted from his
own original principles. For Mr. Shepherd, the Reformer,
was distinguished in former years amongst the severest
of Mr. Canning's Liverpool scourges: and he is at this
time only so far removed from a perfect radical, as the
sense of enormous concession on the side of the Canning
(or anti-reforming) party has led *him* also to swerve a
little from his fanatical rancor, in order to narrow the
trifling distance which now divides them. With respect
to Mr. Huskisson, he says little in effect, that had not
previously, and by implication, been said by Mr. Currie:
but he says it in so much more hearty and cutting a
manner, that we shall extract it: allowing for some misrepresentation, as regards the spirit and temper of that
most conscientious opposition which was made to Mr.
Canning, certainly Mr. Huskisson must have been sensible, that, for all which he concerns himself, it is full of
truth:—

"When Pilot Goderich, alarmed by the stiff breeze
that whistled through his cordage, and, if report speaks
true, terrified by the indiscipline of his crew, quitted the
helm of state, it was consigned to the hands of the Duke
of Wellington, who entered the Cabinet, accompanied by
a strong phalanx of the bitter revilers and persecutors of
Mr. Canning. At that crisis the eye of curiosity was
turned intensely on Mr. Huskisson, eager to see what

partly suppressed something of his marital problems and the
revelation, that his son had not been borne by his wife, was
made more explicit in Southey's review (*Quarterly Review*, XXXI
[1824], 293ff.)

6 Shepherd had published a life of Poggio Bracciolini, in 1802,
and had edited a manuscript of his, in 1807. The quotation is
from Horace, *Odes*, II, i, 7-8: you are walking into fires laid under
deceptive ashes; it was Shepherd's warning to Huskisson.

line of conduct he would adopt on this emergency. As I
was conversing with a Liverpool friend, a sincere admirer
of Mr. Huskisson, and a man of a most ingenuous temper,
he was pleased to say, "Sir, it is impossible that Mr.
Huskisson can join the vilifiers of Mr. Canning,—of Mr.
Canning, his personal as well as political friend,—of Mr.
Canning, who first introduced him to the notice of the
burgesses of Liverpool!" To this I replied, "My dear Sir,
you know very little of human nature. A habit of being
in office, like a habit of drinking, smoking, or snuff-
taking, is extremely difficult to be got rid of. Depend
upon it Mr. Huskisson will find some plausible pretext
or other to get into the new Cabinet. If he cannot enter
by the door he will try the window. If the window fails
him, he will come down the chimney, though in his transit
he may be covered with soot."—(Here some hissing occurring, and the authorities remonstrating against it, the
reverend gentleman remarked, "Let every beast use its
own language," on which the disturbance immediately
ceased, and he thus proceeded.) The event has proved
that my prognostic was right, for here stands Mr. Huskisson, in London, associated with those whom I have justly
described, as the revilers and persecutors of Mr. Canning;
and in Liverpool asking the friends and admirers of Mr.
Canning for their support. It has been said, in the defence
of the right hon. gent. and, indeed, it has been insinuated
by the right hon. gent. himself, that there are circumstances in which a man must sacrifice personal feelings
to a sense of public duty. I grant, Sir, that such circumstances do occur, both in public and in private life. But,
Sir, I am declining into the vale of years. "My days are
fallen into the sear and yellow leaf." With age comes
caution, and perhaps, suspicion; and I am free to confess,
I entertain a very humble opinion indeed of that spirit of
self-sacrifice which prompts a man to leap over the grave
of a calumniated friend, into a Cabinet crowded with

that friend's bitter and uncompromising enemies. I can understand and value a sacrifice where something is lost, but I cannot understand a sacrifice by which much is gained."

But, to quit a subject of what is personal to Mr. Huskisson, a subject which has become curious only from the same cause which proportionably robs it of all moral interest, viz. the Harlequin rapidity of his changes, we may notice, that in his Liverpool harangue, he makes us acquainted with just one article of secret history connected with the late turbulent fluctuations of parties— viz. the appointment, had he been willing or able to accept it, of Lord Grenville as provisional Prime-Minister: for so we interpret the following passage:—"I shall only state, that in the course of December," (this was the time when Lord Goderich's resignation was so generally rumoured, and so peremptorily contradicted by the *Courier,*) "his Majesty had reason to call upon a noble Lord who had retired for years—partly through ill health; and it was proposed to place him temporarily at the head of affairs." By the "noble Lord" here alluded to, we have no doubt is meant Lord Grenville.*[7]

* It is not generally known that Lord Grenville retired from public affairs in consequence of a complaint in his head, connected with one singular symptom, viz. an extraordinary thinness of the skull-bone.

[7] William Wyndham Grenville, Baron Grenville, who had been the Prime Minister of All the Talents; sixty-nine years old at the present time, he and his skull-bone had retired after a stroke in 1823. But De Quincey has a garbled version of Huskisson's words and therefore conjectures wrongly. According to the *Times* (February 7, p. 3, col. 2), Huskisson said that the noble Lord "had retired from public life owing to ill health or advanced years," and the *Times* guessed, rightly, that he referred to Lord Harrowby. Dudley Ryder, first Earl of Harrowby, had been Lord President of the Council in Liverpool's and Canning's cabinets and had retired when Canning died.

The fallibility of the *Courier,* in denying that Goderich had attempted to resign, was discussed at greater length in the *Post*

We ought to add, that Mr. Huskisson was called upon
to vindicate the Duke of Wellington from an attack of
Mr. Shepherd's—on the ground that he had not inter-
posed in a military way to check the fanatic Popish
massacres at Nismes.[8] Mr. Huskisson replied, that the
Duke could not have done so without undertaking the
responsibility of a most unwarrantable and dangerous
interference with the municipal affairs of France. But
such attacks could hardly, in any audience, have the
effect of injuring the Duke of Wellington; and we are
only sorry that against such an assailant, the Duke's
cause should be maintained by such a defender.

*

Two passages in the Liverpool proceedings, we have
forborne to point out to our readers' contempt, for want
of space: We beg to be supposed not to have overlooked
them. One is that passage of Mr. Currie's speech, in
which he called upon Mr. Huskisson to enforce *martial
law* against the great landholders, if they should prove
"refractory" on his new corn bill; *i.e.* if they should refuse
to vote for it. This was heard and tolerated by a British
Minister of State!—The other was a more harmless folly,
from Mr. Huskisson himself, on the religious duty of
political inconsistency.

ATTRIBUTION

This leader is part of the series on Huskisson, of which
the Bodleian MS. and the leader of January 26 are also a
part, and is probably De Quincey's.

De Quincey had known the Rev. Mr. Shepherd, who
figures so largely here, in Liverpool, in 1801. He wrote
about him in *Tait's* in 1837, in the same unpleasant tone

---

of December 22, 1827, p. 260; that article, not reprinted here, may
have been De Quincey's.

[8] In 1815.

and attacking some of the same points: his Poggio, his coarse manner, his pale pink radicalism, his opposition to Canning on the Liverpool hustings (M., II, 123, 128-29, 135-36).

Some of the words and phrases, though not distinctive, are common in De Quincey, including some of the other articles he wrote for the *Post*. "Midsummer madness" (p. 305), the most useful of these, is in the article of October 13, 1827 (p. 160), and references are given there. For *a fortiori* (p. 301) see the article of August 4, 1827 (p. 59) and the further references there. For *a priori* (p. 301) see the article of November 10, 1827 (p. 180) and the further references there; he twice uses the specific phrase "*a priori* necessity": M., VII, 130 and *Blackwood's*, LII (1842), 464. For "rat" (p. 303), see the article of January 19, 1828 (p. 279) and the references there; for "apostacy" (p. 305) the article of November 24, 1827 (p. 208) and the references there. He also uses a couple of the other tags: the construction "by the *lene tormentum* of . . ." (p. 301) is in *Blackwood's*, L (1841), 680, and in "Animal Magnetism," *Tait's*, IV (1834), 467; *chateaux en Espagne* (p. 306) is in M., XIII, 163.

February 16, 1828

[Mr. Huskisson's Character]

Last week we drew the attention of our readers to the
character of Mr. Huskisson, as affected by his own statements at Liverpool. The result was not very favourable
to the honour of that right honourable gentleman. But
what shall we now say after the remarkable disclosures
made in the House of Lords on Monday night?[1] These
disclosures came both from friend and foe; and we must
say, that disclosures more fatal to the reputation of a
public man, never yet were brought forward, nor apparently more incapable of being parried. The nature of the
charge, coupled with the situation of the speaker, is in all
cases a sufficient guarantee of its truth. There were absolutely four separate assaults made upon Mr. Huskisson's
character; two of them affecting his *private* character; all
of them impeaching his official life; and none of them, as
we are persuaded, of a nature to receive any satisfactory
answer.

First comes Lord Clanricarde,[2] and charges Mr. Huskisson with a solemn declaration, made within his own
knowledge, "That nothing would induce him to take part
with those individuals who had exhibited such personal
hostility towards his lamented friend Mr. Canning. He
(Lord C.) would leave the right hon. gentleman to get
over that declaration, and to reconcile it with the fact of

[1] The report is on p. 323 of the same issue of the *Post*, but De
Quincey used fuller reports given in the London press.

[2] Not first in the actual debate but in the climactic order adopted
here. Lord Clanricarde was married to Canning's daughter (see
September 15, 1827, p. 123 above). Canning's wife, it had been reported, considered that Huskisson had gone back on his word and
had betrayed the memory of her husband in joining Wellington's
government. The report was true, and a few days after this she
and Huskisson exchanged very painful letters of accusation and
defence.

312

his present union with those individuals." This was exactly the substance of the letter said to have been written by Lady Canning to Mr. Huskisson. It now appears that, if her Ladyship did not write such a letter, she has sent her son-in-law to deliver its substance publicly, and in the face of the nation.

Next comes Lord Lansdowne, and disavows Mr. Huskisson in his Liverpool statements, so far as they relate to himself.

Thirdly, We have, from Lord Goderich, a full account of the late rupture in his Administration, which he ascribes to the cause generally assigned at the time—viz. the resentment testified by Mr. Herries for the undue interference on the part of Mr. Huskisson with the rights of his place, in nominating (without any reference to him) Lord Althorpe as Chairman of the Finance Committee.[3] Now, as Lord Goderich unequivocally declares that the nomination did, of right, belong to the Chancellor of the Exchequer's place, he thus throws upon Mr. Huskisson the whole *onus* of breaking up the government—and also of a most unwarrantable aggression upon established rights and privileges.

Fourthly, and, with far greater injury to Mr. Huskisson's reputation, the Duke of Wellington flatly denies every one of those stipulations which Mr. Huskisson alleged to the Liverpool *liberals* as pledges of his consistency and his fidelity to Mr. Canning's policy. The contradiction is point blank; and Mr. Huskisson never

[3] John Charles Spencer, Viscount Althorp (a couple of years later Chancellor of the Exchequer and leader of the House of Commons in Grey's government, eventually third Earl Spencer). He had been appointed chairman of a finance committee to inquire into the condition of the revenue; the choice was agreed upon by Tierney, Huskisson, and Goderich, but Herries, Chancellor of the Exchequer, was not consulted. Herries insisted on resigning if Althorp was appointed; Huskisson would do the same if he was not appointed.

can get over it. True it is indeed (according to the manner of public men) that the Duke affects to doubt whether Mr. Huskisson did really hold the language imputed to him at Liverpool; and at the same time marks his contempt for him, by declaring that he had not thought it worth while to question him on the subject. But this will not avail Mr. Huskisson. He is in this dilemma: either he did *not* say the words imputed to him on the Liverpool hustings, and, in that case, he has grossly duped the electors, who returned him upon the belief that he *had*; or he *did* say those words, and, in that case, he is declared by the Duke of Wellington to have uttered what is scandalously false. In any case where the Duke is satisfied, the Electors will *not* be satisfied: and *vice versa*.

But, finally, it is not left open to Mr. Huskisson to make his choice between the Duke and the Liverpool electors. For let the reader consider the nature of the evasion which has been so good-naturedly provided for him by the Duke, and he will find it to be utterly untenable. "Mr. Huskisson," says his Grace, "never could have alleged any specific guarantees given by me, for I gave him none at all; what I suppose him to have said, is, that my general character was a sufficient guarantee." Aye;— this is supposeable as long as we forget the circumstances of the Liverpool election, but utterly without meaning or logic in Mr. Huskisson's particular case. For what was it that the Liverpool supporters of that gentleman apprehended?—The abandonment of Mr. Canning's policy. And why?—Simply on the presumption arising out of the Duke of Wellington's character and avowed principles. Now what rational guarantee could there be against such a case in the Duke's general character? This very character it was that, in the eyes of the Liverpool *liberals*, constituted the danger,—this, and this only: and yet this, we are to suppose, that Mr. Huskisson palmed upon the

Liverpool electors as the guarantee *against* the danger!

No: accomplished as Mr. Huskisson may be in the arts of shuffling, the present dilemma is one which he will never shuffle out of. Falsehood at Liverpool brought him into it, but neither truth nor falsehood at London will now suffice to bring him out. As a public man, Mr. Huskisson is gone, and, henceforward, must submit to bear a tainted name, and to take his station amongst those who, for a private advantage, have, in a public and solemn instance, violated their good faith.

ATTRIBUTION

This continues, and refers back to, the leader of February 9, and it is part of the same series on Huskisson and his difficulties at Liverpool; for that reason it too is probably De Quincey's.

It carries also some of the marks of De Quincey's composition. For *onus* (p. 313) see the article of August 4, 1827 (p. 57) and the further references there. For the use of the dilemma (p. 314) see the article of September 15, 1827 (pp. 120-21) and the further references there.

[The Dissolution of the Late Government and the Constitution of the Present]

The political interest of the week settles exclusively upon the explanations drawn forth on Monday night by Lord Normanby[1] in the House of Commons. These explanations, which come from three quarters—Messrs. Huskisson, Herries, and Tierney, relate to two points—the dissolution of the late government, and the prevailing constitution—in respect to principles and future policy—of the present. The first inquiry, excepting in so far as it involves the views and character of some persons who belong to the new Cabinet as well as the old one, is comparatively a matter of mere speculative curiosity; the other is of high practical importance, and concerns us all. On neither of the two points were the explanations offered such as could satisfy any honest inquirer: On the first they were professedly reserved, not even pretending to tell the *whole* truth; and there is so little likelihood of a plain honest judgment being delivered upon either in the public journals, from the extreme chicanery and spirit of 'trimming' which now govern the political press of this country, that we shall speak rather more at length than might else have been called for.

On the first question, the only person who acquits himself with honour is Mr. Herries. It appears that Lord Goderich's statement in the House of Lords was so far correct, that the case of Lord Althorpe's appointment to the chair of the Finance Committee, was *that* upon which arose the immediate cause for the rupture of the late administration: Perhaps it was no more than the pretext;

[1] Constantine Henry Phipps, a Whig supporter of Canning. The report is in the *Post* of the same issue, pp. 331-32.

at any rate, from Mr. Huskisson's declaration, it turns
out that there was a remote cause of more weight concerned in this event. What that cause was, general ru-
mour stated at the time; and, there is no doubt, stated
correctly: It was this—a determination on the part of
the Whigs to infuse a more decided tone of whiggish
politics into the composition of the Cabinet, to destroy
the equilibrium of the government, and thus gradually to
pave the way for the entire triumph of Whig principles.—
Fortunately either that object, or the means taken to
accomplish it, defeated the intrigue. One of those means
was the introduction of Lord Holland into a cabinet
office.[2] Lord Holland happened to be personally disagree-
able to his Majesty, and was rejected; the Whigs were
inexorable; mutiny insued; Lord Goderich was incapable
of restoring order; and the ministry, the 'harmonious'
ministry, (as Mr. Huskisson persists in calling it) foun-
dered. The nation owes a world of gratitude to Lord Holland for his personal disagreeableness! To be odious at
such a crisis for a man in his position, was the first duty
of a patriot.

Lord Althorpe's case, therefore, was not the true grievance, or not the insurmountable grievance. But, though
not the cause of the dissolution, it was the immediate
occasion which made the true causes available. Hence,
and from the stress laid upon it by Lord Goderich, explanations became necessary from the several parties to that
affair. Two of these parties, however, Messrs. Tierney
and Huskisson, so perplexed their explanations with unmeaning details, as to make it difficult to collect their
final amount: They pursue Mrs. Quickly's method of

[2] Henry Richard Vassall Fox, third Baron Holland, the Whig
statesman. Lansdowne and the Whigs had wanted him in the cabinet. The King refused but not, he said, for personal reasons but
because he wanted the new government to be reconstructed of the
materials of Canning's government; he agreed to admit Holland
at a later date, Easter or thereabouts.

intermingling with the few significant and essential circumstances, a world of others that are wholly impertinent, and involve us in such a labyrinth of dates and abstracts from letters, and endless interviews of the Right Hon. Gentleman with his Right Hon. Friend or his Right Hon. Enemy, as leave us quite at a loss, without more effort than the matter is worth, to settle their exact relations to the point at issue. So much, however, is evident—that the rights of Mr. Herries, as Chancellor of the Exchequer, had been usurped by Mr. Tierney and slighted by Mr. Huskisson. But the counter-charge against Mr. Herries is—that during a critical period of time, (Dec. 2—26.) he remained passive, and allowed it to be supposed that he was reconciled to what had happened, —reserving his hostility to the moment when it would explode with most effect. Such conduct, coupled with such an intention, would certainly have been dishonourable. But Mr. Herries explains it otherwise:—He says that, having once made his remonstrance, he thought it due to his own dignity that the next steps should come from the other party; and, secondly, that the unsettled state of the government at this period, from Lord Goderich's resignation, (Dec. 8), and subsequent restoration, (Dec. 19), made it difficult to know with whom to lodge his further protests—or to what purpose to make any protests at all, where every thing was in hourly fluctuation. This answer seems to us satisfactory; and, even if it were not, it is difficult to see how Mr. Huskisson is aggrieved, who owns that in any case it was his determination to abide by Mr. Tierney's suggestion, to make Lord Althorpe's appointment the *sine qua non* of his own adherence to the ministry, and therefore in no contingency to be influenced by any thing that Mr. Herries could do. The effect of the explanation, so far is to confirm Lord Goderich's view of the case, which loads Messrs. Tierney and Huskisson with the odium of those cabals, which these gentlemen, (though otherwise in hostility with each other) now seek to throw off upon Mr. Herries. This, however, we repeat, is not the point of the explanations which retains any *practical* interest to the nation; nor perhaps to the individuals concerned apart from previous circumstances. Even Mr. Herries, the injured person, admits, that, under that reasonable distrust which grew out of the original cabal to shut him out of office, he allowed a weight to the transaction beyond what would have been either prudent or magnanimous under circumstances calling for a less jealous regard to his own rights and dignity. In itself, and as an insulated transaction, the affair is not much; but as part of a system it became important. What a man of honour will think petty to notice on its own account, and as long as it may be presumed to have been accidental, he will resent inexorably when he discovers in it a settled purpose to lower his dignity or his rights.

From the dignity and rights of an individual, however, to pass to what concerns us all,—the temper and character of the present Administration, which had been brought into a most questionable light by the declarations *attributed* to Mr. Huskisson at Liverpool,—on that head the right hon. Gentleman set all fears at rest, by subscribing unreservedly to the Duke of Wellington's counter-declarations in the House of Lords; but with what result to his own honour, and with what probability as respects the *mode* of his explanation, remains to be examined. We observed, last week, that the dilemma in Mr. Huskisson's case was such that he had no possible escape as regarded the Duke, but by such a course as left him with a manifest taint on his good faith in relation to the Liverpool electors. Now it happens that the Duke is so much more conspicuous an object of public attention than the electors, that Mr. Huskisson having prudently decided for satisfying *him* is pronounced by the thoughtless sycophants of the press (who entirely overlook the other party) to have satisfied the whole question. But how little this is the case, a short statement will show. There is in the composition of the present Ministry a certain peccant part, viz. a small remainder of the Canning, or apostate party, but so inconsiderable for influence or numbers that no jealousy was directed to it when connected and over-ruled as it now is. In whatsoever point the Wellington and Peel policy might diverge from that of Mr. Canning, it was taken for granted that so mere a fragment or rump (to use the old political designation) of a broken faction could be no object for reasonable fears—but that the other party, fortified by the national confidence and occupying the supreme stations in the Cabinet, must, as a matter of necessity, give the predominant impulse to the course of public affairs. This was the general belief; and in this belief most reluctantly the Liverpool friends of Mr. Canning participated. Here lay the great point of their anxiety; and consequently the one sole question as respects the *future*, which they put to Mr. Huskisson, was this:—*Your party in office being now so much decayed, and pretty nearly reduced to the persons of yourself and Lord Dudley, in what way will you relieve our fears that at this crisis you design, or perhaps have already promised, or will soon be compelled, to sacrifice the Canning policy?*" Now then for Mr. Huskisson's answer: the reporters, one and all, London* and Liverpool, no voice dissenting, except that of a man from Leeds, (who first remembered to publish his dissent *after* the Duke of Wellington's speech had raised the question) ascribe to Mr. Huskisson a very rational and pertinent answer, viz. this: "weak remnant as we are of the Canning party, we shall not be compelled to sacrifice his policy; because, before joining the

* The *Sun*, perhaps other journals of the capital had a reporter present.

Duke, we exacted guarantees from him that it should be maintained: thus I relieve your fears." This we say, however false, was a sensible answer. But now, since the Duke of Wellington has insisted that those words (if ever uttered) shall be eaten up,—what is the new version of the answer *(which, be it observed, Mr. Huskisson never brought forward until the old one was denounced?)* Simply this—"That the characters of Lord Dudley and Mr. Grant, so long as they continue parties to the Administration, are guarantees for the maintenance of the Canning policy."[3] Lord Dudley! why he was the object of the jealousy, and of the question, as much as Mr. Huskisson; and only not specially addressed by the Liverpool men, because not personally on the hustings. It was felt, that the Canning party were too weak to resist the other: it was not likely that the other would forego the power which they possessed: and then what became of the Canning policy? Without positive stipulations, it was seen that the whole party collectively were impotent to guarantee themselves as faithful conservators of the Canning policy: could it possibly be imagined then that, taken separately, they could guarantee each other? The Liverpool voters must be simpletons indeed, if upon insinuating a particular suspicion against a candidate, and requiring guarantees against the dangers to which that suspicion pointed, they had been gulled into accepting as guarantees one or two men, somewhat less known to themselves, but otherwise liable to the same identical suspicion.

Next, as the particular *mode* in which Mr. Huskisson would set aside the original report. Against the whole weight of the internal evidence, from the logic and the context, and against the external evidence of all the re-

[3] Dudley and Grant were two other Canningites who had joined Wellington's government; see the article of January 26 (pp. 287, 289 above).

porters, he brings forward the single contradiction of Mr. Shepherd. *Prima facie*, in such a case the presumptions are heavily against Mr. Shepherd. But now look to his letter. It is dated simply *Saturday*, and begins thus: "Sir, on reading my *Morning Chronicle* this evening, it appears to me"—&c.; the object of all which is to leave the impression that this letter was a spontaneous testimony to the truth immediately upon reading the report, and before any interested motive had arisen for tampering with his own genuine recollections. With this view the date of the month is omitted, and we hear no more than the day of the week: but how came Mr. Shepherd to be first reading his Chronicle on a Saturday? Mr. Huskisson's election took place on a Tuesday, about 2 o'clock in the afternoon; by immense exertion, a report was forwarded express to London, (distant 207¾ miles,) printed in the *Sun* of Wednesday evening, and read in Liverpool on Thursday night at 8 o'clock. The *Chronicle*, as a morning paper, would be read in Liverpool one day later,— *i.e.* on Friday and not on Saturday. But, next, *what* Saturday is it that Mr. Shepherd means? By accident it came out in the debate that Mr. Shepherd's letter had reached London on that day, viz. last Monday: so that the Saturday, which is left undetermined by Mr. Shepherd, turns out unluckily to be Saturday last, February 16. But this is in the *wrong week*; every caulker in Liverpool had read his *Chronicle*, on or before Saturday, February 9. Did Mr. Poggio Shepherd first read *his* *Chronicle* on the 16th? There goes to the winds Mr. Shepherd's device for giving the air of an impromptu to his letter; it now appears to have been got up to serve a purpose: and that fact it was sought to disguise, by omitting the date and by substituting for the natural expression—"Sir, on *reviewing* my *Chronicle*," the very inappropriate one of—"Sir, on *reading*," &c.

Do we then suspect the Rev. Mr. Shepherd of de-

liberately stating an untruth? Not altogether *that*. Undoubtedly, as the Roman philosopher, in disputing with
Caesar, was not too keen in pressing the laws of logic
against one who commanded thirty legions, so it is possible that a reverend dabler in politics, who has an
opportunity laid before him for doing a service to a
Secretary of State, which, to the thoughtless, weighs all
the more for coming from a political opponent, (as the
phrase is,) will not be inclined to spoil his favour by too
churlish a severity as to words. But, on the whole, we are
disposed to confide in Mr. Shepherd for all that is *positive* in his statement. We doubt not that Mr. Huskisson
said exactly what he attributes to him about Lord Dudley, and that is not at all inconsistent with the previous
reports; but it is difficult to swear to a *negative*; and we
as little doubt that Mr. H. said or insinuated all that has
ever been attributed to him about the Duke of Wellington. Mr. S. may persuade himself that he did not; but in
a speech of two hours, and where Mr. H. himself supposes so much to have come absolutely *altered* to the
ears of the practised reporters, through the noise which
prevailed,—something (it is just possible) may have
barely *escaped* the unpractised Mr. Shepherd. If not, the
Liverpool electors have been hoaxed,—and there is an
account yet to be settled in that quarter: the logic and
coherency of Mr. H's. speech are violated,—and there is
an account to be settled between the several parts of that
speech; and finally, the reporters* are wrong to a man,

* Mr. Huskisson is in a whimsical distraction about the reporters.
His general practice, according to the Canning precedent, is to
plaister them with flattery. But yet, in this particular instance, the
painful necessity of the case obliges him to tax them with the only
extreme and essential error that a reporter *can* commit—utter violation of the facts; they have all, it seems, reported a mere fiction
and coinage of their own brain. Yet, again, this charge might irritate and rouse them to contradiction: so he soothes them, and
palliates their error, by attributing it to the noise and incom-
modiousness of their situation. Yet, again, *was* their situation in-

and have been so grievously inattentive as to mistake the name *Dudley* for that of *Wellington*; and they have an account to settle with their employers.

So much for the replies of this right hon. gentleman to the late and the present Premier: his answers to the two noble Marquesses, Lansdowne and Clanricarde, are hardly less illustrative of his character. But *ohe jam satis!*

ATTRIBUTION

This is another in the series on Huskisson, his difficulties at Liverpool, and "Poggio" Shepherd; it refers back (p. 319) to the leader of February 16 and Huskisson's dilemma; and like the Bodleian MS. (p. 350 below) it deals with Huskisson's need to "eat up" the "words" of his Liverpool speech to square himself with Wellington (p. 321). It is therefore probably De Quincey's.

On *sine qua non* (p. 318) see the article of November 17, 1827, and the further references there. On Canning and apostacy see the articles of August 18 and November 24, 1827 (pp. 83 and 208) and the references there. On *prima facie* (p. 322) see the article of August 11, 1827 (p. 73) and the references there.

---

commodious? Some angry man amongst them might get up and deny it. So he is careful to add, that, whether on the other hand the situation allotted them was not particularly commodious, is a point of which he knows nothing at all. Oh falsehood and chicanery! how crooked are your paths!

Emigration

On Tuesday, this subject was brought forward by Mr. Wilmot Horton,[1] as the most important that has engaged the attention of Parliament during the present Session. Important it is most certainly, being the only measure yet proposed, which is of a nature to afford the least relief to the true evil under which Ireland groans. That evil, as our readers know, is a redundant population; redundant, not as regards the capacities of the land, but the actual developement of those capacities. Irish population has far outrun the capital disposable for its profitable employment. To apply any remedy to this mighty evil such as could act only for a moment, and would speedily re-act to stimulate its original causes, would be a folly of more than infantine improvidence. Emigration is undoubtedly in its tendency fitted to relieve the evil for a time, but is liable to two great objections; one of the prospective nature here adverted to, viz. that, as fast as it relieves any district from the existing burthen of superfluous population, it will open an encouragement to early marriages which will speedily create a second. The other objection is immediate, viz. the immense cost of emigration conducted upon any useful, (that is, any proportionate) scale. Now the first of these objections Parliament propose to meet by a measure calculated to be effectual, inasmuch as it will lay the axe to the very root of the evil. For what is the main cause of that excessive population under which Ireland, more than any known part of the world, at this time labours? Notoriously it is the principle which governs the occupation of

[1] See October 6, 1827 (pp. 149ff. above). The report of Wilmot-Horton's speech is on the same page of the *Post* as the present article.

the soil: it is the facility of obtaining so much land as will suffice to yield a bare subsistence at that low point of comfort to which the Irish peasantry are unfortunately reconciled. One cure for that evil would be to improve their habits of life, and elevate their standard of respectability. This, however, can be done only by education combined with the light of a Protestant reformation; and these are means of slow and remote progress. Parliament, therefore, have resolved violently to exterminate the evil at one blow, or so much of it as it is possible to exterminate, by putting an end to the extreme subdivision of cabin farms under the present system of indefinite sub-letting. Coupled with such a measure, the emigration scheme will, of necessity, so far succeed, that it will not be defeated *in limine*, and in the very tendency of its principle: as to the *quality* of its results, it will be entitled to every body's approbation; and the only question which can then arise will be as to the *quantity*.

Here, unfortunately, we find ourselves obliged to speak doubtfully. We fear that nothing short of a complete exoneration (so to speak) from one hundred thousand *families* could give any effectual or even sensible relief to Ireland as a nation; and, as to local relief, *that* is not the point aimed at. A million of money is as much as it will be found possible to extract from Parliament; and that sum will not transport above 18 thousand families even to Canada; whereas the plan is to transport some proportion of the whole to New South Wales. With sufficient encouragement from the result, we doubt not that Parliament would make further grants in a couple of years. What we fear is that the result will not be broad and conspicuous enough, owing to the narrow scale of the experiment, to insure a triumphant issue to the next application on this head.

This measure, however, or none, must work the deliverance of Ireland; and it is therefore gratifying, in the midst of our doubts, to find three capital points established in the debate of Tuesday. 1st, That the scheme, even upon its present scale, if not available for the adequate relief of Ireland, would be so for Scotland and England: it would be quite sufficient to absorb that annual tide of emigration to Glasgow, &c. which is gradually forcing this part of the empire into an awful participation in the wretchedness and demoralization of Ireland. 2d, Whatever difficulties may arise at home, none at all can by possibility arise in Canada and New South Wales, to emigration on the most unlimited scale; nor, for many years, at the Cape of Good Hope: that point at last is settled, and it is satisfactory to know, that in a case, where two distinct sets of difficulties might have been apprehended, we are definitively released from one. 3d, We are rejoiced, (and we must say—surprised) to find it unanimously agreed by those who are the best practical judges of that question, that the expenses of emigration would be gradually repaid to the nation after a certain period, by instalments of £.4. per family, annually; provided only that payment were received in produce, and not in money. With the emigration scheme, some persons would combine, or would even substitute for it, a scheme for cultivating the waste lands; which to those, who know any thing of political economy, is insanity. Another proposition for carrying on, conjointly with the emigration measure, great national works of harbours, roads, &c. is more worthy of attention; properly directed, and so regulated as not to stimulate wages, the two measures would aid each other; and this combination would furnish the first genuine hope that has dawned upon unhappy Ireland.

ATTRIBUTION

This brief leader on emigration, with its reference to the cultivation of waste lands as an alternative scheme but an insane one to those who know anything of political economy, sounds like De Quincey. The question had appeared in the companion articles of October 6 and 13, 1827, which are very probably his, and it is in next week's article, March 15, 1828 (p. 337), which is certainly his. In his "Hints for the Hustings," *Blackwood's*, XLVIII (1840), 313-314, he says that emigration is not "relief" to the "evil" of "redundancy of people" because it "stimulates" the evil faster than it abates it.

In limine (p. 326) is a tag he uses a number of times, before and after this date: M., III, 199; VI, 114; IX, 409; X, 340; XIV, 20; XIV, 142; *Blackwood's*, LV (1844), 521.

Edinburgh Review

No. 93.

ART. I. *Poetical Works of Dryden.*[1]—This edition comes from the University of London; and we commend their judgment in the selection. For it has happened—*why* we know not—that editions of this great classic are, and always have been, particularly rare, as compared with those of Pope. The Reviewer maintains, at considerable length, and with great liveliness, a thesis of no particular novelty—viz., the necessary disjunction of the age of genius, and the creative faculty from that of good taste. Hackneyed as this theory is, it has little truth: in the *highest* movement of genius, good taste is always latent. Even Ben Jonson could see, long before Schlegel expanded and illustrated the idea, that Shakspeare was as far superior to other men in judgment and good taste as in genius.[2] One mistake of the Reviewer, in a matter of fact, we must correct. Speaking of Milton, he says, that "his works, at first, enjoyed a very small share of popularity.—To be neglected by his contemporaries was the penalty which he paid for surpassing them. His great poem was not generally studied or admired, till writers, far inferior to him, had, by obsequiously cringing to the public taste, acquired sufficient favour to reform it." This is a common notion, but a most unfounded one: the

1 University Edition (1826). The reviewer was Macaulay; obviously, and unfortunately for us, De Quincey did not know.

No. 93 of the *Edinburgh* is the issue of January 1828.

2 Jonson's poem to the memory of Shakespeare, published in the first folio. A. W. Schlegel's lectures on *Dramatic Art and Literature,* lecture XXIII; see also Coleridge's ["Shakespeare's Judgment Equal to his Genius"] in his *Shakespearean Criticism,* ed. T. M. Raysor ("Everyman" ed.), I, 194ff., with the further references in Raysor's notes.

public taste did not need reforming, as regarded Milton; and, in fact, retrograded rather than advanced for the first 80 years after the publication of Paradise Lost. Addison, and Lord Somers, have each had the credit of bringing this mighty poem into notoriety. But the fact is, that the number and size of the editions published within the first thirty years from the publication, (1670-1700) prove the whole story to be groundless. On this point, see the introduction to the notes of Richardson the painter.[3]

ART. II. *Dietetics*.[4]—Six writers furnish the text of this article, and amongst them Dr. Wilson Philip, whose very important experiments on rabbits ought to have been noticed; since these certainly paved the way for the improved speculations of the present day, on the digestive process. We shall briefly state the result. Let the reader imagine the first portion of what he eats to arrange itself in the stomach into the form of a hollow cylinder. *Within* this cylinder, the next portion eaten will then arrange itself as a second or interior cylinder; the third portion will form a third cylinder; and so on, until we come to the last portion, which will form the axis or innermost cylinder of the whole. Here then we have a column of food in the stomach, composed of a series of distinct cylindrical layers, which, in the rabbits (when killed at various stages of digestion) showed themselves as such, from the different *colors*, purposely selected for

[3] Somers, by his encouragement and patronage of Tonson's 1688 *Paradise Lost*, and Addison, of course, by his critique in the *Spectator*, had been given credit for making the poem known and admired. Richardson is Jonathan Richardson, Senior, who argued that *Paradise Lost* was known and esteemed before there was such a man as "Lord" Somers; see his life of Milton, in *Explanatory Notes and Remarks on Milton's Paradise Lost* (1734), pp. cxvii ff.

[4] Reviewer unidentified. Wilson Philip is Alexander Philip Wilson Philip, physician and physiologist, whose *Treatise on Indigestion and its Consequences* (1826) was one of the titles at the head of the review.

the successive portions of food administered. These premises settled, the rest of the process is easily anticipated. The outermost of all the layers, i.e. that portion first swallowed, is first brought into contact with the gastric fluid; this having been sufficiently saturated, is in some way or other pushed off towards the lower orifice of the stomach, leaving, of course, the next (or penultimate) layer exposed to the action of the gastric juice; *that*, when saturated is pushed off, and in its turn leaves the third layer exposed; and so on to the central layer or nucleus. Upon this theory, it became easy to account for the injurious effects attributed by modern medicine to a liquid diet; since here, from the absence of successive layers or strata, the gastric juice was necessarily applied to the whole bulk of liquid at once. However, this explanation seems doubtful,—the fact, indeed, that fluid of every kind, *as* fluid, and no matter for its quality, in other respects, is peculiarly deleterious to stomachs of diminished tone,—this fact, we say, is put beyond all doubt; and hence it is that cautious medical men will never take soup; but the solution must be sought elsewhere, if it be true (as we now find it asserted upon the authority of Majendie)[5] that all liquid food, before it can be acted on by the gastric juice, must be brought to a certain consistence; and that the superfluous fluid passes off *not* through the pylorus. "Thus, when milk is taken into the stomach, it is first coagulated, the fluid part is then absorbed, and the *solid* mass subjected to the process of digestion. It is the same with all liquids, broths, soups, and even wine," &c. In what way, and by what vessels, this absorption of the superfluous fluid is conducted, for the present remains a mystery. But the fact is certain, as the following curious experiment demonstrates:—A dog was made

[5] François Magendie, contemporary French physiologist.

NEW DE QUINCEY ESSAYS

to swallow diluted alcohol during the process of digestion. Half-an-hour afterwards, the chyle was found to
contain no alcohol at all, whilst the blood yielded, upon
distillation, a sensible quantity. The inference was clear,
that the liquid had been absorbed into the blood directly,
and not carried there by the indirect process of digestion.

We shall conclude with one objection to the logic of
the Reviewer in a particular instance. Wilson Philip
reports an experiment in which it was in vain attempted
to feed a man upon concentrated essences of beef: the
man pined away. Upon this an inference is founded—
that mere nutriment is not enough without a sufficient
distention of the stomach, and distention cannot be
effected without a certain bulk in the food. Now this
may be true; but it is not a necessary inference. All that
is proved by the experiment, is this—that the nutritious
parts of food, in order to obtain their effect, must be
blended with *in*nutritious parts; but, it is possible, that
these innutritious parts may be requisite, not by way of
increasing the bulk, but as a menstruum for extracting
the virtues of the other parts.

ART. III. *Best Method of Funding*.[6]—This article will
be found interesting: it exposes some very important
errors in the mode of funding adopted in England. In
order to obtain an *immediate* advantage, it has been
usual to fund in a stock bearing a low nominal interest,
(as three per cents or three and a-half per cents.) and
to create a proportionable increase of nominal capital.
For example, in 1781, Government, in order to obtain
a loan of twelve millions, created a nominal capital of
twenty-one millions in favour of the lenders, viz. eighteen millions of three per cents., and three millions of
four per cents. Now, had they funded in stock at a higher

[6] The reviewer was M'Culloch; see Fetter, *Journal of Political
Economy*, LXI (1953), 253. Once again De Quincey evidently did
not know.

interest, say six and a half per cent., it would have sufficed to create a nominal capital of twelve millions. And what would have been the benefit of that? Precisely this: that now, when money can be had much cheaper, it would have been possible to reduce the interest to three and a half per cent.; in which case we should have had about the same interest to pay on twelve that we now have to pay on twenty-one millions. For the alternative, in case the stockholders refused to take this interest, would be to pay them back their capital; but this capital is nominally twenty-one millions, which presents a bar to that operation; a bar which would not have existed, had the nominal capital been no more than the real sum borrowed. As it is, we must now go on paying three and four per cent. on a capital of twenty-one millions, instead of three and a half per cent. on one of twelve millions. But is not this evil balanced by the immediate saving in the interest upon the plan of creating a large nominal capital? True: *that* might be, if it were necessary that the higher interest consequent on the other plan must continue until the extinction of the debt; but it is not necessary that it should continue longer than until the return of peace, when the rate of interest must always fall in consequence of the great outlet for superfluous capital (the Government demand for loans) being then of necessity closed.*

Art. IV. *New South Wales.*—A subject so fully discussed some months back in connexion with Mr. Cunningham's book, that the Review may be said to come a day after the fair.⁷

* This writer declares, upon the authority of "persons well versed in the subject," that an addition of from one-fourth to one-half per cent. of interest more than was actually bargained for, would have enabled government to have funded all the loans contracted during the late war, without any artificial increase of capital.

⁷ The review is given to Sydney Smith in W. A. Copinger, *On the Authorship of the First Hundred Numbers of the "Edinburgh Review"* (Manchester, 1895). Cunningham is Peter Miller Cun-

ART. V. *Scottish Marriages of English Parties.*—This, of course, is suggested by the Wakefield case;[8] and the object of the Reviewer is not to propose any alteration of the Scottish law of marriage, as regards Scotland, but only so far as to prevent the monstrous evasion of the English laws, which the decision of the English judges at this time authorises. "All that is necessary to remedy this evil effectually, is to declare that no persons *other than natives of Scotland*, shall intermarry there without a certain length (six weeks), of previous residence." Whatever be the remedy, the evil is undeniably great, for, undoubtedly, as the Reviewer says, "no nation has a right to become the means of destroying another's institutions with respect to that other's proper subjects."*

ART. VI. *Pestalozzi.*[9]—Pestalozzi was a pest and a sentimental humbug during his life. We hope that he is not to survive as a permanent bore by means of his books and his institutions. What is told of him here is the old story: we shall tell a new one, which will place him in a pleasing and amiable light. Our informant was a Quaker lady, much connected with some branches of our Royal

---

* Concurrently with this improvement, and in order to make it complete, the Reviewer suggests "that some restriction shall be imposed also upon Scotch divorces."

---

ningham, naval surgeon, brother of Allan Cunningham (the subject of Article VIII), and his book is *Two Years in New South Wales* (1827). It had been reviewed in *Blackwood's* in November 1827, by Captain Thomas Hamilton, whom De Quincey knew at this time.

[8] Review possibly by Brougham; see New, *Brougham*, p. 443. Wakefield was Edward Gibbon Wakefield, later a most important statesman in the development of Australia, New Zealand, and Canada; at this point in his life, however, he owed his celebrity to the extraordinarily melodramatic style in which he had deceived a schoolgirl of wealthy family into an elopement to Scotland. He was sentenced to a three years' imprisonment, after which he turned his genius to the colonies.

[9] Review by Brougham; see New, p. 443. On the following anecdote about Pestalozzi see below, p. 338.

Family. This lady went to reside at Yverdun for the benefit of Pest's conversation. Pest was at this time seventy years old; no chicken therefore: yet so it was that Pest had not been washed for two generations: without a preliminary purification, our quaker friend found it impossible to admit Pest into her company; and it is a fact, that she paid eighteenpence to have him scowered. This first operation was long, toilsome, and proportionably costly; but, during the rest of her stay, when scowering was no longer necessary, she contracted, at the rate of 4d. a-week, to have Pest mopped down, and thus kept at least as clean as the steps of her front door. This anecdote, for the truth of which we solemnly vouch, appeared to us likely to prove interesting to the Reviewer, or any other Bozzy or Piozzi who may design to write the life of old Pestalozzi. At the end of this article we find some of the latest news from the *March-of-Mind Men*: advertising puffs are given of Mr. Brougham's new Almanack, of Mr. Buckingham's *Athenæum*, and of another journal as yet unknown to fame, (called the *Verulam*) on which still higher hopes are built.[10] Unfortunately, the most interesting item in all this news, is one entire blunder from beginning to end: listen, good reader, and learn how puffs and bounces are manufactured:—in illustration of a general proposition, that, in our days "working-men pass their evenings at lectures, and not at ale-houses," and, "that tradesmen pursue letters as a vocation joined with their peculiar craft;" the Reviewer affirms, "that the most abstruse metaphysical researches have for years been carried on

10 "Brougham's" *British Almanac* was a publication of the Society for the Diffusion of Useful Knowledge. The *Athenæum* had just begun publication, under James Silk Buckingham. The *Verulam* was a weekly scientific, literary and political newspaper that ran from March to May, 1828, after which it was incorporated with the *Athenæum*.

by a working silversmith," and in a foot-note explains
this allusion as referring "to Mr. T. Urrgmann's writings
on the philosophy of Kant, composed while he went
about with silver-plate and scissars to his customers."
A grosser mis-statement cannot be; Mr. *Wirgman*,[11] (not
Urrgmann,) the person here alluded to, a very respectable old blockhead, is *not* a journeyman, but a master
tradesman, with a town and country house,—think of
that in the first place; secondly, he has no sort of connexion with mechanic institutes, or any new lights of
any description, having published his "Metaphysical
Researches," such as they are, many years ago in the
Encyclopædia Londiniensis; thirdly, he is not a person
whom any party needs to be proud of,—having done
nothing but degrade and misrepresent Kant by the heap
of stupidities which he has fathered upon him, and the
absolute Babylonian gibberish in which he has delivered
them.

ART. VII. *Indian Taxation of Englishmen*.[12]—This
paper denounces the New Indian Stamp Act as most
impolitic, unproductive, and expensive in the levying.
So far it agrees with all the other public journals, that
have any accurate knowledge of Indian affairs. But in
all the rest of the mismanagement which the writer
charges upon the East Indian Company, we are obliged
continually to recollect that the statement is an *ex parte*
one, and from a most hostile quarter. That the Company
would deliberately continue to pay £.26 a ton for shipping, at a time when it could be had for £.10 or even
£.8, is really more than we can swallow.

[11] Thomas Wirgman, a noble and pathetic eccentric, who wrote
endlessly on Kant and whose children apprehended and applied
Kantian principles with as much facility as they did their multi-
plication tables; there is a long, interesting account of him in René
Wellek's *Immanuel Kant in England* (Princeton, 1931).
[12] Probably by John Crawfurd; see Fetter, *Journal of Political
Economy*, LXI, 253.

Art. VIII. *Cunningham's Songs*.[13]—Some just compliments are paid to the genius of Allan Cunningham, with a few drawbacks on the score of taste, &c.; rather more severe than, perhaps, the Reviewer would have allowed himself had he known the whole extent of the difficulties and disadvantages with which this very meritorious man has had to struggle.

Art. IX. *Emigration*.[14]—Any thing more obscure than this paper in matter and purpose, or more desultory in logic and connexion, we do not remember to have read. Meantime, the drift of the whole is simply to recommend emigration, assisted by the public purse (i.e. the purse of Government, of local districts, or of parishes) first of all—with some reserve to the surplus rural population of England, (especially in the south and west); secondly, to the manufacturing population of England and Scotland; but finally, to urge it upon Ireland, as a preliminary measure of absolute necessity, for the sake of disburthening the land to that point at which any permanent reforms can commence. The writer expresses himself at times with effect and energy: but the chaotic disconnexion of the whole baffles all analysis.

Art. X. *Sir Harry Moncrieff*.[15]—A notice of Dr. Thomson's Funeral Sermon.

[13] *The Songs of Scotland, Ancient and Modern* (1825). The review is reprinted in B. W. Procter, *Essays and Tales in Prose* (Boston, 1853), except for the actual discussion of Cunningham, which may be Jeffrey's; information from Esther Rhoads Houghton of the *Wellesley Index*.

Honest Allan Cunningham was a self-educated Scotch stonemason, later an assistant and secretary to Francis Chantrey, the sculptor. He wrote varied kinds of poetry and prose and contributed to *Blackwood's* and the *London Magazine*. Carlyle admired him as healthy, stalwart, solid. See also p. 339 below.

[14] Attributed to M'Culloch by Cockburn, though M'Culloch himself does not claim it; information from Esther Rhoads Houghton.

[15] Possibly by Brougham; see New, p. 443. Sir Henry Moncrieff had been a leading figure in the church of Scotland; his funeral

ART. XI. *State of Parties.*[16]—A paper of no interest, because, coming from one who neither is, nor pretends to be, behind the curtain. A lecture to Lord Goderich, and a laudation of Lord Lansdowne; a little anger and a little suspicion directed towards Mr. Huskisson, and a great deal of both towards Mr. Herries, with scorn and malice in such excess as to shew pretty clearly where the shoe pinches,—these make up the article. Our friend the *Standard* is denounced as "a most infamous journal;" and, in short, it is just such an article as we read every day in what we are again happy to call the opposition newspapers.

The whole No., like all Nos. for years back, of the two leading Reviews, is deficient in novelty, in variety, in literature, (politics, as usual, overbearing every other interest) and generally in amusement.

ATTRIBUTION

This carries several strong evidences of De Quincey's authorship.

He tells the same story about Pestalozzi (pp. 334-35) in his "Notes on Walter Savage Landor" (1847), M., XI, 419-20: he identifies his informant, the Quaker lady who had Pestalozzi "scoured," as Mrs. Clermont, and the date of her visit as about 1820.

The details about Dr. Wilson Philip's work on digestive problems (pp. 330-32) are not taken from the article in the *Edinburgh*, which spends its time on the other authors under review and barely mentions Philip; they are contributed by the author in the *Post* from his own knowledge: De Quincey had that knowledge and used some of the same language in discussing some of the

sermon was preached by Andrew Thomson, who succeeded him at the head of the evangelical party in the church.

[16] Reviewer unidentified. Preceding articles in the *Post* will make clear why the Whig *Edinburgh* held the opinions summarized here.

338

same details. He praised Philip and his most valuable book on diet in "National Temperance Movements" (1845), M., XIV, 271: Philip's ingenious "speculations" are supported by his "*experimental* investigations of the . . . digesting processes in rabbits"; his work "explains the reason of a fact" not known until "modern" times—viz., "the injuriousness to enfeebled stomachs of all fluids." De Quincey also refers to "Dr. Wilson Philip's experiments on rabbits," which have partially unfolded the true theory of digestion, in "Casuistry" (1839-40), M., VIII, 354n.

On the deficiencies of reviews, their little literature and much politics (p. 338) see the article of November 17, 1827 (pp. 208-209), which is certainly De Quincey's, and the further references there.

The account of Kant (p. 336) published by Mr. Wirgman in the *Encyclopædia Londiniensis*, and its poor quality, were of interest to De Quincey and he pointed them out in "Kant in His Miscellaneous Essays" (1830), M., VIII, 87-88. In the "Letters to a Young Man" (1823) he referred to Wirgman, but hadn't yet read him (M., X, 68).

On Allan Cunningham (p. 337), his "genius," his occasional singularity of "taste" and his "merits" as a self-taught man who had started in the lowest ranks, see De Quincey's reminiscences of his associates of the *London Magazine*, published in 1840 (M., III, 145-59); it was in the same article that he had written of Taylor's book on Junius.

Ex parte (p. 336), though no evidence of authorship, is used several times by De Quincey: M., VI, 185 and n.; VII, 89n.; VII, 149; "Animal Magnetism," *Tait's*, IV (1834), 461n.

There is one piece of contradictory evidence in this article, at the beginning, where it is denied that Addison and Lord Somers brought *Paradise Lost* into notoriety. De Quincey did deny, in 1847, that Lord Somers had given a powerful lift to *Paradise Lost*, and he is clearly dependent on Richardson for his authority ("Schlosser's Literary History," M., XI, 23). De Quincey certainly knew Richardson's book because he had just referred to it in the first of the essays "On Murder" (1827), M., XIII, 17, and it figures in an important passage on Wordsworth (1839), M., II, 246ff. So far there is agreement. But he also says, in the 1847 article, and again in 1857 (M., X, 407-09), that Addison helped Milton win popular acceptance. I am unable to explain this partial contradiction, unless it is self-contradiction on De Quincey's part after a lapse of years, because the evidence that he wrote the present article is quite strong.

April 5, 1828

[The Corn Bill]

Last Monday night the new Corn Bill was brought forward in both Houses.[1] Upon this measure two questions arise: First, with regard to *a* corn bill (i.e. the principles on which *any* corn bill is to be justified;) secondly, with regard to *the* Corn Bill, (i.e. the provisions of that particular bill now before the House.)

Upon the last question there is little to say which would interest either the general reader or the political economist: The present, like every former corn bill, must be viewed as a merely tentative measure; and, as circumstances change at home or on the continent, many such bills will become necessary. All bills of this description in fact are essentially the same, under different modifications, suited to the varying circumstances of the home and foreign market; and are interesting rather to the mealman and the corn factor, than to the political economist. When the bill is committed, we may perhaps find occasion to make a few remarks upon it: at present it is sufficient to notice that the provisions of the bill are inaccurately stated in the London papers, as though the protecting duty on foreign wheat would be lower than by Mr. Canning's bill of last year upon all the averages below 59s. (Winchester bushel); this is not the case: the duty first begins to be lower when the price in the home market is less than 56s., from that sum to 57s. it is the same: the two duties (Mr. Canning's and

[1] The Corn Bill of 1828, which was passed by the end of June, satisfied no one fully; but it was part of the movement toward free trade which Huskisson had been pushing since 1823. It changed the principle of the bill of 1815, under which the importing of corn was forbidden until the domestic price had reached a certain point, and substituted the principle of sliding duties.

the present) at this point coincide; but after 57s. they again separate—the new duty being continually higher up to 67s., after which the scale declines gradualy, though still considerably higher than that of last year.[2]

Upon the other question, which has long ago been settled to the satisfaction of political economists, it would be an idle thing *actum agere*; nor would a newspaper be the proper place for such discussions. It is notorious that this question cannot be understood without a previous knowledge of the laws which govern *rent*; and we must add, that those laws cannot be understood thoroughly without a much more accurate knowledge of the laws of *value* than is generally to be found even in professed economists. For we do not scruple to affirm, that all objections to the new doctrine of *rent*, rest upon an imperfect theory of value.

Two general errors, upon this subject, we shall here notice, which are current amongst those who profess to understand, and even to adopt the law of rent: They will sufficiently expose their inability to apply it to any practical purpose.

One is the error of those who maintain that the burthens national and local upon the British grower of wheat present an obstacle to a free corn trade. "The farmer at home," say they, "is liable to taxes, poor rates, &c., far heavier than any which press on his foreign competitor: How then is he to stand the competition?" Now this shews a total blindness to the true operation of the principle which governs rent; for the true pressure arises from rent, and never by any possibility from taxation; and, if another Pelion of taxes were heaped upon another Ossa of poor rates, the case would not be changed. Let us illustrate this by a short hypothesis:—

[2] Canning's unsuccessful bill of 1827 had been similar in principle but different in its specific duties. The figures given here are not those of the bill that was later passed.

Suppose that in Great Britain wheat shall be grown upon three qualities of land, viz. No. 1. (or the best) at 6d. No. 2. at 7d. No. 3. (or the worst) at 8d. These sums we shall assume to include *everything*—wages, profits, taxes, which properly make up the cost of production. Under these circumstances what will be the price of wheat? It will be 8d. for the whole; and rent will be equal to the complemental differences upon the several qualities of land; that is to say, on No. 1. it will be two-pence, on No. 2. one penny, on No. 3. nothing at all. Now suppose that from some foreign country we intro-duce corn at 7d. equal in quantity to the whole amount grown upon No. 3. In this case what follows? Two things; 1st, That No. 3 is wholly withdrawn from the cultiva-tion of wheat, and must be applied to some other pur-pose. And this must not be complained of, because manifestly it is in this way that *any* corn bill whatever—the most illiberal that can be conceived—acts and pro-fesses to act. Or, if it *were* complained of, this is not the complaint which we are now meeting. Secondly, then this importation of 7d. wheat under the given circum-stances reduces the price of wheat universally to 7d.; and the effect of *that* is to abolish rent entirely on No. 2, and to sink it by one-half on No. 1. Here then there is room for a loud outcry as regards rent, but not at all as regards taxation: for, by looking back to the supposi-tion, the reader will see that 7d. pays No. 2. for every part of the cost, taxation included.—But is not rent as truly a burthen as taxation? Doubtless, so long as it lasts: but the important difference is—that rent is the consequence of price, and no part of its ground. Hence, all leases will gradually conform to the new state of prices: but, if it were possible to be otherwise, still the true pressure is in rent and not in taxation: Q. E. D.

The other error is simpler: it takes the shape of this

dilemma: we import much, or we import little. In the first case, in proportion as we benefit the consumer of corn, we injure the home-grower: in the second case, in proportion as we spare the home-grower, we give little relief to the consumer. *Answer*: Suppose a consumption of 50 millions of quarters, and the whole grown upon No. 1, 2, and 3, as above, and consequently all at 8d. Next year a small increase of population calls for an additional hundred thousand quarters. But even this cannot be had without resorting to No. 4, i.e. to nine-penny land; and the universal price upon *every* quality of land now rises to 9d. In this crisis import but 100,000 quarters at 8d., and what follows? Universal relief has been given to the consumer, for the price sinks universally to 8d., and yet no injury at all has been done to the grower; for not one acre of land has by the supposition been thrown out of cultivation. But this is a complete answer to the dilemma above stated. For, by truly applying the doctrine of rent, it appears that the greatest relief is given to the consumer with no possible injury to our own agricultural interest.

ATTRIBUTION

This seems to be De Quincey's, chiefly because its handling of the "doctrine of rent" is in the manner characteristic of him, both in his known writings and in other articles in the *Post*, some of which are certainly his; see the article of September 15, 1827 (pp. 118-19) and the further references there.

The use of the dilemma (pp. 343-44) is also characteristic; see the same article of September 15 (pp. 120-21) and the references there. Similarly, on the use of the question-answer style (p. 344) see the article of September 15, 1827 (pp. 121-22) and the references there.

"Q. E. D." (p. 343), by way of pointing up his cleverness, is a small device De Quincey employs on occasion. It is in the "Toilette of the Hebrew Lady," published at just this time (March 1828), M., VI, 156n. See also "The Casuistry of Roman Meals" (1839), M., VII, 35, and "Homer and the Homeridae" (1841), M., VI, 63. "Actum agere" (p. 342), though it is of little importance, he uses a couple of times.

[The Transference of an Elective Franchise]

The transference of the elective franchise from a Cornish borough[1] to the great manufacturing town of Manchester, is the most important measure which has been brought forward in this Session of Parliament. In common with many others, we regard it with great suspicion; not so much for itself (no matter how modified in its progress through the two Houses) as for the yielding temper which it marks, and the spirit of *trimming* in a quarter where we had looked for nothing but uncompromising firmness.[2] No one acquainted with our constitution can be ignorant of the necessity there is that the aristocratic influence should be balanced against the democratic, and a due equipoise maintained between the territorial power in which is lodged the *vis inertiæ* of our political system or the principle which secures its permanence, and the power derived from manufacturing and other shifting modes of property, by means of which it is that our system bends to the influences of the age. This antagonism, it will be said, can hardly be endangered by a change of so little extent as the one in question. Certainly not; and we repeat that it is not for itself, as an insulated measure, that we are disposed to call it in question. It is because, taken in conjunction with the repeal of the Test Acts[3] and other measures, it marks

¹ Penryn. This was the beginning of the incident that led to Huskisson's resignation; see below, pp. 349ff.

² The quarter of Peel and Wellington.

³ Lord John Russell had introduced a bill for repeal of the Test and Corporation Acts in February; it soon became clear that in spite of initial opposition from the government he was going to succeed. Earlier articles in the *Post*, possibly by De Quincey, had deplored the prospect. By the repeal dissenters were allowed

(as we fear) the prevalence of a general disposition to relax the safe-guards of the constitution; and specifically taken for itself, that it expresses a principle of compliance with the revolutionary schemes of Major Cartwright[4] and other Parliamentary reformers. Apart from all this, however, the equilibrium in the different forces of our constitution has been too much disturbed of late years by various events, both in and out of Parliament— to make it possible that we should regard any further attempt upon it, however separately unimportant, as a matter of indifference. These events have passed with little notice; or, if noticed, have had their real character overlooked. Next week, or at some early opportunity, we shall call our readers' attention more fully to the subject.

ATTRIBUTION

This is certainly De Quincey's. Some of the ideas and parts of the language are from Burke, but others are not and are specifically De Quinceyan. In his article "The Present Cabinet in Relation to the Times," written on a similar occasion a few years after this one, he says very much the same thing in very much the same words. After a passage on Major Cartwright, as a democratic revolutionary reformer of Parliament and the constitution who was opposed to the aristocracy and the influences of property, De Quincey attacks a limited reform measure that gives new members of Parliament to leading commercial towns; it is not dangerous in itself except

---

to hold offices from which, in theory, they previously had been excluded. Actually, annual acts of indemnity had been customary for a long time. But De Quincey is right in seeing the repeal as part of a general movement; the next step was Catholic emancipation, as Russell himself predicted; then Reform.

[4] John Cartwright, who had died in 1824; he had devoted a half-century to political pamphleteering and agitation, in advocacy of several causes, but most notably the reform of Parliament.

as it is a precedent of revolution, throwing the balance too much from "the aristocratic influence" to the "democratic"—"the commercial and moneyed interest being naturally opposed to the territorial and aristocratic." The true "equipoise of power is disturbed" by lessening the weight of the fixed and abiding possessors of property, the landed aristocracy and their borough property. It is with the aristocracy that political *"inertia"* is associated. *Blackwood's*, XXIX (1831), 144-45, 146-47, 149. In another article he says, also in reference to an electoral innovation (low electoral qualification), that since he looks upon the root of British grandeur as lying in an exquisite interdependency of "our aristocratic and democratic influences," he naturally views every measure that would destroy "the equilibrium of these forces as ruinous to the constitution." "Conservative Prospects," *Blackwood's*, XLIX (1841), 414.

Furthermore, the Bodleian MS. (pp. 352-53 below) rests part of its argument on the same "antagonism" of "democratic" and anti-democratic "forces" of the constitution which it is necessary to keep in "equilibrium." The same ideas and language are in other of his articles written in these years. Also on the "equilibrium" of "antagonist forces" in the English constitution, see his "French Revolution," *Blackwood's*, XXVIII (1830), 556. Again on "antagonist forces," "the democratic and the antagonist influence in the English Constitution," see his "Toryism, Whiggism and Radicalism" (1835-36), M., IX, 328, 331-32, 337-38; each "principle" and its "antagonist," the "democratic" and "aristocratic," is necessary in the "political system of England." See also the sequel of that, "On the Political Parties of Modern England," written 1837, M., IX, 371-76. Other references to the general principle of antagonism are given in the notes to the article of September 15, 1827 (p. 120 above).

[*May 31, 1828*] (Bodleian MS.
Eng. Misc. d. 271)

[Mr. Huskisson's "Resignation"]

This week we have to record a great triumph of the
principles which we maintain, and a triumph which
was in some measure necessary as the seal of that revolution which overthrew the Whigs in the beginning of
the present year. The cabinet has been reformed: it has
undergone a *lustration* (to borrow a Roman phrase):
and the tainted members of it, persons who in honor
ought not to have joined the Duke of Wellington's government, nor could have done so unless from domineer-
ing views of personal self-interest or (as we are apt to
suspect in one or two cases) with schemes of treachery
to their leader and to the party with which nominally
they were allied, are at length dismissed: according to
the usual *façon de parler* in such cases, they are all said
to have 'resigned'; and some of them, of no political
weight, may have done so: but for the only one amongst
them, notorious for his *vice* and restive habits, the circumstances of the case assure us that he has been dismissed. Mr. Huskisson, it is now formally and definitively
announced, has "withdrawn himself from the administration"; and greatly he has added to the obligation he has
thus conferred upon us all by "declaring his intention to
withdraw altogether from political life."[1]

The cabinet is thus placed at unity with itself, and by
an event which without any great effort of foresight we
calculated upon from the first. On the 26th of January,
speaking of the prospects for the Duke of Wellington's
cabinet, and adverting to the use he would make of it
as a *break* for unruly cattle, we said—"He will keep a

[1] Huskisson's resignation was reported by the daily press on
Tuesday, May 27; this leader, therefore, must have been written
for the *Post* of Saturday, May 31.

tight bearing-rein upon any dangerous subject like M͟r
William Huskisson; and, if M͟r William Huskisson should
jib, or plunge, or shew any vice, he will speedily be
taught who it is that holds the ribbons, and will be
brought into a beautiful state of civilization." The Liverpool election soon followed, in which M͟r Huskisson
"plunged" and shewed a little "vice" at starting; and
though he thought fit immediately to eat up in London
those words which hundreds will swear to his having
uttered on the Liverpool hustings, enough remained to
set the Duke of Wellington upon his guard. The old
soldier watched him; and at length upon the case of the
Retford franchise he caught him at his old practices:
M͟r Huskisson jibbed: the Duke pulled up in a moment;
turned him out of harness; and so ends another tale of
desperate ambition caught in it's own snares, and a most
imbecile attempt to repeat M͟r Canning's game of Machi-
avelianism without an atom of M͟r Canning's talents
and against an antagonist by many degrees more formidable than any with whom M͟r Canning was matched.[2]

[2] For the *Post* of January 26, see p. 288 above; on the Liverpool
election, see pp. 300ff. East Retford and Penryn (p. 346 above)
were corrupt boroughs which were to be punished. But the cabinet
could not agree on their disposition: the more orthodox Tories proposed that the boroughs should be merged with the adjacent hundreds, thereby keeping the votes rural; the Canningites proposed
that the boroughs should be disfranchised and the representation
given to large unrepresented manufacturing cities. The compro-
mise was that Penryn was to lose its vote to Manchester and East
Retford was to be merged with the hundred. But when the Penryn
bill could not get through the Lords, Huskisson voted against the
proposal for East Retford. Having done that he wrote a letter to
Wellington, "affording you," as he said, "an opportunity of placing
my office in other hands." To his surprise the Duke accepted the
opportunity. Huskisson tried to explain that it was a mistake, that
he had not intended the letter to be a resignation. But the Duke,
never a man to fall into the intentional fallacy, was unmoved:
"There is no mistake; there has been no mistake; and there shall
be no mistake."

On the other dismissals, and on the particular reports current with regard to the substitutions in the various vacant offices, we have not grounds enough for enlarging at present: it is enough to say that lord Dudley, lord Palmerston, and Mr Charles Grant, have all resigned, which sufficiently proclaims the auspicious *principle* of the new recast. As to the new appointments, nothing is yet definitively known—whether definitively settled or not. Even in respect to the Colonial Secretaryship, which is most the mark of curiosity and anxious inquiry at this moment, the public voice is almost equally divided between lord Aberdeen and Sir George Murray: and the other arrangements are still more imperfectly anticipated.[3]

But we need no details of the *personel* arrangements to ascertain the spirit in which the public interests will now be administered. The significant language of the several resignations, the immediate occasion of these resignations, and the character of our present all-popular premier, are so many pledges for the general tendency of the changes and the direction in which they will travel. The benefits we shall gain are great, instant, and unequivocal. Amongst them are these:

First, and chiefly we shall henceforward have no particolored government, and therefore no systematic dualism in our councils. It is scarcely to be calculated how much distraction is introduced into public affairs, and what subtle springs of self-contradiction are at work upon the great system of our national interests, whenever a divided cabinet is tolerated even under the firmest leader, and when any open coquetry is winked at between members of the King's government on the

[3] Dudley, the Foreign Secretary, Palmerston, Secretary at War, and Grant, President of the Board of Trade, were Canningites. Aberdeen succeeded Dudley, Murray succeeded Huskisson in the colonial secretaryship.

one hand and their organized Parliamentary opponents on the other. Such coquetry it was, openly carried on under the eyes of a failing and superannuated administration, that opened the door to Mr Canning's intrigues and all the confusions which we have since witnessed. In fact the utter chaos of chance combinations, into which political men were thrown by the dissolution of the old known and constitutional system of parties, would soon have put an end to all divisions on the natural basis of *principles*; and men would have been gradually congregated into little factions and *camarillas* associated upon family or private interest, and held together by no tie of public duty. The great distinctions of Whig and Tory, it can never be sufficiently proclaimed, are not factious distinctions—nor irrelevant (as is now pretended) to the modern aspect of things—nor are they (as the leading Whig journals have recently maintained for obvious motives of self-justification) of a nature ever to become obsolete. That doctrine is ignorance: yes, *pace tuâ* Mr Brougham, mere ignorance. *Whig* and *Tory* are not like the distinction of *Trinitarian* and *Anti-Trinitarian* for example, where both cannot logically co-exist: on the contrary the Whig and the Tory not only co-exist without supposition of error on either side, but in fact are reciprocally necessary, each to the philosophical existence of the other. Whigs and Tories are severally charged with the conservation of two equal and coordinate interests—the popular interest, and the interest of the crown: and both jointly, but neither singly, make up the total constitution of this country. [As respects the conduct of particular Whigs and Tories at particular æras and with regard to questions foreign to the great principle on which they divide, there is undoubtedly room enough for a preference between them. But to talk of any election between two sets of true principles, which by their synthesis only compose the total truth, or]⁴ To suppose therefore that either could ever merge and collapse into the other when their very essence lies in antagonism, or to ascribe a constitutional preference to either, is pretty much as philosophical as it would be to lay more stress on the centrifugal than to [*sic*] the centripetal force in the maintenance of the planetary orbits. These are antagonist forces; but are so far from being on that account hostile and incompatible forces, that each is indispensable to the conservation of the other. So long as the British constitution subsists, so long the democratic and the anti-democratic forces, reconciled as they are in that great effort of human wisdom, will also subsist: and concurrently with those two great distinctions of *things* will subsist the two great distinctions of principles, Whig and Tory, which have reference to them and are built upon their basis: the one distinction is co-eternal with the other. And if ever that time should arrive when no organized bodies of property, talent, and legislative influence will take charge of these two great forces which it is so necessary to keep in equilibrium,—but, neglecting these great objects of their lawful solicitude, shall abandon themselves (according to Mr Brougham's suggestion) to new—sentimental—and childish combinations of *liberal* and *illiberal*,⁵—thenceforward farewell to the monuments of our fathers' wisdom!

Upon this view of things we rejoice heartily that now we shall again have a strong Tory party, really and truly such and not ashamed of the *name*. The Tory banner will be again reared: and the instant consequence

---

⁴ Bracketed material is deleted in the manuscript. There are many other deletions, including some within these brackets, that have not been transcribed here; this one is given because of its similarity to a passage elsewhere in the *Post*, as pointed out below, p. 357.

⁵ See the article of November 24, 1827, p. 198 above.

of *that* will be that the Whigs also will be driven to recombine with all their might: and we the Tories shall have the merit of scourging them back from their fantastic fopperies of last year's growth to the old solemn constitutional duties which they have abandoned and in one of their leading journals have deliberately abjured. Yes: the apostate Whigs will be forced into party union again through hatred of us: and we the Tories shall grow strong again by clearing our camp from their deserters.

Secondly, if there be any meritorious member of the present administration who has been insensibly tainted by communication with liberals and Huskissons and so forth, he will receive at this juncture a salutary shock and warning; and we doubt whether he will now be willing, or whether with his new colleagues he will have the courage, to bring forward his ruinous measure for the regulation of the English currency; a measure which Scotland, as regarded her own separate interest when menaced by the same insane scheme, strangled in it's birth with such summary decision.[6]

Thirdly, we shall now have a chance for putting our feet on the neck of the Popish Anti-Parliament of Ireland.[7] An Anti-Parliament, above all a Popish Anti-Parliament, is no more endurable in the political system than an Anti-Pope in the religious. Delenda est Carthago! And what more auspicious Scipio for our Protestant hopes than the D. of Wellington? Catholic Emancipation, as the villains call it, already sickens at that name. And at the next general election, we anticipate

[6] In 1826 the government had suppressed the issue of small notes by country banks, on the ground that excessive circulation of unsound paper currency had been a cause of the economic crisis. The Scotch, however, were successful in preventing the suppression of the notes of their own banks; this was the occasion of Scott's letters of Malachi Malagrowther. Huskisson had been the man blamed by the Scotch.

[7] See p. 291 above.

that the fine old patriotic chaunt of *No Popery*, by which the modern Whig is stung into more madness than a turkey by a red rag, will ring in the ears of the hollow emancipators from shore to shore.

Fourthly, which we are reminded of by the words *general election*, if there be any House of Commons which has adulterously intrigued with all sorts and successions of public impostors and jugglers until it has grown an unfit engine for honorable purposes, and which very recently has trafficked with great national interests that should have been as sacred in their eyes as the honor of their daughters,

"This false senate, full of gifts and lies,"[8]

will now, thank Heaven! be cashiered as unceremoniously as a Huskisson or any other the meanest of those impostors. Another Session such a house, if any such there be, will hardly have a chance to see: and to the justice of their indignant constituents we heartily commit them.

But these last are slight and partial benefits in comparison of that which we first mentioned—the restoration of our old political landmarks, the termination of our year of confusions, and the recal of our political parties from a carnival of drunken coxcombry to their ancient standards and their venerable constitutional objects. These are benefits to be grateful for: and in consideration of these we are grateful even to Mr Huskisson that he 'jibbed' so soon and so determinately as he did.

*

From Portugal there is further intelligence, but as yet none of a decisive character. Two aspects however of public affairs look ominously upon Don Miguel's designs: the one is the desperate condition of his finances, and

[8] See Coleridge's "Ode to the Departing Year," l. 91.

the other a much more serious disaffection to his person amongst the army than we had been led to expect.

From the theatre of the Turkish war, the only news is that the Russians are now in peaceable occupation of Moldavia, and are rapidly spreading their advanced posts into the heart of Wallachia; as yet without opposition. But of the force and positions of the Musselmans, and of their plans for the conduct of the campaign, no certain accounts have yet reached us.[9]

ATTRIBUTION

That this was written for the *Post* is proved by the *verbatim* quotation (pp. 349-50) of the article of January 26, 1828 (p. 288).

It has also other links, both in subject matter, ideas, and words, with other articles in the *Post*. Huskisson's need to eat up his words (p. 350) seems to refer to the article of February 23, 1828 (p. 321), which, like this one, is part of a series on Huskisson and his problems in his candidacy at Liverpool. The passage on the antagonism of democratic and anti-democratic forces in the constitution and the necessity of their equilibrium (pp. 352-53) repeats a point and some of the key words of the article of April 19, 1828 (pp. 346-47). The essential relationships of Whig and Tory (pp. 352-53) are also a subject of the article of November 24, 1827, and there

[9] The last two paragraphs show that De Quincey must have been doing more work for the *Post* than it is possible to identify or worth identifying except for biographical evidence of the sort of work he was doing.

Don Miguel had just become regent of Portugal; he was opposed by the constitutionalists, whom Canning had tried to help (see the article of August 18, 1827, p. 79 above).

The event feared by the British after the battle of Navarino, a Russo-Turkish war, had come to pass. Both this and the career of Don Miguel had been the subject of reports and comments in previous issues of the *Post*, some of them no doubt by De Quincey.

are verbal identities there too (pp. 198-99). That same article (p. 198n.) makes the distinction made here in the deleted passage on p. 352 between the basic principles of the two parties and the conduct of particular Whigs at particular times. It also, like other articles in the *Post*, attacks the apostate politician (p. 354). The figure of the centrifugal and centripetal forces appears also in the article of December 15, 1827 (p. 225); it is a favorite figure with De Quincey, who used it several times to illustrate the equilibrium of the antagonist forces of Whig and Tory in the constitution: "French Revolution," *Blackwood's*, XXVIII (1830) 556; "Toryism, Whiggism, and Radicalism" (1835-36), M., IX, 331-32; a preface of 1857, M., V, 129-30.

June 14, 1828

West India Property

The great questions of justice and expedience, which have been raised in our days, upon West India property, in its several relations, to the slave—the planter—and the mother country, are of a nature to concern us all.[1] Indirectly we are all interested in the issue as a question of the purse,—a question which will be brought home to the meanest among us, through its inevitable connexion with the national revenue. All of us, again, have an immediate interest in it as a case affecting the national honour; for which of us would be otherwise than heartily ashamed, if our Government were to expose this great country to the laughter of Europe, by legislating in a spirit of Arcadian simplicity, and sacrificing time-hallowed rights to the clamours of an effeminate sensibility, misdirected even where it is not altogether counterfeit, and generally ill-instructed as to facts. Lastly, for the British colonies in particular, those even in which the condition of slavery is unknown, they have special reasons for watching with anxiety the case now pending: for, most assuredly, in the litigation subsisting for sometime between the Supreme Legislature at home, and the different colonial legislatures in the West Indies, the fundamental principles of colonial dependence, its kind and its degree, are silently agitated: the limits of reciprocal rights generally between colonies and the mother country, hitherto but imperfectly defined, are virtually

[1] The movement to abolish slavery in the British empire, successful by 1833, had gained great strength since 1823. In that year the Anti-Slavery Society had been established; and in the same year the colonial legislatures had been charged to pass laws bettering the condition of the slaves (see p. 291n. above): the anti-slavery forces were now insisting that the colonies had done nothing significant and that Parliament should act.

and (it may be thought) prematurely ripening to a final settlement; a settlement which can hardly fail to be modified injuriously to the weaker party by the passion and irritation which at this moment too manifestly govern the stronger. No man therefore can say, no member of the empire can say, '*mea res salva est*'—I am an unconcerned spectator, let the justice of the case tend to what issue it may: for, on the contrary, we are all bound, by many ties, to a participation in its last results; and not merely under the several relations we have pointed out, but finally under the most comprehensive relation of any which belongs to the social state—the relation, actual and contingent, in which we all stand to PROPERTY; a relation which obliges every part of the social world to look with absolute panic on the proposed invasion of its sanctity by the most virtuous assembly in Europe. Mr. Coleridge, in speaking of the French Revolution, used to say, that the whole opposition to it in this country, however cloaked under other names, commenced and moved under the impulse of what he called '*the panic of property*;'[2] a very salutary panic at any rate, however unworthy to have monopolized the national regard; and well it would be if some such panic could arise to irritate the public torpor at this time: well for us all, if not directly as a West Indian proprietor, already injured and traduced, nor generally as a colonial proprietor menaced by analogy, nor as a disinterested patriot shrinking from the humiliating spectacle of his own potent government intermitting its appropriate labors to dally with little schemes of maudlin romance, well, if merely through the universal instincts of the purse, every man amongst us could be roused to an alarm on a level with the occasion. Violations of prop-

[2] *Friend*, No. 10, October 19, 1809, pp. 157, 158; in the 1818 ed., II, 28, 30. See also his *Table Talk*, the entry for April 8, 1833.

erty, under every mode, we may rest assured, are contagious: *Proximus ardet Ucalegon*;[3] the spirit of spoliation has an undistinguishing appetite. We have already had solemn proposals for confiscating tithes and Church Property in Ireland; for confiscating the whole Funded Property of the British Empire; and now, finally, not for confiscating, i. e. adjudicating to the public treasury, but for annihilating (as eventually it would prove) the colonial property of the West Indies. Certainly there is nothing to hinder unprincipled men, even in the most virtuous country, from making unprincipled proposals: The evil is, when the records of great deliberative bodies show that such schemes have been tolerated and entertained in the national councils. *That* raises them into an ominous sign of the times. With this sense of its fearful importance, we have drawn up an outline of the West India case; and next week we shall submit it to our readers. Meanwhile, for the present, we shall add whatever may be necessary to introduce it.

We, the writers of this article, are old enough to remember the first stage of the slavery discussions in this country. That stage was limited strictly to the question of the *trade* in slaves; and the movers of it were most anxious to disavow all ulterior designs upon the condition of the existing slaves, excepting only as regarded their religious improvement. The pioneers of that first period were chiefly Day, the author of Sandford and Merton, (for whose extravagant, and, we must say— foolish life,* consult Miss Seward's Memoirs of Dr. Darwin, Miss Edgeworth's Memoirs of her Father, &c.), Bicknell, Benezet the Swiss, and Granville Sharpe, so

---

* And *foolish death*, we may add: he sacrificed his life to a theory upon colts, pretty nearly as wise as those of the present Anti-Colonists upon the negro slaves.

---

[3] *Aeneid*, II, 311-12; neighbor Ucalegon is on fire.

famous for his hyper-orthodoxy.† These persons, however, were merely the heralds who drew attention by a
flourish of trumpets to the two heroes of this period—
Clarkson and Wilberforce. We place their names in the
order of their merit; and even in placing Wilberforce
next to Clarkson, we must add the old restriction of the
critic when speaking of Virgil in relation to Homer—

† A man of wit once observed to us, that Granville Sharpe was a
super-orthodox member of the Church of England; for that, whereas others of that church believed in 39 articles, he believed in 40;
since he believed in the article—ὁ, ἡ, τὸ. G. S., the reader must
recollect, was the first person in England who attempted to establish the divinity of our Saviour upon the peculiar use of the Greek
article in the New Testament,—a speculation since pursued, but
not exhausted, by the first Bishop of Calcutta and others.[4]

[4] Thomas Day was the author of the *History of Sandford and
Merton* (1783-89), an education novel in the tradition of Rousseau.
There are accounts of Day in Anna Seward's *Memoirs of the Life
of Dr. Darwin* (1804) and in the *Memoirs of Richard Lovell Edgeworth, Esq.*, begun by himself and concluded by his daughter,
Maria Edgeworth (1820). Day was foolish, certainly, but an entertaining, noble eccentric, in the eighteenth-century style. His death
seems apposite to a defender of West Indian interests. In the
words of the more sympathetic Miss Edgeworth, "This excellent
man was, at last, a victim to his own benevolence." Having observed that horses suffer much, in the breaking, from brutality, he
tried to train a horse by gentle means; it threw him and kicked
him in the head. He had written, with the collaboration of his
friend, James Bicknell, a popular poem, "The Dying Negro"
(1773), condemning the West Indian planters; and he was also
the author of *Fragments of Original Letters on the Slavery of the
Negroes* (written 1776, published 1784). But to include Day and
Bicknell among the major pioneers of the opposition to slavery is
to be deliberately mocking.

Anthony Benezet, French by birth and American by emigration,
had been the author of pamphlets against slavery which influenced
Clarkson at the beginning of his great career; Benezet died in 1784.

Granville Sharp, who had died in 1813, had been a most energetic and successful worker for Negro liberation; it was his effort
that obtained the legal verdict (1772) that as soon as any slave
sets his foot upon English soil he becomes free. The footnote on his
super-orthodoxy is a reference to his *Remarks on the Uses of the
Definitive Article in the Greek Text of the New Testament* (Dur-
ham, 1798, with later editions), in which he argued that, gram-

Proximus, sed longo intervallo.[5] Never, indeed, was there
a case that better illustrated the injustice of the world,
always the dupe of glitter and pretence, than the par-
tition of honours between these two champions of the
negroes. The first was the working (or, as it is called
in Scotland, the *operative*) agent for the Black interest,
its indefatigable *chargé d'affaires*; the other was the gay
show ambassador for holiday occasions. What Mr. Wilberforce sacrificed for "his children," was some few
hours of his time; he made a few speeches on their behalf; he attended a few public meetings; and, seated in
an elegant saloon, he wrote or dictated a few diffuse
pamphlets. All this, even apart from the immediate
applause which repaid it a thousand times over, could
not have cost much sacrifice even to a voluptuary; for
Mr. Wilberforce had great natural volubility and com-

---

matically, the use of the article is such that God and Jesus must
be the same person; the point, of course, was crucial in unitarian
controversy. One of his defenders was Thomas Fanshaw Middleton,
a schoolfellow of Coleridge and Lamb, in his *Doctrine of the Greek
Article* (1808); Middleton was later the first bishop of Calcutta.
Another defender of his was Christopher Wordsworth.

[5] Misquoted from the *Aeneid*, V, 320: next, but at a long distance.

Thomas Clarkson, 68 years old at this time, had spent his money
and health in working against slavery; he was indefatigable as col-
lector of evidence and as author. William Wilberforce, now 69,
having been the Parliamentary leader of the successful fight
against the slave-trade and a well-known public figure, received
most of the public credit for its abolition. In fact Clarkson and
Wilberforce worked together, each contributing his special ability.
But others made invidious comparisons between them. Hazlitt, for
example, in *The Spirit of the Age*, had championed Clarkson, not
liking Wilberforce's politics. De Quincey's animus may be based
on his dislike of the evangelical group of which Wilberforce was
a leading figure and with which De Quincey's mother was connected, through her association with Hannah More. The Clarkson-
Wilberforce controversy began in earnest in 1838, with the publication of the life of Wilberforce by his sons; Clarkson himself
responded and he was defended by Crabb Robinson too.

mand both over words and shallow thoughts: His writings show this no less than his speeches. At all times he delivered himself with ease and unpremeditated grace; and, had his matter been weightier, he would have been a memorable speaker. On the other hand, what Mr. Clarkson sacrificed to the blacks was this:—For them he sacrificed his golden youth, and his "fervent prime" (See Mr. Wordsworth's fine Sonnet) : [6] For them he sacrificed his health and firm constitution: So much indeed was his nervous system shattered by the perils and hardships he had sustained, that in middle life he had already anticipated the infirmities of old age, and often started at noon-day, as though persecuted by phantasms, or listening to the noiseless steps of assassins stealing behind him. According to his own account he many times ran the risk of assassination, when hunting for evidence in Liverpool and other great towns. Certain it is, that his labours and his anxieties were like those of the great Apostle of the Gentiles. He was the Luther of that reformation; and of Mr. Wilberforce it is almost too much to say that he was the Melancthon. Yet, whilst the one has been crowned with the civic wreath by applauding nations, the other (except from his friends the Quakers) has received no marks of approbation, little or great, from his own age. So hollow, base, and worthless, is the testimony and praise of the world!‡

‡ It is a remarkable illustration of a remark formerly made in this paper, that we have never had a journal with enough of commanding power to lead and correct the public mind; but that the highest ambition has been cleverly to follow and serve it,—that in an article on Mr. Clarkson's History of the Abolition in the Edinburgh Review, all the compliments paid by Mr. Coleridge (the author of that paper) to Mr. Clarkson were suffered to stand, but were transferred by a stroke of the pen to the use of Mr. Wilberforce—probably under the revision of Mr. Brougham, to whom at that time Mr. Wilberforce's favour was of great importance.—So at least Mr. Coleridge told the story at the time (about 18 years ago).[7]

[6] "To Thomas Clarkson, on the Final Passing of the Bill for the

To return however from this digression, these two servants of the Negro cause were good and conscientious men. Intellectually, indeed, they were *hommes bornés*; not only what the Germans call *einseitige männer*, men that can see things under one aspect only, or phasis; but they were literally men with only one idea. Nobody however could doubt, and hardly any body ever *did* doubt, that their motives were entirely good. Of their present representatives in the service of the Negroes, such as Mr. Buxton, young Mr. Stephens, &c. we may possibly speak a word or two hereafter. But between this last generation, and the original generation of the Clarksons and Wilberforces, there was a second and connecting race, to whom it is that we owe the transition from the purity of the early schemes to the lawless intemperance of the present. As leaders in this second generation we may instance Mr. Zachary Macaulay of Sierra Leone notoriety, and for many years editor of a religious journal;* Mr. Stephens the father, brother-in-law to Mr. Wilberforce, who obtained so much celebrity in the outset of the war with Bonaparte, by his exposure of the fraud of neutral flags (See his "War in Disguise;")

* "The Christian Observer," supported by occasional contributions from Wilberforce, the Thorntons, the Hoares, Mr. Babington, long M. P. for Leicester, and many other respectable Members of Parliament.

Abolition of the Slave Trade. March 1807" (1807), l. 4. In 1838, after the publication of the life of Wilberforce, Wordsworth appended a note in defense of his praise of Clarkson. The Wordsworths were neighbors and friends of the Clarksons, but they knew the Wilberforces too.

7 The remark formerly made is in the issue of November 17, 1827 (pp. 189-90). Coleridge's review of Clarkson's *History . . . of the Abolition of the African Slave-Trade* (1808) is in the *Edinburgh Review*, XII (1808), 355-79; see below, pp. 384-85.

and, thirdly, the factious Mr. Brougham.[8] Of the sincerity
of these persons, the world has long taken the liberty to
speak sceptically. But without allowing to ourselves any
license of that kind, and wishing to think charitably of
all men's motives so long as it is possible, we are yet
obliged to observe that they much sullied any genuine
philanthropy which might mix with their schemes, by
building upon them at every step concurrent schemes
of personal aggrandizement. Doubtless, there is no absolute crime in making a scheme originally of benevolence
carry double, as it were: to equivocate in this way between selfish and disinterested purposes, does not put a
man out of the pale of decent society; it is not absolutely
criminal, we repeat: but it is more disgusting to delicacy
and native goodness than even open rapacity, and far
more of a snare to a man's own heart. Mr. Brougham,
it is notorious, used the negro cause as his own stepping-

---

[8] With the exception of Brougham all the men listed here as the
"second generation" were, like Wilberforce, members of the evangelical group later known as the Clapham Sect. Zachary Macaulay
and his connection with Sierra Leone and the *Christian Observer*
have been noted above (pp. 28, 42). The Thorntons were the sons of
John Thornton (the friend of Cowper), especially Henry Thornton. Henry Thornton and Wilberforce were second cousins and
close friends and Henry's house at Clapham was the center of the
sect; he wrote much for the *Christian Observer*. (He was also the
father of E. M. Forster's *Marianne Thornton*.) The Hoares were
a numerous family, whose money, from the family banking business,
and whose energy were active in evangelical causes; Charles James
Hoare, a friend of Wilberforce and the Thorntons, wrote for the
Christian Observer. Thomas Babington was married to Zachary
Macaulay's sister. There was much intermarriage among these
bright and earnest families. "Mr. Stephens the father" is James
Stephen (grandfather of Sir Leslie Stephen), whose second wife
was Wilberforce's sister; his *War in Disguise* had been published
in 1805 and was followed by the orders in council on wartime
shipping. The "young Mr. Stephens," of the "present generation,"
is his son, George Stephen. Buxton is Thomas Fowell Buxton, who
had succeeded Wilberforce, at Wilberforce's request, as the Parliamentary leader of the anti-slavery forces; George Stephen collected evidence for him; both men were later knighted.

stone into political life.† And others, apparently, are open to the same suspicion. Still it may have happened, and is indeed the thing naturally to be expected, that what began in false and counterfeit zeal, may have ended in true (though still perhaps selfish) devotion to the cause. Long necessity of facing keen opposition naturally leads to that result. A man becomes sincerely wedded to that which he has long defended. But still it is right to notice the taint of worldly views and impulses which distinguished the immediate successors to Messrs. Wilberforce and Clarkson for two reasons; first, because from these mixed and doubtful motives are no doubt derived the licentious plans which are now pressed on the public attention; secondly, because, strange as it

† Poor Mr. Wilberforce, as he advanced in years, gave melancholy proof of the imbecility with which he sank under his *one idea*, by sacrificing to it every other consideration, even such as in earlier life he had regarded as most sacred. Whoever (to use a coarse word) would "humbug" him about the negroes, and *all that*, was sure of his patronage. And hence it was that he, the friend of William Pitt, was absolutely *green* enough to address a very strong recommendation to Lord Lonsdale of ———, the most factious and jacobinical agitator of the times, as a fit person to succeed Lord Muncaster, on the Lowther interest, in the representation of Westmoreland. The cool disdain with which the recommendation was treated led to some remarkable results that, in some future memoirs, will no doubt find a place, and do something to throw light on that person's character. The jacobin, be it observed, was perfectly willing to be the tool of the Lowthers.[9]

9 The unnamed Jacobin is Brougham. In 1806, before he had been able to find a seat in Parliament, he asked Wilberforce to apply on his behalf to Lord Lowther (Wordsworth's patron, Sir William Lowther, second Baron and Viscount Lowther, created Earl of Lonsdale in 1807). Brougham's opposition to the slave-trade had recommended him to Wilberforce; but it was also apparent by now that Brougham was not going to revere the memory of Pitt and Wilberforce wrote Lowther a long, embarrassed letter, enclosing the note he had received from Brougham. Lowther returned the note to Wilberforce the same day, very briefly, "without answer or observation." As Wilberforce knew, the seat had been offered already to his friend Muncaster (Sir John Pennington, first Baron Muncaster in the peerage of Ireland and fifth baronet).

may seem, we are convinced that it is the enthusiasm belonging to the pure schemes of the early abolitionists,—which, transferred through mere ignorance and confusion of subjects, to the present schemes of a very different set of abolitionists, is really the main anchor by which these latter have any hold of the public favour. Startling as the reader may find such an assertion, satisfied we are that in the majority of the Anti-Slavery meetings, if an orator were to rise and speak at length on the horrors of the "middle passage," he would be heard with great attention, and at the utmost hear his blunder whispered to him by a secretary, chairman, or some such official person.

In this situation, what is the plain path for the friends of the West India interest? Manifestly to sharpen the public attention to the true points at issue, and not to suffer an enthusiasm really derived from a legitimate source, to be misdirected to a spurious one. The professed purpose of the opposite party is to promote the abolition of slavery, and at all events its "mitigation." To disabuse the public mind, therefore, of its present delusions, the natural course is,

1st, To present a close and unwordy abstract of the actual condition, both physically, and with relation to religious and civil privileges, of slavery, as existing at this time in the West Indies: In that way the reader will be enabled to judge for himself how far that condition calls for mitigation.

2dly, On the assumption that any mitigation were really called for, to institute a brief inquiry how far those particular innovations which have been urged upon the colonies by the Colonial Secretary, have any true tendency in that direction.[10]

10 Sir George Murray, like his predecessors in the colonial office, was trying to move the local legislatures to action.

3dly, With respect to those who are pressing, not for the mitigation of slavery, but for its immediate and unconditional abolition, to direct their attention to the case of Hayti and its Rural Code, as furnishing some practical data for our speculations on the probable results.[11]

This is the course we propose to take; and we shall abstain from all irritating expressions, not because we profess to feel no indignation towards the abusers of the national mind, and the calumniators of the innocent, but out of deference to the weight and solemnity of the subjects.

[11] The example of Haiti, which, after achieving its independence from France, not only became proverbially bloody but found it necessary to enforce labor, was a favorite of the anti-abolitionists.

West India Property

[*cont.*]

In the year 1807, after 19 years of discussion, the abolition of the Slave Trade being at length adopted by the Ministry, and raised into a Cabinet question—was solemnly carried by a vote of the British Parliament. This great measure was executed by the Government with good faith, corresponding to the wishes of the Legislature. Some evasions of the new law were certainly complained of for a time: nor could it have been otherwise: in a change of that magnitude, it was inevitable that the growing temptations to infringe it should be caught at eagerly by persons in subordinate stations. But the Government stands clear of all connivance in such practices: even the base incredulity of the Continent is at length satisfied on that point: and we may now say, that for 21 years, as regards the permission of British laws, or the countenance of the British Government, or the participation of the British people, this wicked commerce has been absolutely extinguished.

It is false to describe the West India proprietors as repining at that issue. Undoubtedly, and with good reason, the planters of the last generation, contemporary with the course of that dispute, were slow to co-operate in measures of certain injury to themselves. It was no part of their duty to surrender old interests of inheritance, (interests of which they were no more than trustees for the next generation) at the first summons of a revolutionary philanthropy. It did not become *them* to take for granted, that a system was rooted in iniquity which they had received from their fathers, which had been sanctioned by so many illustrious Statesmen, and countersigned (as it were) by a long line of Kings, Parliaments, Councils, and Courts of national justice. Had they indeed been in a condition so readily to yield the questions then litigated, *that* facility—far from being matter of honor to them—would have argued a guilty knowledge on their part of the whole atrocity belonging to the contested system. Whereas, in fact this knowledge was as slowly diffused amongst *them* as amongst us— the neutral part of the nation. And for both parties, for the nation, and for the planters, who were jointly accountable for the maintenance of that system, their common ignorance of its circumstantial features is their common apology. Then first when the attention of this nation was keenly directed upon the slave trade, then first when a blaze of day light began to stream upon its guilty recesses, did it become a crime in every man (according to the degree of his illumination) to exercise or to defend that traffic. Just as in the parallel cases of the foul oppressions of European dungeons exposed by Howard,[1] or the enormities that lurked in the lunatic hospitals of England exposed by Parliamentary inquiry,[2] those abominations did or did not become national re-proaches—as they were or were not adopted into national acts by passive acquiescence in the body of the people.

If even with these equitable allowances for the colo-nists of that day, it should be thought by some, that a case is hardly made out for them amounting to a full justification, if the obligations of a just regard to their own interest do not *entirely* acquit them,—we must next consider the great provocations which they received. As a body it is certain that they were foully traduced: was it in human nature that they should lend them-

[1] John Howard, who in the 1770's and 1780's continually in-spected and reported on prisons in England and the Continent and worked for their reform.
[2] In 1815.

selves to the schemes of the traducers? More especially
when the logic of the case is considered, viz. that these
calumnies were not mere circumstances of irritation,
such as are apt to arise in controversy, and confessedly
extraneous to the argument, but were absolutely relied
on as the argument itself or a main part of it in behalf
of the abolition. (*a*) Not only were the colonists called
on to yield to certain changes, but to yield to them on
this principle—that themselves and their whole order
had cruelly abused their power. Upon that footing the
argument was managed by the most eminent Abolitionists; and he, who adopted the scheme, made himself

(*a*) The fact is that the abolition of the slave trade was placed
upon a false ground. The treatment which the slaves received in
the colonies had no relation whatever, in the way in which that
topic was managed, to the question of the African Slave Trade.
The evidence taken on that point, if it were good for any thing,
was good against the very existence of slavery, an object which
the Abolitionists at that time disclaimed. The only way to connect
the evidence on the *colonial* treatment of the slaves with the question at issue on the trade in slaves, was by the following argument:—That the perpetual infusion of fresh African recruits
amongst the slave population kept up the irritation and insur-
rectionary ferment, which would else gradually subside, and thus
(as an inevitable consequence) obliged the colonists to a much
severer code of laws, penal and preventive, than would be necessary with a purely Creole population. The Abolitionists would
have been consistent, had they supplied this link in their argument.
They would have said—evidence to acts of cruelty in the planta-
tions, is in effect good evidence against the slave trade; because
the excuse and occasion for such acts arises with the new im-
portations, and would die away concurrently with *them*. But,
treated as it now is, and insulated from its proper application, the
evidence is singularly impertinent to the professed objects of the
Abolitionists: it proves nothing against the slave trade, whilst it
leaves the reader to a necessary inference (such as the Abolitionists then deprecated) against slavery. Emancipation for the
slaves was a measure which they disclaimed anxiously, except as a
most remote one in the first place; and, secondly, as a spontaneous
growth from the natural progress of society. And, indeed, let their
secret designs have been what they may, it is clear that regard to
their *immediate* object forbade them in prudence to lose sight (as
in this one instance they have done) of these public professions.

a party to every cardinal principle by which it was supported.

Thirdly, for the mere *manner* of the controversy, omitting its more substantial merits, there is much color of right for the Anti-Abolitionists, especially for those whose attention was quickened by local knowledge. We who were neutral to the question, for any immediate interest that we had at stake, learned occasionally how much there was in the progress of these discussions of garbled and varnished evidence, of evidence dislocated from its appropriate commentary, of evidence addressed to the ignorance of European readers, of evidence, even positively false; many of us knew how much there was of revolting hypocrisy; all of us saw how much of theatrical imposture. Every thing of this sort revealed itself more distinctly to what we may call the learned eye of the colonial reader, and furnished reasons even to good men amongst them for demurring to the merits of a cause managed by such dishonest arts.

But finally, even for the ultimate end of the Abolitionists, and abstracting from the whole body of secondary considerations which may chance to make the very best end a bad one, it was and is to many judgments a questionable measure. We indeed think otherwise, but upon principles which are open to conscientious doubts. The case stands thus: That Europe was the cause of African misery, or that such a mere local irritation or flea-bite as the slave trade stood in any sensible relation to that immense continent, cannot be read without a smile. The very possibility of such a trade arising at all is the best proof that Africa was in no condition to be degraded by it, and is but one more amongst a thousand manifestations of that mysterious fact, that this great continent, through its whole vast area, if we except only those narrow belts, which, from position, have fallen under Asiatic influences, is the only quarter of the globe that in no age has been able to mould itself into great communities, or to take the lowest steps in civilization. Narrowing the question, therefore, to that of the happiness of the poor wretched negroes, surely there would be many more presumptions for *that* in a state of West Indian plenty, security, and (we may now add) of Christian knowledge, than in their native lairs of ferocious anarchy and bloody paganism. In Africa they are level with the beasts of the field; in the West Indies, after one generation, they become a contented peasantry. But this view of the case, which was and is the view of many good men, we for our own parts reject. Outrages upon the rights and independence of our fellow men, which are crimes without further question, must not be perpetrated out of any regard to consequences: *we* have no concern with consequences. The rule for us is eternal—not to do evil that good may come. On this principle the British people enacted the abolition of the Slave Trade; and supposing it possible for them even to have erred in that sacrifice, by estimating the obligations of duty upon too heroic a standard, we must still rejoice exceedingly, and in one view must forever pronounce the abolition to have been the very sublimest act for a national act which the records of this planet present us—inasmuch as it gave the first example of a great nation, king, senate, and people, solemnly uniting to divest itself of large commercial interests on pure considerations of justice. Such a spectacle among political communities had no precedent, and may be looked upon as inaugurating a new era, and far happier prospects for man.

Such is our creed, in its principal heads, upon the question of the Slave Trade; which question, let us now go on to say, for England has long been obsolete. That strife has been over for years: that "warfare is accomplished:"[3] and at this day not a groan ascends to heaven from any child of Africa under authority of British law. Why then detain the reader upon a topic alien to the real question? We answer, for the purpose of meeting a dishonorable antagonist. The case is thus:—A proposition is now before the nation for invading colonial property in ways abominable to British ears. The leading article in this scheme is the emancipation of the West India slaves. Now, it is evident that in a country, where of all upon earth the principles of justice as applied to property are best understood, it would be vain to look for any success in a measure of that nature unless by embarking it upon the support of some misdirected popular feeling. Fortunately, the old dormant body of enthusiasm, connected with the Slave Trade Abolition, still survives: the word '*slave*,' common to both schemes of abolition, facilitates the juggle by which this original enthusiasm might be awakened and made available for the new purposes; and, accordingly, while no person dares to maintain *openly*, upon any fiction or construction, that a connexion exists between the old and new Abolitionists, yet all the benefit of such a connexion is obtained substantially by one of two ways. Either, first, the two questions are boldly confounded; or, secondly, where *that* is impossible, the principles and temper of the first anti-abolitionists are confounded with those of the present; so that, if the new cause is acknowledged to be directed to a new set of objects, it is yet represented as moving under the same influences, and as virtually identical for the moral principles concerned. Now, even if *that* were true, it is worth while to consider how far it ought to vitiate a man's vote, upon this or any question, that he belonged to the opposing party, even upon the first scheme for abolishing the Slave Trade. And with this view we have endeavoured to appreciate with candor the

[3] *Isaiah*: 40:2.

grounds of their opposition; grounds which, in fact, they held in common with multitudes of impartial men. But the truth is, that the justification of that body, the early colonial defenders of the Slave Trade, is now stripped of its *practical* importance; for that body is itself gone, and exists neither personally nor by any modern representatives. They are gone; and in their place have come up a new generation which in succeeding to *their* interests, have not, in that particular, succeeded to *their* views. No class, indeed, regard the abolition of the Slave Trade in a more approving spirit than the West India proprietors of this day. But were it otherwise, so far is it from being true that the old and new abolitionists stand related to each other in that order of succession which is now alleged, and as though the one set inherited from the other its claim upon the public favor, that, on the contrary, the old opponents of the Slave Trade happen to be the only class in this kingdom who are committed by many positive pledges to the support of the present colonial cause. By natural justice we are all committed to that course; but *they* by distinct verbal promises, and by many even angry declarations of faith, and solemn renunciations of objects for which they now contend. In particular, and amongst a thousand other vouchers, we refer to the Edinburgh Review of twenty years back, where the reader will find the distinction anxiously pressed between Emancipation for the Slaves, and Abolition of the Slave Trade, and the patrons of the first measure described as the worst enemies of the other.[4] So much for that dishonesty which now labors to confound the spirit and principles of the two schemes. As to that other and bolder dishonesty, which confounds the very schemes themselves, we fancy that some readers will believe this a chimera of our own; and, when we asserted, (*Sat. June* 14,) that in most of the Anti-Slavery

[4] Perhaps the article of 1804 (IV, 477).

meetings an orator would be heard with attention and respect upon "the horrors of the middle passage," we doubt not that we had credit for a jest. But we know our men. And the very next day after this was published, the *John Bull* newspaper, (of *Sunday, June* 15,) adverting to what is falsely called the *Cambridge* petition against Slavery, (a petition in no degree speaking the wishes of the University,) opens one paragraph thus:— "Mr. Professor Scholefield attended the meeting both of the University and of the town; and after enlarging on the horrors of the African Slave Trade, *and of the Middle Passage*, drew out of his pocket a little printed brief from the Anti-Slavery Society, containing statements as often refuted as repeated."[5] Such was the course actually adopted in a learned University, one of the twin-luminaries of England, by the Regius Professor of Greek,[6] anxious to proclaim himself the blindest of dupes in that very chair once occupied by immortal scourges of spurious pretensions—by Porson, and the eagle-eyed Bentley. Delusions of that magnitude, in situations of so much light, leave us to infer the general condition of the public mind under less favorable circumstances; and make it emphatically necessary at this moment to sharpen the national eye-sight to the distinctions between the two sets of Abolitionists, the old and the new; to distinguish, as to the Anti-Colonists generally, between what they *did* and what they *do* pursue; to allow them no benefit from that philanthropy in the black cause which they now fraudulently misappropriate; and to state the tenor and particulars of that attack which they have already half accomplished upon West India rights.

[5] *John Bull*, p. 190, col. 1. De Quincey omits, after "of the Middle Passage," in his quotation: "for effect, as they could have nothing whatever to do with the object of the petition." This disguises the fact that the point he is making had been made by the *John Bull*.

[6] James Scholefield.

The injustice which we challenge in behalf of the West India Proprietor in its capital heads is this. First of all he is libelled in his moral character; and what fragment of his property his traducers would leave him is tainted in the popular ear by an opprobrium, such as elsewhere follows plunder or fraudulent gains. Is it nothing to a man of honor that he and his order—conscious of a paternal relation to their slaves, in a degree inconceivable to the spirit of our manners—are every-where described as ferocious tyrants, administering a harsher code of laws, and in a harsher spirit than was tolerated even in Pagan antiquity? Is it nothing that his children are to inherit a property which is represented as extorted from the groans of the unhappy, and watered with the blood of the unoffending? (b)

But these are the libels of the ignorant. True: yet they are adopted sometimes by those who are *not* ignorant. Next, however, hear the calumnies of Senates and Universities. In the West Indies of late years there has been

(b) The ignorance of Mr. Stephen, jun. may have concurred to this statement; but there can be no doubt that it began in a spirit of misrepresentation; for it has not even so much of colorable truth as is necessary to a paradox. It would be well, however, that a popular account should be drawn up of the conditions of slaves in the different ages of the Roman state. Upon this subject we must remind the reader that the question is not about extreme cases of cruelty, such as are recorded in past states of West Indian society: these were remembered and brought forward in the evidence on this subject chiefly because they *were* extremes: the question is, how far are such cruelties practised with any countenance from the laws, or reconciled to the spirit of public manners? Now all men of honor, who have visited the West Indies, are agreed that public opinion is as sensitive upon these subjects in the colonies, and as powerful as in England. The Police annals of England, the most humane country of the world, bring up daily instances of savage domestic tyranny. But we do not therefore feel nationally disgraced—we know that the one act of cruelty is put on record, when the million acts of benignity belonging to the same day are allowed to perish; and it is sufficient that this one act is obliterated as any national stain by the general disgust which it rouses.

a steady current of wise and benign reforms, chiefly originating with the West India Proprietor himself. Now, hear his reward. Every-where almost it is believed that they have been carried in his teeth by the British Parliament, or by an order of the Privy Council; and his own bounty is thus turned into a handle of insult against himself. If he refuses any boon called for by the Anti-Slavery Society, he is threatened as contumacious: if he grants it, he is insulted as one overawed.

In the Cambridge petition it is declared, "That the Colonial system is oppression; that *nothing* has been done after five years"—(meaning since the Resolutions of 1823)[7]—"to carry into effect the recommendations of Parliament for meliorating the condition of the slaves; that the colonial enactments are deficient and delusive; and that therefore Parliament ought to legislate for the colonies and abolish slavery."

Hear, on the other side, Government speaking by the Prime Minister, last Monday night: "Upon the whole, I do say that it is surprising to see in so short a time that so much has been done towards the attainment of the object which Parliament had in view." (*c*)

The British Government is here in flat opposition to the *Caput*[8] (five members) of the University of Cambridge. Who can doubt the superior information of Professor Scholefield?

Mr. Brougham, in the House of Commons, uniformly insists that the alleged moral improvement of the West Indian slaves is a delusion, and so slow as to be "absolutely imperceptible to any eye but that of a planter." (*d*)

(*c*) Speech of the Duke of Wellington, as reported in the *Morning Herald* of Tuesday, June 24.

(*d*) Mr. Brougham taxes the Planters with a horrible self-contradiction in this—that, with *their* notions of negro improvement, they still keep back any civil privileges on the plea that the ne-

[7] See p. 291n. above.
[8] The ruling body of the university.

Lord Bathurst,[10] on the other hand, an unfriendly witness, "feels himself bound to state that all the information which he had received regarding the moral improvement of the negroes is in the highest degree satisfactory. The Bishop of Jamaica had given him the most gratifying accounts of the rapid improvement in the morality of the negroes in that island. The Bishop of Barbadoes bore similar testimony."

Some libellers, not content with charging upon the planters inertness, or doing nothing, insinuated, that they did much in an opposite direction. To meet that description of calumnies, we might bring a body of unwilling testimony from Lord Bathurst, (a weak but honorable man), from Mr. Huskisson, and others, in proof that, except upon those points where the local knowledge of the colonists made them upon principle hostile to change, they often outran the expectations of reasonable people at home.

---

groes are not yet in a condition to use them. Few people will find any contradiction in *that*: on the ot . . . hand, it would be hard to find an escape from this . . . . follows:—We have seen how Mr. B. speaks of th . . . . . when his purpose is to traduce the Colonist, or . . . . . . ward the tyrannical interference of Parliam . . . . these bye purposes are forgotten, and b . . . . character of an Abolitionist, he . . . . supposed advancement of the . . . . reason for conceding civil, ... own party than held 9

9 The corner of the newspaper has been torn away. The point evidently is that when Brougham's purpose is to traduce the planters or to advocate Parliamentary interference in West Indian affairs he deplores the degradation of the slaves; but when he advocates abolition he insists that the slaves are ready for all civil privileges.

10 Henry Bathurst, third Earl of Bathurst, sympathetic with the Clapham Sect, was currently Lord President of the Council; from 1812-27, in Liverpool's long ministry, he had been Colonial Secretary. The report of his words, too, is taken from the *Morning Herald* of June 24 (p. 1); the version of his speech given in Hansard is a much less enthusiastic account of the progress of the slaves.

But to pass from these injuries to others more within the level of a universal sympathy, provided only that the avenues to it were not foreclosed by ignorance and prejudice, let us come to that war upon West India property which is now conducted under the name of Emancipation. Emancipation for the slave was not disguised as a final object of the early abolitionists; but they looked for it under three conditions:

1st, *That it should be remote*; because in that way only could it be preceded by those gradual changes in the moral condition of the slave which would fit him for bearing it.

2dly, *Through the Masters*; because upon any other system the slave would be trained to look upon himself and his master as having a divided interest.

3dly, *As the last in a series of Changes*, which would have ended in preparing a fund of free labor fitted to step naturally into the former duties of the slaves. The case is this: climate will not allow of *white* labor in the West Indies: on the other hand, the blacks have never worked but under the stimulus of coercion; and, until they are raised into a capacity of higher influences by gradual admission to civil privileges, by religious culture, and by the whole complex process which we call civilization, it is in vain to expect that they ever will: all the examples of Sierra Leone, Surinam, the Mosquito Shore, Hayti, &c. unite in proving that, unless previously disciplined to higher motives of action, an emancipated negro inevitably surrenders himself to a life of indolence, for which unfortunately a tropical climate offers but too many facilities in most of the West India Islands. Hence the emancipation of the slave should be slow, still more on his own account than his master's. The master might be indemnified: but the negro never can be indemnified if once launched upon independence under a wrong impulse. Twenty-one years ago, upon a motion of the present Duke of Northumberland's[11] for the gradual abolition of slavery, (the principle of which was, that all children born after a certain day should be declared free,) Mr. Wilberforce opposed the proposition, on the ground that the transition for those who must still be reared under parents of servile habits, would be too violent and abrupt; and wisely declared that he would entrust the cause of emancipation to "the diffusion amongst the negroes of those domestic charities which would render them more fit than they now were to bear it." Let this be remembered at present: the sanctities of marriage are now first beginning to take root amongst the slaves: and it is not certainly until one generation has passed away that the most ennobling of its effects will be reaped.

Upon such a scheme slavery would not be violently extinguished, but would expire naturally (to borrow a word of Lord Bacon's) by the happiest of euthanasies.[12] Freedom would not be mechanically manufactured, as it were, by an act of Parliament,—but would evolve itself, by just degrees, like a flower, or any other stage of a natural growth; and the very same steps by which those blessings were secured to the negro, would bring indemnity to his master.

But, as things now are, in what way is Emancipation to be effected?—By compulsory manumission: so much is settled; under which sagacious course Government undertakes the responsibility of all consequences; and, therefore, amongst the rest, of that squalid poverty and immorality which, being once allowed to settle into the

[11] Hugh Percy, third Duke of Northumberland of the third creation; twenty-one years ago he had been Earl Percy and an M. P. See Hansard, March 17, 1807, IX, 143-46; the following quotation from Wilberforce is on 146.

[12] *Advancement of Learning* ("World's Classics" ed., p. 123).

new form of negro life before it has been braced to industry by nobler habits, will probably determine its destiny for many ages. So much for the care of black interests. (*e*)—Next, with what provision for those of the whites? One party declares itself for compensation; and, as this happens to be the prevailing party, compensation there will be. (*f*) Perhaps the reader may find

(*e*) Such is the infatuation which possesses the *soi-disant* friends of the negroes, that some of them think it the highest expression of their sincerity to proclaim that under no circumstances will they tolerate "a state of regulated coercion, as an intermediate state between slavery and freedom;" the very thing of all others which would do the most for negro welfare, because it would train them to the discipline of industry before they were their own masters enough to reject it on the one hand, and yet after they had quitted the brute physical coercion on the other which would stifle the first sentiment of hopeful and forward-looking industry. How often is one compelled to recal the old sagacious prayer—"Save me, oh Lord! from my friends, and I will save myself from my enemies!"

(*f*) What a compensation!—For the most exquisite specimen of charlatanerie on this subject we refer the reader from the middle of p. 87 to the middle of p. 95 of *The West India Question practically considered.* 1826.—(A pamphlet ascribed to Mr. Wilmot Horton in the House of Commons, and not disclaimed.)[13] Mr. Horton seems verily to think that it is the easiest thing in the world to compute the value of a single wheel in a vast machine, all parts of which are dependant on each other; and quite reasonable to say to the master of a steam-boat—Sell me a pound and a half out of your boiler, and a half crown slice out of your paddles. So much "glib nonsense," to borrow a homely expression from Locke,[14] was perhaps never crowded into eight pages. Amongst many perplexing cases where it will be most difficult to assign the true value of a slave, and many still more perplexing cases where two values will arise—one to the proprietor, and another much below *that* to every person beside, (in which cases injustice must be done to the one side or the other)—take the following illustration from this country of a situation to which West

[13] See above, p. 149n. This pamphlet is doubtfully Horton's; but he did write others on the same subject and some contemporary opinion ascribed this one to him.

[14] The closest I can come is "palpable nonsense," in *A Second Vindication of the Reasonableness of Christianity*, Locke's *Works* (1823), VII, 200.

it difficult to believe in the possibility of a second party calling for gratuitous emancipation. Such a party, however, there is.

(In an early Number we shall resume and close this subject.)

ATTRIBUTION

This two-part article may or may not be complete; the installment of June 14 promises a continuation next week, but the issue of June 21 is not extant; the conclusion of the installment of June 28 promises to resume the subject in an early number, but the only succeeding extant issues of 1828 are those of July 12 and 26, and they have nothing relevant. But these promises are not sacred and we may have all that was written. In any case, the writer certainly seems to have been De Quincey.

The article of September 1, 1827, replies to the abolitionist attack upon slavery in the same manner, denouncing it as an attack upon property; and it makes the same distinction between abolition of the slave-trade and abolition of slavery; references are given there

India estates will be often liable. Suppose a great printing-house in which 100 men are employed: in this case, with so large a disposable force, every man retains his own separate value, and is rated without any relation to the other. Next imagine this house to be gradually reduced to the lowest possible number capable of printing this newspaper, entitled *The Post*, which number suppose to be 10. Here (under the West India circumstances, where no substitute is to be had,) the loss of one man will cause no less a calamity to the world than the total disappearance of *The Edinburgh Evening Post*: 10 can, 9 by the supposition can*not*, print it: for, whatever Mr. Wilmot Horton may think, it will be found impossible to sell nine-tenths of a *Post*. Any one man, therefore, by carrying himself off, carries off virtually the entire value of the ten. Now, suppose this man a slave, and his proprietor compelled to manumit him: in that case he is entitled to demand for this one slave a compensation equal to the value of the ten. How hard upon the slave! Yet on any other principle of compensation, how unjust to the proprietor!

NEW DE QUINCEY ESSAYS

(p. 94) to similar passages in De Quincey's known writings, including the article in the *Post* of January 26, 1828, which is certainly his.

On the first stage of the slavery discussion, in which those who were opposed to the trade disavowed abolition of slavery itself (pp. 360-61), see the autobiographical article of 1834, where too he lists Clarkson, Wilberforce, Benezet, and Granville Sharp as participants in this stage (M., I, 19n.). Also on Clarkson and Wilberforce as opponents of the slave-*trade*, see "Political Anticipations," *Blackwood's*, XXVIII (1830), 727n.

To come to more specific evidence. In his "Memorial Chronology" (written c. 1850), M., XIV, 307-08, De Quincey notes the injustice by which the praise of Clarkson's work for abolition of the slave-trade was subordinated to Wilberforce's because it suited the policy of a political faction, a religious sect and a celebrated Review. The same point is made here (pp. 362-63). There are verbal similarities in one of his Lake reminiscences (1840), M., II, 412, where De Quincey writes of Clarkson's "nerve-shattering perils" as the one great supporter of the abolition of the slave-trade; "So much had his nerves been shattered" by all he had gone through, his "labours," toil, suffering, "anxiety," that he could not walk upstairs without tremulous motion of his limbs. The association of Clarkson here with Wordsworth and with Coleridge also points to De Quincey.

Most impressive is the evidence of two of the footnotes, which display information that could have come only from someone personally acquainted with literary and political activity in the Lake country. The first is the note on p. 363, which, in addition, begins by referring the reader to the article of November 17, 1827, an article certainly written by De Quincey. It is not only that the author of the note knows and remembers that Coleridge reviewed Clarkson's book in the *Edinburgh* of two decades past; the review was the only one Coleridge ever wrote for the *Edinburgh,* so that knowledge and remembrance of his authorship must be more than casual. It was an unsolicited review which Coleridge offered to Jeffrey because he was anxious that Clarkson's book not be mauled. Furthermore, Coleridge says in a letter of September 19, 1808, that his review was changed and the change favored Wilberforce: it was not quite, as stated here more spectacularly, that all his compliments to Clarkson were transferred at a stroke of the pen to Wilberforce, but that in an inserted paragraph he had been made to contradict himself "in a nauseous & most false ascription of the Supremacy of Merit to Mr. Wilberforce." See Coleridge's *Collected Letters,* ed. Earl Leslie Griggs (Oxford, 1956——), III, 124-25; there are other references to the review in Coleridge's letters of 1808, including one in a letter to Jeffrey in which he disagrees with Jeffrey on the relative merits of Clarkson and Wilberforce (III, 148-49). These letters, of course, were unpublished, so that the author of the article in the *Post* must have had personal knowledge of Coleridge; the incident of 1808 had occurred shortly after De Quincey met Coleridge, when they were seeing one another and corresponding. Further knowledge of Coleridge's writings that connect the present article with De Quincey is the use of Coleridge's phrase "the panic of property" (p. 359). De Quincey uses it, within quotation marks, and, as here, in reference to the French Revolution, in his "France and England," *Blackwood's,* XXVIII (1830), 702. He uses it again, and again in reference to the French Revolution, and this time with credit to Coleridge, in one of his London reminiscences (1837), M., III, 25. "France and England" (p. 717), we may observe parenthetically, has a further similarity to the *Post* article (p. 360) in that it too denounces the conspiracy against the property of the West Indians, the fundholders and the church, as founded on principles of wicked "spoliation." And "France and England" was published in *Blackwood's* a month before "Political Anticipations," which has been noted already as offering another parallel to the present article.

The other significant footnote is the one on p. 366 about Wilberforce's recommendation of Brougham to Lord Lonsdale, which "in some future memoirs, will no doubt find a place." The letter was not published until 1893, when it was included in the Historical Manuscripts Commission's Thirteenth Report, Appendix, Part VII, *The Manuscripts of the Earl of Lonsdale*, pp. 182-84. As the author of the introduction to the Report said, this "remarkable" document and episode appear to have been unknown to biographers; the first biographer of Brougham to take notice was Arthur Aspinall, *Lord Brougham and the Whig Party* (Manchester, 1927), p. 14. But De Quincey would know about the episode through Wordsworth; he himself had worked with Wordsworth, on Lonsdale's side, against subsequent attempts by Brougham to gain a seat in Westmorland; so he had, especially as editor of the *Westmorland Gazette*, more than a casual opportunity to hear and to remember the story. That Brougham was a jacobin, as the same footnote calls him, had been one of the issues of 1818. De Quincey, following Wordsworth, had argued it at length; see the reprint of his *Close Comments* by John Edwin Wells, *PMLA*, LV (1940), esp. 1109.

Some of the other people whose names figure in these articles were known to De Quincey in one form or another. The Clapham saints (p. 364 and n. 8) he had personal reason to know of and dislike because of his mother's connection with them. As he said in the autobiography, "my mother's views were precisely those of her friend Mrs. Hannah More, of Wilberforce, of Henry Thornton, of Zachary Macaulay" (M., I, 407). In "Dr.

Samuel Parr" (1831), M., V, 25, he lists them much in
the style of the present article, "the Wilberforces,
Thorntons, Hoares, Babingtons, Gisbornes, &c." Cf. also
M., III, 129. Through his connection with Hannah More
he also met a man who had belonged to the coterie of
"Miss Seward, Dr. Darwin, Day, Mr. Edgeworth, &c."
(M., II, 448 and p. 360 above). He also knew the work
done by the first Bishop of Calcutta on the Greek article
(M., V, 203 and p. 361n., above).

To come now to words and phrases. "Euthanasy," a
word used here with some self-consciousness (p. 381),
is in "Political Parties of Modern England" (written
1837), M., IX, 394; "Conservative Prospects," *Blackwood's*, XLIX (1841), 416n.; "The Game Up with Repeal Agitation," *Blackwood's*, LIV (1843), 679; *Confessions* (1856 version), M., III, 420. Some of the foreign
phrases also point to De Quincey, especially "einseitige
männer" (p. 364); "einseitig" is in a number of his essays
around this time. It is in "Lessing" (1826-27), M., XI,
159; it is in "Charlemagne" (1832), M., V, 354, where
a note he added in 1859 points out that at the time of
original publication the term needed an apologetic for-
mula, so that he obviously thought of it as semi-private
property; in a portion of his autobiography published in
1834, M., I, 268; in an article on Wordsworth in 1839
and in another in 1840 (M., II, 287, III, 204), where the
term is "einseitigkeit." "Homme borné," in the same
sentence (p. 364), is in M., XI, 27. For *"soi-disant"* (p.
382n.) see the article of August 4, 1827 (p. 57) and the
references there. For "charlatanerie" see the article of
September 15, 1827 (p. 122) and the references there.

Among the quotations, one of which is hackneyed, the
other perhaps not, Ucalegon (p. 360) is in M., XIII, 279,
and the warfare accomplished (pp. 373-74) is in M., I, 106.

Mr. O'Connell and the Clare Election

This most important contest has terminated on the 5th day;* and, as all our readers are by this time aware, with the election of Mr. O'Connell. For this result we are right thankful: unfeignedly we rejoice at the crisis which has thus suddenly ripened into a form of perilous magnitude,—a crisis which must now *compel* the great Irish landholders and the Government into active measures, whether the House of Commons do or do not persevere in flinching from their duty. At the Waterford

---

* So early a termination is in itself remarkable. We ventured last week to call in question the probability of a report then credited both in Edinburgh and in London, that Mr. Fitzgerald had withdrawn himself on the Tuesday, (the first day's polling); and it has since turned out that we were right. The ground, however, on which we rested, entitled us to anticipate that Mr. Fitzgerald would poll out the county; in which case, and with the proper demurs on the part of his counsel, the contest would not have occupied much less than the legal period of 15 days; at any rate not less than 12. In an English county containing not one half the votes, or pretended votes, which might have been brought forward for Clare, supposing that party feeling runs high, that frauds are numerous, and rigorous inquisition therefore necessary, —a keen contest will seldom terminate before the 8th or 9th day; provided that the assessor is impartial, and the counsel vigilant. Hence we conclude one of two things—either that Mr. Fitzgerald has had bad legal agents; (and in fact nothing is rarer than a good electioneering lawyer, great talent for bullying being required, which certainly may be had in Dublin, but then in connexion with an elaborate knowledge of election law, such as can hardly be found out of London); either this, or a foolish complaisance in Mr. F's. party in sparing their antagonists what they would call a "vexatious" opposition. Both causes have perhaps concurred to the sudden termination of this important contest. If a scrutiny had been demanded at the close of the polling, we have little doubt that the 40 shilling votes would have been reduced by two thirds: and as to "vexation" in a conflict of this description, it was the duty of the landed proprietors to vex, teaze, harass, and embarrass their adversaries by every means which the law opens to their service.

Election the mischief was yet in the green ear; but it now
stands ready for the reaper's sickle. Had the Catholic
Association continued to dispossess the landlords of their
natural influence by means of *Protestant* tools, the
disease would have crept into the vitals of the State
without forcing itself upon the national eye. But now,
with the *avowed* purpose of wringing from the Legislature, in utter scorn and defiance, the very foremost of
those boons which have been so long refused under the
name of Catholic Emancipation, and, for the achievement of this purpose, putting forward a Popish incendiary, such as Mr. Daniel O'Connell, doubt there can be
none that the Popish Anti-Parliament will at last have
awakened an alarm proportioned to the danger. The
season for torpid security is forever gone by; and for
that it is that we are thankful. Let us briefly consider
the results of this election to the several parties concerned.[1]

[1] After Huskisson's departure the other Canningites resigned
from the cabinet; Charles Grant, President of the Board of Trade
and Treasurer of the Navy, was among them. He was succeeded
by W. Vesey Fitzgerald, member for County Clare, who then had
to stand for reelection, in what was expected to be a routine affair: Fitzgerald was popular in Clare and a consistent advocate
of emancipation. The forty-shilling freeholders, who were expected
to vote for him, were in fact tenants who had been created bogus
freeholders, and therefore actual voters, by the landlords, to extend the power of the landlords. But at the Waterford election in
1826 the forty-shilling freeholders had elected a nominee of O'Connell's, defeating Lord George Beresford, of the very powerful and
anti-Catholic Beresfords, who had held the seat for twenty years;
and this after the Beresfords had created recently eight hundred
new freeholders. The Clare election was conclusive proof that the
forty-shilling votes were weapons that had turned upon their
masters. But it was especially impressive because the successful
candidate was the bold O'Connell himself, the leader of the Catholic Association (see p. 291 above), who, as a Catholic, would
not be able to take his seat even if elected. The power of the
Association in organizing and leading the masses made it plain
that emancipation had to come soon. The price of emancipation,
when it did come in 1829, was the establishment of a ten-pound
franchise.

First, for the SHERRIFF, there can be no question that he was right in declaring Mr. O'Connell duly elected, (making, however, a special indorsement on the writ of the peculiar circumstances belonging to the case.) On this point we are surprised that any question should have been raised. Such a question was, however, argued before the Assessor at great length; and, as we conceive, upon grounds not entirely right. The distinction taken was this—That, though disqualified for sitting and voting in the House, Mr. O'Connell was not disqualified for being elected. But what *we* say is this—1st, That, supposing Mr. O'Connell to be not merely incapable of sitting and voting, but absolutely ineligible as a Papist, still the Sherriff has no legal means of knowing him to be such: and, 2dly, That in fact so far from being disqualified for election, Mr. O'Connell is not even disqualified for sitting and voting simply as a Papist, (for *that* the House have no right to know,) but as a recusant to a certain test, viz. Oaths of Abjuration and Supremacy, and Declaration against Transubstantiation. Now, this test has not yet been proposed to him; nor was it in the power of the Sheriff to propose it; nor in the power, therefore, of Mr. O'Connell to put his recusancy on record. Consequently, for anything that could legally fall under his cognizance, the Sheriff is bound at present to suppose Mr. Dan. as sound a member *in posse* of the Honourable House as Mr. Speaker himself *in esse*, of whom everybody knows that he has the good fortune to be son to the Archbishop of Canterbury.[2]

Secondly, for Mr. O'Connell himself—for this prince of *boutefeus*, whom for the absolute unity of his profligacy, for the systematic outrageousness of his sedition, (alas! how painfully contrasted with the base cowering

[2] The Speaker of the House was Charles Manners-Sutton, son of Charles Manners-Sutton the Archbishop of Canterbury. Both father and son were opposed to the Catholic claims.

timidity of our Protestant champions!) we do verily hold in something like reverence,—how will this election operate for *him*? Will it crown his hopes, or will it wreck them? Will the guilty demagogue take the test, a thing that has been done (under the peculiar casuistry of *his* church) by Papists as bigoted as any that is likely to breathe the atmosphere of the four courts of Dublin in 1828? Will he do this? or, on the other hand, will the guilty House, guilty by more than one vote of a virtual violation offered to that very identical test, liberate him basely from his dilemma by conniving at his silent admission without any test proposed,—a thing which has been done, both inadvertently, and perhaps intentionally, by a better House of Commons than any we now see, or are likely to see? Neither one nor the other. And why? Simply for this reason—that neither party *dares* to do it; Mr. O'Connell from fear of the Association, the House of Commons from fear of the nation. A general election cannot be very far distant; as *that* approaches, every House of Commons shrinks and cowers, like a hound under the uplifted lash, before its constituents: and for the feeling on this point of those constituents, consult any of these gentlemen who had in 1826 to affront the terrors of the hustings. Ask Lord Milton, or Mr. Marshall, for instance, what was the feeling in the immense county (the nation in fact) of York. Ask Lord Howick for the *real* state of Northumberland. Ask Mr. Brougham for a *sincere* report of Westmoreland—where even the veriest Jacobins (to our perfect knowledge) fell away from his interest under that sublime instinct of Anti-Popery which both in Scotland and in England has for two hundred and fifty years victoriously survived all local, personal, temporal, perishable motives.[3]—No: weak

---

[3] All these men were "Catholics" and all had faced difficult contests in 1826 for that reason. Lord Milton was Charles William Wentworth Fitzwilliam, later third Earl Fitzwilliam in the peerage

are those who imagine that Mr. O'Connell catches at the peacock's feather of a seat in the House of Commons for the bauble of distinction which it confers. Such idle interpretations of his conduct we have seen, and in Irish papers. But this is folly. He flatters himself with no seat in the House of Commons. How much better as a means of notoriety, supposing that his lucrative profession left him at leisure to court that influence, that he should be the first man in Ireland—the *great commoner* (to borrow a cognomen of the first Lord Chatham)—the successor of Grattan in power[4]—far more than his successor in the affections of the people,—the bearder, the adequate antagonist, the defier to the teeth, the challenger *à l'outrance* of the British Government,—a potentate to be numbered in the dreams of the Prime Minister, not with Mr. *this* or Lord *that*, but with Spain—with the Netherlands—with France—with the Empire!—Yes! how much better all this than to be confounded with a mob of common-place Members of Parliament, which assuredly he would be if ever he should show his brazen face in the House of Commons! There he would be tamed and emasculated. In 1825 this Mr. O'Connell exhibited himself in London. He came as the leader of a deputation from the Catholic Association to petition Parliament against dissolving it; and at the Crown and Anchor—

of the United Kingdom, at this time Viscount Milton and member for York county; John Marshall of Headingly was also member for York. They had been elected but only after a fierce contest in which the county also returned two "Protestants"; Sydney Smith had written his *Letter to the Electors upon the Catholic Question* in their support. Lord Howick was Henry George Grey, Viscount Howick, son of the second Earl Grey, the Whig leader, and afterwards himself the third Earl; he was at this time member for Winchilsea, having lost in Northumberland, the Grey seat, on the Catholic issue. The same election had been Brougham's third unsuccessful attempt to defeat the Lowthers in Westmorland.

4 Henry Grattan, the Irish statesman who had died in 1820; in his last years he had worked chiefly for emancipation.

(or where was it?—some place or other in the Strand)—
he spoke for four hours on the Catholic claims, in the
presence of an immense multitude.⁵ We appeal to every
man who heard him on that day, whether the caitiff did
not tremble before a British audience—did not falter—
did not (to use a slang word of Eton) *funk* exceedingly
for the first quarter of an hour. He felt that the thought-
lessness of an Irish audience was necessary to support
his loose incoherence. In fact, he is a very minor Edward
Irving.† And we say *minor,* comparing him in degree,
because he is identical in kind. Take away from him the
region of scorn, indignation, intemperate invective, and
he is stripped of the very element in which his wings
are able to expand. To him the forms of the House of
Commons would be a complete extinguisher. These
forms, the gentlemanly self-restraint, the necessity of
courting the ear of the House, would be a curb-chain to
him, and compel him to draw in the vulgar team of men,
unless he could carry into the House two hundred ruffians like himself, and, in fact, change the tone of that
assembly. Not to mention that his coarseness and brutality, wheresoever he was met by opposition, would
engage him in ten duels during the first month; one or
other of which would liberate the world from O'Con-
nellism. But all this is to speculate on an impossible
event: Mr. O'Connell will *not* enter the House of Com-

† Mr. Canning's opinion of an orator we should not quote as
generally decisive. But in Mr. Irving's case it may be taken to be
so, because Mr. Canning's classical taste may be taken to be dia-
metrically opposed to *his.* Being asked in 1826, by Mr. Wordsworth,
what he thought of Irving, Mr. C. replied—"A great orator, undoubtedly a magnificent orator!"—giving it to be understood, in
the little which followed, that he also thought him—as to the
matter of his orations—a great fool.⁶

⁵ It was at Freemasons' Tavern, February 26, 1825. O'Connell
himself said he had a great success; Protestant accounts, naturally,
were less enthusiastic.

⁶ See below, p. 397.

mons—how could he? His profession he could not afford
to renounce; on the contrary, he makes an eternal boast
that he sacrificed as much as Horatius Cocles[7] in quitting it for six weeks; and by taking the oaths he would
cease to be the head of the Association. On the other
hand, to allow any silent evasion of the oaths to a person
so notorious—is more (as we said before) than the
House of Commons durst venture upon; though it is
much that they would venture upon in such a cause;
for had it not been for the House of Lords, let us remember, that at this moment there would have been nothing
left for Mr. O'Connell to ask. Such then is the case: Mr.
O'Connell cannot take the test; the House dare not wink
at his evading it. Yet upon this it is that he calculates.
He says to himself—This is a case which concerns the
House of Commons separately. I will rely upon their
weakness in a matter where the Upper House cannot
control them. Once gained, it will be impossible to deny
the privilege to others; and thus, however little I may
use it myself, I shall have paved the road to others. The
funds of the Association, and the influence of the Priests,
will then have an open career; the counties, unless it
were in the north, will all be carried; and a large majority
of the Irish Members will be servile tools of the Popish
cause.—Thus we interpret Mr. O'Connell's audacious
enterprize; and it is clear that, if in this one instance
the interest of the House of Commons should keep them
firm to their duty, this audacity will recoil with a weight
of disgrace upon himself,—fatal, perhaps, to his own
interests, and, through him, to those of the Association,
whose sole principle of cohesion lies in his ability for
leading.

Thirdly, for the LANDLORDS and TENANTS, their connexion is now dissolved; and new measures will hence-

[7] The Roman hero of the bridge, later celebrated by Macaulay.

forward be adopted. To introduce a clause into leases, binding a tenant affirmatively to vote for a particular person, or perhaps for a particular interest, would be amenable to the bribery laws; not so to introduce a negative clause restraining the tenant generally from voting for any Papist, or for any Protestant who stands upon popish support—whether that of the Priests, or the Catholic Association. Something of this kind will now be done; if not, there are other remedies in reserve, and the benefit of the present case is, that it will effectually rouse all landlords to employ them. Else the agrarian balance, so well developed by Harrington in his Oceana, is sapped; and if ever there was such a thing in this world as an *imperium in imperio*, we have it now in Ireland, where the Church is arrayed against the State, the tenant against his landlord, and even the humblest dependent against his benefactor.*

Finally, for our GOVERNMENT. How will *that* be affected by this unparalleled event? Speaking generally, a British Government, as it is distinguished amongst all European ones for its integrity, and the personal respectability of its members, is no less distinguished for its feebleness—irresolution and timidity as regards public opinion. More or less this must always be true of a popular government; but from the death of Mr. Pitt in 1805,[8] up to the end of last year, this infirmity has been a scandal to the nation. Who can forget the many instances in which both Executive and Legislative bodies have trembled before a popular journalist? Who can remember, without shame, the inexorable insolence (as we might almost call it) of the Ministry and the House of Commons, in putting down the Catholic Association

---

* Clare was one of the counties which suffered most in the last season of distress, and was most largely indebted to its resident gentry.

8 For 1806.

by paper decrees, and the abject timidity with which they have since submitted to the kicks, spurns, and mockeries of that same Association, menacing and defying them to their teeth? Oh! for a Burke, in such times of feebleness, to arise and THINK! Oh! for a Chatham to ACT!—But hush! We *have* a Chatham since Christmas last presiding in our Government; and though the first step in the retribution which we seek must come from a house in whose public virtue the nation has little confidence, the next may chance to depend upon *him*. In a spirit of confiding hope, therefore, at this extraordinary crisis for Ireland and the empire, let us wait and watch.

ATTRIBUTION

Certainly De Quincey's.

O'Connell was one of his favorite subjects during and after these years and he was always violent on it of course. He wrote about O'Connell, the Catholic Association and Emancipation, drawing a contrast, as here (p. 395), between present weakness and the vigor with which Pitt acted, in "The Duke of Wellington and Mr. Peel," *Blackwood's*, XXV (1829), 294-302; that was after the battle had been lost and his hopes betrayed. The distinction made here between O'Connell's power as a member of Parliament and his power in Ireland is made also in "Political Anticipations," *Blackwood's*, XXVIII (1830), 734-35. His other political articles for *Blackwood's* return continually to O'Connell: XLVIII (1840), 135, 142, 144; XLIX (1841), 407-14; LIV (1843), 264-74; LIV, 549-50; LIV, 679-86; LV (1844), 521-26, 531-32; LVII (1845), 647, 648, 651-52. He refers to him and the Clare election again in "The Marquess Wellesley" (1846), M., V, 174.

The reference to James Harrington's *Oceana* and the

agrarian balance (p. 395) is a more specific sign of De Quincey. It appears frequently in his political writings where he is interested in constitutional balance: "The Present Cabinet in Relation to the Times," *Blackwood's*, XXIX (1831), 147; "The Prospects of Britain," *Blackwood's*, XXXI (1832), 577; "Conservative Prospects," one of the articles that attack O'Connell, *Blackwood's*, XLIX (1841), 416; "Toryism, Whiggism, and Radicalism," (1835-36), M., IX, 320-21. There are other references to Harrington in "Rosicrucians," etc. (1824), M., XIII, 432, "The Aristocracy of England," *Blackwood's*, LIV (1843), 52, and the *Confessions* (1856 version), M., III, 254.

The perfect knowledge of politics in Westmorland claimed by the author (p. 391), especially when it is combined with the private knowledge of Wordsworth (p. 393n.) are even better indicators of De Quincey. Most specifically, Canning's poor opinion of Irving's oratory is cited by De Quincey in an article of 1840 (M., III, 125); the same paragraph also criticizes Canning's oratory in terms used by an earlier article in the *Post* (p. 84 above). Wordsworth's name is not given in the 1840 article, but the occasion of Canning's oral opinion—a visit to Mr. Bolton of Storrs, on Windermere— we know from other sources to be an occasion when Wordsworth was present, in the summer of 1825. See Lockhart's *Life of Sir Walter Scott* ("Everyman" ed.), p. 478, and Wordsworth's letter to Lockhart, April 27, 1838, in Wordsworth's *Letters*, ed. De Selincourt, *Later Years* (Oxford, 1939), II, 928; also Dorothy's letter of 1825, I, 226. Cf. M., III, 20.

The Eton word *funk* in the same passage of the present article (p. 393) is used and identified as an Eton word by De Quincey in "Mr. Schnackenberger" (1823), M., XII, 338 and n. (and used again on 352); and it is used and so identified by him in the first of the papers "On Murder" (1827), M., XIII, 26 (and used again on 29). The word is also in "Richard Bentley" (1830), M., IV, 143. Furthermore, the identification with Eton seems to be De Quinceyan, since other sources offer an Oxford origin.

All of the foreign phrases, though not important here, do appear elsewhere in De Quincey. *In posse . . . in esse* (p. 390) is in one of the Junius articles, certainly written by him for the *Post*, and in his known writings (p. 276 and the references there). *Boutefeu* (p. 390) is in the article of January 26, 1828 (p. 284), which is certainly his. *À l'outrance* (p. 392) is in a couple of the autobiographical articles, M., I, 255 and III, 194n. *Imperium in imperio* (p. 395) is in M., V, 87 and VII, 437.

Index

Italicized numbers refer to the text of De Quincey's articles in the *Post*; others refer to editorial matter. Where the editorial matter is on the same page as the text, reference is made to the text only.

Details within long passages quoted or translated by De Quincey are not indexed.

Peers are indexed by the title they held, or were known by, in 1827-28.

INDEX

INDEX

INDEX